The Cinderella Service

The Cinderella Service

British Consuls since 1825

D C M Platt

Archon Books, 1971

© D. C. M. Platt 1971

This edition first published in the United States of
America, 1971, by Archon Books, Hamden, Connecticut, 06514

ISBN 0 208 01209 5

Printed in Great Britain

JX
1784
.P65

Contents

Abbreviations	vii
Preface	viii
Introduction	1–4
1 British Consuls before 1825	5–15
2 The General Consular Service in the nineteenth century	16–67
Functions	16
Recruitment	21
Training	25
Conditions of service	27
Financing the service (fees)	30
Allocation of salaries and allowances	33
Salary levels	37
Pensions	44
Promotion and incentives	48
Consuls and the Foreign Office	54
Control and inspection	58
Accounting control	64
3 The General Consular Service in the twentieth century	68–124
Recruitment	69
Examinations	71
Training	75
Salaries	81
Allowances	83
Personnel administration and inspection	88
Promotion	94
Career planning	99
Consular functions before 1914	103

Contents

    Consular functions after 1914   110
    Amalgamation: social objections   114
    Amalgamation: educational objections   116
    Amalgamation: functional objections   117
    The amalgamation   121

4 The Levant Service   125–179

    Commercial functions   126
    Political functions   130
    Judicial functions   136
    Consular courts   146
    The condition of the consulates before 1877   152
    The formation of the Levant Consular Service   163
    Recruitment and training   166
    Movement towards amalgamation   168

5 The Far Eastern Service   180–230

    Origins   180
    Recruitment   183
    Language training   185
    Legal training   188
    Career prospects   192
    Salaries   195
    The problem of scale   200
    Relations with British residents   206
    Exterritoriality   211
    Political conditions   214
    Conditions of service before 1914   217
    Conditions of service after 1914   221
    Amalgamation   225

Epilogue   231

Appendix   240
    Private letter from Sir Hughe Knatchbull-Hugessen to Sir Alexander Cadogan, 20 January 1939 [Diplomatic Service objections, on social grounds, to the inclusion of consular officers in a combined Foreign Service].

Contents vii

Bibliography 243

Index 251

Maps
Salaried posts in the Levant Service, 1900   128
Salaried posts in the Far Eastern Service, 1900   184

Abbreviations

PRO.FO Public Record Office, London; Foreign Office Papers
PP Parliamentary Papers
Parl. Deb. Parliamentary Debates
HC Deb. House of Commons Debates (after 1909)
HL Deb. House of Lords Debates (after 1909)

Preface

As a pioneer in British consular history, I have chosen to set my own terms of reference. I might have attempted an omnibus history—what a critic once described as 'a sort of egg-laying pig which produces wool and milk'. But I was persuaded by the diversity of the consular service and the nature of the surviving material to give a first priority to establishing the common ground among so scattered and isolated a body of officials, to defining the main issues, and to describing in outline the development of the service.

One result has been to diminish the political and diplomatic content. It is doubtful, in any case, whether a satisfactory diplomatic history of the consular service can be written. Consular and diplomatic functions often overlapped and consuls, as individuals, might find themselves playing important political roles. But the diplomatic functions undertaken by consuls were a product of individual circumstances and tastes; there was no common rule. Short of writing a dictionary of consular biography—an unenviable task for many of these unrecorded, minor officials—the diplomatic record of the service as a whole can never be established; it is merely the sum of many hundreds of individual, unrelated contributions.

There is one sense alone in which the consular service, and more particularly its Levant and Far Eastern branches, can be said to have had a common influence on British foreign policy. Officials serving at isolated posts overseas are notably sensitive to local conditions of service, to the traditions and prejudices of their area. It can hardly be denied that the British official outlook in the East was influenced by the restricted educational background of our consuls, by the emphasis exclusively on language proficiency at the expense of administrative, commercial, and judicial expertise, by the 'orientalizing' of British consular officers, by their divorce from the local British communities, and by the parochialism implied by a career structure limited entirely to one area of the world. Nor can it be disputed that the overwhelming weight of judicial and police functions set strict limits to the value of consuls as policy makers, or that consular influence, and with it British influence generally, were tarnished by the corruption so often associated with consular courts and jurisdiction in the East. For all the great merits of the officers in the specialist services—and they were often fine scholars and dedicated officials—the reaction against those services in the 1930s was in part a recognition that their character and limitations were damaging to British policy in important areas of the world. In a sense, then, these group characteristics were as influential locally on British policy in the East, as the Germanophobia of the Foreign Office clerks in the West, the impact of which has been described so convincingly in Zara Steiner's recent study, *The Foreign Office and Foreign Policy 1898-1914* (Cambridge, 1970). It is extraordinarily difficult to reach a firm conclusion on questions of influence and partiality. Since I would never lay claim myself to a detailed, blow-by-blow acquaintance with British diplomatic history throughout the world, I am not prepared to take this any further. But I hope that specialists will be able to use the information which I have provided on the mentality of the services, on social conditions and on administrative reform as a background to the reinterpretations for which they are so much better qualified than I.

I have an apology to make. It is perhaps inevitable that an historian of the consular service should become partisan. The members of the consular service suffered more than most from the snobberies of government service. Certainly for the nineteenth and early twentieth centuries, when high social position was regarded as indispensable for diplomacy, the social gulf between the diplomats and consuls was enormous, practically unbridgeable. That social gulf was translated into all kinds of distinctions—privileges for the diplomats and disadvantages for the consuls—which poisoned the air between the diplomatic and consular services and penetrated into practically every corner of consular administration. An historian can hardly escape this, and indeed he would be writing curious history if he did, since social injustice was so fundamental a part of the history of the consular service. But in writing the Epilogue to this book I have quite openly exchanged the role of historian, in which I am supported by ample documentary evidence, for that of social commentator and critic. I believe that I am right in projecting some of the long-standing Foreign Service attitudes into the postwar period, though without access to official archives for these years I cannot confirm it. But before I am accused of jumping to conclusions on entirely insufficient evidence, I should point out that the basis of what I have said, in most instances, is the material collected in those respectable documents, the Plowden and Duncan reports.

In writing this history I owe a particular debt to two former officials, Sir Godfrey Fisher and Sir David Scott. The late Sir Godfrey Fisher, the historian of the 'Mercantile Consuls', completed the groundwork on the x Preface

early consuls without which it would have been difficult indeed to estimate the significance of the Canning reforms of 1825—the reforms from which one can date the origins of a consular 'service'. Sir David Scott of the Foreign Office, the official to whom the consular service owed so much in the 1920s and 30s, has given me the benefit of his unmatched experience. His advice and approval have been a great stimulus in bringing this book to completion, and no one is better qualified than he to judge whether the theme which I have pressed so strongly is justified or not. I must also acknowledge, with warm thanks, the help of the Foreign Office Library in gathering published material on the service; transcripts of Crown-copyright records in the Public Record Office appear by permission of the Controller of Her Majesty's Stationery Office. My wife, Sarah, and my brother, Dr Colin Platt of Southampton University, have generously advised me at every stage.

D. C. M. P.
Queens' College, Cambridge

Introduction

The history of the British consular service is a reminder of two related and unpleasant truths: first, that reform seldom follows from the spontaneous recognition of injustice by those in authority; and second, that the avenue to change is by way of loud, persistent, and self-interested complaints, and that it will be reached most swiftly by those best organized and most centrally placed by the seat of government. The consuls, by contrast, were lonely, fragmented, distant, and unable to communicate among themselves. Accordingly, in a nation which in so many respects led the world in civil service reform, the British consular service remained as the last stronghold of the old system, as a conclusive warning against any predisposition to depend on the disinterested benevolence of official, or indeed social superiors.

The nineteenth century, during which the consular service first developed in any recognizable form, was a period in which social class was openly at the forefront of public affairs. The consuls, chosen, as Borel said, 'parmi les citoyens d'une fortune mediocre', were ill-placed from the start to take their full share of the 'plums' of the public service, and the distance which separated them from the centre where decisions were made detached them from civil service reform when it came. Their crowning misfortune, which they themselves, with social pretensions of their own, were slow to recognize, was their subordination to a Department, the Foreign Office, where social distinctions and snobberies were really important. The consul was ill-regarded by his social superiors, and it was from among his social superiors that his official superiors were drawn. The distinction between diplomats and consuls, between diplomatic and consular functions 'lower in dignity, as belonging rather to individual interests than to those of the state', was certainly a delusion, caste-created—Sir David Scott pointed out—and not really arising from the less exalted nature of consular work.[1] But the *tache*

---

[1] Memorandum on the 'Amalgamation of the Diplomatic and Consular Services', dated Foreign Office, 21 January 1938: PRO.FO, Confidential Print 15334.

2 The Cinderella Service

consulaire was a real factor in the history of the service, and a serious barrier to any equality in the distribution of the fruits of office.

The distinction was marked in a dozen different ways, some trivial, some more important, but all irrational and irritating. The consular uniform was embroidered with silver, the diplomatic with gold. A consul-general was entitled to a mere nine-gun salute, no more than the salute given to a British factory (trading station) abroad; a consul might expect only seven. Consuls-general of whatever seniority rated in precedence after the most junior Third Secretary in the Diplomatic Service, and even, at one point, after the honorary attachés. Diplomats did not call on consuls, nor did they share the same clubs. The St James's Club in London existed for the Foreign Office and Diplomatic Service alone; it was 'known to harbour a strong prejudice against admitting members of the Consular Service'. To a diplomat, said Francis Oppenheimer, the consular official was regarded as a maid of all work. His place was below stairs, 'while the diplomatic representatives, lording it over him, basked in the leisurely atmosphere of the *bel étage*'.[1] Of the two main European clubs at Constantinople, the *Cercle d'Orient* was the preserve of diplomats, financiers and the uppermost levels of society; merchants and men of the second rank, including consuls, patronized the *Club de Constantinople*. The embassies and legations at Pera were the great centres of social life, while the diplomats lived in a high and rarefied atmosphere of their own. 'We junior consular officers', Andrew Ryan reported, 'were very distinctly of a lesser breed, men profane to the mysteries of diplomacy and apt to be infected with a disease known in the language of Olympus as *Morbus Consularis*, or *l'esprit capitulaire*.'[2]

A social distinction, in a society already so rigidly stratified, might just have been acceptable—a cause of amusement, perhaps, rather than of bitterness to the consuls themselves, if casting a heavier blight on their wives. Unfortunately contempt was translated into more physical terms. It came to be applied to the casual administration of the consular service, to the indifferent staffing of the Consular Department at the Foreign Office, to the continual failure to divert resources, on which there was always a prior claim, to the satisfaction of legitimate and widely recognized consular grievances. The Departmental Committee of 1939 explained that the inferiority of the consular service to the diplomatic service, which undeniably

---

[1] Sir Francis Oppenheimer, *Stranger Within. Autobiographical Pages* (London, 1960), pp. 152, 167.
[2] Sir Andrew Ryan, *The Last of the Dragomans* (London, 1951), pp. 27, 48.

existed in the *minds* both of the services and of the public, was indeed a *fact* as regards consular status and prospects:

> There is a considerably larger proportion of major posts in the Diplomatic Service as compared with the Consular Service; and the rank and pay and eventual pension attaching to the major posts in the Consular Service are lower than those of Heads of Missions. Having regard to the similarity of work and responsibilities over large areas of the world, to the similarity of professional conditions, to the parity of age as between the two Services, and to the fact that both Services are responsible to the Secretary of State for Foreign Affairs, the discrepancy in reward between the two classes of officers cannot fail to be noticed.[1]

Treated as second-class citizens within their own Department, British consuls, without a friend in Parliament or in the Press, fell victim to the Victorian obsession with economy in government expenditure. When the consular establishment was examined by the Commons, it was generally with the intention of reducing expenditure. The evidence brought before committee after committee was overwhelmingly in support of substantial *increases* in consular salaries and allowances, but it was not until after the First World War that consular emoluments even approached a realistic level, or after the Second that they actually reached it. The British Government consistently refused to face the real cost of maintaining the consular establishment. It depended, to a degree unknown in the Home Civil Service, on the supplementation of official salaries by private means. It was content to exploit both the Victorian ambition for the status attached to an official position, and the desperate contemporary pursuit of some respectable occupation for those unfortunate young gentlemen who found themselves unable to join their family businesses or to live off their own estates.

By the twentieth century a more liberal and rational view was taken of a government's responsibility to its servants. But the consular service was fixed in a mould of penny-pinching economy and social inferiority from which, it seemed, there was no escape. Ultimately, it was the irredeemably low status of the British consular service which destroyed its credibility as an efficient, independent organization.

Sir Malcolm Robertson, in the memorandum which guided Anthony Eden in his decision to amalgamate all three branches of the overseas services (diplomatic, commercial and consular) into one common service, based his

---

[1] Report dated January 1939: PRO.FO/366/781.

recommendations first and foremost on the endemic inferiority of the consular branch. It was essential, he argued, in the competitive conditions with which Britain was likely to meet after the war, that the Foreign Service should work together in closest harmony, and that no section of it should have any justification for feeling that it was regarded as of inferior standing either in the Service itself or outside it: 'I regard this as of vital importance for the future.'[1] The 1943 reforms of the Foreign Service were intended to achieve just this; but the barrier was too formidable, as it turned out, to be breached by amalgamation alone.

[1] Report on the Reform of the Diplomatic Service, dated 12 May 1941: Foreign Office Library, FO Print No. 16050. (The Report was drafted in the main by Ivo Mallet.)

Chapter 1

British Consuls before 1825

This is the history of an organization, the British consular service, and not of those individuals who, at one time or another, have called themselves British consuls. A 'service', in any real sense of the word, with systematic recruitment, control, transfer and promotion, did not exist before 1903, and the history of the British consular service, properly speaking, extends simply from the first approaches to a service in Canning's Consular Act of 1825 to the amalgamation of the service into a combined Foreign Service in 1943. But the office of 'consul' is ancient, even in that post-classical phase when, as Gibbon said, the great name of consul 'finally settled on the humble station of the agents of commerce in a foreign land'; and its early history is part of the background to the consular system which Canning attempted to establish in 1825.

It was a natural development that merchants overseas, trading in alien and occasionally hostile cities, should band together, and that they should then appoint a spokesman or leader to conduct affairs of common interest with the local authorities. The local authorities, in turn, found it an advantage to delegate the detailed regulation and government of foreign merchants to their own leaders, often holding those leaders personally responsible for the good behaviour of their nationals. While methods of justice remained primitive, as in medieval Europe, or while they depended on an entirely distinct system of religious beliefs, as in the Islamic Levant, it became convenient also to permit foreign merchants to live among themselves under their own laws, with their leader or his delegate as magistrate. Local leadership and magistracy, then, formed the basis on which the office of consul developed. It was an office which had already become familiar in the Mediterranean by the end of the fifteenth century, when traders specifically described as 'consuls' were first appointed under the English crown.

Over the next 150 years a modest network of consulates was established in the Mediterranean, and more particularly on the Iberian peninsula. 'The peculiar feature of our factories in Southern Europe and the consulates connected with them', Sir Godfrey Fisher points out, 'was that their development owed little or nothing to governmental assistance or control.'[1] The system of what Sir Godfrey calls 'the Mercantile Consuls' emerged as a result of the initiative of the merchants themselves, personally responsible for the choice and election of their consuls and for the regulation and payment of the fees on which those consuls existed. The royal authorization of consular appointments at this time, where it was felt to be necessary at all, was no more than a useful addition to the consul's authority with the resident English community and, more doubtfully, to his position with the government of the nation in which he served. What was important was not the royal appointment, but recognition by the local sovereign, and, of course, the cooperation of the English merchants themselves. The relationship between merchants and their consul was described by Sir John Coke, Secretary of State, in 1631, when he concluded wryly that 'the power given is to govern and assist: wherein how far the word govern may extend the merchants doubt: for the rest they find it reasonable'.[2]

The functions of consuls at this time, though less extensive than they have since become, had much in common with those of a modern 'state' consul. The 'mercantile consuls', appointees as they were of the merchants, had no direct concern with the political interests of England overseas. Though they might occasionally have acted as sources of political intelligence, they were under no obligation to do so and, indeed, had they done so they would normally have been out of line with the traditional neutrality, or even the local loyalties of the English factories they served. Merchants themselves, the mercantile consuls took no official part in the promotion of trade; their fellows feared nothing more than the use of an official position to further individual trade or to discover trade secrets. Their consular duty was limited to ensuring that the local factory regulations were observed, that the interests of the factory as a whole were maintained, and that outsiders were excluded from trade.

The consuls' first concern, in the sixteenth and seventeenth centuries as in the nineteenth, serving as they did invariably at sea ports, was with maritime affairs—the protection and regulation of British ships and seamen. These were centuries when piracy was a common experience, when a seaman unfortunate enough to fall into pirate or enemy hands ran the risk of sale into lifelong slavery, when there was virtually no provision for the sick or the poor,

---

[1] Sir Godfrey Fisher, 'Our Old Consular Service. The Era of the Mercantile Consuls, 1485-1648', unpublished typescript, p. 176.
[2] Quoted by Fisher, 'Mercantile Consuls', p. 163.

when conditions on board were atrocious, when the ships themselves were unseaworthy and seamanship primitive or non-existent, when in consequence only the scum of the earth risked their lives on the sea and the seamen, if this were possible, were rougher, more ignorant, more intoxicated, rapacious, and riotous than they were even under the Victorians. When all this was so, the maritime functions of consuls could make demands on the persons and purses of Tudor mercantile consuls fully as exacting as those on their more professional successors in the nineteenth and twentieth centuries.

Yet there is a fundamental distinction. Consuls before the middle of the seventeenth century were not state officials. They were traders, appointed by fellow-traders in England and abroad to serve functions of common interest to a particular mercantile community. They were not employed to serve the general interests of Englishmen, whether commercial and political, and though they certainly acted on occasion as Englishmen rather than as the representatives of a particular private interest, they did so as a matter of personal choice and not of duty.

In this respect the consular system changed entirely during the seventeenth century, when for the first time consuls were nominated and appointed by the state. Still operating mainly in Mediterranean ports, they retained their important maritime functions and their status as leaders of the British mercantile community. But they were now state officials, with a first loyalty to the British nation. Their local functions expanded to include matters of national interest: political intelligence, naval agencies, and, eventually, information for the promotion of British trade. The contrast is most clearly marked, perhaps, in the last of these. As an employee of the merchants, it would have been an act of disloyalty for a Tudor consul to reveal trade secrets or to point out opportunities for traders outside the limits of his own factory. As a state official, it came gradually to be accepted that the first duty of the consul was to the English commercial and industrial community as a whole, and that where this clashed with local interests, it was the latter which took second place.

This shift in allegiance, which was of first importance to the creation of a modern consular system, developed out of the military and naval requirements of both parties in the English Civil War. The Commonwealth party, faced with the problem of safeguarding the important Iberian and Mediterranean trade and of reconstructing some system by which relations with foreign states could be continued, became aware of the importance of obtaining a hold over the trading communities overseas. On 12 March 1649 the Council of State instructed the trading companies to present for approval by the State the names of any persons to be employed as ambassadors or consuls, for 'we think that those employed on merchants' affairs as ambassadors, consuls etc should be persons of approved fidelity and sufficiency and well affected to the present government'. Some months later, Parliament commanded the Council of State to 'take care for employing consuls and agents in all parts beyond seas for maintaining a good correspondence with foreign states'; and the appointments which followed under the Commonwealth and Protectorate were unquestionably of state officials with political and naval duties in addition to the more conventional functions of the old 'mercantile consuls'.[1] The Royalists acted along similar lines, and a number of appointments were made or confirmed in France, Italy, Portugal and Spain to further the royal cause.

After the Restoration in 1660 the practice of consular appointments originating with the state was maintained, and a Commons protest was met with the answer, based on most questionable authority, that:

> His Majesty finds that the Nomination of Consuls, in the Factories abroad, hath always been in the Crown, and kept there; because, in most Parts, they are Agents, to maintain the Privileges of the Nation, and the Articles of Peace made for the Advantage of it: That, if His Majesty should grant what is desired to the Merchants here, it would manifestly disoblige the rest of the Kingdom, equally engaged in the Trade.[2]

The consul as a public servant dates, then, from 1649. From the point of view of the public interest it made sense to claim some national hold over the loyalties of consular officials overseas, more especially if, by continuing the system of fees, this meant no appreciable increase in demands on the public purse. In the narrow sense of political advantage, the conversion of consuls into public servants was an unqualified success. But this was where it ended. The distribution of consulates, when not determined purely by the desire to find a comfortable sufficiency for a political supporter, was directed either by tradition—the fact that a consulate had always existed at that particular spot—or by the necessities of naval strategy. National trading requirements simply faded out of the picture. The 'mercantile consuls' may have served a narrower interest, but at least, as Sir Godfrey Fisher argues, 'whether the

---

[1] Fisher, 'Mercantile Consuls', additional typescript A, pp. 2-3.
[2] Quoted by Violet Barbour, 'Consular service in the reign of Charles II', *American Historical Review*, 33, no. 3 (April 1928), 560.

consul was appointed directly by a factory as in the ports of Andalusia or by some overseas authority as at Leghorn or Lisbon he was practically always a resident merchant properly qualified for the position by his standing and long experience'.[1] Charles II, while affirming his right to nominate consuls, had promised that the consuls would be 'fitly qualified' and acceptable to the merchants. But the pleasures and profits of patronage kept these good resolutions unfulfilled. Writing about a century later, Wyndham Beawes, himself a former consul, lamented the passing of that 'laudable Custom' by which consuls had been elected by British merchants from amongst their own numbers:

> In process of Time, the Corruption of Court Favour and Court Influence extended itself to this as well as to all other Offices held under the Crown. Ministers of State established a Claim to dispose of all Offices of Honour and Profit, subject to the Jurisdiction of their respective Departments. Their Recommendation, then, whether proceeding from Friendship or Purchase, was substituted in the Place of that of the Merchant; and Men were appointed from Home, who were so far from being qualified, that very often they had not had a commercial Education.[2]

Shortly before the Canning reforms, *The Times* was complaining that in a great proportion of consular appointments men were selected who were wholly unfit for the office—'either military men, Court retainers, or other persons quite ignorant of commercial affairs'.[3] And Castlereagh's appointments, it seems, included 'a ruined gamester, a singer (presumably foreign) at his wife's parties, and a particularly notorious Irish informer, who to his embarrassment continued to draw the consular emoluments under his eyes in London'.[4]

Quite apart from the problems created by political and social patronage, 150 years of government control had left the consular system in a state of confusion and inadequacy for which there was no remedy short of complete and radical reform. In the first years of the new state system, war and patronage had required a large number of experimental and normally shortlived appointments. Professor Barbour records the existence of no less than thirty-

---

[1] Fisher, 'Mercantile Consuls', p. 188.
[2] Wyndham Beawes, *Lex Mercatoria Rediviva or, a Complete Code of Mercantile Law* (London, 5th edn, 1792), p. 295.
[3] *The Times*, 23 April 1822, 3e.
[4] Fisher, additional typescript G, p. 4.

four foreign ports at which Charles II, at one point or another, had consular representation. But it is significant that the only two lists she was able to find mentioned thirteen and fourteen consulates respectively.[1] Certainly, in 1740 there were only fifteen consuls, and their distribution was still overwhelmingly Mediterranean—eleven at Mediterranean ports and one at Lisbon, while the remaining three were in Flanders, Denmark, and Russia. In 1750 this number had increased to thirty-nine, but there were still only three in northern Europe, and it was another thirty or forty years before the distribution began to shift markedly towards the north. In 1790, the last date before 1815 for which a fair comparison can be made, there were forty-six consular stations, of which eleven were in northern Europe, three in the United States, and the rest in and around the Mediterranean and the Iberian Peninsula.

The state consulates, then, for well over a hundred years followed the pattern established by the mercantile consulates in the sixteenth and early seventeenth centuries, a pattern which reflected the early importance of Mediterranean trade while taking little or no account of trading developments in the eighteenth century. But trade was not the first consideration. The state had taken over the responsibility for consular appointments for political reasons, and the Mediterranean, while it had lost much of its early importance as a trading area, was crucial to the naval strategy of the eighteenth century. The state was prepared to pay for political intelligence and naval supplies, not for trade, and as late as 1786 the modest Civil List allocation of £4888[2] to consular salaries indicates that even here the state's requirements were limited.

The state in any case was not adequately equipped to deal with questions of trade. The mercantile consuls, locally appointed from among men experienced in the details of trade, were efficient enough at the limited range of functions they were called on to execute, and merchants after the Restoration continued for some decades to have a limited say in consular appointments. But the drift towards patronage, in the hands of the governing classes, meant that in time the mercantile classes found themselves excluded from the consular posts in which their experience would have proved invaluable. The new men, well-intentioned though they may have been, had no knowledge of trade and no means of acquiring it, while their political and social

---

[1] Barbour, *American Historical Review*, 33, 578.
[2] This figure excludes the salaries for the Barbary consuls (who by this time had come under a different state department from the remaining consuls, and who were regarded as having diplomatic rather than consular functions).

background made them inclined increasingly to regard their position as state functionaries as standing above mundane and trivial matters of trade. Consular commercial reports in the eighteenth century, as for much of the nineteenth, were fitful, incomplete, and commercially almost valueless. The central government had no organization capable of handling a consular system overseas. The Board of Trade barely existed. Consular administration was divided between the Secretaries of State; the few consuls appointed to northern Europe were under the direction of the Secretary of State for the Northern Department, while those in and around the Mediterranean were appointed and administered by the Secretary of State for the Southern Department. It was only in 1782 that a separate Foreign Office was created with its own Secretary of State, and it was another forty years before a Consular Department was established within the Foreign Office to administer and watch over Canning's new consular service. A Foreign Office memorandum of 1809 maintained stoutly that the most important duties of a consul were '1st to Watch over the Commerce of a Country where he resides, and to point out the measures by which that of his own may be most benefited—2ndly To prevent as far as possible the Revenue of his Country from being diminished by smuggling or other frauds'. But it went on to say that

> it has unfortunately for many years been the Custom of the Foreign Office to send Consuls abroad like lost sheep in the Wilderness, without any sort of instructions or any information respecting their duty, in consequence of which they have been obliged to follow the steps of their Predecessors, and are generally considered by Merchants as doing more injury than service to the Trade which they are intended to protect[1]

The real point of friction was that the merchants themselves were bearing by far the major part of the expense of a system increasingly out of touch with their needs. In the years immediately preceding the 1825 reforms, the total cost of the consular system to the nation averaged some £100,000 a year, to which the government contributed £30,000 for salaries from the Civil List, while British merchants and shipping produced the other £70,000 in the shape of fees.[2]

If there had been any logic or equity in the distribution of salaries or the levying of fees, the existing system might have been more acceptable. But

---

[1] Anonymous memorandum bound up in PRO.FO/95/592.
[2] Anonymous memorandum, dated from the Foreign Office, January 1831: PRO.FO/95/592.

by the beginning of the nineteenth century a consular organization had developed so irregular and confused that in many cases, while providing nothing of benefit to the mercantile interests, it was acting as a positive barrier to trade. In some of the most important commercial consulates, such as Rotterdam or Danzig, the consuls were local traders, with no salary and only a small revenue from fees. In others, such as Rio de Janeiro, where the trade was considerable, the salaries were also high; at Rio, indeed, which was the *cause célèbre* of the day, the consul-general, Mr Chamberlain, had received no less than £57,567 in salary and fees between 1814 and 1820.[1] At still others, ports such as Emden and Venice, the consul depended entirely on a salary and there were few, if any, fees. There was no general rule, applicable either to ports or countries, even for those ports to which there was known to be a considerable trade.

> The Consul at Bourdeaux has a salary as well as fees. The Consuls at Marseilles and Havre have no Salaries. The Consul at Antwerp has a Salary —The Consul at Rotterdam none. The Consul at Stettin has a Salary— The Consul at Dantzic none—The Consul at Madeira has a Salary—The Consul at the Azores none.[2]

The system of fees was as irregular and ill-coordinated. Charles II, in what had appeared at the time to be an enlightened concession to the legitimate demands of the merchants, had admitted the right of merchants to set such allowances as they saw fit at their respective factories for the maintenance of the king's consuls.[3] This was a satisfactory arrangement to begin with, but not unnaturally the consuls saw to it that the scale of fees became irremediably fixed and sanctified by usage at whatever rate most suited them at a particular moment in time. In any case, the situation in 1822, as Joseph Hume complained to the Commons, was that an English ship of 150 tons would have to pay £1 17s 6d for the certification of her papers by the British consuls at Hamburg and Rotterdam, 'but let her go to Rochelle, and she would have to pay £5. 16s 8d; at Bourdeaux, £8. 2s 6d; at Naples, £4. 8s 10d; at Leghorn, £3. 8s 9d; at Genoa, £3. 15s, and so on; the charge varying almost in every port, but exorbitantly high in all'.[4]

[1] The Rio affair, which was one of the principal factors in the events leading to the 1825 reforms, is fully documented in *Correspondence relating to Consulage in the Brazils*, PP 1822 (604) XX.
[2] Memorandum by Huskisson on the reform of the Consular Service, 4 November 1823: PRO.FO/95/592.
[3] Barbour, *American Historical Review*, 33, 560.
[4] 7 *Parl. Deb.*, 2s, 367 (7 May 1822).

Then there were no less than three entirely distinct principles on which fees might be levied. A fixed charge might be payable by all British vessels, large or small, as at Leghorn. A certain sum (say 7s 6d) might, as in Portugal and Brazil, be levied on each hundred pounds sterling of imports and exports in British ships. Or the system might be the one followed by the British consuls in France, that is, a levy on the tonnage of the vessel, 6d for each ten tons for the consul and 3d for the vice-consul. All three principles were open to objection. The Leghorn system penalized small vessels; the Brazilian system, while not unsuited to ships operating over long distances, was impossibly costly to shipowners whose profits depended on short and frequent voyages on low profit margins; the French system subjected all cargoes of a certain bulk to the same fee, irrespective of the value of the cargo itself.

Joseph Chitty, in a choice understatement, concluded his chapter on consuls with the observation, published in 1820, that 'Great Britain certainly appears to have paid less attention to the office of consul, and the regulations respecting it, than some other of the states of Europe'.[1]

Canning's Consular Act of 1825, limited as it was in many respects and ineffectual in others, was a genuine attempt to convert a group of individual state servants overseas, whose only common denominator was the name of consul, into a single government service of full-time officials, paid and pensioned by the state. Pressure in the Commons, from the merchants, in the press, and from within the Government itself (particularly from Huskisson at the Board of Trade) made it impossible for reform to be delayed. The Foreign Office circular of 26 November 1825, announcing the Canning reforms to all British consuls abroad, admitted that

> the System under which the British Consular Service abroad has hitherto been conducted, has been so little settled or uniform, the Duties and Position of Consuls so undefined, and the manner in which they were remunerated, partly by Salary, and partly by Fees (the legality of which latter was liable to question) so unequal and uncertain, that it became apparent that some fixed and general system ought to be adopted for the regulation of His Majesty's Consular Service.[2]

But an important additional factor in determining the timing of the reform was the immense expansion in the scale and cost of the consular system

---

[1] Joseph Chitty, *A Treatise on the Laws of Commerce and Manufactures, and the Contracts relating thereto* (London, 1820), I, 72.
[2] Copy bound up in PRO.FO/369/2464.

over the previous few years. In 1790 there had been a total of forty-six consuls. By the restoration of peace in Europe in 1814, the number had increased to fifty-seven. By 1824, by which time the consulates in the United States were reopened after the Anglo-American War and no less than eighteen additional consulates created for the newly independent states of Latin America, the number was 107. Furthermore, the eleven Turkey consuls, excluded from the 1824 total as employees of the Levant Company, had been absorbed into the service of the state on the winding up of the Company's affairs in 1825. Although many consuls still drew their main or sole income from fees, salaries on the Civil List had risen from £7493 in 1790, to £23,233 in 1814, and £30,000 in 1824, with a further £36,400 voted in Supply to cover the salaries and expenses of the new service in Latin America.

The question of remuneration of the consuls themselves and of payment for their services had been under discussion within the government since 1823. The dissatisfaction of merchants at the levying of fees on cargoes and tonnage, the refusal in some cases by masters of vessels to pay any fees at all where these were based on no authority other than usage, and the behaviour of some consuls, for the sake of fees, in such a way as to be actually in restraint of trade, forced the government to consider what alternative means existed of financing the consular system.

After some discussion between departments, it was agreed by officials that the least objectionable of the methods examined was the levying of a percentage on trade at English ports. But commercial opposition to this particular solution was so strong that action was postponed until 1825. The 1825 reform, in order to dispense with the detailed objections of the commercial interests, placed the burden of the expense of the consular system overseas on the country at large. The consuls were to be remunerated in future, as were other classes of civil servants, by salaries assured to them under the sanction of Parliament: they were to be prohibited from taking fees, with the exception of certain notarial fees the level of which was fixed by Act of Parliament; and the principle was to be adopted in all new appointments, and as far as was practicable in existing appointments, that British consuls should not in any way be concerned, directly or indirectly, in commercial pursuits.

It is true that by modern standards the 1825 Act barely began the movement towards a genuine consular service. It made no attempt to solve the problems of patronage and of the appointment of unsuitable candidates to consular posts at all levels and at any age; it introduced a system of salaries, based initially on an estimate of the expenses of each post, which made no attempt at uniformity and no allowance for adjustments in the cost of living; it introduced no logical grading of posts and no system of promotion between posts; and no effort was made to equalize rewards or to recognize merit. It is true, also, that the attempt to create an exclusively salaried service came to grief almost immediately in the wave of economy which struck the government services in the early 1830s.

But whatever their imperfections, Canning's consular reforms of 1825, when taken in common with the great expansion of consular offices in the early years of the nineteenth century, were the first uncertain steps towards the creation of a modern consular service. A salaried service, represented however inadequately in most parts of the civilized and semicivilized world, replaced a disparate and geographically restricted body of overseas servants whose remuneration came almost exclusively from whatever they could extort, on dubious authority, from the mercantile community. The relationship of this new salaried service with British mercantile and shipping interests overseas, no longer at the mercy of the whims and avarice of the individual consul, was determined in future by a fixed scale of fees, authorized by Parliament. In some respects most important of all, a Consular Department was created at the Foreign Office to administer the reformed consular system. The new Department, though far from active itself as a source of advance and reform, gave consuls—an unusually fragmented group of state servants—a centre around which a service might ultimately develop.

Chapter 2

The General Consular Service in the nineteenth century

Functions Canning's reforms were intended to develop a new approach to consular functions. The consuls in the Mediterranean and in northern Europe, where they had not served simply as suppliers of naval stores or political intelligence, had existed for the regulation of British seamen and shipping. Yet the range of functions expected of the Latin American consuls and of the newly incorporated Levant consuls was far larger. Both in the Levant and, more particularly, in Latin America, consuls acted as agents for the expansion of British trade.

Canning himself felt that these trading functions were of the first importance; it was in this area in particular that the consular system deserved to be expanded. His view was reinforced by the arguments of a new and vigorous Board of Trade. William Huskisson, in a strongly worded memorandum from the Board of Trade in 1828, urged the extension of the consular system in the eastern Mediterranean:

> There is no occasion to ask in what positions British Consuls ought to reside. The places are sufficiently obvious. Here are Producers and Consumers. Here are large, wealthy and Luxurious Towns. Here is a demand for the Manufactures of Europe and the productions of our East Indian Territories. Our European Rivals are sedulously securing to themselves the Market. . . . We ought to resolve that we shall by judicious degrees, but without delay, as well in the Interior as on the Sea Coast, plant Consuls in all the principal Towns . . . Too much time has already been lost. The appointment [at Damascus] should be immediate; but it should be only the commencement of a more general system.[1]

But expansion was brought to a halt almost immediately by a wave of economy which overtook all government services after 1829. The spirit which characterized government attitudes to the consular service for the

[1] PRO.FO/95/592.

rest of the century was one of rigid economy. Expansion came only where it could not be avoided (as in the opening of Africa), and even then it was at the cost of reductions and consolidations elsewhere. When Lord John Russell was under attack in 1861, on the size of the consular establishment, he explained that he was 'constantly being importuned to appoint new Consuls in various parts of the world—at Liberia for instance—but [his] uniform course had been to make no new appointments that were not called for by absolute necessity, and to abolish as far as possible the number now in existence'. He was supported by Seymour Fitzgerald, who observed that Foreign Office policy of late, whether under Clarendon, Malmesbury, or Russell, had been 'marked by a desire to sweep away every unnecessary appointment in the consular service'.[1]

Economy, in fact, was taken to extraordinary lengths. In the decade 1880–1890, a decade which included so much of the partition of Africa and so formidable an extension of foreign competition in the world's markets, the net charge for salaries and allowances in the General Service was actually *reduced* from £115,761 to £92,701, in spite of an addition of over £10,000 to the Estimates for Africa alone.[2] Over the last three decades of the century, during which Britain's foreign trade had nearly doubled and her shipping tonnage trebled, the net cost of the entire consular service rose only by £30,000, from £200,000 in 1872 to 230,000 in 1903.[3] It is true that these net figures conceal a substantial increase in the Exchequer's revenue from fees following the recommendations of the 1872 Committee, so that the actual increase in consular expenditure might have been nearer £100,000. But the sums were still remarkably modest, and they bore little relation to the expansion of trade and of merchant shipping over the same period.

The tradition of economy in Whitehall was one factor in restraint of expansion, while government complacency was another. After all, it was Palmerston who told the Commons in 1855 that he was really not aware that any improvement could be effected in the consular system, and Hammond whose view it was, before the 1870–72 Committee, that the consular service was operating perfectly satisfactorily and that there were no changes of importance in contemplation at the Foreign Office.[4] But underlying both

---

[1] 164 *Parl. Deb.*, 3s, 1077, 1081 (18 July 1861).
[2] Minutes of Evidence, *Report of the Royal Commission on Civil Establishments*, pp 1890 (c. 6172-1) XXVII, QQ 27,257-9.
[3] 129 *Parl. Deb.*, 4s, 602 (8 February 1904).
[4] 138 *Parl. Deb.*, 3s, 907 (22 May 1855); Minutes of Evidence, *Second Report of the Select Committee on Diplomatic and Consular Services*, pp 1871 (386) VII, QQ 1565, 1579, 1682.

economy and complacency was the rejection of the shortlived Canning/ Huskisson belief in consuls as trading agents, and a return, dating effectively from 1831, to the traditional view that the first, and overwhelmingly the most important, function of a consul was maritime.

It was only at exceptional posts, in the General Service, that political duties were given any priority. The consul-general at Warsaw kept watch over the movements of the advance guard of the Russian army, for Poland at the time was the most important *arrondissement* in Russia, commanded by the first generals in the Imperial Service. The vice-consul at Bremen kept himself and his government informed on proceedings at the naval station of Wilhelmshaven. A number of inland European consulates, in particular Leipzig, Frankfurt, Cologne, and Milan, were maintained in the 1850s and 60s to collect political information during the unification of Italy and Germany. The consul at Cherbourg at all times kept an eye on a naval base menacingly close to Southampton. The consul at Brest reported regularly on the naval base and dockyard. The consul at Tonnay watched the arsenal at Rochefort. But these political duties were discharged as unobtrusively as possible. During the Foreign Office inspection of French consular posts in 1873 Lord Lyons, the ambassador at Paris, warned Lord Granville that if there should be any question of making the inspection reports public, 'some caution should be observed with regard to those parts of them which relate to the appointment of Consuls for the particular purpose of obtaining military or naval information'.[1]

Then, standing alone as the representative of Britain at so many isolated posts overseas, the consul found himself the sole resort of British subjects and foreigners alike for advice and assistance. A town council might apply to him if it wanted to lay out a public garden in the English style, or to get a supply of English lymph for vaccination. Discoverers of perpetual motion requested him to bring them to the notice of the Royal Society, while artists of unappreciated genius expected him to provide them with an opulent English patron. An English lady had carelessly left her handbag, containing a few trifles, an interesting notebook or a scent bottle, in some railway carriage. A gentleman's fowling piece had been stopped at the frontier, while another's wife had run away with a dragoon. A traveller in the Levant needed a trustworthy dragoman; another wanted to check the movements of steam packets and railway trains. A solicitous relative required to know whether the climate of the place was suitable for a rheumatic lady

---

[1] Despatch dated Paris, 13 June 1873: PRO.FO/366/1133.

or for a person suffering from bronchitis. A governess lost her employment; the remittance man's cheque failed to arrive. Certainly, the Distressed British Subject was a constant worry, for the Foreign Office was most reluctant to finance derelicts overseas. A consul, faced with a pathetic case on his doorstep, had no alternative other than to reach into his own pocket for relief. What could he do, one consul asked, when a British subject, often an educated man, strolled in and said: 'Here I am, penniless. House me, or I'll sleep in the street. Feed me, or I'll die on your doorstep. And send me away, or you'll have to house and feed me forever.' The same consul complained that he had had D.B.Ss. walk boldly up to his house complete with suitcase, proposing to stay there. He had even found one fast asleep on his bed, full of his whisky.[1] Indeed, the consul at Taganrog (Russia), called upon to describe the range of his duties, complained that 'with the exception of the administration of the Sacrament of baptism and exercising the business of executioner, it would be difficult to say what duties I can not be called on to perform'.

Even if the possible range of duties was almost infinite, even if some consuls were appointed deliberately to open up a trade—at Trebizond, Erzurum, Diarbekr, Mostar, Murzuq, Ghadames, Susa, Iloilo, Sual, Rosario —and others were posted to watch a frontier region, to assist in the suppression of the slave trade, or to safeguard the interests of colonial coolie labour, the normal Victorian consulate was sited at a port. The official duties of the consul were largely restricted to the regulation of British shipping. 'The Consul acts as a sort of special providence on behalf of shipowners, shipmasters, and crews,' Consul Brackenbury wrote from Lisbon in 1871, 'interposing to save them from the effects of their own negligence, rashness, quarrels, and misfortunes.' Another consul complained that the Board of Trade regarded consuls as a kind of dry-nurse to the seafaring population— 'bearded but helpless foster-children, who, to the number of 4,000 to 5,000, fall to my lot in the year'.[2] The numbers were not exceptional. Seamen engaged, paid off and discharged, left in hospital, reported deserted, and dead, amounted at the New York consulate in 1871 to 17,930. The consul-general at Odessa in 1885, with only a vice-consul and a clerk to help him, entered and cleared 669 steamers, the crews of which aggregated over 15,000 men. At Antwerp, at the turn of the century, nearly 16,000 seamen were

[1] W. A. R. Wood, *Consul in Paradise: sixty-nine years in Siam* (London, 1965), pp. 9–10.
[2] *Further Reports relative to British consular establishments, 1858 and 1871*, Part II, PP 1872 (c. 501) LX.

engaged, and rather more discharged. The consul at Santos, his consulate thronged with aggrieved or distressed British seamen, had wire-netting to the ceiling to prevent them from throwing things at him. Consul Brackenbury explained how he would have liked to enclose in his report a photograph of the Lisbon consulate as he had often seen it

> filled to overflowing at one and the same time with half-a-dozen shipmasters desiring to report arrival, or note protest; with a shipwrecked crew waiting to have their claims to clothing investigated, to be provided for, and be sent home; with six or eight Portuguese police officers in charge of double the number of police cases from the Channel Squadron; with a shipmaster ready for sea, clamouring for copies of his protest and surveys; with travellers waiting for passports; and residents begging for attestations of powers of attorney to be sent off by the day's post; and all this to be attended to by three persons, who comprise the whole of the Consular staff, and who would generally have quite enough to occupy them during office hours in the clerical work alone.

In all this hubbub it was not surprising that commercial work, at the busier maritime consulates, was neglected or passed by altogether. But it was not so clear at the time that the merchants themselves would have welcomed more consular intervention. The nineteenth century was a self-reliant age in which government intervention was treated with great suspicion; *laissez-faire* and non-intervention were the ideal for businessmen and officials alike. Until the 1870s, British merchants and manufacturers found themselves with as much trade as they could handle overseas, and although competition became serious in the 1880s it was long before the traditional attitudes changed. By the last decade of the century the more far-sighted officials were anticipating an expansion of the commercial role of consuls. But a genuine shift in attitudes towards further commercial functions and a return to expansionism in the General Consular Service had to await the twentieth century. 'If the leading traders and manufacturers were asked whether they required assistance from our Consular agents', Lord Cranborne (the Under-Secretary of State) told the Commons in 1902, 'they almost invariably said "No! we mind our own business; we understand it twenty times better than your consuls; we have our own representatives, and this is part of the enterprise in which we are engaged".'[1]

---

[1] 111 *Parl. Deb.*, 4s, 296 (15 July 1902).

Recruitment It would be difficult to imagine a group of public servants more diverse than the Victorian consuls—the dandies, Beau Brummell and Thomas Raikes; the explorers, David Livingstone, Harry Johnston, Robert Schomburgk, Richard Burton, and Henry Kirk; the archaeologists, Henry Rawlinson and Charles Newton; Kitchener and Gordon among the soldiers; and, above all, the men of letters, Charles Lever, William Synge, W. Gifford Palgrave, Grenville Murray, Oswald Crawfurd, James Hannay, R. Lambert Playfair, and G. P. R. James.

Diversity had a reason and a price. Throughout the nineteenth century, consular appointments remained in the private patronage of the Secretary of State for Foreign Affairs. Admittedly it was not uncommon for consular clerks or vice-consuls (normally unsalaried at this time and appointed personally by the consuls themselves) to receive promotion to permanent salaried office; nearly 100 out of some 300 salaried consular appointments existing in 1858 were filled by officers who had previously served in such subordinate positions.[1] But the usual method of appointment, as recently as the turn of the century, especially to the pleasanter posts, was by selection from a list of candidates kept by the Secretary of State. And a name might reach this list only through the personal knowledge and interest of the Secretary of State or by recommendation from some aristocrat or politician whose own name carried weight at the Foreign Office.

For the first half of the nineteenth century a patronage of 170 appointments with annual salaries totalling nearly £100,000 still had substantial political value. Indeed, one of the most frequently repeated arguments against civil service reform was that administrations, in those days of less well-developed party loyalties, would find government impossible without the support they could buy through the distribution of offices—support not only from those who were lucky enough to receive office, but from those who nominated them, backed them, were related to them, or themselves hoped later for a share in the spoils.

As the electorate enlarged, and as party lines became sharper, political bribery shifted to the wider area of promises in party programmes. But there still remained the common human desire, by the distribution of favours, to please friends, placate possible enemies, display charity, and satisfy vanity. It so happened that by the end of the nineteenth century the consular service

---

[1] Return printed as Appendix 3, *Report from the Select Committee on Consular Service and Appointments*, PP 1857-8 (482) VIII.

remained one of the few areas of unrestricted patronage; the *refugium peccatorum* which Dr Bowring had denounced so forthrightly in the Commons in 1843 could still, as late as 1903, be described by a knowledgeable critic as 'a harbour of refuge for retired army officers and for failures whose only recommendation is aristocratic, official, or personal influences, or an easy source of reward for persons to whom the Government of the day is in some way indebted'.[1] One consul, at the turn of the century, was reputed to owe his appointment to his mother's place as wet nurse to Queen Victoria. And a story was in circulation of a duke who, many years before, had refused to pay his tailor's bill, but who had offered to make the tailor's son a consul instead.

So obsolete a tradition could hardly expect to survive into the twentieth century. In important debates in the Commons in 1902 and 1903—the years preceding the drastic reforms in consular recruitment introduced by the Walrond Committee—two former Under-Secretaries of State for Foreign Affairs, Sir Charles Dilke and James Bryce, sharply criticized the continued existence of patronage in an important branch of the public service. Dilke called attention to notorious cases with which he was personally acquainted where Secretaries of State had 'jobbed' totally unfit nominees into consular appointments, 'and the interests of the country had suffered in very high degree in consequence'.[2] Bryce spoke of there being 'far too much of the element of mere patronage in appointing consuls' and 'far too much patronage in regard to promotion'.[3]

The appointments which both had in mind were spelt out by William Redmond, the Irish leader, in the course of the 1903 debate: the appointment of a fifty-four-year-old Foreign Office clerk as consul-general at Valparaiso; the gift of the consulate-general at Le Havre to the chief clerk in the Treaty Department at the Foreign Office; the appointment of a diplomat to the consulate-general at Chicago; the translation of a prominent official in the Primrose League to the consulate at Samoa, and of a hussar officer to the consulate-general at Tahiti; the offer of the consulate at Montevideo to a former Conservative M.P. for Rye, as a reward for his political services and as compensation to a popular Member for his enforced departure from the House.[4] Other cases as disturbing were reported in a Return printed for

---

[1] J. H. Longford, 'The Consular Service and its wrongs', *Quarterly Review* (April, 1903), 618.
[2] 111 *Parl. Deb.*, 4s, 308 (15 July 1902).
[3] 126 *Parl. Deb.*, 4s, 1000 (30 July 1903).
[4] 110 *Parl. Deb.*, 4s, 730 (3 July 1902).

the House in 1902.¹ The majority of appointees could claim previous experience either as unpaid consuls or as consular clerks. But one, now consul at Piraeus, was a former secretary to the Governor of Mauritius; two, consuls at Brest and Cherbourg, were employees of the South-Eastern Railway Company; four were army officers; and five had served in one capacity or another as government officials in the new African Protectorates. The problem of finding suitable employment for imperial officials who, for health or other reasons, could no longer continue at their original posts was already serious, and the consular service was one of the few such outlets left to the government. As the Under-Secretary of State (Lord Cranborne) explained, there were large numbers of devoted public servants governing with admirable success the great African Protectorates:

> The work is extremely arduous and dreary, and after men have served a large number of years in that service it is no abuse of patronage that they should be removed to consular appointments in other parts of the world. Being men of ability, they can undoubtedly perform the duties admirably, and without such a system I think it would be impossible to maintain the service at its present level.

The attractions of the consular service as a source of patronage were enhanced, both to candidates for the posts and to those who were able to offer them, by the fact that no special qualifications were felt to be necessary for the General Service. Palmerston always maintained that the duties of consuls, important and detailed though they might be, required no particular previous education and could be carried out by any man of good sense. One of the more unfortunate results of this attitude, which was generally shared by Foreign Office officials until late in the century, was that the duller youths, who had failed to distinguish themselves in any particular branch of education, were felt still to be in the running for a consulate overseas. It meant, as *The Times* once put it, that the Secretary of State was 'perpetually assailed by all the influential relations of half the blockheads in the kingdom'. It also gave a long list from which to nominate. Though cautious parents may have disliked the consular service for its meagre pay, poor to non-existent prospects, and promise of unbroken exile, there was never in practice any shortage of applicants for positions. The salary and prospects were to some degree unimportant; there was simply, as any reader of

¹ *Return of the Names, Ages, and Previous Employment of Persons appointed to the Salaried Consular Service 1897 to 1902*, PP 1902 (Cd 1074) CIV.

Middlemarch will know, an appalling shortage of secure, respectable positions where a man might lay claim to some of the prestige attached to office, hope for reasonable security against bankruptcy, and supplement an exiguous private income inadequate on its own to maintain his wife and educate his children. In any case, Thomas Wood, giving evidence to the 1835 Committee, felt that there would be many, even among successful merchants, who would 'realize a certainty and take even a small salary to hold so respectable an office', and his confidence was borne out by the 'very great number' of applications reported by Edmund Hammond to the 1858 Committee. Posts were still much in demand in the last decades of the century when *Vanity Fair* reported, as an example, a vacancy at Bordeaux for which there had been no less than 130 applicants.

> If your doubt is as to the talents and energy of the young men of this country [W. M. wrote to *The Times* in 1854], I say, only let the Foreign Minister throw open to fair competition the next appointment of £150 a year that he has on his hands.... I know something of the young men of the present day who are seeking to earn their livelihood and to retain a respectable position in society, and, as one of them, I appeal to you to do them justice.[1]

Unfortunately, the existence of this constant reserve of applicants encouraged the Foreign Office in its resistance to the introduction of a logical system of recruitment. But there were theoretical objections, too, to the adoption of the French system of consular *élèves*—young men recruited after examination into a tiered service, trained, and offered prospects of promotion. The Secretary of State's discretion to 'pick out a good man wherever he could find him' was defended on the grounds that the qualities needed for each consular post were so distinctive, whether in languages, local knowledge, commercial or shipping expertise, diplomatic or legal skill, that no common pool of talent could be expected to produce the right man at the right time. It was considered unwise to send out young men, without status or experience, to fill independent posts overseas. Few British consulates in the nineteenth century were large enough to employ subordinate staff, other than the occasional, locally engaged clerk. Short of a massive and expensive expansion in the staffing of each consulate, there were no subordinate posts which young vice-consuls might fill while they matured sufficiently to win the respect and cooperation of the local inhabitants at independent posts.

[1] *The Times*, 12 June 1845, 12a.

Whether the fault lay more with traditional conservatism at the Foreign Office, with staffing and financial problems, or with the continued existence of a more than adequate list of applicants for consular posts, it was certainly the case that a conjunction of the three prevented the competitive principle, gradually extended to the rest of the Civil Service since the establishment of the Civil Service Commission in 1855, from reaching the General Consular Service until 1904. The Order in the Council of 21 May 1855 had made provision for testing the qualifications of young men proposed for appointment to government posts, and the Earl of Clarendon, Secretary of State for Foreign Affairs, had accepted that it should be applied to new appointees to the consular service 'whenever the circumstances of their being resident in England on their first appointment, or of their passing through England on their way to take up such first appointment, may admit of their being subjected to examination'.[1]

Clarendon's proviso was widely interpreted, since it came to include, amongst others, senior officials such as ex-colonial civil servants and military men for whom an examination was felt to be inappropriate. Of the eighty-two salaried consuls serving at the turn of the century, only thirty-four had passed the examination; of the sixty-six salaried vice-consuls, only thirty-three. But the real point was that the examination, when taken at all, was simply a qualifying test of a most elementary standard. It was not competitive, and the Secretary of State's nominee for the particular consular post sat it as scarcely more than a formality. It was no test even of competence —the limited objective of the 1855 proposals—let alone, as entry to the Civil Service under open competition later became, an attempt to recruit the best of the national talent for the public service.

Training Edmund Hammond, Permanent Under-Secretary 1854-73 and pillar of the Foreign Office for so much of the nineteenth century, was possibly as reactionary an official as any government department has had to endure. But in his attitude towards the commercial experience required by consuls and to their recruitment and training he was certainly representative. He was asked, when giving evidence before the Select Committee of 1858, whether he attached much importance to having mercantile men for consuls. 'Not the slightest', he replied:

---

[1] No. 4, *Correspondence respecting the Examination of Persons appointed to situations under the Foreign Office*, PP 1856 (2029) XLVI.

> I believe there is nothing which a consul is required to perform, which a man of sense, temper, and judgment might not learn to do efficiently, after an experience of six months in his office. . . . I think the manner in which our consuls are selected is better calculated to produce good public servants for our purposes than any more exclusive system.[1]

Admittedly, there were difficulties in the general nature of consular duties and in the part which was necessarily played in them by common sense rather than book-learning, which made it impossible, even in the twentieth century, to develop an entirely satisfactory training scheme for consular officers. But this was no excuse for the continual failure, throughout the Victorian period, to make an adequate and systematic attempt at training consular officers before despatching them, in the words of the 1809 Memorandum, 'like lost sheep in the Wilderness', to their isolated stations overseas.

The Times had argued as early as 1842, in answer to Lord Palmerston's observations on the impracticability of devising any specific education for consular office, that there was a variety of matters, not generally included in the education of an English gentleman, such as knowledge of the principal European languages and of the elements of commercial and maritime law, which might very easily be made the subject of a specific course of instruction. Once a consul had been posted overseas, his opportunities for acquiring further general information were slight indeed, and it was therefore of great importance that his capacity should be enlarged and his mind stored, at the commencement of his career, with 'a thorough knowledge of geography, a tolerable supply of political economy, and a more accurate acquaintance with modern history than is usually acquired in a merchant's counting house or a mess-room'.[2] But the farthest the Foreign Office was able to get towards a system of training, in spite of a barrage of suggestions from outside experts and from the Select Committees and Royal Commissions of the Victorian period, was the three months at the Foreign Office prior to first appointment which Lord Clarendon had introduced in 1855. No attempt was made to recruit, on any systematic basis, men who had already had the advantage of some commercial training or experience. 'I never missed a man from the Manchester Exchange', said the President of the Manchester Chamber of Commerce in 1864, 'who had taken a consular appointment', and he reported a conversation with an experienced consul some years

---

[1] Minutes of Evidence, *Report from the Select Committee on Consular Service and Appointments*, PP 1857-8 (482) VIII, Q 270.
[2] *The Times*, 16 March 1842, 5a.

before in which he had asked the consul in what manner he had become acquainted with his duties and responsibilities. The consul had replied: 'When I received my appointment, I inquired where I was to go for instruction and advice touching commerce; and the answer I received was, "You must rub against the next consul you meet; your information will come by friction".'[1]

If the three months of preliminary training at the Foreign Office, later shared with the Board of Trade, had been intelligently applied (of which there is no evidence, since the training thought most appropriate to a Foreign Office clerk at the time was to set a man to copying, registering, and sealing despatches, sometimes for years on end), or if the so-called 'technical subjects' set for examination, such as a knowledge of *Smith's Compendium of Mercantile Law* or of *Bishop Colenso's Arithmetic*, had had any relevance to consular functions, at least something might have been achieved. As it was, more often than not even those three months, the bare minimum required by Lord Clarendon, were dispensed with. Until the early years of the twentieth century there was no reserve of consular probationers to fill posts falling vacant, and when a man died or retired it was necessary to appoint a replacement specifically for that post. For one reason or another it was often, perhaps even normally, considered important to send out a replacement at once. Furthermore, a fair proportion of posts were filled direct by the promotion of unpaid vice-consuls or consular clerks, who had been locally recruited in the first place and who, though skilled in consular routine *en poste*, had no direct experience either of the Foreign Office itself or of British commerce and industry.

Conditions of service In the normal course of events a Victorian consul arrived at his first overseas post direct from his father's parsonage, from the barracks at Aldershot, from a stool in Whitehall, from the quarterdeck of a man-of-war, or from Grub Street. He arrived with no knowledge of his duties, commercial or otherwise, and with his stock of influence at home exhausted on winning the patronage to which he owed his appointment. What, then, were his prospects?

Unless his influence had extended to an appointment to one of the neighbouring European consulates or to an important port with a large resident

---

[1] Minutes of Evidence, *Report of the Select Committee on Trade with Foreign Nations*, PP 1864 (493) VII, QQ 946-7.

English community, the consul faced a life of discomfort and exile in a selection of dreary posts. One of the more melancholy grievances aired before the 1914 Royal Commission was that Britain, by taking so many of the pleasantest parts of the world for herself, had deprived her consuls of the more agreeable posts now open only to the consular services of other Powers. Buenos Aires, it is true, had improved from the days when Lord Ponsonby described it (in 1826) as a 'depraved country', a beastly place, the vilest place he had ever seen, in which he would certainly have hanged himself if he could have discovered a tree tall enough to swing on. But Charles Lever found even Trieste a vile place, 'half Holywell and half Wapping', where 'whatever is not skipper is Jew' and where the whole talk of the people was molasses and elephants' teeth. Richard Burton described Santos, which he hated, as a place where the climate was beastly and the people 'fluffy', and where 'the stinks, the vermin, the food, the niggers are all of a piece'. Puerto Rico, said Captain Galway, was a very sociable place to send an English gentleman: 'The best society he could enjoy of his own nation would be some bankrupt shopkeeper of the City who had emigrated to that Land of Monkeys and opened a store there.' A consulate on the West Coast of Africa was defined as a corrugated iron case with a dead consul inside. And Curzon, after visiting the British consulate at Muscat where the summer climate was 'indeed, an exceptional horror', quoted Abdur Rezak's description of a heat 'so intense that it burned the marrow in the bones; the sword in its scabbard melted like wax, and the gems which adorned the handle of the dagger were reduced to coal. In the plains the chase became a matter of perfect ease, for the desert was filled with roasted gazelles.'

Life was hard enough for the consul (and for such of his family as he could not afford to maintain and educate at home) in those long years before his retirement, on a modest pension, at the advanced age of seventy. His food was primitive, there was no ice or air-conditioning, no music, theatre, books or company.

> Dear life! [wrote Sir Rutherford Alcock from his exile in Japan] what could make it so in such an exile as this—in total isolation, under sentence of banishment from all that enters into and constitutes *existence* in a civilized country? The ringing laugh of merry childhood —the soft voice and familiar tones of women—the interchange of ideas and intellectual intercourse continually fed by new materials for thought—all are wanting, as absolutely as though an evil destiny had

cast me into a clearing in the backwoods of Canada or Texas! . . . What could be more dispiriting or more *fossilizing*?[1]

The hardships, almost unendurable as they must often have seemed, were infinitely multiplied by inept regulations for leave and travel. For some consuls regulations existed to be ignored. Charles Lever, as vice-consul at La Spezia, never troubled to live at his post at all. After his promotion to Trieste he was heard to remark that he 'looked in at the Consulate once in three weeks or so'. In London on one occasion, having dispensed with the formality of asking for leave, Lever met the Foreign Secretary at dinner with Lord Lytton. Clarendon could not recall his leave application, to which he replied, with great presence of mind: 'No, my Lord, I thought it would be more respectful to your Lordship to come and ask for it in person!' But this took some nerve, backed by the security of a fashionable literary reputation. For the ordinary unbefriended Victorian consul, the entitlement was to a month of leave on full salary in every year, which he was not permitted to accumulate. Travelling time was included within this month, which might leave the consul at Calais with twenty-eight days but which, for a Levant consul, gave him the opportunity, as Sir Philip Francis complained, 'of spending four weeks of seasickness in arriving at his native country and coming back again, with perhaps three days over, to recruit his health in Liverpool'.[2] And Francis was more fortunate than some of his colleagues; it would have taken him six weeks in each direction from Valparaiso.

Fares were not paid, either for the consul or for his family; full salary for one month and half-rate thereafter was supposed to take care of his expenses. But from China in the 1850s it might cost him from £90 to £113 in each direction, or £60 or £70 for his passage from South America; and the addition of family fares made the total prohibitive. Consul Pedder explained in 1869 that the cost of travelling from Amoy to London for himself, his wife and one child was £350.[3] And two years later Consul Robert Cumberbatch reported from Smyrna, one of the 'plums' of the Levant Service, that he had never, during his twenty-seven years in the service, been able to afford to absent himself from his post.[4]

---

[1] Sir Rutherford Alcock, *The Capital of the Tycoon: a narrative of a three years' residence in Japan* (London, 1863), I, 361.
[2] *Reports Relative to British Consular Establishments, 1858 and 1871*, Part III, PP 1872 (c. 530) LX.
[3] Inclosure 10 in No. 8, *Reports on Consular Establishments in China, 1869*, PP 1870 (c. 44) LXIX.
[4] *Reports Relative to British Consular Establishments*, Part III, PP 1872 (c. 530) LX.

It was not until 1874 that consuls were allowed to accumulate leave, that travelling time was no longer counted in with that leave, and that an allowance of half the consul's own fare and a third of his family's was made on return on leave of absence after five years. Substantial though the improvement was, married men with families were still finding it difficult to take their leave. Fares, if leave were taken at all regularly, absorbed (even with the government's contribution) an inordinately high proportion of a consul's income; and the state, while now permitting a consul to accumulate up to six months of leave, would do so only if he were prepared to forgo all leave in between (a painful decision in a trying climate), and if, after the first two months at full salary, he accepted reduction to a three-quarter rate for the remaining four. There were exceptional problems for those with children of school age or with marriageable daughters. Unless they wished their children to run the risk of disease or of 'going native', they had to maintain an establishment at home in addition to all their other burdens. 'Is it any wonder', Consul Michell asked in 1918, 'if a man who for all those years [25/30] has had little or no domestic comforts... living in enervating climates, with poor prospects, and the cares of a family at home for which he can do very little, became irritable and liable to take to drinking, gambling or immorality?'[1]

Financing the service (fees) One of the first administrative problems faced by consular reformers in the nineteenth century was to determine the best method of financing the service and of paying the consuls. What it amounted to was that there was a choice between a service financed as far as possible directly by fees from those who most benefited from it, or, alternatively, a state salaried service, the cost of which was borne by the community as a whole.

The mercantile consuls of the sixteenth and seventeenth centuries had existed on their fees, and since their services were direct to the English merchants, their ships and their factories overseas, direct payment by the customer seemed appropriate. But when the state, during the Commonwealth period, first made serious demands on the political services of consuls, and when it became obvious that a politically valuable post did not necessarily coincide with commercial duties adequate to earn a living wage from fees, the state began to supplement fees or to replace them altogether by salaries on the Civil List.

---

[1] Memorandum dated 25 June 1918: PRO.FO/369/1047.

Civil List salaries had reached a total of some £30,000 by 1824, together with a further £34,000 voted by the Commons to provide salaried consuls in the semipolitical posts just established in Latin America. Discussion at the time, prompted both by the scale of these salaries and by the scandalous abuses and irregularities in the levying of consular fees, turned on whether the state should make itself responsible for the consuls as an ordinary branch of the civil service, or whether the whole or part of their maintenance should come from some form of tonnage dues levied on British and foreign shipping. Canning's decision, embodied in the 1825 Consular Act, was in favour of the first of these alternatives. The country as a whole was to bear the burden of the new consular service; consuls were to be paid entirely by salaries, and prohibited from taking any fees other than those levied for notarial purposes on a scale sanctioned by Parliament.

Canning's reasons were plain enough. The levying of substantial fees was a running sore in the relationship between consuls and the communities they existed to serve. Fees were both a temptation to the consuls to feather their nests and an inducement to evasion among traders and shipmasters. It was almost impossible to negotiate a system of fees which would represent at all fairly the use made of consuls in so many different parts of the world, by British merchants, shipowners, seamen, travellers and residents; the problem became insoluble when, to all these different interests, were added the political and commercial intelligence functions of consuls, intended to benefit the community as a whole. Then, practically *any* system of fees, whether levied on size of ship, weight or value of cargo, imports or exports, in home ports or in foreign ports, would fall as an additional charge on British trade; and if the fees were substantial enough to be worth gathering to meet the costs of the consular service, they would put British trade at what might become a serious competitive disadvantage in foreign markets. The financing of the consular service by fees or by vote of Parliament was merely a question of taking the same money from different British pockets. The overseas consuls in 1825, taking fees and salaries together, formed a total charge of £134,200, with the burden falling very largely on British traders (more particularly on merchants in Brazil and in the Levant). The cost of the new system in 1826, excluding the notarial fees which were relatively insignificant at the time, was £119,000, falling on the state.

Canning's reasoning, sound as it was, left one thing out of account—the fact that the charge on the state, which was the charge brought most directly before the notice of the public and of the House of Commons, rose dramatically from £66,400 in 1825 to £119,000 for the reformed service in

1826. By 1830 this total had been reduced to £99,600, but it was still an open target to Whig and Radical economists. Sir James Graham explained in the Commons on 11 June 1830 that he had never been entirely happy about Canning's substitution of salaries for fees. He argued that consuls served only a small section of the community, and that it was reasonable to expect this section, the merchants, to pay for the services; fees, he thought, gave consuls an interest in doing their job and in remaining at their posts; fixed salaries destroyed that incentive. Joseph Hume, speaking at the same debate, denied any responsibility whatever for the system of salaries established in 1825, and argued strongly for a return to the system of giving consuls permission to trade, either as a supplement to a small salary paid by the state or in entire substitution for that salary. Sir Robert Peel, speaking for the government, conceded what he took to be the failure of Canning's experiment, which, he repeated, had been tried out at the recommendation of the House; he concluded that it was a 'subject worthy of serious consideration whether we ought not partially to return to the old system of remuneration by fees'.[1]

In the event it was Joseph Hume's suggestion, rather than Sir James Graham's, which was adopted. It was generally agreed on both sides of the House that the cost of the overseas services had risen beyond reason. The expenditure on the diplomatic and consular services in 1792, Sir James Graham had pointed out, had been £113,927; in 1829 it was £366,000. The whole charge for the civil government, diplomatic and consular expenses of the United States was £52,420, not half of the cost of the British consular establishment alone. But the solution adopted by the British Government after 1830 took the form of savage reductions in consular salaries, in conjunction with a general permission to trade; no return was made to a system of financing the service exclusively from fees. Poulett Thomson, Vice-President of the Board of Trade, in reply to a request from the Foreign Office for a departmental opinion on the whole question, felt that 'upon the whole the payment of the consuls by the State appears the simplest mode'.[2] When the question was brought before the Select Committee of 1835, with particular reference to the suggestion of a system of fees charged on the tonnage and imports entering the ports where consuls were stationed, the Committee confirmed that, in their opinion, 'the mode at present in force, of payment by annual Vote of Parliament, is to be preferred'.[3]

---

[1] 25 *Parl. Deb.*, 2s, 260-81 (11 June 1830).
[2] Memorandum on Consular Arrangements, Board of Trade, 1832: PRO.FO/95/592.
[3] *Report from the Select Committee on Consular Establishment*, PP 1835 (499) VI.

Proposals to finance the consular service by the levying of dues on its principal beneficiaries were revived from time to time, but there, in practice, the matter rested. The cost of the consular service continued in the main to be met by the state.

Allocation of salaries and allowances Canning, when he decided to substitute salaries for fees, selected a system for allocating these salaries which, though it seemed reasonable enough at the time, became the main obstacle to the development of a modern consular service.

Canning and his officials were impressed by the difficulty of assigning uniform salaries to consular officers when the local cost of living and the volume of work varied so much from post to post. Instead of adopting the modern practice (which would have been to draw up a regular and uniform scale of consular salaries, with variable allowances to cover different costs of living and a higher rank for the more important posts), Canning followed an earlier tradition of administration. Patronage, in the eighteenth century and earlier, had taken the form of the appointment of individuals to particular posts to satisfy their own demands or those of their friends. These posts then became virtually the freehold of those fortunate enough to possess them. There was no grading or salary scale by which a man, appointed originally perhaps by patronage, would start at a comparatively low post and work his way up through the service. Canning applied this old tradition to his new salaried service, and there is much point in the argument that the consular service in the nineteenth century was less a service than an aggregation of individual posts. The salary was not attached to the consul as an officer at a certain point of seniority; it was attached to the post he happened to hold.

Taking a short-term view, there was obviously something to be said for salaries allocated to posts. As Canning understood the position of consular officers in 1825, consuls were the individual owners of consular freeholds, and some of those freeholds, by virtue of the circumstances of the original appointment or by accident of a shift in the pattern of world trade or politics, were more valuable than others. Furthermore, at some the work was heavy, at others light, and in no case were the rewards even remotely equalized. Canning's principle was to fix the salaries for each post, not so much with reference to whatever emoluments those ports had enjoyed to date, but rather according to some estimate of the extent of the duties at the post and of the local cost of living.

This remained the principle on which posts were valued until the end of the century. Sir Percy Anderson, senior clerk of the Consular Department at the Foreign Office, in his evidence before the Ridley Commission in December 1889, explained that there was no ladder in the consular service: 'The whole service is more or less on the same level; some posts are better paid, but the better pay does not always represent a better post. The better pay is given because the climate is worse, or the country is more expensive.' Anderson added, ominously, that consular salaries were always adapted to what the Foreign Office thought were the requirements of the post, 'and those we watch with the most rigid economy'.[1]

A principle so attractive in theory had serious disadvantages when put into effect. For one, the system of salaries attached to posts meant that it was very difficult to recognize or reward merit without damaging the interests of the state. An officer who might be doing particularly good work at one post could be rewarded only by a transfer to some post to which a higher salary was attached, in which case the very services which had gained him recognition were lost. For another, the system led to gross inequalities in pension rights. Pensions, calculated at one-sixtieth of the terminal salary for each year of service, naturally varied substantially according to the salary attached to the post held at retirement. While a salary of £1,200 p.a. for the consul at Panama in 1858 may arguably have compensated for the higher cost of living in Central America as compared with Ostend (where the salary was a mere £300 p.a.), there seemed to be no logic in the fact that when Mr Perry retired to Cheltenham he enjoyed four times the pension of Mr Curry in the next street.

Both recognition and pensions—but more particularly pensions, since the Foreign Office rarely felt the need to recognize merit among consuls—were serious grievances in the service. Furthermore, they were responsible for such absurdities as the transfer of expert consuls-general, capable still of excellent political work in the Levant, to large ports in the Western Hemisphere. There, for the last three years of their working lives they buried themselves in the affairs of merchant seamen, simply in order to qualify for a better pension.

More serious than either for the future of the service was the emphasis given by Canning's salary allocation to the fragmentation of his new service into an aggregation of posts, independent of each other, with virtually no interchange, and with what amounted to freehold rights until death or retire-

---

[1] Minutes of Evidence, *Report of the Royal Commission on Civil Establishments*, PP 1890 (c. 6172-1) XXVII, Q 27,231.

ment. Reorganization of consular posts throughout the nineteenth century was hampered (and sometimes blocked altogether) by the property rights of individual consuls. The consulate at Seville, for example, which was recommended for abolition in the early 1860s, was still in existence ten years later. When Murray, the Assistant Under-Secretary in overall charge of the Consular Service during the 1860s, was questioned on the point in 1871 he admitted that there had been no returns for the last ten years and that the Seville consulate was useless. He explained, however, that he had never urged that any person should be turned out of office; he thought that was unfair. If that was the case, he was then asked, why, when Seville had fallen vacant in 1866, had a further appointment been made and the post actually *raised* from a vice-consulate to a consulate with a salary of £300 p.a.? Murray's reply was that 'it was merely the son succeeding the father, because the father had been consul there for years and years, and it was thought that this man had done a great deal of work for his father; and a great deal of local interest was made for him, as well as I can recollect'.[1]

The consul's freehold and his entire responsibility for a particular post were recognized in other administrative curiosities. In the Levant and Far Eastern Services, where the embassy at Constantinople and the legations at Peking, Tokyo and Bangkok were responsible for staffing and regulation, posts were manned continuously by salaried officers. In the General Service, consuls were themselves uniquely responsible for finding their own replacements while absent on leave or for reasons of health. Apart from a formal notification, the Foreign Office had no knowledge of the person selected to represent Britain at what might be an important consular post for months, sometimes years at a time. Roger Casement, who spent so much of his service absent from his post investigating 'atrocities' in the Congo or the Upper Amazon, explained to the 1914 Commission how it had been entirely up to him to find his own replacements, and to pay them if necessary:

> I could lay my hands on a publican or a nigger, or anyone I pleased, and appoint him as consul in the Congo, and notify the Secretary of State that I had done so, and ask for sanction—purely a formality, which will be given because I am supposed to exercise my discretion. In a place like the Congo, Delagoa Bay, or Para I have to get anyone I can.[2]

---

[1] Minutes of Evidence, *Second Report of the Select Committee on Diplomatic and Consular Services*, PP 1871 (386) VII, QQ 2011-14.
[2] Minutes of Evidence, *Fifth Report of the Royal Commission on the Civil Service*, PP 1914-16 (Cd 7749), Q 38,520.

Casement argued strongly that the pay should attach to the office of consul and not to the post, so that when a consul went on leave or was compelled to leave his post for reasons of health, another officer of the same grade was at once appointed to replace him.

In his evidence before the 1914 Commission Casement raised another consequence of the curiously irresponsible and detached attitude adopted by the Foreign Office towards individual consular posts. Not only were the salaries fixed independently for each post, but so were the small office allowances allocated to Victorian consuls for the renting, furnishing and staffing of their consular offices. These allowances, once established, were entirely uncontrolled and at the discretion of individual consuls. Many regarded whatever they could save out of the allowances as a supplement to their salaries, and a low rent was the most obvious economy. The New York office in 1860 was 'up three pairs of stairs in a back street', which, as *The Times* said, was 'beyond what even republican plainness ought to demand'; the consulate-general in Buenos Aires in 1914 was described as 'housed in three semi-dark rooms in an unsanitary backyard entered from a narrow street'; the consulate-general in Rio was up two very long flights of wooden stairs above a 'third-rate cook-shop'. 'To put the matter brutally', Consul-General Maxse reminded Victor Wellesley in 1917

> you are doubtless aware that several, if not many, Consular Officers have in pre-war years made a distinct profit on their office allowance, and that Consular Offices in many instances were kept in a manner which, to put it mildly, did not redound to the credit of the British Empire.[1]

Even furniture which had been bought out of the office allowance was regarded until 1914 as the consul's personal property. The usual practice was for a consul to take over from his predecessor such furnishings as he cared to leave and at whatever inflated price he chose to ask—it was too expensive at the time to transport bulky furniture around the world, and the Foreign Office certainly made no provision for removals. Sir Roger Casement was slow off the mark, and when he reached his first post in Delagoa Bay he found the consular office denuded of every stick of furniture, every scrap of stationery—all of which had been auctioned-off by his predecessor before he arrived.

---

[1] Letter dated 8 September 1917: PRO.FO/369/971.

Salary levels It was not long before the salaries assigned in 1825 came under attack. When labouring men were living on ten shillings a week in England, and Whitehall clerks were satisfied on £300 a year, it was difficult to defend salaries of £2500 for the consul-general at Rio and the consul at Lima, or £2000 for the consul at Bogota. Admittedly, a dollar only bought a shilling's worth of goods in Buenos Aires. A suitable house for the new consul-general cost over £500 a year, while his seven servants—from whom he could expect half the labour of their English equivalents—came to another £340 in wages alone. Woodbine Parish told Planta at the Foreign Office in November 1825 that he would willingly exchange £3000 p.a. in Buenos Aires for £1500 in England.[1] But then, even £1500 set a standard substantially higher than the British public was prepared to pay for. In 1831 Palmerston undertook a total revision of consular salaries as a result of which the bill for consular salaries was reduced by as much as a third. This was not a percentage levy on all salaries. Each post was examined separately; all consulates-general were abolished except for those 'political' appointments which existed primarily for diplomatic purposes; and every consulate suffered a reduction in salary according to an estimate of the duties and the expenses of the office.

One of Canning's main objectives had been to remove the abuses which followed from a consul's connection with trade—that is, the temptation he was under to use his official position or knowledge to boost his own trade or damage his rivals'. But Palmerston, under pressure to reduce salaries, reversed Canning's principle so that permission to engage in trade as a supplement to a reduced salary became the rule rather than the exception.

The issue of whether or not consuls should be permitted to trade, like the parallel issue of whether foreigners should serve as British consular representatives overseas, was never fully resolved. Raised time and again by critics of the service, among consuls, and within the Foreign Office itself, there were still some 350 unsalaried consular officers in the service by the late 1930s, most of whom were in business and a fair proportion foreigners. It was never reasonable to employ salaried career officers at every minor post where a consular officer might from time to time be required, and it was as difficult, at these minor posts, to be sure of finding a British subject capable of taking unsalaried office. Honorary consuls, if need be foreigners, were the only solution.

It was a solution which had some curious results. A traveller, calling at a

---

[1] Quoted in N. L. Kay Shuttleworth, *A Life of Sir Woodbine Parish* (London, 1910), pp. 298-9.

British vice-consulate, admired the variety and splendour of the imperial, royal, and ducal escutcheons over the doorway. The vice-consul replied: 'Oui, monsieur, moi et mon frère nous representons toutes les Puissances'; and he went on to explain, with emotion, the apprehension with which he looked forward to an outbreak of hostilities and a suspension of intercourse with himself. The dilemma was not wholly unreal, more particularly when it took the form of action by a foreigner, in his capacity as British consul, in conflict with his own national inclinations or interest. Theodore Küchen, British consul at Frankfurt and a native of Frankfurt-on-Main, found himself, as British consul, protecting Prussian subjects, naturally his enemies, in 1866. Then, as a native of Frankfurt-on-Main, and in opposition to the Prussian military authorities, he had protected the subjects of Hesse. Lastly, in 1870–71, as a Prussian, in the midst of the general enthusiasm of the war, he had fulfilled his duties as consul in protecting French subjects and prisoners-of-war.[1]

All the same, Palmerston's reversion to trading consuls was a serious blow both to the concept of a salaried, state service, and to the individual consuls themselves. Some may have been equipped to take advantage of permission to trade, but the majority had no knowledge of trade, no wish to engage in it, and no trade to engage in even if they had felt so inclined. Palmerston's new 'trading' scales were in practice a net reduction in the income of most consuls, bringing that income down to a totally unrealistic level. There were vigorous protests, and a long and pathetic list exists in the Foreign Office archives of 'Representations rec.d from H.M.'s Consuls of the inadequacy of the Salaries assigned to them', prepared no doubt for the Select Committee of 1835.[2] But the opportunities at the time for alternative official employment were non-existent and for commercial employment, slight. The consuls had to take what they could get.

The only rule for consular salaries, Lord Stanley told the Commons in 1852, was that 'the sum fixed should be the lowest for which the services of a well-qualified person could be procured'.[3] While there existed a constant and considerable reserve of applicants for consular posts, many or even most of whom could expect some kind of private capital or income to make up the difference between what they were paid by the state and what they actually needed to keep alive, state salaries could be maintained at an absurdly

---

[1] *Reports Relative to British Consular Establishments, 1858 and 1871*, Part V, pp 1872 (c. 551) LXI.
[2] PRO.FO/95/592.
[3] 122 *Parl. Deb.*, 3s, 111 (7 June 1852).

The General Consular Service in the nineteenth century 39

low level. There were certainly cases of Victorian consuls who tried to survive off their official incomes, but if the well-informed George Stevens, consul at Nicolaev (Russia), is to be believed, there were not ten career consuls, if so many, who could live comfortably without supplementation from private means. The rest, as he said, lived from hand to mouth, 'many in perfect exile or precarious climates, all without means of educating their children as the age demands, and without the least possibility of making the smallest provision for their future'.[1] Richard Burton's predecessor at Santos, who 'lived over a spirit shop and washed his own stockings', was probably one of these.

It was really a question, as Burton said, of how one chose to live. An English gentleman, in the nineteenth as in the twentieth century, was rarely prepared to adapt his customs and his standards to the local way of life. To take this stand was to face some heavy additional expenses, yet Consul-General Crowe could insist, even from so civilized a post as Christiania (Oslo), that an Englishman could not be expected to live on a par with foreign officials: 'Foreign domestic habits and hygiene are so different to what an Englishman has been brought up to that it becomes a real hardship to him to have to conform to them.'[2]

Edmund Hammond, in his evidence before the 1858 Committee, argued that in every career of life it was normal to expect a young man to receive some assistance from his family, and the state had the right to expect the same. The right extended, it seemed, well beyond youth. Hammond himself admitted before the same Committee that a consul's salary was 'inadequate in most instances to keep him without the assistance of whatever private means he has', while two of the consuls giving evidence, W. P. Mark (Malaga) and G. W. Featherstonhaugh (Le Havre), were quite open as to their dependence on private resources, to the tune, in the case of Featherstonhaugh, of several hundred a year.[3] When returns were called for in 1871 Charles Lever from Trieste described his official salary as 'a mere contribution to my yearly expenses'. Consul-General Playfair reported from Algiers that he could not by any exercise of economy live on his official salary. The consul at Nice, required to make ends meet at an expensive and fashionable winter

---

[1] *Reports Relative to British Consular Establishments, 1858 and 1871*, Part V, PP 1872 (c. 551) LXI.
[2] *Further Reports Relative to British Consular establishments, 1858 and 1871*, Part II, PP 1872 (c. 501) LX.
[3] Minutes of Evidence, *Report from the Select Committee on Consular Service and Appointments*, PP 1857-8 (482) VIII, QQ 579, 738, 4046-51, 5139.

resort on £200 p.a. and £100 office allowance, reported understandably that his salary and allowance were 'perfectly inadequate' to meet the calls made on him, and that after seventeen years' service he remained dependent on his private means to meet the expenses of a moderate household. H.M. Consul at Savannah lived with his wife and child in a single room in a cheap boarding house, and spent more than his salary to keep alive. Richard Burton may have been the reverse of Gladstone's ideal, the 'rigid economist', but he was probably not too far wrong when he told the 1872 Committee that a shilling in England had the purchasing power of 27 pence in Brazil and of a dollar (4s 4d) at Fernando Po; in any case, his salary at Fernando Po was £750 and he spent £3000 of his own, at Santos it was £700 and he could not live under £1200, and at Damascus salary and office allowance amounted between them to £1000 p.a., and he never spent less than £1500.[1]

Private means were the normal safety valve, but there were other sources of income available to consuls, officially sanctioned but most unevenly distributed, which helped the more fortunate to 'preserve the respectability of their position'. Some of these were curious survivals from the old, pre-reform days. The consul at St Petersburg drew £1100 p.a. from the so-called 'agency money' of the former Russian Company. The Russian Company had ceased to trade and the agency money represented no service whatever to British shipping (on which the burden lay). But it is a comment on the strength of the 'consular freehold' that the Under-Secretary of State (Austen Henry Layard), while admitting that this addition to Michell's salary was 'exceedingly objectionable in principle', felt unable to bring the abuse to an end so long as Michell remained at his post; 'It would scarcely be fair to deprive an efficient and long-tried public servant of the salary he had enjoyed for so many years, and which was attached to the office before he accepted it, without adequate compensation.'[2]

Consul Michell's income (salary and agency money combined) reached the comfortable total of £1850 p.a. A more representative budget was Consul Mark's at Malaga, where the salary in 1858 was £300 with permission to trade, together with £100 office allowance. Fees averaged £175 a year, and some money came in, irregularly, from the agency of Lloyds in shipwrecks.

The fees levied at Malaga were for the notarial functions authorized under

---

[1] Minutes of Evidence, *Select Committee on Diplomatic and Consular Services*, PP 1872 (314) VII, QQ 2047-8.
[2] 179 *Parl. Deb.*, 3s, 1282-3 (8 June 1865).

Canning's Act and for certain of the shipping services assigned to consuls under a series of Victorian Shipping Acts. £175 p.a. was probably a reasonable average for consulates in general, but some drew considerably more. In 1857 fees paid to the consul at Pernambuco amounted to £1000, to the consul at Callao £1100, and to the consul at Boston no less than £1600. The 'impropriety of the present incidence of fees', the irregularity of benefits, and the uncertainties and fluctuations of fee levels, persuaded the 1858 Committee to recommend that all fees should in future be collected on government account. But though the recommendation was accepted by the government, it applied only to new appointments, and it was not until the 1870s or even the early 80s that fees, now paid with only slight and unimportant exceptions into government account, genuinely ceased to form part of the income of consuls *de carrière*.

The other addition to the salary at Malaga in 1858 was an agency fee from Lloyds. Consuls had a general permission to act as Agents for the Post Office, for Lloyds, and for mail steamers, whether or not they were permitted to trade. The consul at Rio collected £500 a year from his Post Office agency in the 1860s, the consul at Valparaiso £320, the consul at Puerto Rico £300, and a number of others from £100 to £225. The consul at Puerto Rico, again, received about £400 p.a. as agent for the Royal Mail Steam Packet Company, though the next highest receipt was £127.[1] The consul at Brest, one of the fifty or so consuls and vice-consuls acting as Lloyds' agents, considered that his appointment as a Lloyds' agent (at between £800 and £900 p.a.) was more lucrative than his consulate. But most non-trading consuls held no such agencies, and for those that did, average receipts were no more than £50 p.a.[2] Agencies could act, no doubt, as a useful addition to a consul's income, but the size of the income derived even from the best of them was often deceptive. The Post Office agency at a place like Valparaiso meant the establishment of what amounted to a British Post Office, with office space and permanent staff; what was left of the agency fee belonged to the consul, but it might not be very much.

The most troublesome question with respect to consular salaries in the nineteenth century was clearly the permission to trade. The 1858 Committee, after hearing a great deal of evidence on the point, recommended that all consuls should be prohibited from trading, but that respectable merchants

---

[1] *Return of Consuls restricted from trading and of Appointments other than Consular held by such Consuls*, PP 1872 (c. 472) LXI.
[2] *Ibid.*, and Minutes of Evidence, *Report of the Select Committee on Diplomatic and Consular Services*, PP 1872 (314) VII, Q 850.

might be employed as British consular agents in places where the presence of a salaried British official was not required.

Like so many of the recommendations in the 1858 Report—the most sensible of the Victorian reports on the consular service—this particular recommendation, though long postponed, was finally adopted in the last decades of the century. But in the short run, the proposal to divide the service into strict 'career' and 'honorary' categories, distinguished by salary and permission to trade, was blocked by the officials. The committees of officials which met in 1859 to consider the Select Committee's report of the previous year advised the government not to carry out the recommendation that consuls should be restricted from trade, except with respect to consuls exercising important political or judicial functions, especially in the East. The Treasury, welcoming the officials' report, congratulated them particularly on this point, noting that this counterrecommendation appeared to Their Lordships as

> calculated, on the one hand, to promote efficiency, and, on the other, to prevent undue expense, which must have been the result of acting on the Report of the Committee of the House of Commons, to abolish trading without a careful discrimination of the cases in which Commercial Consuls, at moderate salaries, may be sufficient, or even preferable.[1]

Economy and official conservatism delayed the only logical solution of the problem until after the subject had again been fully considered before the Select Committee of 1872. The 1872 Committee recommended the division of the consular service into two classes: a salaried class restricted from trading and accounting for all fees to the Exchequer, and an unsalaried class rendering services gratuitously but retaining such fees as it collected to cover office expenses. Within the next few years this recommendation was put into effect, and the service of salaried consuls *de carrière*, which Canning had intended to create as much as half a century before, finally came into existence. By 1903 only two salaried consuls and six salaried vice-consuls still survived with permission to trade.

The resurrection of a separate salaried service, restricted from trading and accounting for all fees to the Exchequer, made it possible to take a more sensible view of consular salaries. Once the existence of fees or the possibility

---

[1] Nos. 11 and 13, *Correspondence on the subject of the Report of the Consular Committee of 1858*, PP 1860 (2661) XXXIX.

of trading profits could no longer be used as a convenient distraction from the serious business of establishing a living wage for each post, it became necessary to rethink the whole problem of salary levels in the General Service. A major revision of the salaries at each independent post was undertaken in the early 1880s, when Hugh Childers was Chancellor of the Exchequer. Sir Percy Anderson felt confident, in his evidence before the Ridley Commission in 1889, that a fair level of salaries had been arrived at. Anderson could not himself think of any particular post which was either overpaid or underpaid, although, as he admitted, he only knew of one post in which he thought an officer could lay by anything out of his income, and that was on the West Coast of Africa, in such a pestilential climate that the unfortunate consul was at that moment lying at the point of death at Madeira.[1]

However that might be, and it seems unlikely that any review of salaries under a Gladstone administration would have erred on the side of generosity, the point which must be made in connection with the whole question of Victorian consular salaries is that, in this as in every other respect, consuls had no bargaining position as against their employer. The Report of the 1872 Committee, a Committee dedicated to economy, illustrated the kind of attitude with which the consuls had to contend. The evidence presented to the Committee, both verbal and written, which included detailed cost-of-living estimates from every consulate, was overwhelmingly in favour of a sharp increase in consular salaries. Even Hammond, the reactionary Permanent Under-Secretary, reported in his evidence that the general feeling in the Foreign Office was that the consular service was miserably paid, and he was supported by James Murray, the Assistant Under-Secretary recently in overall supervision of the service, and by W. H. Wylde, the current Senior Clerk and Superintendent of the Consular and Commercial Departments.[2] In spite of all the material brought before the Committee, it expressed itself 'strongly opposed to a general and indiscriminate raising of salaries'. The Committee agreed that many consuls were underpaid, and recommended that careful attention should be given to this subject when the next Estimates were prepared. But it found it impossible to read the complaints pervading the whole of the reports from consulates abroad

> without some misgiving that consuls are too apt to regard the question of salary from their own point of view exclusively, and that one which

[1] Minutes of Evidence, *Report of the Royal Commission on Civil Establishments*, PP 1890 (c. 6172-1) XXVII, QQ 27,254-5; 27,511.
[2] Minutes of Evidence, *Second Report of the Select Committee on Diplomatic and Consular Services*, PP 1871 (386) VII, QQ 1688-9, 2186-7, 2569.

cannot be justified by the interests of the country. The cost [of a general salary rise] would be too great, and the operation would inevitably require to be repeated a few years hence. In fact, the same statements of pay inadequate to expenditure, and of prices having been raised 100 per cent, appear to have been made to the Committee which sat fifteen years ago.

The reasoning was obviously at fault, but the Committee was perfectly aware that it ran no danger of revolt or of an exodus from the service. Continued competition for consular posts, the existence of a tradition of private means employed as a supplement to official salaries, the social status attached in a class-conscious society to an official appointment (however remunerated), and, above all, the fragmentation of individual salaried posts, with no common salary structure on which to base negotiations and no meeting ground on which to coordinate proposals and protests—all these factors meant that public economy could be satisfied unthinkingly at the expense of the individual.

Pensions The existence of pension rights has always, and rightly, served as an excuse for keeping salaries at a lower level in the public service, and this was more particularly the case in the nineteenth century when private pension schemes barely existed. Canning had promised consular officers in 1825 that, by the Consular Act, they would be 'placed on the footing of other classes of Publick Servants, by the assurance (if deserving) of a Retirement proportioned to the length and nature of their Services'.[1] Consuls, unlike members of the Diplomatic Service (which until 1928 had its own peculiar pension scales), were placed on the ordinary Civil Service scale of one-sixtieth of terminal salary for every year of service, up to a maximum of forty-sixtieths (altered, by the Superannuation Act of 1909, to one-eightieth, with a lump sum allowance equal to one-thirtieth of the annual salary and emoluments multiplied by the number of completed years served).

These non-contributory pension rights formed an important element in attracting men into the service. Insecurity was the recurrent nightmare of the Victorian middle class; commercial failures and bankruptcies were far more frequent than they are today, investments were hazardous and insecure, and in the days of social ostracism and the workhouse destitution in old age held

---

[1] Foreign Office Circular, 26 November 1825: PRO.FO/369/2464.

special terrors. The Civil Service offered one of the few opportunities for those without adequate private means to live outside the shadow of bankruptcy; and the existence of a pension, even if attainable only at the age of sixty-five/seventy after a lifetime of exile and discomfort, was the final promise of security to the grave which, as Civil Service employers knew very well (and recognized in the astonishingly generous compensation given in the nineteenth century for abolition of office), drew a constant, satisfactory and, in the long run, economical flow of applicants for whatever vacancies the Secretary of State might care to offer.

But there were serious imperfections in the arrangements for superannuation, some of which survived until the consular service itself was discontinued in 1943. One of the problems which, to some extent, found a solution in the nineteenth century was the allowance for service in unhealthy climates. For the first half century after Canning's Act, no differentiation was made between the pension entitlement of a clerk who spent his working life at a desk in Whitehall, and of a consul whose career took him to posts notorious for their damaging climates and high mortality. As Edmund Hammond told the 1858 Committee:

> It is a most melancholy thing to see the number of men that have died in the China service since its establishment. I yesterday received from Siam, which is a cognate climate, intelligence that one very valuable servant was expected to die in a few hours, and another is expected to come home in broken health.[1]

Thomas Ussher, the consul-general in Haiti, explained to the same Committee how Europeans fell victim to the climate shortly after they arrived at Port-au-Prince. The consular office was situated near a swamp, 'from which daily exhale effluvia as noisome and more poisonous than the present exhalations from the Thames'. Vice-Consul King, a healthy young man, had died of yellow fever within six months of his arrival, and another vice-consul, Gretton, in the prime of life, 'died in six weeks of black vomit, his wife having fallen victim to the same fearful malady on the day previous'.[2]

The 1858 Committee made no recommendations specifically on the subject of pensions and retirement, and it was only as a result of the evidence presented to the 1872 Committee that the Foreign Secretary introduced, in

---

[1] Minutes of Evidence, *Report from the Select Committee on Consular Service and Appointments*, PP 1857-8 (482) VIII, Q 387.
[2] Ibid., Q 5094.

1874, the principle of permitting two years' service in certain, designated unhealthy climates to count, for pension purposes, as three years. This was certainly an improvement, even if, as one official put it after experience of the system in operation, the advantage in respect of pension only applied where life was usually shortened and was therefore generally never enjoyed.[1] But the effect was diminished still further by the refusal of the Treasury, to the end of the service, to make the same kind of calculation when determining the date on which a consul might be permitted to retire. The curious result was that a consul in an unhealthy climate might have accumulated full pension rights (two-thirds of his terminal salary) a decade before the permitted retirement age, after which, unless he could find a cooperative medical officer, he watched his advantage whittled away either until the climate killed him off altogether, or until he came to retire at the normal age in precisely the same position as a consul who had spent a lifetime at Calais or Le Havre.

The point has already been made that until the introduction of regular salary scales in 1903 the pension entitlement of consular officers varied extensively according to the salary attached to the particular post at which they passed their last years in the service. Further, the level of fees at a particular post, on which the salary itself was determined, was not taken into account in calculating pension rights. Lousada, the consul at Boston, who in the middle of the last century enjoyed a handsome revenue of some £1500 from fees, was paid a salary, in consideration of this income, of a mere £200. Yet it was on the £200 salary that his pension, and those of consuls similarly placed, was calculated.

Salaried consuls permitted to trade, perhaps the majority after the 1831 economies but a decreasing minority after 1858, were denied any pension rights, presumably on the grounds that they could apply the profits of their trade to a private insurance. *Ex gratia* pensions were sometimes conceded to consuls who could establish that they had never availed themselves of the permission to trade, but it was still the case, right up to the formal separation of the salaried and unsalaried services, that a sizeable proportion of consuls *de carrière* had no claim as of right to a pension from the state.

The main deficiency in consular superannuation throughout the history of the service was the failure to make any appreciable allowance for widows and dependants. The failure was not peculiar to the consular service. It was

---

[1] Algernon Law's minute on E. MacDonell's proposals for the reform of the Consular Service, 20 January 1909: PRO.FO/369/266.

not until 1949 that civil servants generally were given pension rights for widows and dependants, and even then only on a contributory basis. But consuls, at distant posts far removed from contact with the friends and relations who might have been expected to help in an emergency, were in a particularly unenviable position.

For most of the nineteenth century, no provision whatever was made for the widows and dependants either of retired or of serving officers. Widows of retired officers were entitled merely to whatever portion of their husbands' pensions remained unpaid at the date of death, and the families of consuls dying at their posts were not even provided with the fare to bring them home. After the 1887 Act a case could be made out for compensation if a consul died either on or just after service as a direct and traceable result of injuries (or, to some degree, of physical conditions) on service, in which case a small pension might be awarded. More than twenty years later the Superannuation Act of 1909 provided for a gratuity equal to one year's salary and emoluments to the legal personal representative of a consul dying while still in service, or to a gratuity calculated on the basis of one-thirtieth of the annual salary for each year of service, whichever was the greater. But the sums were ludicrously small. In the normal course of events the widow of a serving consul before the First World War might expect to be left with a lump sum varying from about £500 to £800.

'There is a delusion in some quarters', Algernon Law wrote in 1909, 'that every one has a private fortune which he puts by', and Law suggested, as had been suggested before and was to be proposed (unsuccessfully) again, that the pension scheme enjoyed by Army and Navy officers should be applied to consuls.[1] The Treasury refused to consider the introduction of legislation, for fear that it would raise the whole question of such pensions for the Civil Service in general.[2] The only loophole in cases of particular merit or hardship, was by way of an annual grant out of a sum set aside from the Civil List for the purpose of compassionate allowances—a fund which amounted for all such claims from any direction to a mere £1200 p.a. just before the First World War. This was still the situation in 1945 when R. K. Law, Minister of State, reported in answer to a question in the House that there were three pensions still being drawn from the Civil List by widows of diplomatic and consular officers: £150 by Lady Alice Portal, in recognition of the late Sir Gerald Portal's distinguished services; £100 by Mrs

---

[1] Minute on Consul MacDonell's memorandum, 20 January 1909: PRO.FO/369/266
[2] For example, Treasury to Foreign Office, 16 January 1913: PRO.FO/369/536.

McMaster in consideration of the murder of her husband while discharging his duties as consul at Beira; and £100 by Mrs Venables, in recognition of her husband's services and of her 'necessitous circumstances'.[1]

Faced with such grim prospects, most consuls made some sort of provision through life assurance for their dependants, whether individually or, in the case of the China consuls, as a group, through the China Widows Pension Scheme. But life assurance could be, and generally was, a severe drain on already inadequate salaries. One consul, writing from Salonica in 1871, reported that the premium for insuring his life so that his family might have a yearly income of £100 after his death was upwards of £50 p.a.; that is, 10 per cent of his total income. Life assurance in the 1860s cost, on average, nearly three times as much in China as it did in England, and the outlay which a China consul had to be prepared to make even to match the pensions payable automatically to widows and children of naval and military officers of equivalent rank formed a very large element in his annual expenses. Perhaps 75 per cent of salaried civil servants at the turn of the century were making provision by life assurance for their families. But whereas annual payments by home civil servants averaged about 5 per cent of their salaries, consular officers were paying at the rate of 8-10 per cent, and sometimes more.

Promotion and incentives *The Economist*, concluding a series of articles on Civil Service reform, argued in August 1855 that capacity and merit would be attracted to the state service by adequate payment and just promotion, and that these, rather than a new scheme of examinations, should form the focus of reform. For able men 'the only necessary, and the indispensable, inducements are reasonable emolument, the certainty of just appreciation, and a fair prospect of prizes'.[2] None of these existed for a Victorian consul.

The consular service in the nineteenth century had no promotion ladder, no regular policy of transfer or promotion, few prizes, and fewer honours. Entry into the service was at an age between twenty-five and fifty. A first appointment might be offered at any level, as vice-consul, consul, or consul-general with nothing laid down as to previous service in a junior capacity. An officer could request transfer but, as Sir Percy Anderson told the Ridley Commission, once appointed to a post there was no reason why he should not stay at that post all his life: 'He may be changed to another; he would

---

[1] 140 *H.C. Deb.*, 5s, 1385 (2 May 1945).
[2] *The Economist*, 4 August 1855, 841.

The General Consular Service in the nineteenth century 49

rarely be changed to another against his will, but there is no rule as to whether he may or may not be changed.'[1] Nor was there any all-seeing Providence to distribute justice even in the most obvious and deserving cases. Mr Meagher served for nearly sixty years at the consulate at Lisbon, for some fifty of which he held the rank of vice-consul. He was consulted confidentially by every British Minister at the Court, receiving their high testimonials and the approval of the Foreign Office. Yet, when he retired, he had had no step in rank and his only reward was his pension. 'Had he been in the French Service', said Consul Brackenbury in his Return from Lisbon in December 1871, 'it may safely be affirmed that he would have worn the ribband of the Legion of Honour during his life, and could have died a Consul-General.'[2] Lord Palmerston, as Secretary of State for Foreign Affairs, was asked whether there was any progressive promotion through the ranks of the consular department under the Foreign Office. He replied that there was none; it was 'entirely at the discretion of the Secretary of State to appoint whom he pleases to any vacancy which may happen, whether that person has or has not been in the line before'.[3] And this, in theory at any rate, was still the position in 1903.

A number of objections were raised to consular promotion and to a properly constituted promotion ladder which, taken together, were considered to be of sufficient weight to postpone the creation of a genuine consular 'service' until 1903. The 'modern official tendency', said *The Times* in 1871, is

> to make each department of the public service a close profession, into which men shall enter early, by an examination more or less competitive, and in which, when they have once gained a footing, they shall not be disturbed by interlopers, but shall rise either by seniority or by a limited competition among themselves.[4]

Promotion in the nineteenth-century consular service was neither by seniority nor by merit, and there was certainly no guarantee against interlopers.

The main objection, as far as the consular service was concerned, to the

---

[1] Minutes of Evidence, *Report of the Royal Commission on Civil Establishments*, PP 1890 (c. 6172-1) XXVII, Q 27,231.
[2] *Further Reports relative to British consular establishments, 1858 and 1871*, Part II, PP 1872 (c. 501) LX.
[3] Minutes of Evidence, *Report of the Select Committee on Miscellaneous Expenditure* PP 1847-8 (543) XVIII, Q 7568.
[4] *The Times*, 30 May 1871, 9c.

tendency which *The Times* detected (and which it had confidently expected 'to prevail to a greater or lesser degree through the whole service of the State'), was that each post in the consular service had separate requirements and a separate identity. It was felt necessary to preserve the Secretary of State's discretion to appoint whomsoever best fitted the job, whatever his age, and whether or not he had had prior consular experience. It was this objection which vitiated the Ridley Commission's recommendation, as late as 1890, in favour of a graded service with a system of promotion, and which had led it to conclude, feebly, that although it hoped that the recommendation might be considered, it felt that in any case 'meritorious services of consuls might, to a larger extent than heretofore, be rewarded by honorary distinctions'.

In the nineteenth century, during which wide areas of the world were still only beginning to be opened to trade, it was quite true that it did not always make sense to appoint career consuls, in strict rotation, to entirely new posts, the duties of which could often only be carried out effectively and usefully by someone with local knowledge. Lord John Russell, defending a proposal to appoint an adviser to a proposed consulate at Abeokuta in 1861 (with the object of developing the cultivation of cotton and the growth of the cotton trade), told the Commons that he must endeavour to find a man of experience who would be useful in promoting the interests of British trade. He did not think it would be advisable to send a person there who had no knowledge of the country, however deserving the particular individual might be of consular promotion.[1]

There was some point too in the argument against the creation of a regular service raised by Edmund Hammond before the 1858 Committee: that is, the desirability of keeping consuls as 'stationary rather than migratory officers' so that the public could gain advantage from their local knowledge and influence; the notion that a consul, for the work he had to do, 'should be, in great degree, a man of the world, and not a stickler for strict forms, which a person regularly educated for a "career" has a tendency to become'.[2]

These were arguments against the creation of *any* service. A certain inflexibility and loss of discretion (as far as the Secretary of State was concerned) had been recognized as the price of the introduction of promotion prospects, incentives and rewards for seniority and merit into most departments of

---

[1] 161 *Parl. Deb.*, 3s, 820 (22 February 1861).
[2] Minutes of Evidence, *Report from the Select Committee on Consular Service and Appointments*, PP 1857-8 (482) VIII, QQ 683, 696.

state and into the diplomatic service itself in the third quarter of the nineteenth century. The problem with the consular service was the low esteem in which it was held by its official superiors in the Foreign Office and even by some of the consuls themselves. The 1872 Committee considered the conflicting views of George Brackenbury, consul at Lisbon, and Oswald Crawfurd, consul at Oporto. Brackenbury supported the creation of a genuine service on the French model. Crawfurd was opposed. 'A close service', Crawfurd argued, 'would lead to a strong *esprit de corps* among its members.'

> I can imagine nothing so injurious. It would encourage ambition, emulation, over zeal, a desire for change and movement, in a service where the reverse of all these qualities constitutes a useful consul . . . The ten or twelve ablest and most efficient consuls in our service are men who have been content to continue in one post. . . . The motives to a quiet and unambitious existence (the ideal of a consul's career) might be seriously interfered with by holding out prizes to ambition or vanity.

The 1872 Committee was inclined to accept Crawfurd's argument, and quoted his views ('which seemed entitled to great weight') extensively in their report. They might not have done so if they had realized that Crawfurd had every reason for satisfaction with his comfortable European post. His 'consumptive tendencies', fortunately never realized, enabled him to spend May to October of each year at Queen Anne's Mansions. The remainder of the year he passed *en poste* at Oporto, out of reach of the London fogs, researching pleasantly into the local Portuguese dialect and compiling anthologies of northern Portuguese songs.

It was not that merit or seniority were *never* rewarded in the Victorian consular service. There was simply no guarantee that they would find their reward and no machinery for making certain that their claims would even be considered. If a Victorian consul showed outstanding talent, if he happened to be around at the right place and at the right time, and if he had a few friends or admirers well placed at the ear of the Private Secretary of the Secretary of State—at that time the sole fount of patronage and promotion within the diplomatic and consular services—then there was a chance that he might find himself promoted. Isobel Burton worked wonders for her husband. A well-timed tearful collapse in Layard's office in 1862 brought four months' leave from Fernando Po. Two years later, persistent canvassing gave Richard Burton his transfer from the pestilential West African coast to the consulate at Santos. Later still, when Burton had exhausted his interest in exploration and botanizing in the interior of Brazil, Isobel, working through her Arundell connections, found him the perfect post at Damascus.

Burton, whatever his merits in other directions, was at a far remove from the perfect consul. Men of much greater official merit than he were simply passed over. There was many a man, said the *Pall Mall Gazette*, who would rather have a C.B. than an extra hundred a year, but when the C.B.s and C.M.G.s were scattered about, very few came in a consular direction. Foreign Office officials, when under attack on the subject of the lack of promotion prospects and incentives in the consular service, were liable to produce a well-worn list of names of consuls who had been admitted into the higher ranks of diplomacy—Sir Charles Wyke, Sir Rutherford Alcock, Sir Harry Parkes, Sir Ernest Satow, Sir Spencer St John, Sir William White, William Gifford Palgrave, Sir John Jordan, Sir Lionel Carden, Sir Claude Mallet. Yet under examination, in nearly every one of these cases, the circumstances turn out to be quite out of the ordinary—appointments, usually, to emergency posts where specialist knowledge was unmatched by anyone in the regular diplomatic service. In practice, transfers to the diplomatic service were rare, and to European posts unknown. Sir William White, congratulating himself in 1879 on his entry into the diplomatic service as Minister at Bucharest, made a special point of the fact that while four other former consuls occupied similar positions their appointments, unlike his, were out of Europe; in Europe it was almost unheard of for anyone who was not a 'scion of the nobility or a Court favourite' to reach ministerial rank.[1]

Fitful promotions were not uncommon in the Victorian consular service. Some Secretaries of State were more conscientious in this respect than others. Lord John Russell welcomed, as 'one of the best recommendations' of the 1858 Committee, the proposal that consuls should not be without the encouragement given by promotion, and should sometimes be employed in diplomatic duties.[2] The Earl of Derby, in his evidence before the 1870 Committee, considered that the great deficiency of the consular service was that there was no security for a man who did well in it that he would get promoted to a better post, and explained that he himself as Foreign Secretary had endeavoured, as far as he could, 'to remedy that defect by appointing whenever an eligible consulate fell in, preferentially, someone who had

---

[1] Quoted in H. Sutherland Edwards, *Sir William White, his Life and Correspondence* (London, 1902), p. 271.
[2] 161 *Parl. Deb.*, 3s, 818 (22 February 1861).

done his duty well in an inferior post'.[1] The Consular Service Order in Council, 1896, actually laid down that 'promotion of officers in the Consular Service shall be strictly according to merit'.

But without the posts to fill or the machinery to select the men to fill them, Russell and Derby were the exceptions and the Order in Council inoperative. Palmerston, during the 1831 economies, had cut out all the 'commercial' consulates-general; the remaining 'political' posts (the consulates-general in Latin America and in East Europe) had been appropriated almost immediately by the diplomatic service. By 1858 Hammond could think of only two 'commercial' consulates-general, Christiania and Odessa, to which the entire consular service could look for promotion; by the time he gave evidence to the 1870 Committee, he had come to consider that it was the large commercial *consulates*, such as Marseilles and New York, with their high salaries and local status, which were the prizes to be looked for in the consular service.[2]

By the end of the century the situation was vastly improved, and there were forty consulates-general on the Foreign Office List for the General Service. But the figures were broken down by an ex-consul, J. H. Longford, in a critique of the service in the *Quarterly Review*, April 1903. Of the forty consulates-general, only twenty-five were held by *bona fide* members of the consular service (the others were diplomatic or honorary posts), and of these twenty-five, only thirteen had risen from vice-consul (seven had never fallen below consul, and five, apparently, had received their first post as consul-general). Furthermore, of the eighty-two salaried consuls at the time, two were in the anomalous position of salaried officers permitted to trade, five were officers in the employ of the India Office and the Colonial Office, and of the remaining seventy-five, twenty-four had entered the service at the rank of consul. The rest had first passed through the rank of vice-consul, but there was no uniformity in their length of service at that grade. The consul at Baltimore had served five years as a consular clerk and seventeen as a vice-consul, while the prior experience of the consul at Paramaribo amounted to three months as a vice-consul. After a further examination of all three branches of the consular service—General, Levant and Far Eastern—Longford concluded that without the magic charm 'influence', consular

[1] Minutes of Evidence, *Report of the Select Committee on Diplomatic and Consular Services*, PP 1870 (382) VII, Q 2288.
[2] Minutes of Evidence, *Report from the Select Committee on Consular Service and Appointments*, PP 1857-8 (482) VIII, Q 756; Minutes of Evidence, *Report of the Select Committee on Diplomatic and Consular Services*, PP 1870 (382) VII, Q 261.

officers had very little chance of regular promotion leading ultimately, as a reward for merit and prolonged service, to one of the prizes of the profession. *Lasciate ogni speranza voi ch'entrate*, he considered, was the legend over the consular gate.[1]

Consuls and the Foreign Office The first essential for promotions, other than for promotion based purely and simply on seniority, was adequate information, and this the Foreign Office never achieved. Currie, the Permanent Under-Secretary, was asked in 1890 by what means the Foreign Office, once consular officers were appointed, came to know what they were doing and how they were getting on. He replied that consuls were in constant communication with the Foreign Office; that when they came home they came to the Foreign Office, were seen, and could be judged from their reports; and that they were under the superintendence of the minister or ambassador of the country in which they served.[2]

It would have been far closer to the truth to have said that consular communications, unless they were of great political interest, were never seen by anyone who had the least influence on a consul's promotion; that the normal reception to be expected by a consul at the Foreign Office was chilly and dispiriting, and he was lucky if he saw anyone of higher rank than a junior clerk; that commercial reports were barely glanced at in the Foreign Office, and then forwarded unedited to the Board of Trade; that, except in the Levant and Far East, the supervision exercised by legations over consuls was nominal.

Currie's impression, no doubt honestly held, confirms the minimal contact existing at the time between senior Foreign Office officials and the consuls nominally under their supervision. One of the difficulties was the disparity in size between the consular service, the staff in the Foreign Office, and the diplomatic service. Both the Foreign Office and the diplomatic service, in practice independent services until as recently as 1943 (though in theory united after the First World War), were small services of social equals, in which everyone knew everyone else, either personally or by repute. The consular service, by contrast, even at the turn of the century, employed some 260 salaried officers, 75 assistants and student interpreters, and 450

---

[1] 'The Consular Service and its wrongs', *Quarterly Review* (April, 1903), 611-13, 619.
[2] Minutes of Evidence, *Report of the Royal Commission on Civil Establishments*, PP 1890 (c. 6172-1) XXVII, Q 28,829.

unsalaried officers. Furthermore, the officers came obviously from a different milieu with which social contact was slight and unevenly distributed. Their social position at the Foreign Office, Bruce Lockhart once wrote, was 'a kind of purgatory suspended between the Heaven of the First Division and the Hell of the Second'.

Precisely because of this the Foreign Office itself, conscious of the ease with which merit was recognized and rewarded among Foreign Office clerks and diplomats, seems to have been extraordinarily slow to wake up to the need for an adequate personnel department; it was entirely unable to think itself into the position of consuls. In fact, it was not until after the amalgamation of the Foreign Office, diplomatic and consular staffs in 1943 that the Foreign Office realized that its own officials and diplomats might themselves be lost in the throng, and it was only then that a Personnel Department was actually established.

For Victorian consuls nothing of the kind was even considered, and the contrast between their chances of winning recognition and those of the clerks and diplomats was painfully obvious. Even the most junior diplomats at isolated capitals lived in close contact with their chiefs. As they progressed in their profession they found not infrequent opportunities to bring their merits directly to the attention of the Secretary of State, often while acting, in their chiefs' absence, as *chargés d'affaires*. But, for consuls, Consul Cowper's complaints from Puerto Rico in 1871 summed up the situation only too well. A man might have sufficient influence to enter the service, but if he were appointed to a distant post it became difficult for him to place himself in personal communication with his chief, and death gradually diminished the numbers of his influential friends. When a vacancy occurred, other men more favourably situated, nearer home, stepped in and obtained it, before he had even heard of its existence. 'No system', Cowper concluded, 'could be more depressing to the hopes and spirit of the corps, or more detrimental to its zeal for the public service. With the generally expressed approbation of my chiefs I have received neither promotion nor other recognition of my services for thirty years.'[1]

The irony was that it was only at the point when it was realized that consuls were creatures who actually liked, and sometimes deserved, promotion, that the Foreign Office lost detailed contact at a high level with its consuls overseas. In the long years during which Palmerston and Hammond

---

[1] *Further Reports relative to British consular establishments, 1858 and 1871*, Part II, PP 1872 (c. 501) LX.

presided over the Foreign Office—years in which a consul, appointed to a particular post as an act of pure patronage, had no expectation of transfer or promotion, and, indeed, no consulates-general to which he might hope to be promoted—consular despatches on all except the merest routine reached an absurdly high level. Palmerston used to boast that he saw everything going in and out of the Foreign Office, including every consular despatch. Even the commercial returns required of consuls as a matter of annual routine were seen regularly by the Secretary of State before they went to the Board of Trade, and were frequently circulated to the Cabinet Ministers.[1] At the time of the 1858 Committee, Edmund Hammond was seeing anything consular which was more than purely a matter of form: 'Anything that requires a letter, the transmission to another department, or an answer or anything to be done upon it, is invariably sent to the Under Secretary of State.'[2] Iliasu puts this down primarily to a decline in the quality of the senior clerks.[3] But the evidence suggests that the reason lay rather in a failure to work out any satisfactory system of delegation. At any rate, Lord Russell, even after appointing a capable Assistant Under-Secretary (James Murray) in overall supervision of the department, still insisted that all consular despatches and letters, other than formal or routine business, should be sent up by Murray to one or other of the Under-Secretaries, to be submitted by him to the Secretary of State, 'the Consular business being so closely connected with the political business as to render it indispensable for the Under-Secretaries to have constant and regular cognizance of what may be passing in the Consular Department'.[4]

By the last decades of the century the situation was transformed. Although the consular service itself remained remarkably static, the volume of political business handled by the Foreign Office increased to such an extent that the old practices were no longer humanly possible. Among the first victims of the need, by now universally recognized, to channel and refine papers reaching the higher levels of the Office, were routine consular returns, correspondence, and commercial reports. After a shortlived attempt to

---

[1] Evidence given by John Bidwell, first Superintendent of the Consular Service: Minutes of Evidence, *Report of the Select Committee on Miscellaneous Expenditure*, PP 1847-8 (543) XVIII, Q 6303.
[2] Evidence given by T. L. Ward, senior clerk in the Consular Department: Minutes of Evidence, *Report from the Select Committee on Consular Service and Appointments*, PP 1857-8 (482) VIII, Q 835.
[3] A. Iliasu, 'The role of free trade treaties in British foreign policy, 1859-1871', London thesis, 1965.
[4] Minute dated 24 December 1859: PRO.FO/366/386.

concentrate foreign trade functions in the hands of a new Commercial Department in the Foreign Office—an attempt which had even extended to the disbandment of the Commercial Department at the Board of Trade in 1872—the Board of Trade soon resumed its responsibility for commerce overseas, and the Foreign Office reverted to its former position as a mere Post Office, for commercial matters, between consuls and the Board of Trade.

The effect on the contact between consuls and the Foreign Office in what was already their most easily evaluated function (the compilation of periodical reports) was disastrous. Currie had claimed that consuls were judged by their reports. In actual fact, as the Select Committee on Steamship Subsidies established after closely questioning Sir Harry Bergne (the head of the Commercial Department), there was nobody at the Foreign Office who was responsible for studying the reports before they were sent on to the Board of Trade. Sir Harry himself sometimes 'skimmed through' them, but he could not claim that he read them all through.[1] Edward Fitzgerald Law (commercial attaché in Russia, Persia, and the Asiatic provinces of Turkey) told the Ridley Commission in 1890 that the first that the ambassadors themselves saw of the reports from their own consuls was when these reports returned as printed matter, together with all the other printed papers, confidential print and so forth which came regularly in large quantities from the Foreign Office. Law pointed to the contrast between this and the treatment received by diplomatic secretaries. The ambassador would see his secretary's commercial report

> and the secretary of the embassy is there beside the ambassador, and if the ambassador thinks it good he not only compliments him upon his work but he writes a despatch, and says that he encloses Mr So-and-So's very valuable and highly interesting report, and the gentleman whose report it is, does thus receive that little encouragement which I think the consul would like to receive.[2]

It was unfortunately true that the only contact which the Foreign Office had regularly with the quality of individual consuls was through the complaints of aggrieved British subjects. In other respects, the Foreign Office was aware merely of deficiencies—the failure, according to the record, of a

---

[1] Minutes of Evidence, *Report of the Select Committee on Steamship Subsidies*, PP 1901 (300) VIII, QQ 323-4, 346-51, 390-9, 433-4.
[2] Minutes of Evidence, *Report of the Royal Commission on Civil Establishments*, PP 1890 (c. 6172-1) XXVII, Q 28,571; 28,478.

particular consul to make such-and-such a return, the number of annual reports received and the date, late or otherwise, of receipt. It knew nothing about the quality of the reports or of the merits of the consul behind them; regularity, whatever the value of the returns, was its only yardstick. In their all-important shipping functions Victorian consuls communicated direct with the Board of Trade, and their commercial reports were communicated unread to the Board of Trade. The morale of the consuls suffered, and some officials at the Foreign Office had the sense to see it. Victor Wellesley, commenting on the mental and physical isolation of British consuls and commercial attachés, without official contact or adequate instructions, was reminded irresistibly of a blind man in a dark room seeking a black cat which did not exist. There was nothing, he said, so discouraging and disheartening as the 'stultifying effect which is produced by the continual pumping of information into what has aptly been described as the "capacious but silent maw" of the Home Departments without the slightest inkling as to the merits, utility, or otherwise of the work performed'. Yet, as he said (and he was writing in August 1918), 'this has been our practice hitherto'.[1]

Control and inspection When Canning took the first steps towards an organized consular service in 1825, he established 'for the better carrying into effect the new system and for ensuring a watchful Supervision of its numerous details', an independent Consular Department at the Foreign Office, with John Bidwell, the first Senior Clerk, as its Superintendent.[2] If the new Department had been allowed to take its proper place in the Office, if it had been sufficiently manned with staff of adequate calibre, then it might have developed over the years into an acceptable nucleus of control within the service. Under Bidwell, a capable man of wide experience, it came within reach of this ideal—so far as the circumstances of the day permitted. But Bidwell, by the end of his long tenure in 1851, had allowed it to become grossly understaffed. His successor, Staveley, reported to the Secretary of State that while the papers handled by the Consular Department (10,240 in 1851) were more than half the aggregate number handled by the four political divisions of the Office, the Consular Department, with an establishment of four clerks, was no larger than any single one of the political

[1] Memorandum on the Future Training of Commercial Attaché and Consular Services, 20 August 1918: PRO.FO/369/1319.
[2] Canning to the Treasury, 25 November 1825: PRO.FO/366/386.

divisions. The work of the Department included political correspondence of high importance; in addition to the daily correspondence with other government offices and with merchants and others, at home and abroad, there were about 500 consuls, vice-consuls and consular agents (some 230 of whom were salaried officers) whose correspondence came under its control.[1]

Two further clerks were appointed to the Consular Department on Lord Malmesbury's recommendation, but the problem was as much quality as numbers. In fact, when Murray discussed the Department's problems in 1860, he felt that numbers were relatively unimportant; what was required, and what was more indispensable in the Consular than in almost any other branch of the Office, was that the men serving in it should be '*able* and *willing* to do the work'. Murray pointed out that no less than twelve juniors had passed through the Consular Department within the last eight years and that the position among seniors was much the same—eight men in eight years:

> there is not a man who is put into the Consular Dept. who does not, from that moment, try to get out of it again—The work is too grinding; too methodical; too uninteresting. It is less agreeable than that of the Political Division. It is considered a hardship to be placed there; and, if held to be very clever, men are thought too good to be there at all.[2]

Murray wanted all junior clerks in the Office to spend four years at least in the Consular Department 'in order to remove all invidious distinction between Junior Clerks who have and have not to be sent into the Consular Department'. But his proposals were rejected by Hammond.

Half a century later the situation was precisely as it had always been. The Consular Department was headed by Lord Dufferin, a kindly, well-meaning but lethargic official with a passion for neatness and red ink, who at least took a sympathetic interest in his consuls and even consented to see them when they came home on leave. But Dufferin had reached the end of the line, and Bruce Lockhart, who served briefly in the Department in 1911 as part of his vice-consular 'training', was correct in describing the senior clerkships as habitually held by men who had lost all ambition and abandoned hope of further promotion, 'a last stepping-stone to honourable retirement and a pension'.[3] The Consular Department was still the 'Cinderella of the

---

[1] Memorandum dated 22 May 1852: PRO.FO/366/386.
[2] Memorandum dated 27 February 1860: PRO.FO/366/386.
[3] R. H. Bruce Lockhart, *Memoirs of a British Agent* (London, 1932), p. 46.

departments' when Sir David Kelly spent some unhappy years there in the early 1920s, and although, for a period during the 1930s, it came under unexpectedly good management, it has remained the Cinderella to this day. The opportunity which Canning's independent Consular Department had provided to develop a centralized control over the Victorian consular service was lost: it fell victim to economy and to the internal caste system of the Office. Such alternative methods of control as were developed before the First World War were primitive, piecemeal, and generally ineffectual.

There are two more or less distinct but interconnected areas over which control, in any organized service, needs to be exercised—the cost and quality of the personnel, their distribution and their operations on the one hand; on the other, the accuracy of their accounts. For the first, there was no systematic control until the consular inspectorate came fully into operation in the 1920s. The Consular Department itself, staffed by Foreign Office clerks, had no experience of the duties of consuls or of the working of a consular office. From time to time consuls on training, between posts, or on leave, joined the Consular Department for a few months, but no attempt was made until the 1930s to introduce a regular arrangement by which a senior consular officer served in the Department. The result was that the Department which was supposed to control the service, and which had to decide on questions as they came up, had no experience on which to base its decisions.

The almost total absence of informal contact between consuls and the Foreign Office at home was one of the most positive barriers to consular reform. It was one of the ironies of modernization in the Foreign Office that the abolition in 1870 of the 'agency' system—a vicious system in many respects, by which consuls paid a substantial commission to certain Foreign Office clerks for the privilege of having their salaries collected and their mail forwarded—put an end to the sole form of direct, personal, and lasting contact between consular officers and Foreign Office clerks. It destroyed, too, the consuls' chances of having their names brought forward at the right moment when vacancies occurred. Though consuls were occasionally given the opportunity to ventilate their grievances in reply to such circular enquiries as were set in motion by the 1858 and 1870-72 Committees, or in the evidence which one or more of their number might give to the periodical Select Committees and Royal Commissions, there was no real, experienced voice for consular grouses and grievances within the Foreign Office itself. 'Most of the clerks in the Foreign Office', Sir Henry Austin Lee told the

1914 Commission, 'can have no idea of what takes place in a consulate.' Without that knowledge, there was not much they could do to control it.

At a local level the situation was not much better. The archetype of a consul-general was of a consular officer, serving at the capital, with functions coextensive with the country as a whole; the consul, by contrast, was limited to a district. The extent to which one was in a supervisory capacity over the other and the overlap which necessarily existed between their functions were never clearly defined, and the consuls-general established in some numbers after the defeat of Napoleon had a tendency to become picturesque and valuable additions to the Crown's patronage rather than functional officers overseas. 'What was the use of Consuls-General?' George Robinson asked pertinently in 1831:

> They were generally ignorant of mercantile affairs, and were only known by enormous salaries and large retirement allowances. What have we to do with Consuls-General at Washington, at Paris, and Madrid, all being far distant, the latter several hundred miles, from the sea?[1]

The argument was appealing, and the consuls-general disappeared as a result of the 1831 economies. Such consuls-general as existed in the middle years of the last century, where they were not at political posts (like Warsaw and Budapest) staffed by diplomats, survived either because other Powers had appointed consuls-general and it was felt necessary to match the level of their appointments, or, as in the case of the consuls-general at Naples and New York, as a rare form of reward or compliment for long service. With some very occasional exceptions, such as the consul-general in Syria, they had lost any claim to supervisory functions.

In theory, consuls came under the orders of the Ambassador or Minister and were supervised by him. According to a Memorandum on Consuls, prepared in the Foreign Office in 1822 for the information of Lord Clanwilliam, 'the Consul is desired to obey the Envoy, in default of Instructions from home, and to acquaint him with whatever passes of interest, at his Post, and to make application where necessary for his Support'.[2] In practice, difficulties of transport and communication, the high cost of postage, the absence of cheap or easy copying facilities, and, only too often, the social barrier which has traditionally cut consuls off from direct personal contact

[1] 5 *Parl. Deb.*, 3s, 276 (25 July 1831).
[2] PRO.FO/95/592.

with H.M.'s diplomatic representatives, have blocked this theoretical subordination of consuls to diplomats even to this day. In countries like Brazil, for example, where overland communication was impossible before the days of air transport, it made no sense to channel all consular business through H.M.'s representative. The same was true of great empires like Russia where, as Sir J. Crampton reported in 1864, all communications had to go through the censored public post and confidential reports from a post as distant as Odessa travelled via Constantinople and England herself before they reached the embassy at St Petersburg. Some consuls, Lord Lyons had complained from the Washington legation at the beginning of the 1860s,

> seem to think it correct to follow up a case for some time, under instructions from me, and then, in the midst of it, to apply with or without informing me for instructions to the Foreign Office. Some, when I write to them for a report on a particular subject, to be considered in conjunction with information from other sources, deem it proper to send their reports separately to the Foreign Office themselves; some, I believe, address despatches, in substance the same, to your Lordship and me simultaneously; some send me copies of despatches which they write to your Lordship; some, I suppose, write political despatches to your Lordship, which I know nothing about.[1]

Hammond undertook to put this right, and Lord Russell's circular of 2 May 1861, which established that the consular service was 'in all matters strictly subordinate to the diplomatic service', was the result.[2]

But nothing could overcome the sheer practical difficulties of direct communication. Instructions were issued as recently as 1934 requiring consular officers to visit or be summoned to the Mission periodically, and a Foreign Office committee admitted a few years later that 'the extent to which these instructions are observed varies greatly with the individuality of the Heads of Missions and Consulates'.[3] It was still the practice after the Second World War for the bigger and more remote consulates in foreign colonial territories to communicate direct with the Foreign Secretary, even on political matters. All consulates continued to correspond independently with the Foreign Office on questions of staff, administration, and consular business, while they worked directly with other government departments on

---
[1] Quoted by Layard: Minutes of Evidence, *Select Committee on the Diplomatic Service*, PP 1861 (459) VI, Q 517.
[2] Printed as Enclosure in No. 25, Appendix 2, *ibid*.
[3] Memorandum dated January 1939: PRO.FO/366/781.

The General Consular Service in the nineteenth century 63

the problems with which those departments were concerned (shipping, labour, trade).[1]

When neither the Consular Department at the Foreign Office nor H.M.'s diplomatic representatives overseas could claim contact, as a matter of course, with individual consuls overseas, it became obvious, even in the independent, *laissez-faire* days of the Victorian consular service, that some more direct form of contact would have to be developed. Nineteenth-century consular inspections were not intended as a species of accounting control; they were substitutes for the control over the quality, distribution and operations of consuls which the Consular Department and the diplomats had singularly failed to establish. The first formal inspection seems to have been the inspection of the Baltic consulates by Lord Augustus Loftus, then secretary of legation at Berlin, in the mid 1850s. Consul John Green, in an elaborate memorandum on consular reform dated from Alexandria, 3 December 1857, argued convincingly in favour of a regular system of inspectors. He pointed out that the Foreign Office, generally speaking, only knew consuls by their correspondence; it had no official means of discovering whether consular duties were well or ill performed, whether the consulate itself was on an adequate footing, in what state the consular archives were kept, whether the consul's social position was such as H.M. Government had a right to expect, or whether the consul might not, for local reasons, be better transferred elsewhere. Green's remedy was to appoint inspectors

> to whom a rank should be given removing them beyond the influence of cajolery or slight, fully capable of pointing out to the consuls the necessity of alterations in their practice, thoroughly acquainted with the details of the service in all its bearings, and with instructions to do all in their power to improve the service without personal complaints, except in extreme cases.[2]

Green was more than half a century in advance of his time. A visit by C. M. Kennedy, First Assistant in the Commercial Department, to Constantinople in 1870 to investigate certain local grievances against the operation of the consular system developed into a general inspection of the Levant consulates in 1870-71. The success of Kennedy's tour and its value to the

---

[1] Foreign Office Memorandum dated December 1950 and printed as Annex 12, *Minutes of Evidence taken before the Select Committee on Estimates (Sub-Committee F)*, PP 1950-1 (242) V.

[2] Appendix No. 4, *Report from the Select Committee on Consular Service and Appointments*, PP 1857-8 (482) VIII.

Select Committee of 1870-72 stimulated further inspections of the consulates on the coast of France, in Italy, in the Iberian peninsula, and around the Baltic. In the remaining decades of the century, Sir Clement Hill reported on consular establishments in the West Indies and other parts of the Spanish Main, Dudley Saurin (and later Ian Malcolm) reported on the United States consulates, and Henry Howard reported on the consular service in China.

The reports were useful for general organizational purposes, but they were much less valuable than they might have been, both to the Foreign Office and to the consuls themselves, simply because they were conducted by Foreign Office officials and diplomatic secretaries, none of whom had firsthand contact with consular work. When Sir Percy Anderson, senior clerk of the Consular Department, was questioned on this point in 1889, he explained that further consular inspection tours by Foreign Office officials were not in contemplation at the time. Since the perfection of telegraphic correspondence, he argued, the Foreign Office kept in touch with consuls without the expense of visits, and the practice was now to send round secretaries of legation rather than organize inspections from home, 'when probably the consul has his house swept and garnished in order to receive the visitor'.[1]

It was not until 1913 that the Foreign Office and the Treasury finally came round to the view put by Consul Green so many years before. Green wanted systematic inspections by specially appointed officers of sufficient status. But he insisted, sensibly enough, that those inspectors should have a detailed knowledge of consular work, which they could use to practical purpose in putting consular houses in order actually during their tours of inspection.

Accounting control A proper system of control over consular accounts, more particularly over money taken in fees, was remarkably slow in developing. When fees were taken on the personal account of the consul himself, it was expected that salary and fees together would cover office expenses. In the circumstances, office accounts were of no great interest to H.M. Government. But when, with the development of the salaried service and the payment of fees into the Exchequer, it became necessary to consider *government* provision for office expenses, the solution adopted was the allocation of a block grant to each consulate, to be spent precisely as the consul

---

[1] Minutes of Evidence, *Report of the Royal Commission on Civil Establishments*, pp 1890 (c. 6172-1) XXVII, QQ 27,430-4.

wished. The system was pleasantly simple and straightforward. It spared Whitehall the task of a detailed auditing of accounts. But of course it made no provision for office allowances to be spent exclusively for the benefit of H.M. Government.

As some sort of check over the level of fees, consuls from 1825 were required to exhibit the fee table in some prominent place in their offices, and to transmit home on oath, at the end of each year, a return in duplicate of the total of such fees received. At the same time, they were expected to make an annual return of all their receipts and disbursements for any purpose (with the exception of their own salaries), backed by the appropriate vouchers, to be transmitted to the Treasury and forwarded by them to the Commissioners for Auditing the Public Accounts.

This may have looked impressive on paper, but in practice it was only a very partial check. Other than salary, the consul's income came from fees, and consuls returned what fees they pleased. The fact that they were under oath, in a century when this was taken rather more seriously than it is today, had a deterrent effect, and there was always the danger of complaint should the overcharging become too blatant. The career consul, with his name, his security, his job and his pension at stake, was likely to take these complaints seriously, and the Foreign Office was quick to investigate them when they came.

The real trouble was not with the salaried career consuls, against whom remarkably few complaints were actually confirmed in the nineteenth century, but with the host of vice-consuls and consular agents, of many nationalities and as many degrees of honesty, with whom the public generally had to deal. As one Member of Parliament put it in 1856, nine times out of ten the consul himself did not deign to touch his fees, but handed them over to a subordinate who very often touched too much.[1] The nature of the day-to-day clientele at British consulates—illiterate and ignorant working men, sailors, Maltese, Gibraltarians, British Indians, Ionians—made it only too easy for a consular officer to use his official position to blackmail his victims into silence or to delude them into the belief that the charges he was levying were legitimate. It was to combat this kind of abuse, rather than to introduce any check on the career consuls themselves, that the 1858 Committee called the attention of the government to the system of collection by stamps issued against the receipt of fees, 'which has the merits of convenience and security'. Unfortunately, this was one of the many

---

[1] 141 *Parl. Deb.*, 3s, 1019-20 (14 April 1856).

recommendations of the 1858 Committee which the Foreign Office chose to ignore. Murray raised it in a desultory fashion with officials of the Inland Revenue, decided that it was impracticable, and let it drop. It was only after further examination before the 1872 Committee that the system was adopted.

A stamp system, as an accounting device, depends first and foremost on a frequent check on the stock of stamps. The stamps held by an officer must relate precisely, and at any time, to the fees paid into government account. If the stamps issued amount to a higher value than the money paid in, the officer has obviously pocketed the difference and can be held to account. Incredible though it may seem, the Foreign Office, for decades after the adoption of the stamp system, made no systematic check on the stock of unissued stamps (as against the sale of stamps returned). The only official check which existed was on the stock of stamps taken over by a consul following a transfer or retirement. This might well have been a sufficient deterrent to a man whose pension was at stake. But it did not prevent 'borrowings' from money intended for government account. Nor did it solve the far more serious problem of defalcations by unsalaried officers who might expect either to die in office or, when the reckoning came, to make good their escape.

The inadequacies of the stamp system, as applied by the Foreign Office, were exposed before the Public Accounts Committee in 1892. Very occasionally the Comptroller and Auditor General made arrangements for officials from his department, the Exchequer and Audit Department, to visit a group of consulates and inspect their accounts. The Foreign Office, though it disliked the visits, did not feel able to resist them; the Chief Clerk admitted, on the occasion of such an inspection at Yokohama and New York in 1908, that 'unfortunately we cannot say that we ourselves organize inspections, because inspection by diplomatic secretaries does not cover details of accounts and fees'.[1]

It so happened that on the first of these visits, in the autumn of 1891, the Comptroller and Auditor General himself inspected a number of Mediterranean consulates. His report caused some concern, and Henry Hervey, the Foreign Office representative before the Public Accounts Committee, was asked for an explanation. Sir Charles Ryan (the Comptroller) had called attention particularly to the fact that there was no fixed provision, so far as he was able to learn, for obtaining independent evidence of the stated balance of stamps at a given date at the various consular offices. On his visit to the

[1] PRO.FO/369/186.

The General Consular Service in the nineteenth century 67

vice-consulate at La Goulette, the port of Tunis, he had been able, by counting the counterfoils of the documents, to make an independent check on whether or not stamps had been issued. He found that there was distinct evidence from the counterfoils that documents had gone out with the consular seal but without stamps—the stock of stamps after nearly two-thirds of the quarter had elapsed was actually larger than it had been at the beginning of the quarter. Hervey, questioned on the point, considered that the general overseeing arrangements by superintending consuls were adequate and that there was no justification for introducing an expensive system of periodical inspections; to which Ryan replied that he had asked at the consulate at Tunis whether they had made any inspection of the five vice-consuls in the consular district: 'They said, certainly not; they knew irregularities were going on, but they had not considered it their duty to go and verify the stock of stamps for themselves.' A member of the Public Accounts Committee asked why it was that the vice-consul concerned had not been prosecuted, but had been permitted quietly to resign; he did not know, he said, how the Foreign Office would describe it in diplomatic language, but in a police court it would have been called embezzlement. Hervey, after a feeble attempt at denying that this *was* a case of embezzlement, added a comment which summed up the deficiencies of the system: the vice-consul at La Goulette 'was an unpaid vice-consul; he was a Frenchman in Tunis. It would have been impossible to obtain a conviction before a court of law there.'[1]

The Public Accounts Committee accepted Ryan's view of the importance of a check which would enable the Foreign Office to obtain independent evidence of the stated balances of stamps at the various vice-consulates: 'The mere adoption of the Stamp System is not a sufficient safeguard without such a check.' But there is no evidence that, before the establishment of the consular inspectorate in 1913, any steps were taken to put this recommendation systematically into effect. '[It is] one of the weak points of the consular system', the Earl of Derby explained to the 1870 Committee, 'that everybody's business is nobody's business, and inefficiency in a consul, as long as he does not get into scrapes, is not very quickly or very easily detected.'[2] The Foreign Office remained dependent on the receipt and investigation of complaints, and as anyone acquainted with the Mediterranean consulates knew only too well, control by this method was no more than nominal.

---

[1] Minutes of Evidence, *Fourth Report from the Committee of Public Accounts*, PP 1892 (277—Sess. 1) XI, QQ 1531–76.
[2] Minutes of Evidence, *Report of the Select Committee on Diplomatic and Consular Services*, PP 1870 (382) VII, Q 2543.

Chapter 3

The General Consular Service in the twentieth century

Canning's 1825 reforms had been intended to convert a miscellaneous group of semi-public officials, variously remunerated, into salaried, full-time state servants drawing a fixed income by vote of Parliament; they had not extended to the organization of a public service. As a result of government economies, even this limited intention was not permanently realized for half a century, and the General Service in 1903 was still an agglomeration of independent, individual posts with no systematic recruitment, grading, transfer, and promotion, and no adequate overall control.

The failure to create a service was not for lack of precedent or excellent advice. The French consular service, for one, had been graded since the beginning of the century into consuls-general, consuls *de 1re classe*, and consuls *de 2e classe*, with salary scales attached to the grade, admission by competition, and a training grade known as *élèves* consuls with a regular expectation of progress to the higher grades in the profession. Then, within the British consular service itself, the Far Eastern Service, developed under distinctively different conditions from the General Service, had followed much the same pattern as the French service, to be followed in turn, after 1877, by a new subdivision within the British service, the Levant Service.

From the earliest days of the Canning consuls, it was suggested that they should be organized into a genuine, graded service. Consul John Brackenbury, before the 1835 Committee, had urged that the service should be placed on a 'fixed and permanent basis'.[1] The 1858 Committee, while reluctant to fetter the Secretary of State entirely in making appointments at all levels to the service, had asked for a limited number of consular students, a graded service with promotion between grades, and salaries attached, so far as possible, to grades rather than posts. The 1872 Committee, reviewing the recommendations of the 1858 Committee, had concluded that though the Service was still too varied in its character and arrangements to be

---

[1] Minutes of Evidence, *Report of the Select Committee on Consular Establishment*, PP 1835 (499) VI, Q 1125.

organized and classified as were other branches of the Civil Service, if the Committee's own further recommendations were carried through, 'then it would be both practicable and convenient to introduce changes in that direction'. The Ridley Commission, twenty years later, felt that though the Far Eastern and Levant Services had proved their merit, the real objection to the introduction of a similar organization into the General Service was the need to recruit at all levels. But it was broadly in favour of some form of competition, and it considered that 'an attempt should be made to grade consulates and vice-consulates according to the salaries which appear necessary for the various posts . . . so as to afford promotion from third to second and first class places'.

For one reason or another each of these proposals had fallen on stony ground. But it became impossible to ignore the dissatisfaction both within the Service and without, more particularly at the continued and archaic abuse of unrestricted patronage. In 1902, with a move towards a regular service in mind, the Walrond Committee was appointed, with Sir William Walrond as Chairman, supported by Lord Cranborne (Under-Secretary of State for Foreign Affairs), Sir James Mackay (of MacKinnon Mackenzie, representing business), and Bonar Law (Parliamentary Secretary to the Board of Trade). Its recommendations (published in 1903), unreservedly in favour of a genuine, organized service, were adopted by the government at once and almost without exception.

Recruitment The first recommendations of the Walrond Committee were that the existing recruitment by patronage should be brought to an end, that admission into the General Service should be by limited competition, and that the age for admission should be from twenty-two to twenty-seven. Power should be reserved to the Secretary of State to appoint any person, regardless of the age limit, to one of the higher posts for which special qualifications might be required. 'But such appointments should be rare, as in the Diplomatic Service, and should only be made in exceptional circumstances, and when they are clearly in the public interest, so as to avoid lessening the attractions of the Service, and blocking the promotion of deserving officers.'

Unfortunately, although the Walrond recommendation put an end to unrestricted patronage, the Foreign Office found it difficult in practice to deny itself so convenient an outlet for its unemployables. Certain appointments, for which particular skills are required, must always continue to be at the discretion of the Secretary of State, and Secretaries of State have reserved their rights in this respect. But by no stretch of the imagination could these considerations have applied to the appointments of Philip Somers Cocks, after twenty years of chronic inefficiency as a Foreign Office clerk, to the consulate at Lisbon in 1907, or in 1914 of Gaston de Bernhardt and Godfrey Hertslet, both clerks with long service in the Librarian's Department of the Foreign Office, as consul at Nantes and consul-general at Trieste respectively. Nor was it true of William J. Lamont's appointment as consul at Boma in 1911, which was quite openly a reward for his excellent service as financial adviser and receiver of customs to the Republic of Liberia. These were the appointments of Sir Edward Grey who had assured the Commons, shortly after becoming Secretary of State, that it was his intention that 'the Consular service should only be entered by young men, after examination, who have special *prima facie* qualifications for the service, and that important posts should be filled up by men who have entered the public service by showing that they have the qualifications for it'.[1]

The continued exercise of patronage even after the Walrond recommendations did not escape the attention of the House, nor, indeed, of the Treasury. Unlike the Foreign Office, the Treasury, guided by the longstanding rejection of patronage for Home Civil Service appointments, was particularly sensitive in this respect. When the Foreign Office opened negotiations in April 1917 for an increased consular establishment after the war, Stanley Baldwin (Financial Secretary to the Treasury) explained in reply that considerable increases in numbers and salaries would mean that there would be a large amount of patronage to be dispensed, and further that the men selected would remain with the Foreign Office for thirty or forty years and make or mar the consular service during that period. He argued that it was essential to have a good parliamentary defence against possible parliamentary accusations of favouritism, and that it would therefore be better if the overseas appointments were made not by the Secretary of State alone but on the recommendation of a suitable committee which should include the First Civil Service Commissioner.[2]

The Foreign Office was inclined to resent interference of this kind. But the Treasury continued to insist, first, that any appointments made directly after the war or before the re-establishment of the normal, peacetime competitions, should be kept to a minimum, and second, that they should

---

[1] 153 *Parl. Deb.*, 4s, 189 (5 March 1906).
[2] Stanley Baldwin to Lord Robert Cecil, Treasury, 5 May 1917: PRO.FO/369/970.

be made by a committee of selection. When the time came, such a committee was in fact established. But in the three years after the 1918 Armistice it was bypassed for no less than fifteen consulates and consulates-general, filled by outsiders without examination or certificate. The Treasury protested strongly against one of these, the appointment of Alan Napier to a consulate in 1921, as 'opening the door to accusations of patronage'; it enquired about similar appointments and demanded (unsuccessfully) that Napier's appointment should be suspended. Its protests were met with the unhelpful reply that the Secretary of State (Lord Curzon) was 'prepared to meet any criticism with regard to his exercise of this right [of direct appointment]', and that, in the specific case of Napier, 'we are committed to his appointment and we cannot possibly turn him down now'.[1]

The understood rule in the service at all times after 1903 was that men were not introduced from outside over the heads of existing officers. Algernon Law, Comptroller of Commercial and Consular Affairs, told the 1914 Commission that so far as he was concerned he would always resist such introductions because they were damaging both with the public and with the service itself.[2] But exceptions were far too frequent and by any standards often unjustifiable, and the appointment of outsiders remained a serious grievance within the service. It was still very much of an issue in the 1930s. The consular officers giving evidence to the important consular committee of 1932-33 were unanimous in feeling that entry into the service except through the normal channel was open, for service reasons, to the strongest objection. The Committee supported their view and considered that 'only the most exceptional circumstances justify the admission of candidates who have not qualified for entry into the service in the usual way'.

Examinations Patronage survived into the reformed service, but after 1903 the normal entry was by limited competition. Whereas 'open' competition, which before 1914 had meant written examinations with no *viva voce* test, was by now generally applied to entry to the Home Civil Service, the Foreign Office and Diplomatic Service had not progressed beyond 'limited' competition—that is, competition restricted to a limited list of candidates who had secured a nomination to compete from the Secretary of State. No

---

[1] PRO.FO/369/1680. In justice to Napier, it should be said that this appointment, unlike many others at the time, was an unqualified success.
[2] Minutes of Evidence, *5th Report of the Royal Commission on the Civil Service*, PP 1914-16 (Cd 7749) XI, QQ 42,953-4.

competition existed for appointments to the General Consular Service; and when the Walrond Committee, deciding that it was necessary to introduce some element of competition, considered the form appropriate to consuls, it came down unanimously in favour of limited competition. The Committee argued that a precedent already existed in the Diplomatic Service; it chose to ignore the precedent established in precisely the opposite sense for entry to the Far Eastern and the Levant Consular Services. Limited competition was necessary because even if recruitment were reserved for 'British subjects', the compass of the term was sufficiently wide to include 'certain persons' not suited to serve in a representative capacity overseas.[1] The method chosen for weeding out these 'certain persons' was a Board of Selection, consisting of Foreign Office officials exclusively, which met periodically, interviewed all candidates whose names came before it, and nominated suitable candidates for a written examination conducted by the Civil Service Commissioners.

Apologists were inclined to argue, between the wars, that no social disqualification was intended. Unfortunately, there is no doubt about it. The minutes of evidence taken before the Walrond Committee in 1903, which were not published, make it perfectly clear that a central objection to open competition was the admission of the 'Board School' man.[2] But it was true, nevertheless, that the line of social acceptability was drawn much lower for nominations to the consular service than it was for the diplomatic service—as it had to be at the time, since one of the main objects of the Walrond reforms was to attract candidates of commercial experience.

There were other reasons. Gentlemen of colour were not to be admitted. When the question of Vice-Consul Watt's recruitment to the career service was considered (he was unsalaried vice-consul at Port-au-Prince, very highly spoken of by his official superior), Lord Dufferin minuted: 'He is not quite white, being a native of Dominica, and I think there would be an objection to taking a "pale yellow" man into the Regular Service.'[3] More generally, Algernon Law, the Chairman of the Board of Selection, felt that the main function of his Board was to ensure that the service was not flooded out by men brought up and educated abroad—a type of candidate not particularly desirable in a service intended to represent Britain, but favoured in the consular examination, with its heavy emphasis on languages. Law told the

---

[1] As explained by Lord Cranborne, a member of the Committee: 126 *Parl. Deb.*, 4s, 1016 (30 July 1903).
[2] Minutes of Evidence, *Report of the Committee appointed to inquire into the Constitution of the Consular Service*: Foreign Office, Confidential Print 7973.
[3] PRO.FO/369/966.

The General Consular Service in the twentieth century 73

1914 Commission that between 5 and 10 per cent of the salaried consular service as it then existed was of part-foreign origin, and he was backed on his general point by H. A. Roberts, Secretary to the Cambridge Appointments Board, who added that, although the argument for preselection was not one of class, it was to the good if the Selection Board could also ascertain that candidates had 'quiet, good manners without aggressiveness, offensiveness, or any marked peculiarity'.[1]

Roberts was pointing to what was really the main difficulty before 1914. There was something splendidly impartial about the Victorian concept of open competition, where a man was judged and employed purely and simply on the standard of his written answers, without reference to his personal acceptability. But as sensible men realized at the time, the state was taking an unnecessary gamble. If any method could be found by which birth, fortune and connections could be kept out of it, there was everything to be said for some sort of *viva voce* test. So long as open competition implied no such test, it was perhaps understandable from many points of view, illiberal or otherwise, that nomination and a board of selection should have been preferred.

It was only after the First World War, rather disturbingly, that the peculiarly exclusive attitude of the Foreign Office to appointments came completely out into the open. As a result of the recommendations of the Royal Commission on the Civil Service, 1912-14, it had been decided to include a *viva voce* examination in the general competition for the Civil Service. Sir Samuel Hoare, introducing a debate on the Foreign Service in 1919, argued most strongly that a single board should conduct the interviews for the whole Civil Service, Home and Foreign; special 'weeding-out' interviews, conducted by the Foreign Office itself, did more harm than good: 'They do harm by leaving the impression upon the public outside that the service is still a close borough, restricted to a particular class, and on that account they shake the confidence of the country in the Service.'[2] But his arguments were ignored, and a candidate for the diplomatic and consular services, until as recently as 1939, had to undergo two interviews—a preliminary board of selection (on which the Foreign Office was represented) where a candidate's suitability for 'representational' functions was determined, followed by the usual 'viva', forming part of the Civil Service competition conducted by the Civil Service Commissioners, to which he

---

[1] Minutes of Evidence, *5th Report of the Royal Commission on the Civil Service*, PP 1914-16 (Cd 7749) XI, QQ 37,356-8; 41,575-6.
[2] 116 *HC Deb.*, 5s, 493-4 (21 May 1919).

was allowed to proceed only if he had satisfied the board. The board was no formality. In the late 1920s the average rejection rate was 36 per cent, a substantially larger percentage than under the prewar system.

One of the reasons, of course, why there were more rejections in the 1920s was simply that, since the examinations had been assimilated to the normal Civil Service Class I competition, the number and social range of candidates was larger: the consular service, associated with the other Civil Service vacancies, had become known to a much broader group of possible candidates. A simple device to restrict too broad a candidature for consular nominations before 1914 had been a refusal to advertise the examinations. Few applications for nominations were turned down—perhaps only one among the twenty or thirty applicants seen by the selection board in a day of interviews.[1] But then, it was unlikely that anyone outside a fairly narrow social range would have had any idea that the interviews were taking place. A proposal to begin advertising for applicants had been discussed within the Foreign Office in 1908, when it was nipped in the bud by the Private Secretary to the Secretary of State on the grounds that the number of candidates on the Secretary of State's lists already ensured an adequate supply, and that he (the Private Secretary) would 'deprecate our resorting to means of advertisement except in case of the supply failing us'.[2] Providentially for the social composition of the service, the supply did not fail. When Miss Haldane raised the subject before the 1914 Commission, it emerged that the Foreign Office was still making no attempt to advertise; that the schools and universities, especially in Scotland and Ireland, knew very little about the General Consular Service; that the examinations, to make things more confusing, were not even held at regular intervals or at a fixed time of year; and that the nomination system, though not in reality a very considerable hurdle, was certainly regarded as such by those who had no reason to think otherwise.[3]

Most successful of all among the social barriers to entrance to the consular service, and one which endured to the end of the service's independent existence, was again the simplest of devices—a stringent language qualification. It was obviously important for consular officials to have a reasonable command of foreign languages, especially at a time when English was not so

---

[1] Minutes of Evidence, *5th Report of the Royal Commission on the Civil Service*, PP 1914-16 (Cd 7749) XI, Q 37,367.
[2] The file is in PRO.FO/369/186.
[3] Minutes of Evidence, *5th Report of the Royal Commission on the Civil Service*, PP 1914-16 (Cd 7749) XI, QQ 38,824-5; 40,543-4; 43,751.

widely spoken overseas. In 1916 one vice-consul went so far as to propose that candidates for consular appointments should be examined 'very searchingly' in French and German, compulsorily in Russian at an easier standard, and optionally in Spanish, Italian, Swedish, Norwegian, Danish or Dutch—a proposal which produced the comment, scribbled in the margin,

> *And still the wonder grew*
> *That one small head, etc.* . . . .[1]

There is no reason to doubt that a genuine language requirement for the efficient performance of consular duties was the original motive for the language test. The effect, nevertheless, was to exclude all except those who could afford the extensive private tuition and the years of study abroad needed to meet the exceptionally high standards demanded. The requirement of two languages was reduced to a single language in 1927 in order to improve the field of candidates. But the standard still remained very high indeed and this, together with the £300 bond which was introduced, inexplicably, for all probationers for the consular service in 1933, acted as a substantial disincentive to lower-middle-class and working-class recruitment.

Training The twentieth-century consular service was no more successful than the Victorian service in solving the problem of the experience it should require of new entrants, and of the training it should be prepared to give them before they were sent to their first post. It was a problem which deserved a solution simply because there were so many independent posts in the service. Even in the larger posts a new vice-consul might expect, within a few weeks of arrival, to find himself in charge while his chief went absent for weeks or months at a time.

In the twentieth century as in the nineteenth there was a standard cycle in training proposals for consuls. A committee would take evidence which indicated a widespread desire, particularly in industry, for more adequate training arrangements for recruits to the consular service; the committee reported in favour of more training and suggested a scheme; the Foreign Office rejected the scheme as too ambitious, but substituted a compromise scheme of its own which was then put into effect; within a few years the compromise scheme had been discontinued. The reasons for failure were always the same: the expense of the scheme, doubts as to its practical value,

[1] PRO.FO/369/912.

and, above all, the chronic problem of finding the time and the staff to permit the secondment of officers for training. The result was that even in the early 1960s, the Foreign Office was spending less than £25,000 p.a. on training programmes.[1]

The most constant desideratum for consular recruits was commercial experience, and demands for such experience were the more strident as consuls, with the turn of the century, became less preoccupied with routine maritime functions and more with the promotion of British trade. The solution experimentally adopted by the 1903 Committee was to widen the normal civil service recruitment age to twenty-seven in the hope that young men who had already spent four or five years in commercial houses might be persuaded to apply. The Committee realized that such 'commercial' candidates would be at a disadvantage in competing, in a purely academic examination, with men fresh from the universities, and they felt that it would be necessary to give this some weight in the examination.

The Committee's experiment failed. Young men with the right kind of commercial experience did not come forward. Of the sixty-nine successful candidates for the consular service, 1907-13, only seventeen had any kind of business experience (commercial, banking and insurance), and of these, only five had the kind of commercial experience which could be regarded as of value to a consular career. 'I think we may say', Lord MacDonnell (chairman of the 1914 Commission) concluded, after examining the details with the President of the Associated Chambers of Commerce, 'that the rules of 1903 have been practically inoperative in procuring for the consular service men with commercial experience.'[2]

One of the reasons, quite clearly, was that the salaries offered to new entrants to the consular service—£150 p.a. while on probation, £300 on appointment abroad with annual increments of £20—were not attractive to good men who were already making their way in business. But though this was the reason which the Foreign Office liked to put forward, there was more to it than that. The two members of the Walrond Committee who could actually claim commercial experience, Sir James Mackay (later Lord Inchcape) and Andrew Bonar Law, had been convinced that there was a substantial reserve of young men in commercial houses who, though of some aptitude, had realized that they had no prospect of a partnership, and

[1] *Report of the Committee on Representational Services Overseas*, PP 1964 (Cmnd 2276) XI, para 403 (this was exclusive of the cost of the Middle East Centre for Arab Studies).
[2] Minutes of Evidence, *5th Report of the Royal Commission on the Civil Service*, PP 1914-16 (Cd 7749) XI, QQ 41,950-64, and Appendix LXXVIII.

who would readily consider employment elsewhere. When businesses were still generally small and partnerships very much within the family, when the lack of opportunities for promising young men without the right connections was still driving such men abroad in large numbers to administer railways or public utilities in Argentina, Chile, India, or the Dominions, it was likely enough that Mackay and Law were right. But there is no evidence that the Foreign Office ever gave the experiment a real chance.

For one, no scheme was worked out by which men of business experience, necessarily away from their books for a number of years, might be given an advantage at the examination. Admittedly it was very difficult to devise any kind of examination which would give proper weight to commercial experience, and the Civil Service Commissioners were aware of the problem. Recruits to the consular service came severally direct from their homes, from the universities, and from commercial employment; it was, as the First Commissioner (Stanley Leathes) told the 1914 Commission, 'a very difficult examination to make at all satisfactory... a very troublesome examination'.[1] The solution adopted was to make the examination itself, except for the language papers, a relatively elementary affair for which candidates at all levels might be entered, and to depend on competition among candidates to sort the sheep from the goats. But an examination of this kind, with fixed subjects and assigned textbooks for arithmetic, commercial geography, the principles of British mercantile and commercial law, and political economy, in addition to English composition and two modern languages, was a gift to those 'cramming' establishments which flourished with such devastating effect in late Victorian and Edwardian England. Not only were commercial candidates put out of the field but so, to the chagrin of the Cambridge University Appointments Board, were graduates of the ancient universities—unless they too were prepared to enrol with one of the principal crammers.

The failure to put the 1903 Committee's recommendation into effect was probably in itself a decisive blow to the whole experiment. Without some weight given at the examination, the odds were very much against the commercial candidate. But the odds were increased still further by the failure of the Foreign Office adequately to advertise its new recruitment policy, followed only two years after the experiment had begun, by its decision to eliminate the one slight element of preference for commercial candidates which had existed. The notice of the 1906 examination, for example, inviting applications from 'candidates with commercial knowledge and experience

[1] *Ibid.*, QQ 38,789-90.

who have spent three years in the employment of a firm of good standing', gave only two weeks for those applications to reach the Private Secretary—effectively precluding candidates who might be serving with British mercantile houses overseas (as they would almost certainly have had to be to acquire the right level of language ability). Furthermore, the notice, which appeared once only, was printed in small type and tucked away at the bottom of the Colonial and Foreign News page of *The Times*.[1] It was hardly surprising that few commercial candidates, of sufficient quality or otherwise, actually put forward their names. Yet this was the reason given for discontinuing (after the 1906 competition) the reservation of a proportion of the vacancies specifically for candidates with commercial experience.

No doubt some of this was due simply to inexperience at the Foreign Office. The Foreign Office knew nothing about publicizing its wares and cared less. There had never been any difficulty in filling the Secretary of State's nomination lists—quite the reverse—and it was, in fact, an established practice that while the Civil Service Commissioners made it their business to advertise 'open' competitions, they did not advertise competitions for which nominations were still necessary. But even if inexperience is a possible excuse, it cannot be denied that Foreign Office officials were not enchanted by the idea of 'commercial' candidates. E. W. P. Thurstan, an experienced consular officer serving temporarily in the Foreign Office, prepared a memorandum in 1917 on the qualifications of candidates for the consular service in which he emphasized the diplomatic and representational functions which a consul was called on to perform. He felt that one of the 'essential qualifications' was that candidates should be 'gentlemen in the best sense of the word', for:

> It must be remembered that not only the British public, but, which is vastly more important, the foreign public, will in the days to come, look up to these officers as representatives of the British Empire, not only as representatives but as the 'beau ideal'. It is useless to shirk the issue of the question.

J. A. C. Tilley, the Chief Clerk, agreed with Thurstan that the consul required diplomatic qualities. While a consul, he argued, might be strong on commercial questions, he might well be incapable of the sort of work currently handled by Robert Bruce Lockhart at Moscow, Edward Vicars at Lyons, and Ernest Maxse at Rotterdam—'It is therefore important that

---

[1] *The Times*, 25 May 1906.

we should not be misled into selecting "business men".'.[1] Some of the consuls themselves felt much the same. Philip Sarell, Consul at Dunkirk, concluded a memorandum on the reform of the consular service with a strong and passionate objection to bringing 'businessmen' into the service: 'Make a Merchant Prince Ambassador at Washington or Constantinople, if you like', he said generously, 'but don't open the door of the Consular Service to the leavings of Trade.'[2]

By 1917 the Walrond Committee's plan for recruiting existing commercial experience, except at occasional high-level commercial posts, was already discredited, and the alternative—of selecting candidates of a good general educational background for commercial and economic training *after* recruitment—had gained the day. The 1914 Commission was satisfied that the Walrond Committee's experiment had failed, and the Commission's thinking developed along the lines of proposals which it had already made for the rest of the Civil Service—that is, the consuls should be recruited by the examination suggested for the new Senior Clerical Class (later to become the Executive Class) at the end of their schooling, after which they should undergo two years' special study at an approved university or college designed to fit them for their consular duties. 'Experience shows', the Commission concluded, 'that we cannot recruit ready made the finished product; let us recruit the sound raw material, and fashion it as we think right.'

The general principle of the 1914 Commission's recommendations was accepted. But it was decided in the later years of the war, when it had become widely agreed that there was a real need to expand and develop the consular service to meet expected foreign competition, that the level of recruitment should be set rather higher. The question in 1914 had seemed to be whether it was better to aim at getting the pick of the boys coming direct from school, or whether the consular service should be prepared to take the leavings of the Class I examination—'leavings', because the Indian and Home Civil Services offered far better prospects and inducements. The 1914 Commission preferred the first; the 1917-19 reformers, the second. In 1920, when the normal Civil Service competitions were restored, the consular service was brought into line with the other higher branches of the Civil Service. It was recruited in future at graduate level from men at the end of their educational careers, who were no longer expected to have previous

---
[1] Memorandum dated December 1917, and minutes: PRO.FO/369/971.
[2] Memorandum dated 19 December 1916: PRO.FO/369/912.

commercial experience. The reduction of the maximum age limit for entry from twenty-seven to twenty-four marked the conclusion of the Walrond experiment.

The new principle of recruitment direct from a general education made sense only if the Foreign Office were prepared to make itself responsible for training. Before 1914 the theory was that all new entrants to the service, commercially experienced or otherwise, spent three months before posting at the Foreign Office and the Board of Trade. Since this was entirely unsystematic, such descriptions as survive are universally uncomplimentary— a 'sheer waste of time'; 'three months' semi-idleness' during which vice-consuls were made to feel 'useless interlopers'; 'little more than a formality and a waste of time'.[1] The postwar scheme, based as it was on a different philosophy of recruitment and training, was far more ambitious. Sir Arthur Steel-Maitland, Parliamentary Secretary of the new Department of Overseas Trade and the moving force behind consular reform at the time, explained to the Commons in February 1918 that what he had in mind was to give new recruits a year of commercial education at one of the modern universities, Leeds for example, where they would receive not only an academic training but firsthand experience in neighbouring factories, followed by a definite course in banking, currency, finance and transport.[2]

When it came to the point, probationers in the General Service were sent to the London School of Economics for a two-year course in currency, finance, industrial organization, transport, commercial geography, and commercial and industrial law—an unhappy locale, as Foreign Office officials soon realized, for 'the atmosphere at the London School of Economics leaves something to be desired', and the probationers were transferred to the unpolluted air of Cambridge in Michaelmas 1923.[3] Three years later new entrants were despatched direct to their posts and the whole elaborate training scheme abandoned. It had fallen victim primarily to the current wave of government economy, but doubt persisted over the practical value of such courses, and the belief was never entirely suppressed that consular work was best learnt on the job. A preference for training *en poste* governed thinking until the end of the service, and, until recently, continued to influence such training programmes as existed in the reformed Foreign Service. A scheme devised in the late 1930s to give 'selected, highly promising

---

[1] Lockhart, *Memoirs of a British Agent*, p. 46; *The Times*, 31 August 1917, 4a; Fisher, additional typescript F, p. 32.

[2] 103, *HC Deb.*, 5s, 1297-8 (26 February 1918).

[3] PRO.FO/369/1830.

officers' a training in the City after their first leave came to nothing; it proved impossible, as always, to spare the men for secondment.

Salaries The General Service after 1903—a salaried, graded service into which officers were introduced at the beginning of their working lives and given some expectation of a career—was administratively a much more complex affair than it had been under the Victorians. It would be pleasant to record that contemporaries realized this, and that the administrative and personnel arrangements of the Foreign Office were at once brought up to date to cope with it. But this, though true enough in some respects, was untrue in rather more.

Though consular salaries and pensions were never raised to an entirely satisfactory level, the Walrond Committee's recommendations did introduce a new and workable basis which survives to this day. The constant problem in establishing salary levels for overseas posts was, and is, the variation in the cost of living from post to post, sometimes over a very wide range indeed. Canning recognized the problem in 1825 (see p. 33 ff. above). But the solution he adopted was to set a salary for each post independently, calculated on an estimate of the local cost of living; thus the consuls at Pernambuco and Bahia were allocated salaries of £1200 p.a., in contrast to the £500 p.a. available at Calais and Le Havre.

Superficially a sensible arrangement, the Canning system had all the disadvantages of inflexibility and inequity already discussed, and the alternative of a graded service, with salaries attached to grades rather than to individual posts, had been under discussion for many years before its final adoption in 1903. The Walrond Committee realized, in fact, that the most satisfactory method of solving the peculiar problems of an overseas service was to apply what had by now become standard practice in the Home Civil Service, the attachment of salaries to grades, but with the addition of a system of local allowances to account for variations in the cost of living overseas. The General Consular Service was accordingly divided into grades in which consuls-general were to receive, according to their standing and the importance of their posts, salaries of £1200, £1000, or £800; consuls, £800 or £600; and vice-consuls, £350 rising by fixed increments to £450, or £300 to £500. Supplementation in the form of local allowances was to be supplied for the really expensive posts.

Local allowances were not entirely new to the consular service. Under considerable pressure a few local allowances had been introduced at consular posts around the turn of the century. The Walrond Committee's contribution was to put these local allowances on a regular basis, extend them to a large number of posts, and attach them to a system of salaries calculated according to grades.

There were two respects in which the new system fell short of perfection. In the first place, the local allowances paid before 1914 were never applied to the consular service as a whole. They were payable only at what were described as the 'expensive' posts, and little attempt was made to define this category systematically. At Buenos Aires, which was generally recognized to be a very expensive post, the consul in 1914 received £500 local allowance on top of his £800 basic salary. At New York, the consul-general was earning the top salary of his grade, £1200, together with a £2000 or £1500 local allowance. But the Treasury set its face against giving local allowances for posts in Europe, even though at some posts the cost of living was markedly higher than it was in the United Kingdom.

The second criticism, and perhaps the more serious, was that the Walrond Committee's grading proposals did not allow enough flexibility for transfers and promotions within the service. The pay of consuls remained attached to the posts at which they were stationed. Automatic increments of salary were received only at the vice-consular grade, after which consuls were posted to £600 consulates, to £800 consulates or consulates-general, and to consulates-general at £1000 or £1200. The result was that if a man had reached a point on the seniority list which entitled him to rise to the ranks of an £800 consul, no matter how good he was at his existing £600 post and how inconvenient it might be to transfer him, he had to be moved to a consulate to which an £800 salary was attached. The situation was at its worst at the level of consul-general, at which there were only four posts, Antwerp, Hamburg, New York and San Francisco, at the top salary of the grade (£1200 p.a.). There was no way of rewarding good work, even at an important post like Marseilles, short of moving the officer to one of the four £1200 posts; and since the pension was related to terminal salary a difficult choice had often to be made between the personal interests of the consul-general and the interests of the state by which he was employed. Lord MacDonnell, the Chairman of the 1914 Commission, took a close interest in this particular problem. His own experience had been that it was better that the pay should be personal: 'I have had experience in the Indian Civil Service of the system of attaching the pay to the place; an officer, on promotion, had to leave the place, where he was wanted, for another in which he was not so useful. The system worked very inconveniently, and was abandoned.'[1]

There was obviously something to be said for attaching some scale of values to senior posts. It was absurd, while more important posts were staffed by men of lower salaries, to pay an officer at a high rate at an unimportant post simply because regular increments had taken his salary to the top of the scale. But this was a matter for personnel planning. It was the total inflexibility of the system introduced by the Walrond Committee (slightly modified to include increments for second-class consuls after the 1912 Committee) which was at fault. In 1919, as part of Sir Arthur Steel-Maitland's proposals for the reorganization of the consular service, the War Cabinet sanctioned a new salary scale in which the salaries were substantially improved and incremental conditions attached to all grades (vice-consuls: £300 by 20 to £600; consuls: £800 by 25 to £1000; consuls-general: £1200 by 50 to £1500). This, with its far greater degree of flexibility, was the scale which remained in force until the Second World War.

Allowances In general, however, the substantial improvement which took place in consular salaries between 1903 and 1943 took the form rather of better and more logically applied allowances than of a radical revision of consular salaries; it is sometimes surprising, indeed, to see how little variation there was in the salaries attached to certain posts between 1826 and 1939. At no point in the history of the consular service did the Foreign Office take the final step to what has come to be recognized, since 1947, as the only logical basis for allowances—the acknowledgment, as one Foreign Office official defined it, that foreign allowances should be 'the amount considered necessary to make up the difference between what a man gets in salary and what he needs for his job'. Allowances at particular posts remained relatively inflexible, unrelated often to the actual needs of the post, haphazard, and inconsistent one with another. But at least some attempt was made to allow for the real expenses of a representational post overseas.

A first reform was in the allocation and control of office allowances. The old system, by which consuls received a fixed office allowance for each post to be spent entirely at their discretion, had opened the door to some notorious abuses, some of which were unavoidable. In a post such as Moscow in the

---

[1] Minutes of Evidence, *5th Report of the Royal Commission on the Civil Service*, PP 1914-16 (Cd 7749) XI, Q 43,017.

years immediately preceding the First World War, it was quite impossible for the consul to live on his official salary; the result inevitably was that the entire office allowance was absorbed into the salary, while the British consular office became a small anteroom in the consul's own shabby flat. The institution of a system of inspectors in 1913 made it possible to identify cases such as this and to recommend the necessary increases, and as a minor improvement in 1914 it was decided that all office furniture purchased in future out of the office allowance should become the property of H.M. Government. After 1919 all furniture and stationery for consular offices were supplied by the Office of Works and H.M. Stationery Office respectively, and remained government property.

More important was the principle, laid down in the Steel-Maitland Committee's Report of 19 March 1919, that consular offices 'should compare favourably with those of business firms of good standing', a recommendation which actually seems to have been put into effect over the next decades. Fixed office allowances were preserved for simplicity of accounting, and the balance, or deficit, carried forward in the quarterly accounts. The level of allowances was based on experience and intended to cover the rent of an adequate office, the employment of staff, and expenditure on telephones, telegrams and newspapers. But it appears from Sir Frederick Butler's evidence before the Estimates Committee in 1937 that a reasonable amount of flexibility was permitted, and that allowances were commonly readjusted, either up or down, as local circumstances changed.[1]

Entirely new principles were introduced in the two forms of allowances added to all consular salaries without distinction after 1919; rent allowance and 'representation' allowance. Consular housing had always been a problem, and there was no uniformity in its solution. In the Victorian Far Eastern Service and for one or two of the Levant consulates, official residences had been supplied at the expense of H.M. Government. For both of these areas, some of the consulates were on an impressive scale. The consulate at Foochow in the early days (the mid-1840s) was a picturesque collection of detached temples, shaded by banyans and pines, and reached by a stiff climb up terraced paths above the city. From the 'monastic solitude of the temple-consulate', the consul looked down on a matchless view, over the battlemented walls and watchtowers of the city enclosing a sea of green-tiled roofs broken by the red patch of a temple or a mandarin's palace, and then out

---

[1] Minutes of Evidence, *Report of the Select Committee on Estimates*, PP 1936-7 (86, 143) VII, Q 1481.

across a spacious and undulating plain, closed in by an amphitheatre of hills.[1] Twenty years later, the Foochow consulate was still sited in a temple, as were the consulates of Newchwang and Chinkiang. But styles of life were becoming more rigidly Europeanized, and an official inspector described T. T. Meadows's temple at Newchwang as 'not at all adapted for the residence of a family'. Major Crossman found the consul at Tamsui (Formosa) in a Chinese house in the middle of the Chinese town, where he had lived for five years under conditions which, the inspector felt, would not have been tolerated by any Englishman for a week.[2]

At Smyrna, the Levant Service had inherited the Levant Company's splendid consular compound, rather decayed but on a substantial scale with its living-quarters, chapel, infirmary, stables, offices, and warehouses. Harry Johnston, who himself (as consul-general at Tunis at the turn of the century) enjoyed the amenity of a country palace at La Marsa, described a visit to the British consulate-general at Tripoli. The exterior of Thomas Jago's residence, in the Eastern tradition, was aggressively blank: 'But inside it was a delightful Moorish palace, with patios and hanging galleries, bananas, palms and flowers, rich carpets, and an array of curiosities, classic and mediaeval.'[3]

Yet, with the exception of the few official residences, the housing of consuls before the 1919 reforms had depended entirely on what they themselves were prepared and able to allocate from their own resources, whether out of official salaries or private incomes. Richard Burton may have had the private resources to rent a great house at Salahiyyeh, fifteen minutes' ride from the walls of Damascus. But the British consul at Jerusalem, the unfortunate, hag-ridden James Finn, chronically short of money, lived in the old parsonage house, next to the Anglican cathedral. There were six rooms, apart from the underground kitchen: three bedrooms, two sitting-rooms (which, thrown into one, had to serve for the consul's business and receptions), and a single living-room, ten feet by twelve, which was all the space available to his family even in the heat of a Palestinian summer.[4] It was to avoid such conditions and to provide some sort of minimum standard that

---

[1] As described by Stanley Lane-Poole, *The Life of Sir Harry Parkes* (London, 1894) I, 104-5.
[2] *Reports from Major Crossman and Correspondence respecting the Legation and Consular Buildings in China and Japan*, pp 1867-8 (315) XLVIII.
[3] Sir Harry H. Johnston, *The Story of My Life* (London, 1923), p. 345.
[4] Mrs Finn's editorial note to James Finn, *Stirring Times or Records from Jerusalem Consular Chronicles of 1853 to 1856* (London, 1878), I, 99-100.

a rent allowance was initiated in 1919 on the scale of £250 to a consul-general, £200 to a consul, and £100 to a vice-consul.

The rent allowance itself was a recognition that British officials overseas, in the national interest as much as in their own, should be properly housed. But the representational functions of consuls were acknowledged more formally in an actual 'representation allowance' (consuls-general, £300; consuls, £250; vice-consuls, £50-£250 depending on posts and seniority). During the nineteenth century, the official attitude to social expenditure by consuls had been quite uncompromising. Consuls, as distinct from diplomats, were not expected or intended to entertain. It was an attitude which took no account of the minimum obligations of consuls to their countrymen overseas or of the value that entertainment might have, if properly distributed, in widening contacts and improving information. The inadequacies or non-existence of hotels made it impossible at many posts for consuls to refuse hospitality to their countrymen, especially when those countrymen, as they so often did, had taken care to furnish themselves with a sheaf of letters of introduction from important persons at home. At some posts such as Cairo (a favourite stopping-off place on the route to India) and Tientsin (an inevitable stage on the road to Peking), consular officers were put to considerable expense by a continual stream of highly placed English globe-trotters, for whom adequate hotel accommodation simply did not exist. The rule laid down inflexibly by the Treasury and the Foreign Office was that foreigners of distinction, officers of rank in Her Majesty's Naval and Military Service, British diplomats and consular colleagues might be provided with accommodation, for which, in the China services at least, a small entertainment allowance could be claimed. But as Lord Clarendon explained in the case of Tientsin, 'there seems no reason why persons travelling on business or pleasure should find quarters at Her Majesty's Consulate, and be entertained at the public expense'.[1] What the fate of these travellers was to be, nobody except the consular officer concerned ever felt it necessary to ask, and in practice any general hospitality which the consul felt compelled to offer came out of his own pocket.

As for the entertainment of foreign business and political contacts—now esteemed so highly among Foreign Service functions that modern representation allowances are payable practically to the level of Chancery guards— no allowance whatever was made. Yet it was obvious by the later decades

---

[1] No. 1, *Correspondence respecting diplomatic and consular expenditure in China, Japan, and Siam*, pp 1870 (c. 69) LXVI.

of the nineteenth century that in some countries social negligence could be a short-sighted economy. Woodbine Parish had complained from Buenos Aires as far back as 1825 that a man's weight depended very much on his ability to give expensive balls and dinners on the extravagant scale common in *porteño* society.[1] Much the same was true in other societies; and as it became more important for consuls to act as sources of commercial intelligence for their countrymen, it was as necessary to widen the range of their social contacts.

In two inspection reports which reached the Foreign Office in 1912, both Henry Cooke, on the basis of what he had seen of the British consulates in Russia, and Guy Locock, on his tour in the United States, urged the importance of some kind of allowance for consular hospitality. 'The best and fullest information,' said Cooke, 'even on business matters, not to mention subjects of general or political interest ... is obtained socially, whether sought from the consul's colleagues or from prominent local business men.'[2] Locock felt that the view was 'wholly erroneous', more especially in the United States, that it was unnecessary for a consul to entertain or to play any part in the social life of his post. It was expected that a consul should keep up some sort of position, and resented if he did not. By social intercourse he could become acquainted with the views of the business men who mattered in the community, and whose views provided a more reliable index to trends than the newspapers on which a consul must otherwise depend. Business in America was largely carried out informally, and it was 'far easier to obtain information from a man in America by asking him out to lunch than by calling formally at his office'.[3]

In the general rethinking on consular functions in the early years of the century, the justice of these arguments was at last recognized. They formed in part the basis of the recommendation of the Foreign Office Committee of 1912 in favour of higher salaries, and they were strongly urged on the Treasury by A. J. Balfour, the Foreign Secretary, in his claim for a 50 per cent increase in many consular salaries early in 1917. It was essential, the Foreign Office argued, to enable consuls to live in a style befitting their position, not simply for personal considerations, but in the public interest:

There is every reason to believe that had they been able to enter more freely into social life, British interests might have been considerably

[1] Shuttleworth, *Sir Woodbine Parish*, p. 299.
[2] Report dated 27 April 1912: PRO.FO/369/536.
[3] Report dated 11 June 1912: *ibid.*

furthered in the past; and Mr Balfour regards as indispensable to their full utility the ability freely to enter the best social and commercial circles of the countries in which they reside. In almost all foreign countries the possession of considerable resources is the most important means to secure this end.[1]

In 1919 representation allowances were given to all consular officers specifically to 'meet the cost of official entertainment and of other representative duties of this nature'.[2]

Curiously, the opportunity to consolidate all these allowances into a general foreign service allowance was not taken. Indeed, Sir Arthur Steel-Maitland's proposals included yet another form of allowance: a 'local allowance' payable to all consuls at a low basic rate, to be increased as the expense of particular posts demanded. The Treasury refused to accept this. The normal consular allowances after 1919, received by all consuls, were the representation and rent allowances. Then, as a continuation of the 'war bonus' introduced as an emergency measure to cope with the substantial rise in the cost of living at some posts, some consulates received a 'cost-of-living bonus' on a *part* of their emoluments, intended to represent a *percentage* of the difference between the base figure of 100, representing the price level in 1914, and a figure calculated to represent the current level of prices. Still other consulates—those regarded as 'expensive' in the prewar years and already in receipt of local allowances—were permitted to retain their local allowances. The remainder, such as it was, received no local allowance at all.

It was all very selective, arbitrary, and unsatisfactory, and a far cry indeed from the system as it exists today—that is, a consolidated foreign allowance with automatic adjustments for changes in the cost-of-living index and in the rate of exchange.

Personnel administration and inspection Readers of *The Times* were warned, even after the 1919 reforms, that consuls were overworked, badly housed, and underpaid, and that no one should think of joining their ranks unless he were prepared to face up to this, or possessed adequate private means.[3] But if feeble in practice, the theory behind both salaries and allow-

---

[1] Foreign Office to Treasury, 28 February 1917: PRO.FO/369/969.
[2] Memorandum on the History and Organization of the Consular Service, prepared at the Foreign Office in March 1933 for the benefit of Mr Baldwin: PRO.FO/369/2316.
[3] *The Times*, 10 January 1922, 6d; also leading article to the same effect, 28 December 1921, 9a.

ances in the twentieth-century service was far in advance of the Victorians. Where the Foreign Office really failed to meet the challenge presented by the 1903 reforms was in an area in which it had always been at its weakest: personnel administration.

It has already been suggested that a reason for the failure to develop personnel administration in the Foreign Office was the diminutive size of the diplomatic and Foreign Office establishment; there may well have seemed little point in evolving an elaborate system when everyone was known, warts and all, to everyone else. But this did not apply to the consular service, for the administration of which the Foreign Office had always insisted on making itself responsible. An arrangement which may have worked after a fashion for a small, self-contained, inbred and socially exclusive group of diplomats and Foreign Office clerks made no sense at all for the large, diverse, and scattered service of nearly 350 salaried officers and trainees which they attempted to control. Some informal personal records were kept by the head of the Consular Department himself, but incredible though it may seem, there was no Personnel Department at the Foreign Office with complete records on which to base recommendations for appointments, transfers, and early retirements, until after the 1943 reforms. The Burgess and Maclean defections, a result of this curiously relaxed view of personnel responsibilities within the Office, were perhaps the least of the troubles to which it contributed.

Personnel administration must aim at a balance between the most efficient employment of those whom it administers and their satisfaction (itself an element in that efficiency) both as individuals and as members of a service. While constantly observing the needs of the service, it should attempt at the same time to establish a fair distribution of posts and an even flow of promotion, with an acceptable compromise, in both respects, between the claims of seniority and merit. It must take care to plan each man's career so that his talents are used to their full advantage and so that his efforts may meet with adequate reward. Above all, it must make sure that the man himself is aware that it is doing so.

Measured against these criteria, the Foreign Office before 1943 fell alarmingly short of the ideal, although it must in fairness be said that in many, though not in all respects, the Treasury was as much to blame. The Foreign Office, as one consul explained, sat as Court of First Instance on any proposal for reform or improvement. If this ordeal were successfully passed, the Treasury then sat on the case as a kind of Court of Cassation, whose duty it was, if possible, to refute the consul's arguments and quash his application.[1]

The first object of the Walrond Committee had been to make the consular service into a career. Lord Cranborne, a member of the Committee and Under-Secretary of State, told the Commons at the time that it was not the pay in the consular service which was so unattractive to good men. The pay was 'not so very bad'.

> But what undoubtedly did act as a deterrent was that the service did not offer any certainty of a career. A man might enter the service, and might be successful in rising in it; but again he might not; and no able young man, choosing his career for life, would embark on one in which the prospects were so uncertain as the Committee found them to be.[2]

The Committee, by establishing systematic recruitment and grading, went a long way towards solving the basic problems. But it failed to establish what was almost as important, a machinery by which the steps in the career it had created could be planned and directed to the full advantage both of the consular officers and of the state. The Consular, Commercial, and Chief Clerk's Departments in the Foreign Office before 1914 were not equipped to administer in any general sense. The Consular Department concerned itself with trivia; the Commercial Department, with only a section of consular functions; the Chief Clerk's Department, with consular accounts. Though their chiefs could collaborate in the production of a sensible report on the subject of consular reform in 1912, no single one of them had the responsibility, authority, or staff to act as the real administrative core of the service.

Victor Wellesley, Algernon Law's successor in 1916 as Comptroller of Commercial and Consular Affairs, had the honesty to admit that the trouble lay in the administration in London. After referring to the total state of 'atrophy and stagnation' of prewar days, he argued that the consular and commercial diplomatic services overseas would inevitably relapse into that condition unless there was some real vitality in the home administration. 'In short,' he concluded, 'the Central Controlling Authorities at home must endeavour to generate a current of directive energy flowing outward and homeward, and they must never be lacking in that human and electrifying

---

[1] Memorandum dated 2 August 1917: PRO.FO/369/971.
[2] 126 *Parl. Deb.*, 4s, 1015 (30 July 1903).

touch in which the secret of success very largely lies.'[1] Reflecting, a year later, on the great postwar expansion promoted with such energy by Sir Arthur Steel-Maitland from the new Department of Overseas Trade, Wellesley noted that his own view was that the weak spot in the consular service was not so much insufficiency of numbers as general inefficiency through lack of proper direction. To increase the service without at the same time effecting radical changes in the system of administration would amount to little more than multiplying the units of inefficiency.[2]

It was one of the minor tragedies of the interwar years that the consular service, in what had become its major function, commercial affairs, fell victim to an administrative experiment. One of the great problems in government relations with overseas trade had been the appropriate division of responsibility between the Board of Trade, which understood commercial policy, and the Foreign Office, which knew virtually nothing about commerce but which had been entrusted with the management of British relations overseas. The first responsibility for overseas trade had shifted already on a couple of occasions during the nineteenth century. But the position in 1914 was that the Board of Trade, with its subordinate Commercial Intelligence Branch, had become the authority to which overseas traders looked for support, while the Commercial Department of the Foreign Office referred most matters of importance, other than the negotiation of commercial treaties, to the Board of Trade. From the point of view of the consular service this was an unsatisfactory arrangement, since its important commercial duties were supervised by a Department which had no responsibility for its promotions, transfers, or general administration.

During the war, with the prospect of a great expansion in government activities on behalf of overseas trade after the return of peace, the squabble between the two Departments reached a new pitch, and a compromise solution was finally evolved which created a joint sub-Department, the Department of Overseas Trade, under a Parliamentary Secretary responsible both to the Foreign Secretary and to the President of the Board of Trade. It was intended that the new Department should take over the overseas trade functions of both major Departments, which, in the case of the Foreign Office, meant taking over the commercial attaché service, the Commercial Department, the Consular Department, and the consular service itself. Somewhere something went astray. The commercial diplomatic service

---

[1] Memorandum dated 20 August 1918: PRO.FO/369/1319.
[2] Memorandum dated 2 October 1919: *ibid.*

became the sole responsibility of the Department of Overseas Trade, and the Commercial Department at the Foreign Office was disbanded. But the Consular Department, charged with the administration of the consular service, remained at the Foreign Office, while consular *commercial* functions, under the supervision overseas of the commercial diplomatic service, passed at home to the Department of Overseas Trade. In fact, exactly the same 'dualism', with precisely the same ill-effects, was conscientiously re-created for the postwar consular service. H. Montagu Villiers was speaking for many of his colleagues when he complained that consuls no longer knew to whom they should address their despatches and reports. They seemed suddenly to have two masters for one job. Correspondence direct with the Department of Overseas Trade on commercial matters meant that 'Ambassadors and the Foreign Office, under whom Consuls always have been and always must be, got to know less than ever of what the Consuls were doing commercially'.[1]

As for the Consular Department at the Foreign Office, now as formerly charged with the administration of a service of which, in one of its principal functions, it remained ignorant, it seemed headed for early disaster. 'I know from my own experience', said the Earl of Drogheda in the Foreign Service debate of 7 November 1945, 'that the non-political Departments in the Foreign Office have a way of not always attracting the best men in the Service.'[2] And under Ernest Gye, an official of the old school who had little time for his consular subordinates and who, according to Sir David Kelly, was even less inclined to be on intimate terms with visiting consuls ('in fact he very seldom consented to receive them at all'), the outlook was bleak indeed. A 'Consular Officer', writing to *The Times* in 1922, reported that the degree of callousness and indifference with which consuls returning from abroad were habitually treated by the Foreign Office had to be experienced to be realized, and there was nothing more demoralizing than to be treated with absolute indifference; what the service mainly required at the time was 'a capable chief to pull it together, to protect its interests and to secure it a dignity and prestige of its own'.[3] By what, for the consular service, was an extraordinarily rare stroke of good fortune, this was precisely what happened. Gye's immediate subordinate and successor, Sir David Scott, was a man of real ability and sympathy who for once took a close interest in the fortunes

---

[1] H. Montagu Villiers, *Charms of the Consular Career* (London, 1925), pp. 165–6.
[2] 137 *HL Deb.*, 5s, 736.
[3] *The Times*, 10 January 1922, 6d.

of the service, and who became a major factor in the administrative developments and controversy leading to the amalgamation of 1943.

Sir David Scott's achievement cannot be exaggerated; the existence of a first-class official in the Consular Department was undoubtedly the most substantial administrative improvement of the interwar years. But the new attitude which he created within the service and the reforms for which he was responsible owed something to the information now available through the new consular inspectorate.

Periodical inspection of all consular posts was one of the recommendations of the 1903 Committee. It was taken no further at the time, but the creation of an organized, consular inspectorate continued to be canvassed within the Foreign Office. When the point was raised in Consul E. MacDonnell's memorandum on consular reform in 1909, Algernon Law noted against it: 'Have advocated this system for 25 years', and W. Langley added that this should be one of the first points to be considered in any full-scale review of the service.[1] One outcome of the review which followed soon afterwards (the Departmental Committee of 1912), was a recommendation for a system of regular inspections, with specially appointed inspectors serving for periods of two or three years and assigned to definite districts. A pilot scheme was started with the appointment of four visiting consuls early in 1914. It ran into some initial opposition among senior consuls, who took it as a reflection on their personal honesty and efficiency (which indeed it was). But some consular officers were sensible enough to realize from the beginning that a consular inspection gave consuls an excellent forum for their grievances and a rare opportunity to make their mark with the Foreign Office. War in August 1914 put an end to the experiment, but Sir Arthur Steel-Maitland's Committee recommended the continuation of the inspections, of which it said (perhaps rather prematurely) that 'experience has shown that, although the idea of inspection was repugnant to senior Consular Officers, it has in practice been welcomed even by those who were disposed to resent it'.

During the 1920s and 30s a staff of between three and four inspectors general was maintained, covering the posts in theory at three-year intervals, in practice at five. The original idea had been that inspectors should make themselves responsible for a thorough overhaul of all aspects of a consulate—its accounts, its archive system, its methods and conditions of work, housing and equipment—and that the visits should be unexpected and at irregular

[1] Memorandum dated 20 January 1909: PRO.FO/369/266.

intervals.¹ This was not to be the case. The Public Accounts Committee was disturbed to learn in 1935 that consuls were given weeks, or even months of notice of a coming inspection, which, as one of its members pointed out, might be an inspection in certain respects, but could not be one from the point of view of finding out if anything was wrong 'because a man would be a complete ass if he had anything wrong with all that notice beforehand'.² After some confusion, the Foreign Office produced a memorandum on the inspection system in which it was explained that a shortage of inspectors, the need to save time and expense by calling for information and statistical data in advance, and the impossibility of keeping an inspector's arrival unknown to consuls in the area, had made surprise visits impracticable, quite apart from the damage which such visits might do to the good feeling and spirit of collaboration which had gradually been built up from the system's beginnings. Inspections as they were currently carried out were not financial inspections at all, except in so far as they helped the consul to apply proper methods of supervision to his vice-consuls and office staff. The only safeguards against dishonest practices by the consul himself were (a) the fact that he had won his position by a stiff public examination and by careful selection, and (b) that the opportunities for making away with sums in any way comparable with the capitalized value of his pension were negligible. Inspections were

> not intended to be inquisitorial visitations whose main object is the prevention of an assumed tendency to defraud His Majesty's Government, but to be the means of securing ... the increased efficiency of Consular Officers and also greater uniformity and improved methods in the Consular work. It is expected, moreover, that the system will enable His Majesty's Secretary of State for Foreign Affairs to obtain a more intimate knowledge of the Consular Officers, and at the same time of the extent and quality of the work performed by them as well as of the possible requirements of their respective posts.³

Promotion Whatever the limitations of the consular inspections, it was true nevertheless that from the point of view of consular administration,

---

¹ Algernon Law's evidence: Minutes of Evidence, *5th Report of the Royal Commission on the Civil Service*, PP 1914-16 (Cd 7749) XI, QQ 37,498; 37,507.
² Minutes of Evidence, *Report of the Select Committee on Public Accounts*, PP 1934-5 (93, 99) V, QQ 865-6.
³ Printed as Appendix No. 5, *ibid*.

accurate, periodical and reasonably up-to-date information represented an enormous advance on the nineteenth century. This was particularly the case with the handling of personnel, in which, as the Steel-Maitland report made clear, the 'first essential' was 'to devise some means by which real merit might become known and rewarded, and inefficiency may receive its deserts'. An additional, if sometimes irregular, source of information was provided by the 'annual' reports on consuls from their immediate superiors, for long resisted as 'inquisitorial' but started, under pressure of war conditions, rather apologetically in 1916. For all that, it cannot be said that the problems of personnel planning—balanced recruitment, postings and transfers, promotion and the recognition of merit—were fully resolved in the interwar years.

The Walrond Committee, though recommending the formation of a graded service with recruits starting at the bottom and working their way up through the grades, had made no suggestion for the machinery by which promotions might be regulated. Traditionally all promotions and transfers within the Foreign Office, the diplomatic service and the consular service were handled by the Private Secretary to the Secretary of State. While the consular service remained, as it was before 1903, a service in which transfers and promotions were exceptional and where both followed only from personal requests, the system, whatever its theoretical disadvantages, was at least workable; the Private Secretary could cope with the volume of movements within the service. This was no longer the case with the graded service after 1903, and when Sir William Tyrrell became Private Secretary in 1907 he realized that the privilege he had inherited was extraordinarily ill-adapted to the needs of the new service. The Private Secretary, under the burden of all his other work, had no chance of investigating the merits of each case, nor did he have the personal knowledge of the consular officers or of their work on which to base a decision. A system which depended on personal representations from the consuls themselves or from their friends was undignified, unfair to those less outspoken, more distant or less befriended, and inconsistent with the principle of seniority which became necessarily applied to an organized career service. Tyrrell formalized the consultation with Foreign Office officials which had always been, to a greater or lesser extent, the practice in consular appointments; he surrendered his direct patronage to a committee consisting of the Comptroller of Commercial and Consular Affairs, the head of the Consular Department, and the Assistant Private Secretary.

Tyrrell's committee was still relatively informal and limited in its composition, but it consisted of officials who in theory were supposed to know something about the consuls whose careers they were considering. A formal Promotions Board was established after the war, in 1919, with representatives from a wider and more knowledgeable field, including the Department of Overseas Trade. In 1932 the Board was strengthened by the inclusion of the senior available inspector of consular establishments, and a further Board was formed to consider and recommend transfers from post to post where no question of promotion was involved.

The problem, by the end of the consular service, lay less with the machinery developed to deal with promotions and transfers than with the basis on which recommendations were made. The old complaint that officers at isolated posts overseas tended to be forgotten and their interests bypassed by those closer to home with friends in the right places, was to some degree remedied, though it is a complaint which has had some justification in all large organizations at all times. But it proved far more difficult to strike a satisfactory balance between the competing claims of seniority and merit.

Most of the Select Committees and Royal Commissions which had considered the question of Civil Service promotions had come out in favour of consideration for merit. Certainly, when the Walrond Committee established a graded service, it made a point of recommending that the Secretary of State should not promote simply on the basis of seniority, but should take merit also into consideration. In theory this was the case even in the unreformed service. The Consular Service Order in Council of 6 March 1896 had laid down quite categorically that 'promotion of officers in the Consular Service shall be strictly according to merit'. And in a service where there was no entitlement to, or expectation of, promotion, seniority could be left out of account.

When the new service was formed after 1903, it was no longer possible to ignore the claims of seniority in determining the proposed, regular movements between the grades. The Consular Instructions of 1907 and 1916 established that 'promotion in the Service will go as far as possible by seniority, but merit and special qualifications will be taken into account in considering individual claims'. Algernon Law, questioned on the point by the 1914 Commission,[1] explained that the principle which guided promotion was purely and simply seniority until the grade of consul, when an element of merit was considered for promotion to the better consulates, and when

---

[1] Minutes of Evidence, *5th Report of the Royal Commission on the Civil Service*, pp. 1914-16 (Cd 7749) XI, QQ 42,966-79.

merit alone was taken into account for promotion to consul-general. This again was the practice described by the 1933 Committee. The Committee considered the question of promotion by merit in some detail, and concluded that whereas varying conditions and opportunities made it difficult to select meritorious vice-consuls for promotion out of turn, promotions from consul to consul-general depended largely on merit, which by this point of seniority was well known to the Department. A consul could not expect to be promoted in order of seniority, or, indeed, at all, unless his record justified it.

The theory was excellent, even if to a vice-consul in the interwar period, who might well have been forty years old by the time he reached the top of the seniority list, fifteen to twenty years might have seemed rather long to wait before the Foreign Office could be expected to take merit into account. Apart from that, the pity was that when it came to making promotions to consul-general in this period, seniority so often was the real determining factor. Algernon Law's description of the operations of the pre-1914 committee—'we take the list according to seniority, and go through them and say would he do, or the other do, and so on'[1]—at least suggested that, though seniority came first, merit or its reverse could decide whether or not a man would 'do'. Surprisingly, the attitude among Foreign Office officials seems actually to have hardened in favour of seniority during the interwar period.

The issue came up for discussion in the particular case of a proposal by the British Minister at Peking, Sir Miles Lampson, to bypass a senior consul, who had reached the top of the list, for promotion to a vacant consulate-general in 1927-8. Ernest Gye warned Sir Miles that, in cases such as this, 'the very fullest consideration should be given to the claims of *all* senior officers'; in the opinion of the Foreign Office, the senior consul should be promoted. The Minister replied angrily that of course such consideration would be given, as it had been in the past. But his own recommendations must be made on merit, plus seniority; he was not prepared to recommend duds. His general principle was to recommend the most senior man who, in his opinion, was fit to discharge the duties and responsibilities not of a particular post in a higher grade but of that higher grade generally. Transfers and leave arrangements would be made even more difficult than they were at present if men were capable only of filling one particular post, an easy one, and only then when times were quiet: 'It was, as you will recollect, to get rid of this disability, that the reform was instituted of appointing men not to posts but to grades.'

---

[1] *Ibid.*, Q 37,335.

Gye's comment was that at least the letter was a frank statement of Sir Miles's views on what he regarded as the proper way of dealing with the China Service. Without knowledge of the facts one would assume that that service was composed of a large number of officers totally unfitted for the higher posts. But this was not the case. China consuls were appointed after a very stiff examination. They spent their entire official careers in China, and though some may well have profited more from this experience than others, Gye refused to believe that there was so wide a difference in their value as public officials towards the end of their careers as to unfit a number of them for the highest posts in that service. Every man, he concluded, who passed the consular examination and went to China had a right to expect one day to become a consul-general. If a man, against whom it was admitted that no actual charge of misconduct or incompetence could be brought, was not promoted, the whole service would soon lose such hope and courage as it still possessed.

In deference to Lampson's decided views and to some rather unfavourable private reports received on the Foreign Office candidate from former consular officers in London, the senior consul was not in fact promoted. But Sir Miles was warned that future promotion was to be in accord generally with the principle of seniority formulated in Gye's original letter.[1]

Ten years later the Foreign Office attitude was confirmed in response to a proposal, in 1937, that the system of promotion in the higher grades should be defined. Mr Allchin, in a long minute on the subject, explained that promotion normally depended purely on seniority, with the exception that a positively inefficient officer would suffer delay or not be promoted at all (and there were usually one or two unsatisfactory vice-consuls and four or five consuls 'clogging the top of their respective lists'). But it would be wrong to suggest, as had the 1933 Committee, that promotion to consul-general was largely by merit. Personally, Allchin thought that the present system with regard to promotion could not in practice be bettered ('provided the brand of "demerit" is not too sparingly applied'):

> In view of the fact that consuls are spread all over the world, working under varying conditions at multifarious and different duties, enjoying unequal opportunities, and being reported on by chiefs of every shade of taste and character, I do not think it would be possible without real injustice to give more weight to 'merit' than is now accorded to it. The most that can fairly be done, I believe, is to pick out a few officers

[1] The private letters, despatches and minutes on this case are in PRO,FO/369/2017.

as being below the standard of the flock and perhaps an occasional man as deserving of special advancement. Moreover, a system of promotion by merit, besides being unfair and whimsical, would provoke a feeling of uncertainty in the Service, with tiresome jealousies among its members, and would encourage a distasteful outbreak of 'window-dressing'. It would thus, I think, tend to destroy the tone of the Service as well as making the work of the Promotions Board invidious, difficult and indeed well-nigh impossible.[1]

Career planning It is at least arguable that promotion by seniority rather than merit may ultimately be in the best interests of a service, particularly of a service where no great demands are likely to be made on its members. It may, and in the consular service did, lead to dissatisfaction and discouragement among the young, the ambitious and the 'trouble-makers'. But the competent rump would have had few grounds for complaint. General comfort and competence may be as high as it is sensible, on balance, to aim.

It made sense, nevertheless, from any point of view to make sure that men did not wait too long, in the course of a normal career, for their promotion, and that when finally it came it gave reasonable satisfaction. Satisfaction was important even at the head of the profession. Sir Andrew Ryan wrote bitterly of the contrast between the rewards available to the diplomat and to the consul—a contrast driven home by the close conjunction in which both services worked. In the diplomatic service, there was a legation and a K.C.M.G. for the merely competent, and glittering embassies for the high fliers. In the consular service, consuls might look no further than a consulate-general, which a man might reach in his forties or early fifties, and after which, no matter how great his ability and experience, he could look for nothing further.[2] The ablest of the consuls suffered most. Sir Andrew Ryan himself was one. Richard Wood, one of the most active and influential of Victorian political consuls, complained from Tunis on precisely this point. It was difficult, he said, to trace the reasons why one class of Her Majesty's servants abroad should not be permitted to advance beyond a certain position, while to others the highest posts in their profession were open. The

[1] Minute on Inspector General T. D. Dunlop's memorandum of 28 October 1937 PRO.FO/369/2464.
[2] Sir Andrew Ryan, *The Last of the Dragomans* (London, 1951), pp. 252-3.

natural effect on the 'humbled class' was 'discouragement, much heart-burning and dissatisfaction'.[1]

This could be of interest only to the élite. The grievance common to the whole consular service in the interwar period was the block in promotions, and the complete failure of the Foreign Office or the Treasury to do anything about it. In 1937, according to the Principal Establishment Officer at the Foreign Office, there were no less than forty-two prewar entrants into the consular service who had not yet reached the rank of consul-general. This was worse, he said, than in any other branch of the public service at home or abroad.[2]

The 1914 Commission had insisted on the importance of regulating recruitment in accordance with a percentage calculated on the experience of wastage from resignation, death, transfer or retirement:

> If this calculation be taken over a reasonably long period of time, be revised at short intervals and be, at such revision, increased or diminished as the conditions of the Service then suggest (only fractional alterations are ever needed) the result will be the retention of a proper and even flow of promotion.

Sir Arthur Steel-Maitland's Committee (1919) took these calculations seriously, and its whole elaborate scheme of consular expansion rested on the proper proportion of consulates-general, consulates and vice-consulates so as to ensure that a vice-consul should be entitled to expect promotion to consul at the age of thirty-five, and that promotion to consul-general should follow at about forty-eight. The proportion needed to achieve this result, assuming a retirement age of sixty, worked out on an actuarial estimate at 38 per cent, 37 per cent, and 25 per cent for vice-consuls, consuls, and consuls-general respectively.

These, ideally, were the principles on which recruitment and promotion in a modern service should have been conducted. But they were dependent on some slight measure of stability, and it was hardly the fault of the Foreign Office that this stability never existed. The First World War began while the 1914 Commission was still collecting its evidence, and within a few months prospects in an important branch of the service, the Levant Service, were

---

[1] Appendix 4, *Report from the Select Committee on Consular Service and Appointments,* PP 1857-8 (482) VIII.

[2] C. Howard Smith's marginal note on Hoyer Millar's minute of April 1937 (which had suggested that the current block in the diplomatic service might be eased by appropriating some of the prizes of the consular profession): PRO.FO/371/20630.

thrown into complete confusion. Promotion was suspended, and by 1918 the absurd situation had been reached that the senior vice-consul was forty years old and the next ten on the list ranged between thirty-four and forty. The Foreign Office had begged the Treasury in 1917 to ease the block by promoting four of the most senior vice-consuls, irrespective of the fixed establishment of consular posts. But the Treasury refused to consider a concession based on the need to increase the flow of promotion rather than on the requirements of the work to be performed.[1] When approached on the same theme a year later it explained, unhelpfully, that 'the flow of promotion in Public Departments varies greatly from time to time: and it is only in the most exceptional circumstances that the numbers in the various cadres can be varied in order to counteract this tendency'—an explanation which brought this understandable retort from Victor Wellesley:

> It is not only unjust but it is stupid, obstructive and diametrically opposed to the best interests of the Treasury itself. It is the kind of obstruction which tends to produce that remarkable characteristic of the British race—collective inefficiency coupled with a great deal of individual ability.[2]

The Treasury, as a Foreign Office official once put it, was 'very fearful of new "principles"'. It was difficult to allow for particular hard cases in the public service when, no matter how sound the reasoning might be, action might, in the Treasury's view, be used as a 'principle' in all similar cases well into the indefinite future. This was certainly the attitude adopted towards the severe promotions block which had developed as a result of an abnormally large number of postwar appointments, followed almost immediately by a severe pruning of all government services in and after 1921. Even the modest proposal of the 1933 Committee that senior vice-consuls, whose promotion had been delayed through no fault of their own, should be given a slight increase in salary after fifteen years' service or on reaching the age of thirty-eight, met with strong Treasury opposition. The Treasury complained that it had continually to resist claims, in one form and another and in all parts of the Civil Service, that failure to obtain advancement to higher pay and higher duties should be compensated financially.[3] The Foreign Office, which realized that one of the main objects of the 1933 Report (a 'remedy

---

[1] Treasury to Foreign Office, 29 June 1917: PRO.FO/369/971.
[2] Treasury to Foreign Office, 11 May 1918, and minute: PRO.FO/369/1052.
[3] Treasury to Foreign Office, 2 June 1933: PRO.FO/369/2317.

to the serious feeling of discouragement which exists in the consular service') was at stake, would not allow itself to be overruled, and the Treasury was finally compelled to relent.

The whole promotions block might have been eased very considerably if the principle of early retirement, introduced with such universal applause in 1943, had been accepted twenty years before. In the armed forces it had long been accepted that officers who had failed to make the step to a senior grade could be called on to retire; apart from the advantages it had for promotion, there was the simple physical reason that officers in junior positions might be expected to carry out duties beyond the strength of an older man. But this could hardly be said to apply to a civil servant. As far as nineteenth-century thinking went—and the Treasury remained in many respects in a nineteenth-century cocoon until the Second World War—the state's interest was best served by squeezing the last drop out of a man before releasing him from the service and putting him on the 'non-effective' list. Where civil service functions continued to be, up to a very high level, extraordinarily routine, this might well have been true—an old consul, after all, could sign on seamen and issue passports as well, or better, than a younger, less experienced man. But it came to be less true as the responsibilities of consuls widened, and officials at the Foreign Office woke much earlier than their colleagues at the Treasury to what has since become a commonplace—that in the long run it is cheaper and better to get rid of a man once his inefficiency is recognized, even if it should be at the cost of a pension or a gratuity.

The 1912 Committee recommended that the Secretary of State should be given the discretion to retire a man at fifty-five; Algernon Law, one of its members, wanted the age to be fifty. The Treasury felt unable to introduce legislation for this object, 'which would raise questions not confined to the consular service'.[1] An Order in Council in 1921 gave the Secretary of State the power to retire consuls at sixty (the normal age was still sixty-five), but although the power was employed from time to time, it was never used as it might have been. As a Foreign Office official put it at the time, it was 'a delicate matter', if a consul were performing useful work, to call on him to retire simply because he was approaching the age limit.[2] Until as recently as 1943 ill-health remained the only means by which the Secretary of State could retire a man with a pension before the age of sixty.

---

[1] Treasury to Foreign Office, 16 January 1913: PRO.FO/369/536.
[2] H. Kelsey, memorandum, 1921: PRO.FO/369/1642.

The General Consular Service in the twentieth century 103

It was the Treasury, and the Treasury's interpretation of opinion in the Commons (false, as it turned out), which proved the stumbling block. 'So far as the *Spectator* articles are concerned,' Sir Alexander Cadogan, the Permanent Under Secretary, assured R. S. Hudson in 1939, 'I should be only too happy if it were possible to apply the remedy suggested, namely, the pensioning-off of certain senior diplomats who may no longer be quite equal to their jobs, but as I expect you know this is a solution against which the Treasury have up to now resolutely set their face.'[1]

Consular functions before 1914 The administrative difficulties of the twentieth-century consular service, compounded for so much of its existence by its subdivision into five watertight compartments (General, China, Japan, Siam and Levant), were a permanently discouraging feature of its history. Though there was some progress after the very substantial changes introduced in 1903, real modernization was blocked time and again by short-sighted economies and a continual failure to give the service the undivided attention, direction, planning, and encouragement that it so desperately needed. The twentieth century does, however, introduce the much broader interpretation of consular functions, which, in the end, was to bring the diplomatic and consular service together in the amalgamated Foreign Service of 1943.

Victorian consuls had developed into marine superintendents; their increasing responsibilities under the Merchant Shipping Acts left them no alternative. By 1871 a Crimean consul was speaking for every seaport official when he claimed that the Consular Instructions, with their numerous Annexes, required a consul 'to possess a head of Medusa, first, to contain them all, and secondly, to terrify shipmasters into implicit obedience'.[2] Commercial reporting and assistance to British traders took second place. A consul, considering the distribution of consular time before 1914, estimated that 20 per cent, as devoted to purely commercial work, would be a generous average; at some posts possibly 60 per cent or more of the time was spent on commercial work, but at others as much as 90 per cent went to political work, shipping, or even to 'general' work, 'for it must be borne in mind that the Consular Officer is the representative of His Majesty's

---
[1] Cadogan to the Rt Hon R. S. Hudson, MP, 3 May 1939: PRO.FO/366/781.
[2] *Further Reports Relative to British Consular Establishments, 1858 and 1871*, Part II, P 1872 (c. 501) LX.

Government at his post in every sphere of activity'.[1] Since, as he went on to demonstrate, the average hours spent daily by a consular officer in his office in peacetime did not exceed six, and might even be less, the total effort devoted by prewar consuls to their commercial functions was often negligible. This was particularly the case in the Far East and Levant Services, where consular officers, overburdened with political and judicial functions and totally untrained in commerce, were inclined to regard trade as something altogether detached from their normal duties.

The only commercial function universally recognized for consuls before 1914 was the production of commercial information. British consuls had always been expected to prepare an annual report on the trade and navigation of their particular districts, and they were also instructed to report any new developments or matters of immediate commercial interest when they arose. As foreign competition developed in the later decades of the nineteenth century, more importance was attached to this side of their work, and emphasis was given less to routine annual reports describing general developments within the district, than to special reports on particular developments, containing immediate suggestions for the expansion of British trade.

But the problem with consular reports before 1914 was their extraordinary variety. Some of the reports were first-class—conscientiously prepared, based on solid statistical information, and presented in a way which made them of real value to the commercial community. But far too many, whether as a result of local difficulties in collecting information, lack of time or opportunity, or inertia on the part of the consuls themselves, were totally useless, conveying, as William Redmond told the Commons in 1903, 'no other impression than that the men who wrote them were not fitted to represent this country in any part of the world'.[2]

It would have mattered less if the valuable reports had reached the commercial public in time, or even if the annual reports had been published rapidly and regularly: an annual report has some value for establishing trends, even if it has never put a man in the way of business. But in spite of the very real efforts which were made to speed up publication of commercial information, particularly with the production of the *Board of Trade Journal* after 1886 and the establishment of the Commercial Intelligence Branch of the Board of Trade at the turn of the century, reports still arrived irregularly and often long after their practical value had evaporated. The annual report

---

[1] E. W. Thurstan's memorandum, Foreign Office, December 1917: PRO.FO/369/971.
[2] 126 *Parl. Deb.*, 4s, 1010 (30 July 1903).

of the consul-general in Chile for 1902 was published towards the end of August 1904, which, *The Economist* said, might make it of interest to antiquarians, but disqualified it as a source of information for businessmen.[1]

The more conscientious among the consuls were aware of these criticisms and inclined to share them, especially with respect to the annual reports. When the whole subject was discussed at length before the 1914 Commission, the comment of one of its members was that no businessman giving evidence before the Commission had spoken of the consular reports more contemptuously than some of the consuls themselves.[2]

If this were genuinely the value of almost the sole commercial function devolving on consuls, and if commercial duties occupied barely more than an hour of the average consular day, consuls can hardly be defined as commercial officers before 1914. Yet the Cave Committee, in its 1919 report, was already describing consuls as 'largely concerned with commercial functions'. And Sir Frederick Butler (of the Department of Overseas Trade), addressing the Hull Luncheon Club early in 1922 on the work of British consuls abroad, protested that while in prewar days commercial intelligence was rather a 'Cinderella' function, there had been a great improvement since 1917; the deliberate policy of the consular service was now to put commercial intelligence right in the forefront of a consul's duties.[3]

Commercial functions had certainly come to occupy a more important place in consular duties in the decades before 1914, but the real revolution was their transformation into the *most* important of consular functions—a transformation recognized in the final recommendation of the Steel-Maitland Committee of 1919, where it was considered, in principle, desirable that 'wherever possible, due regard being had for shipping interests, the higher grade Consular post should be at the chief commercial and industrial centre of any district, rather than at the port'.

There were a number of distinct reasons for this. In part, at least, it was a belated recognition of developments quite independent of official policy. It had never been consciously determined that Victorian consuls should become marine superintendents to the exclusion of all else. The mercantile marine had vastly expanded; legislation had been introduced to keep some control over it; and this control, which involved a very great deal of detailed if routine work, had been imposed on the only suitably placed British officials

[1] *The Economist*, 27 August 1904, 1414.
[2] Minutes of Evidence, *5th Report of the Royal Commission on the Civil Service*, PP 1914-16 (Cd 7749) XI, Q 42,073.
[3] Reported in *The Times*, 11 January 1922, 5e.

overseas—the seaport consuls. Since nobody ever thought to expand their number, and since most consuls, with no promotion or honorary rewards to look to, saw no reason to overexert themselves, shipping functions soon absorbed an altogether disproportionate amount of disposable consular energy. It was only a matter of time, which in consular reform is measured in decades, before someone saw the need either to limit the shipping functions or to increase the number of consular officers available to perform them.

Then, one of the basic principles of the Northcote-Trevelyan civil service reforms—the need to employ intelligent men intelligently while leaving routine to the clerks—was at length to be applied to the Foreign Office and to the services it controlled overseas. A Foreign Office memorandum during the First World War described the work at a busy consulate-general (Antwerp) as divided in the following proportions: 50 per cent for shipping; 30 per cent 'general'; 20 per cent commercial. It went on to point out that, of this work, only about a fifth of the shipping duties was such as to need the personal attention of a consular officer for decisions on points of law, or the settlement of disputes, whereas the proportion of 'brain work' in the other two categories was three-fifths and four-fifths respectively. The rest was simply routine which could be performed perfectly adequately by competent clerks.[1]

Obviously, it made good administrative sense to delegate shipping functions, while emphasizing the commercial side of a consul's duties. This had been the case in New York even before the First World War, with the appointment of an officer specifically to handle shipping. The Foreign Office Committee of 1916 agreed that the shipping work was the 'most wearisome and distracting' of consular duties. Taken as a whole, it probably occupied more time than the whole of the rest put together and the Committee recommended that it should be taken entirely off the consuls' shoulders by junior vice-consuls and shipping clerks. A scheme was tried out after the war of seconding a number of deputy superintendents of mercantile marine (from the Board of Trade) to the charge of the principal consular shipping offices, with the local rank of vice-consul.

Since the middle of the nineteenth century it had, in fact, been seriously considered whether it might not be better to divide off the *commercial* functions of consuls. Two distinct classes of officer might be created: the administrative consul dealing with routine administration, the handling of estates, the affairs of British subjects, and the regular shipping work; and the

[1] Undated, anonymous memorandum, probably written in 1917: PRO.FO/369/973.

commercial consul, specifically appointed to look after and report on commercial affairs. Something of the sort existed in the French consular service, though the lines were drawn more narrowly between the consul and his *chancelier*; and in the British diplomatic service the commercial functions of diplomats had already been delegated in certain major geographical areas to a new class of commercial attachés. For a brief period (1899-1907), the experimental appointment of a number of 'commercial agents' seemed intended to achieve just this for the consular service. But the overlap in functions was too irreconcilable, and the appointments were withdrawn. Some years later before the 1914 Commission, Sir Roger Casement was still arguing strongly that the consul's 'representative' and Board of Trade functions were best divided. The consul, he explained, whatever he may have been in the past was now a full-time government official, with state duties occupying practically his complete day: 'The possibilities of his aiding the commerce of his country, as a commercial agent, are nil—that is my experience.'[1]

The immense expansion of British commercial and financial interests overseas, the great increase in trade and in travellers, commercial and otherwise, compelled some rethinking on the role of British consular representatives throughout the nineteenth century. The real pressure for change came from foreign competition in Britain's traditional markets overseas. British businessmen saw, or thought they saw, a more wholehearted promotion of trading interests by the consuls of their foreign rivals, especially the Germans and Americans, and they demanded the same treatment from their own. For many years the British Government resisted any suggestion that its officers should become actively engaged in the promotion of British trade. As the pressure built up, in the 1880s and early 90s, and again, after a period of relative prosperity and complacency, in the years immediately preceding the First World War, it was impossible to hold out any longer. The 1912 Committee, in the conclusion to its report, drew attention to the following resolution passed at the recent conference of the Association of Chambers of Commerce of the United Kingdom:

That in view of the growing activity and utility of the principal foreign countries competing with the United Kingdom in the markets of the world, the British Consular Service should be strengthened and improved in a manner commensurate with the requirements of British

[1] Minutes of Evidence, *5th Report of the Royal Commission on the Civil Service*, PP 1914-16 (Cd 7749) XI, QQ 38,588-90.

traders, and that this association assures His Majesty's Government of its full support in any measures, financial or otherwise, which will conduce to that end.

And the recommendations of the 1912 Committee were directed at improving the *commercial* efficiency of the consulates.

It was the war itself which provided the final impetus to change. Practically overnight Germans were transformed from friends and kinsmen into implacable enemies, and their trading rivalry, alarming perhaps but relatively friendly until now, became, as suddenly, black villainy. In the intervals which British businessmen, members of Parliament, and officials could spare from hunting out and expelling honorary vice-consuls with German grandmothers, minds were turned to the problem of using the consular service as a powerful weapon in the cut-throat trade rivalry to be expected once peace was restored. 'We are now committed', said the Foreign Office Committee of 1916, 'to a national trade policy which will enter largely into the conduct of our foreign relations and may dominate them. . . . Trade and finance can no longer be things apart, outside the sphere of normal diplomatic work.'

In the early months of 1916 the whole question of the reorganization of the consular service came before the public in the Commons, in the press, and in the form of resolutions before the commercial associations. The first reaction in the Foreign Office was cool. Algernon Law, in a minute on a proposal to establish a committee of officials and businessmen to examine the service, complained that many commercial men refused to learn anything about the recent developments and improvements in the service 'because they liked to hide their own apathy and want of organization and cooperation in the past behind the alleged deficiencies of the Consular Service'.[1] Sir Eyre Crowe, contemplating the daunting prospect of consultation with the Association of Chambers of Commerce on consular reform, trusted that the Association would not be encouraged to believe that nothing would be decided without them: 'They are really nothing more than a very incompetent debating society. I believe no important man of business would ever dream of taking their advice in anything concerning his own business.'[2]

Under steady pressure, the Foreign Office reluctantly decided that the best way to forestall further interference would be to form its own committee. Crowe headed a committee of officials charged with the task of examining

[1] Minute dated 1 April 1916: PRO.FO/369/912.
[2] Minute dated 5 April 1916: *ibid*.

the best form of government organization for the promotion and assistance of British trade, and it was this committee which came to the conclusion that a national trade policy must enter largely into the conduct of British relations overseas. Its proposals for the expansion of government services had an immediate effect on the consular service—'the base on which alone any proper commercial intelligence system can rest'. It now became a revealed truth at the Foreign Office that the consular service should expand substantially after the war, and that the direction of this expansion should be towards a service concentrated at the main commercial and manufacturing centres overseas and entrusted foremost among its duties with the promotion of British trade. The Committee argued that in future the relative value to Britain of the trade of a country should form some indication of the consular staff required. In France, with a total trade of £588 million of which £63 million were with the UK, Britain had four consuls-general, seven consuls, and sixty-five vice-consuls, with total salaries of £16,000; in Argentina, by contrast, with a total trade of £180 million of which £67 million were with the UK, she had only one consul-general, one consul, and sixteen vice-consuls, with total salaries of £7800. 'The explanation of this discrepancy', the Committee concluded, 'is, of course, to be found in the number of sea ports in each country and the extent of the shipping work, but it indicates the undue extent to which this consideration has dominated the distribution of consular posts.'

In the rash of committees which followed—Lord Faringdon's Committee, the Consular Salaries Committee, the Consular Appointments Committee, Viscount Cave's Committee, Sir Arthur Steel-Maitland's Committee—the priority of commerce in consular functions was maintained. When towards the end of 1916 the Association of Chambers of Commerce was foolhardy enough to support the recommendation of its own private committee in favour of a division of the consular service into two branches, administrative and commercial—a respectable enough suggestion in its day—Victor Wellesley's comment was that the report struck him as a 'singularly feeble production'. Eyre Crowe, appreciative as always of the efforts of the 'commercials', described it as a 'jejune' production, 'typical of these commercial bodies who do not realize their ignorance respecting the essential principles of the problems they airily discuss. . . . We shall get no real assistance from these people.'[1] After two further years of committees, private, official and

---

[1] Minutes on Association of Chambers of Commerce, 'Report on the Reorganization of the Consular Service': *ibid.*

110   The Cinderella Service

mixed, Crowe complained that the wretched consular service had become 'the corpus vile on which anybody and everybody appears ready and anxious to experiment'.[1] A few days later, with yet another Committee in prospect (the Steel-Maitland Committee, of which he had just heard), Crowe protested that outside interference had been allowed 'to an extent altogether unprecedented in any public service of any country', and that if the consular service were again to go into the melting pot, it seemed essential to lay it down that 'all other cooks than such as belong to this Office or the D.O.T. shall be excluded'.[2]

Consular functions after 1914   One of the first results of the 1916 Committee had been a circular addressed to all Heads of Mission, enclosing a copy of the Committee's Report and requesting detailed recommendations as to the *post bellum* requirements of each country. The Committee had argued that both the number of officers attached to each post and the number of posts themselves would have to be 'largely augmented'; the first in order to leave the consul or consul-general free from all routine duties so that he could devote his time to commercial intelligence; the second so that officers might be established at growing trade centres around the world, more particularly in such promising markets as Russia and South America.

It was not surprising that the recommendations received back from the Missions were almost universally expansionist in tone; indeed, on the rare occasions when they were not (Argentina and Colombia) Victor Wellesley's reaction was that the minister was not doing his job. But the information on which these recommendations were based, gathered in the course of 1917 when no one could really be expected to foresee exactly what would be the position after the war, was, as Wellesley later admitted, often 'quite inadequate, unconvincing and lacking in any proper appreciation of the subject'.[3] The Salaries Committee, the terms of reference of which were rather wider than its title suggests, used this information, for want of anything better, as the basis of its recommendations for a total increase of 115 posts, not including enemy countries; and the same information was used again by the Steel-Maitland Committee for its larger scheme of no less than 167

[1] Minute on Sir Maurice de Bunsen's telegram from Montevideo, 24 May 1918; PRO.FO/369/1052.
[2] Minute dated 3 June 1918: *ibid*.
[3] Memorandum dated April 1918: PRO.FO/369/1319.

new posts—a scheme, Wellesley said, which was worked out with the utmost care and exactitude but for which there was 'no gainsaying the fact that it rests on an even still greater conjectural basis than did the recommendation of the Salaries Committee'.[1] When the Steel-Maitland scheme was presented to the War Cabinet, it was met, not unnaturally, with strong opposition from the Treasury. A Treasury representative had sat on the Salaries Committee, and the Chancellor was perfectly aware of the imprecise data on which its recommendations had had to be made; the same applied with even more force to the Steel-Maitland recommendations. In place of the 167 new *posts* asked for, the War Cabinet authorized the appointment of thirty additional *officers* (or so the Treasury claimed), after which any further appointments would require Treasury sanction. The position in 1921-2 was that, including additional appointments made during the war, there were fifty-seven salaried officers more than in 1913-14, allocated almost without exception to the General Service, with the Levant and Far Eastern Services remaining limited to their prewar establishment.

The whole new concept of a 'commercial' consular service, under pressure almost immediately during those periodical bouts of frenzied economy which attacked all government services in the 1920s (the Treasury's '20 per cent Circular' in 1921, the Geddes axe, the Churchillian economies of 1927) was virtually unrealized. 'I do not know whether the Government is really in earnest as regards re-establishing our international trade (which I myself consider vital),' Sir Arthur Steel-Maitland explained in his letter of resignation from the Department of Overseas Trade in July 1919, 'but at least, so far as I am concerned, I cannot continue to take the responsibility for work under such conditions that I cannot develop it or, indeed, carry it on properly, and when I am constantly hung up as, for example, with the Consular and kindred services.'[2] In practical terms, the rise in the number of posts turned out to be relatively insignificant, since although fifty-seven additional officers had joined the service between 1913 and 1921, the Foreign Office, under the Geddes axe, was compelled to recommend the abolition of six consulates, the reduction of five further consulates to vice-consulates, and the abolition of nineteen vice-consulates, all in the General Service.[3] During the 1930s the tendency was actually to reduce still further the number of salaried posts; the Foreign Office had persuaded itself that *salaried* consuls were not

---

[1] Memorandum dated 2 October 1919: *ibid*.
[2] Printed in *The Times*, 9 July 1919, 13e.
[3] Foreign Office to Treasury, 29 December 1922: FO/369/1792.

particularly indispensable, and that very often *unsalaried* consuls, even at some of the more important posts, could do the work just as well.

Worse still for the general efficiency of the service was the failure, again under pressure of economy, to strengthen the consular staff with a service of home-recruited, Second Division clerks. The main objective of the several plans for the reorganization and expansion of the consular service was not so much the opening of new *posts*, though these were to play an important part, as the strengthening of the staff at existing consulates so that consuls could spare the major part of their time for commercial work. The Commercial Intelligence Committee had urged precisely this as far back as 1898, and the point was reaffirmed at each of the subsequent committees before which the whole subject was raised.

Victorian consuls had been dependent entirely on such local labour as they could hire either from their scanty office allowances or, when they still drew fees, from the fees collected at their ports. The general experience was unsatisfactory, but occasionally consuls had found good men simply because a clerkship at a consulate was a recognized back door into the consular service (the majority of the consular officers recruited around the turn of the century had some such experience). After 1903, with entry by examination and the reduction of the age limit for entry from fifty to twenty-seven, this opportunity no longer existed, and the quality of the clerical labour available to consuls noticeably deteriorated. One senior consul, writing to another in 1917, complained that in a great many places consuls were compelled to employ 'broken-down British subjects, who ask for charity', and that these people, taken out of charity, were kept on for the same reason, to prevent them from becoming distressed British subjects.[1] Even at Buenos Aires, where there was a large resident British community, the consul-general, complaining of his desperate position during the war, reported that it was hard enough in peacetime to find a man 'sufficiently reduced in circumstances as to render the modest pay offered a powerful enough inducement for him to enter an occupation in which he knows there will be no promotion, no social standing, not the remotest chance of saving and no provision for old age'.[2]

Local staff of a kind could normally be found, and in many cases, whether for purely routine jobs or for duties of greater complexity, they were as efficient as any. But the real problem, in an age when national tempers were

---

[1] PRO.FO/369/971.
[2] Memorandum dated 1 May 1917: PRO.FO/369/915.

The General Consular Service in the twentieth century 113

always rising, was to get British subjects, of sufficient competence, to handle the consular archives, deal generally with confidential material, and satisfy the prejudices of Britons themselves. The prejudices could hardly be ignored. Relatively recently Allan Manson, Assistant General Secretary of the National Union of Seamen, complained indignantly of his experience at the consulate at Port Said, to which he had gone to discuss a particular subject with the British consul: 'All I saw was an Arab clerk. I did not want to talk to an Arab clerk; I wanted to talk to the British consul; but I could not see him, so I went back to the ship and told the rest of my shipmates: "That is your British Consul." That goes on right round the world.'[1]

The only practical means of meeting the need for security and efficiency was the creation of a service of permanent consular clerks. But it was a subject which, as Lord Dufferin put it, 'bristled with financial, geographical and climatical difficulties'.[2] Victor Wellesley, who had put forward the proposal of a Second Division service many years before (only for it to be rejected on the score of expense), tried it out again in the more experimental atmosphere of the consular committees. The Steel-Maitland Committee decided to accept provisionally the principle of such a service, to be called the 'Chancery Service', and a circular was sent out asking for reports on the number of Second Division staff required. But economy set in, and the scheme was abandoned. During the 1920s some Home Civil Service clerks were seconded for work at the larger consulates, and in China there were enough of them by the late 1930s—fourteen clerical officers altogether—to consider themselves, unofficially, a separate service.[3] The Civil Service Commissioners even held periodical examinations for the Consular Clerk Grade for some years after the war. But in 1930 the examinations were suspended, and three years later a Foreign Office memorandum, describing improvements in the consular service since 1914, merely reported that the subordinate staff at consular posts were appointed by the consular officer concerned and were not members of the Civil Service.[4] This system, which the 1943 White Paper was to describe as 'objectionable from every point of view', survived as long as the consular service itself.

---

[1] Minutes of Evidence, *Report of the Select Committee on Estimates* (Sub-Committee F), PP 1950–1 (242) V, Q 2159.
[2] Memorandum dated 1 September 1917: PRO.FO/369/972.
[3] Memorandum on the origin of the Clerical Officer Service in China: PRO.FO/369/2461.
[4] Memorandum on the History and Organization of the Consular Service, March 1933: PRO.FO/369/2316.

Amalgamation: social objections The postwar commercial renaissance of the consular service was a feeble affair. Few posts were created, and consulates were almost as understaffed and overburdened with routine as they had always been; an Edwardian consul would have been hard put to it to recognize the difference. But there was a change in the character of the service which was to end with the achievement of an ambition long dear to its members—amalgamation with the diplomatic service. And it was this change, rather than the urge for administrative reform, which became the dynamic element in consular history after 1903.

Social, educational, and functional differences were said to form the basis of the division of state officials overseas into two distinct services, the diplomatic service and the consular service. A purely practical objection to amalgamation was that the scale of living expected of members of the diplomatic corps had always required the assistance of a substantial private income. Though consuls might themselves often have had some private means, they were not generally drawn from a group in society which could guarantee the minimum of £400 p.a. considered necessary for the diplomatic service. The £400 requirement was dropped officially in 1919. But a diplomat dependent on his salary alone could not expect to follow his vocation at all freely. Until the new allowances were introduced in 1947, posts at the more expensive capitals were simply beyond the means of a man without substantial private resources. It would, as Edmund Hammond had warned back in 1858, have been a 'great delusion' to consuls to have held out prospects of advancement in the diplomatic career which they could not have afforded to enter on the existing rates of salary.[1]

Assuming that salary rates were immutable, there was something to be said for this. But the social argument depended rather on the disqualification which class imposed, for one reason or another, on the conduct of diplomacy. Sir Augustus Paget, Minister at Rome, and Sir Andrew Buchanan, Ambassador at St Petersburg, agreed in their evidence before the 1871 Committee that young men without the right social background would not be admitted to society in the main capitals of the world, and it was only in the salons that access to information could be gained. Foreigners, Paget argued, were particularly punctilious in this respect; he found that the first questions asked about a new man appointed to his legation were who he was, what were his relations, what class of society he belonged to. Buchanan was asked

---

[1] Minutes of Evidence, *Report of the Select Committee on Consular Service and Appointments*, PP 1857-8 (482) VIII, Q 757.

whether people in St Petersburg were aware of the class to which his secretaries or attachés belonged, and whether anyone would actually find out if a son of a butcher were to be posted there. He replied that they were always aware of class, and that they would find out the origins of the butcher's son 'to a certainty'.¹

In the governing circles of Victorian Europe social origins were undoubtedly important. Unjust though it was, the interests of the nation were best served in these circumstances by diplomats recruited from the aristocracy. Stanley Leathes, the First Civil Service Commissioner, was asked by Philip Snowden, during his evidence before the 1914 Commission, whether the 'other qualities' than those of a scholar, which he had said were important for the post of a Foreign Office clerk or attaché, included high social connections and the qualification to take part in the 'society' of the country to which he went. Leathes replied that this was the case, 'as the world is at present constituted'.²

But traditional social values, even by 1914, were under attack. In prewar Europe, it was probably only at St Petersburg, and to a lesser degree at Vienna, that social connections were still indispensable. In Paris, Arthur Ponsonby told the 1914 Commission, society was in a little backwater by itself and had no contact with the government of the day: 'A man may go out into high society and have a very good time without being of the least use diplomatically.' Sir Henry Austin Lee, after twenty-seven years' experience in Paris, felt that the social duties of young diplomats were 'very much exaggerated', and added that the most efficient junior he ever remembered at the Paris embassy had been a young married man who never went into society at all. Sir William Tyrrell, Grey's Private Secretary, while admitting that he was not quite orthodox on this point, discounted the social role of diplomats, except in so far as it genuinely led to personal contact with the people that really governed the country. Speaking of the only country with which he was personally acquainted as a member of a diplomatic mission, Tyrrell said that 'society, so-called, and government are divorced; it is very rarely that you meet in any drawing room the people who really govern Italy'.³

Yet the arguments used privately by the diplomats on the Departmental

---

¹ Minutes of Evidence, *First Report of the Select Committee on the Diplomatic and Consular Services*, PP 1871 (238) VII, QQ 63, 222; 270-1, 307-8.
² Minutes of Evidence, *5th Report of the Royal Commission on the Civil Service*, PP 1914-16 (Cd 7749) XI, Q 38,751.
³ Ibid., QQ 39,379; 41,894-5; 40,996-10.

Committee of 1938-9, appointed by the Secretary of State to consider the whole question of the amalgamation of the diplomatic and consular services, were very much on the old, socially exclusive lines. Sir Hughe Knatchbull-Hugessen, with the consent and collaboration of the two other diplomatic members, Hoyer Millar and Howard Smith, sent a private letter (printed below as an Appendix) to the Permanent Under-Secretary, Sir Alexander Cadogan, putting the diplomats' case. It is a real classic of its kind.

The letter spelt out those arguments against amalgamation which, Knatchbull-Hugessen felt, 'would have been difficult and delicate to include in the body of our report'. There were certain requirements of the diplomatic service, it seemed, which were 'in some sense intangible and difficult to state without creating an impression of exclusiveness'. Though personality, 'address', and *savoir-faire* were naturally of great importance in the consular service, it was in the diplomatic service that these 'rather intangible qualities' were most essential. A diplomat had to be able to 'deal as an equal with foreign colleagues, Cabinet Ministers, Prime Ministers and Heads of State; to hold his own with Sovereigns and other royalties and to fraternize with the governing class in no matter what country'. This meant that 'all suspicion of an inferiority complex must be absent from his make-up'. Identical qualities were required from diplomatic wives, where it was most important that they should be suitable 'adequately to second their husbands in all that concerns the representative and social side of the profession abroad'. The wife, in her capacity as 'Chefesse', had a most important part to play in the diplomatic life, and great attention had to be paid to this consideration in the selection of officers for service abroad.[1]

Amalgamation: educational objections The educational distinction between consuls and diplomats became more identifiable once the consular examination was introduced in 1904. The prewar examination for the General Consular Service, apart from its stringent language tests, was an elementary affair which made no great intellectual demands on the candidates; it was of a distinctly lower quality than the Class I examination for Foreign Office clerks and diplomatic attachés. The nature of the examination actually had a dissuasive effect on university entrants, and Algernon Law was

[1] Private letter, dated 20 January 1939: PRO.FO/366/781.

bound to admit that the Service, as recruited in 1914, did not often get men with an Honours degree.[1]

The MacDonnell Commission (1914) selected the 'more cautious procedure' and the 'much higher educational standard' of recruitment for diplomacy as its main reason for supporting the Ridley Commission in rejecting an amalgamation of the two services. Its recommendation that the consular examination be reduced to the kind of test suited to boys direct from school would, if accepted, have created an absolute educational barrier between the services. But opinions changed during the war, and recruitment to the consular service in the interwar period was by the ordinary Administrative Class examination. The diplomatic service examination in the 1920s and 30s still demanded rather more subjects and a higher total of marks, but candidates for both the consular and the diplomatic competitions came from the same educational base, were of the same age, and needed the same scholastic qualifications.

The difference between the diplomatic and consular entrants in the interwar years was the difference which exists today between entrants to the Administrative Class of the Home Civil Service and to the Tax Inspectorate; it was quite distinct from the very much sharper age and educational line drawn between the Administrative and the Executive Classes. The parallel can be taken further, for consuls, like H.M. Inspectors of Taxes, were often candidates who had failed to collect quite enough marks to qualify for the more favoured service. The fact was that the educational distinction, which for many candidates had been sharp before 1914 and perhaps absolute in the old days of patronage before 1903, was whittled down by the 1920s and 30s to the addition of one or two papers and some extra marks in an entirely parallel examination. It was a slight basis indeed for the enormous disparity of opportunity and reward between the two services.

Amalgamation: functional objections The most genuine distinction between the diplomatic and consular services was not social or educational but functional. The duties of consular agents, Palmerston told the Commons in 1855, were entirely different from those of diplomats; consuls 'are chiefly confined to seaports, and have no reference to diplomatic relations between two Powers'.[2]

---

[1] Minutes of Evidence, *5th Report of the Royal Commission on the Civil Service*, PP 1914-16 (Cd 7749) XI, QQ 41,726; 37,460.
[2] 138 *Parl. Deb.*, 3s, 907 (22 May 1855).

In the early days of the Victorian consuls, there was a great deal of truth in this, and diplomats liked to reinforce the distinction by insisting that there was some sort of mystique attached to the practice of diplomacy which mere consuls would find difficult or impossible to grasp. Edmund Hammond argued that while there was no complication attached to the consular profession, the tact and discretion required for dealing with political questions could only be acquired by previous training in the diplomatic career.[1] Henry Howard, First Secretary at Peking, told a Royal Commission in 1890, thirty years later, that a consul had not had the same diplomatic training as an attaché; 'he has not been copying for ten, twelve or fifteen years; he has not been ciphering for all that time; he has not learnt the legends and traditions of the service.' Nor, Howard added, did he have the training, as a rule, to cope with the social duties of a diplomat.[2]

Naturally, these arguments were resented by those who knew something about the duties actually falling on both classes of officers. Consul Frederick Bernal, who had just returned from four years at Madrid, told the 1858 Committee that from what he had seen of the working of the legation, there was nothing there that he could not have done himself if he had been transferred to the diplomatic service—'I never saw any mysteries in their service'. Richard Wood, who at the time was discharging both diplomatic and consular functions with energy and skill at Tunis, explained to the same Committee that diplomatic functions, compared with the ordinary range of consular duties in the Levant, would be 'deemed easy' by consuls.[3]

When the amalgamation of the two services was imminent, David Scott was not himself prepared to accept that diplomacy was a delicate and difficult task, only practicable to those who had served a long apprenticeship.[4] The reforming members of the Departmental Committee of 1938 felt the same. Apart from the ceremonial and social side of diplomatic life, there was no special diplomatic technique which they considered beyond the reach of any intelligent officer whose previous experience had been limited to consular work.[5] Even Hoyer Millar, who was later (as a diplomatic service member of

---

[1] Minutes of Evidence, *Report of the Select Committee on Consular Service and Appointments*, PP 1857-8 (482) VIII, Q 758.

[2] Minutes of Evidence, *Report of the Royal Commission on Civil Establishments*, PP 1890 (c. 6172-1) XXVII, QQ 29,294; 29,423.

[3] Minutes of Evidence, *Report of the Select Committee on Consular Service and Appointments*, PP 1857-8 (482) VIII, Q 5681, Appendix No. 4.

[4] Memorandum on the Amalgamation of the Diplomatic and Consular Services 21 January 1938: PRO.FO, Confidential Print 15334.

[5] Report dated January 1939: PRO.FO/366/781.

the 1938 Committee) to discover all kinds of objections to giving consular officers access to diplomacy, had minuted his opinion in March 1937 that although a good consular officer could do diplomatic work as well as his own without much difficulty, the average diplomat would have no idea how to set about consular work.[1]

However that may be—and there was no great mystery in fact attached to either profession—as they expanded the two began to cover more of the same ground. The Foreign Office, even in the days when no self-respecting Foreign Office clerk or diplomat would have been seen dead with a consul as a colleague, argued for and against the overlap as the occasion served. A. J. Otway, Under-Secretary of State for Foreign Affairs, driven to it by the contention that consuls, as mere commercial agents, should properly be transferred to the Board of Trade, argued that 'he would be a clever man who could tell where in the conduct of consular functions a matter ceased to belong to the province of commerce and to enter that of diplomacy; there was hardly a single question a consul had to treat that might not become a question of diplomacy'.[2] And when Edward Spring-Rice was under examination before the Public Accounts Committee on the proposal to throw together the Diplomatic and Consular Service Votes, his reply was that it was considered in the Foreign Office that a single vote would represent more truly the facts of the case; the duties of the two services 'overlap considerably and are perhaps tending to overlap more'.[3] Indeed, in 1963 the Plowden Committee could insist that 'within his district, a Consul has the same broad representational responsibilities as an Ambassador or High Commissioner has in relation to an overseas country as a whole'; there were places where 'the general range of activities carried out by Consuls-general and their staffs transcends in importance that of minor embassies'.

There had always been a number of shared functions between a consul and a diplomat. Both existed to protect British subjects and their interests, one in a local district, the other before the central government at the capital. Both were instructed to report developments, political, social and economic, within their areas. Both, as officers of the Crown, acted as the head of the local British community. So long as consuls remained preoccupied with shipping matters, this overlap, which had always existed, remained in the background.

---

[1] Minute dated 31 March 1937: PRO.FO/371/20630.
[2] 299 *Parl. Deb.*, 3s, 548 (18 February 1870).
[3] Minutes of Evidence, *Third Report of the Committee on Public Accounts*, PP 1890 (177) x, Q 1374.

But it became more obvious as consular functions developed in two distinct areas.

In the first, that of politics, it was undeniable that many consuls, particularly in the Levant, in Africa and in the Far East, were asked to perform functions entirely political in scope and intention. Palmerston, who was responsible for that sharp distinction between 'seaport consuls' and diplomats, had admitted some years before that all consuls in the Danubian principalities (which had semi-independent status under Turkish suzerainty) had diplomatic functions of a kind, and that consuls generally, though not strictly diplomatic agents, were necessarily authorized to make what amounted to diplomatic representations on behalf of injured British subjects, in some cases without reference to the legations.[1] Sir Donald MacAlister, in a skilful series of questions at the 1914 Commission, drove two distinguished diplomats, Sir Maurice de Bunsen (Ambassador at Vienna) and Sir Arthur Hardinge (Ambassador at Madrid), to the conclusion that the functions of the consular service and of the diplomatic service in the Levant and the Far East ran into each other so closely that there was no longer any real point in distinguishing between them.[2]

But it was commerce, the second area in which the overlap took place, which was ultimately to prove decisive in the amalgamation of the two services. It has already been suggested that increasing competition overseas in the last decades of the nineteenth century created a rising public demand for consular services to British trade, pre-eminently for the production of commercial intelligence. Even diplomats found themselves drawn inexorably into an increasing range of commercial functions. Sir Maurice de Bunsen was not exaggerating when he told the 1914 Commission that certainly half the time of a diplomatic mission was by now taken up with commercial work, in backing up British traders with grievances and pushing British commercial interests.

Diplomatic responsibility for commerce developed slowly, and it was still at a relatively primitive level by 1914. But the First World War, and the damaging international competition with which Britain was faced in the interwar years, compelled the British Government to take a more positive part in the promotion of overseas trade. The effects of this were felt in the Foreign Office and in the diplomatic service, as they had been in

---

[1] Minutes of Evidence, *Report of the Select Committee on Miscellaneous Expenditure*, PP 1847-8 (543) XVIII, QQ 7593, 7600.

[2] Minutes of Evidence, *5th Report of the Royal Commission on the Civil Service*, PP 1914-16 (Cd 7749) XI, QQ 38,056-7; 38,264-5; 38,392-4.

the consular service. Sir Donald MacAlister had suggested, back in 1914, in an ingenious addition to the argument by which he had already brought Sir Arthur Hardinge to admit the possibility of a fusion of the diplomatic and consular services in the East, that the development of the commercial functions of Missions even in the West had created an area of functions in which consulates and missions were distinguishable only by the extent of the districts for which they reported. Sir Arthur felt compelled 'in principle' to agree.[1]

The amalgamation Both in the scale of the overlapping functions and in a whole range of detailed, largely routine duties, consuls remained, and remain, unquestionably distinct from diplomats. They dealt with districts rather than nations, with local authorities rather than central governments, with local trade enquiries and trading prospects rather than national tariffs, trading regulations, and broad economic trends. It was this real distinction, among others less respectable, which delayed the amalgamation of the service over the interwar years, and which, it will be suggested later, contributed to the relative failure of the amalgamation when at length it came.

The Foreign Office in the 1920s seemed irreconcilably opposed to an amalgamation. Even the amalgamation of the Foreign Office and the diplomatic service (officially in force after 1919) was illusory, and interchange of staff rarely occurred. In practice, it proved impossible to send Foreign Office clerks overseas on the existing salary scale (which for many posts was still dependent on supplementation from private resources), and almost as difficult to ask diplomats to sacrifice their foreign allowances and return to the standard of living available at London rates of pay. As for the consular service, even the Labour Government (in this respect, as in others, *plus royaliste que le roi*) refused to consider an amalgamation. Arthur Henderson announced, in reply to questions in the House, that the time had not yet come for such a move, and that there was no intention to appoint a committee of enquiry to consider it; the duties of the services were 'in many respects different, and call for somewhat different qualifications', and experience had shown that the existing practice, whereby officers were transferred from time to time from one service to another according to their individual aptitudes, was preferable to any rigid system of unification.[2] Since, as the Lord Chancellor (Viscount Simon) was to point out when

[1] *Ibid.*, QQ 38,395-8.
[2] 239 *HC Deb.*, 5s, 1269 (28 May 1930) and 240 *HC Deb.*, 5s, 1591 (30 June 1930).

speaking for the Government's new proposals in 1941,[1] there was in fact 'no interchange at all' and the consular service was 'a separate institution, a separate service', this was not a particularly encouraging or even intelligent reply.

But Geoffrey Mander's unanswered Supplementary—'Does the right hon. Gentleman intend to allow the past system to continue indefinitely unchanged?'—showed from which direction the wind was blowing, and on the whole it was not from within the Office itself. The Foreign Office was not unaware of mounting public criticism, especially of the monopoly which the 'upper 400', conservatively inclined, were believed to enjoy over posts in the diplomatic service. The pressure for amalgamation came now not only from the consuls themselves, but from the people and the politicians, aware of the need to spread the social net for Foreign Office recruitment much wider. The Labour Party, by the late 1930s, was firmly established as the second party in the two-party system; sooner or later, the natural electoral swing would bring it again to power, and the opinions which Mander expressed would gain a sympathetic hearing. In the memorandum which resurrected the whole question of amalgamation in January 1938, Sir David Scott emphasized the need to forestall criticism by bringing the amalgamation into being on terms negotiated by, and acceptable to the Foreign Office; the danger was that it would otherwise be forced on the Foreign Office by 'people who would probably be prejudiced, who would almost certainly know little about the subject and who would be in a hurry to do something spectacular'.[2]

When the amalgamation finally took place, as a major part of the general Foreign Service reform of 1943, the first motive of reform was to broaden the basis of the service. Both the 1943 White Paper and Richard Law's speech (by which the reforms were introduced to the Commons) made a point of answering, and to some extent surrendering to public criticism on this very point. In the circumstances Lord Strang's observations, in the Whitehall series handbook on the Foreign Office prepared within the Foreign Office, are not uninteresting. 'It is worth mentioning here', said Lord Strang, after a laborious defence against the charge of social exclusiveness within the services between the wars, 'that the main impetus towards the reforms came from within the supposedly closed circle, from members of the Foreign Office and Diplomatic Service':

---

[1] 119 *HL Deb.*, 5s, 625.
[2] PRO.FO/366/781.

The necessity both of amalgamating the services and of widening the field of choice was urged most strongly by precisely that 'mandarin' class of British diplomatists which was popularly supposed to be so jealous of its privileges and oblivious of its deficiencies.[1]

Admittedly, officials of the Foreign Office itself and of the Department of Overseas Trade were responsible for much of the move towards reform in these last years before the amalgamation, even if they acted often under pressure from without. But it was the representatives of 'the "mandarin" class of British diplomatists' who had signed the minority report against amalgamation in January 1939, and who were responsible for that curiously archaic letter to Sir Alexander Cadogan on the social disqualifications of consuls and their wives.

The arguments for and against amalgamation, which were raised in David Scott's memorandum of January 1938 and before the subsequent Departmental Committee, covered the same social, educational, and functional ground. There were some additional points of detail connected with the actual amalgamation, such as the problem of arranging for suitable periods of London service in a combined organization of 650 officers, where only eighty-seven on the present establishment were required for London duties. There were other points, such as the desirability of extending the commercial experience of members of the diplomatic service, which had become of greater importance over the past few years.

But the emphasis in Scott's report, and in the special report prepared by Sir Malcolm Robertson which formed the last stage in the move towards amalgamation, was on the need to find some way, in the interests of general efficiency, of solving the position of inferiority in which consuls had always found themselves in relation to their diplomatic colleagues. Scott's conclusion, after examining the arguments for and against the amalgamation, had been unequivocally in favour. An amalgamated service, he explained, given good and impartial administration, would have an *esprit de service* in which the diplomat's contempt for the consul and the consul's envy of the diplomat would disappear: 'It would be worth a lot to alter a state of affairs which produces these feelings so prejudicial to efficiency.'

In the end it was a combination of social and economic arguments which carried the day. The conduct of international affairs, Richard Law argued in introducing the reforms in 1943, had altered in two vital respects. The first was the disappearance of the governing class, which made it desirable

[1] Lord Strang et al., *The Foreign Office* (London, 1955), p. 77.

that today, as distinct from the past, members of the Foreign Service should be representative of the whole nation, of every class and section of the community, and able to deal with whole nations overseas. The second, and perhaps the more important, was the fusion of politics and economics in foreign affairs. Disraeli, a hundred years before, had introduced a motion calling for the amalgamation of the diplomatic and consular services on the grounds that politics and commerce were indistinguishable. Now, a century later, the Foreign Office spokesman was advocating the same thing for the same reasons. The day, said Law, had 'quite clearly gone for ever when the diplomat can concern himself solely with those fascinating questions of high policy and leave the bread and butter questions of economics to more vulgar minds'.[1]

[1] 387 *HC Deb.*, 5s, 1361-2 (18 March 1943).

Chapter 4

The Levant Service

The formal independence of the Levant Service dates only from 1877, but in practical terms it had made its own enclave in the General Service from its first years under the Crown. In 1825, at the request of H.M. Government, the Levant Company quietly wound itself up, and its consular establishments passed to the Crown. The Company was not unsuccessful in representing British interests and developing British trade, but by the nineteenth century the state had expanded to a point where it was no longer necessary to delegate functions, such as consular representation, which properly belonged to the state itself. Nor, in those days of growing popularity for free and unrestricted trade, was it easy to justify the continuation of the Company's monopoly and of the levies, amounting to some 2 per cent, which it had imposed on British trade. Canning, as part of the preliminaries to the Consular Act of 1825, entered into negotiations with the Levant Company for the transfer of its consular agents to the Crown and for the surrender of its monopoly. The Company raised no objections. It was obvious that the development and expansion of British trade in the Levant required some form of official protection, and the Directors themselves were not insensible to the arguments for freer trade. At the meeting during which the surrender was considered, *The Times* reported Lord Grenville, the Company's Governor, as eulogizing 'with proper warmth' the advantages of unrestricted trade, which, he said, were first imparted to mankind from 'this favoured nursery of science and liberty, England':

> If [the report of the speech continued] the same spirit shall animate, the same resolution shall uphold the Legislature; if full and uncompromising effect shall be finally given to a system (that of throwing open commerce) thus confirmed by experience, thus sanctioned by public applause, not this age nor this country alone will have reason to bless our exertions: there is no period so remote, there is no nation so barbarous, in which we may not confidently anticipate that these successful researches of British policy will become, under the favour of

Providence, a pure and ample source of continually increasing human happiness.[1]

Commercial functions   When H.M. Government took responsibility for the Levant consular establishment it received from the Company some £60,000 of consols and about £10,000 cash in the hands of the treasurer.[2] But the contribution was as nothing to the real expense of a service which rapidly developed into one of the most costly and elaborate branches of the whole consular establishment. The problem was in part the scale on which the Company's consuls had lived. At Smyrna, which was one of the most important of the Company's factories, there were elaborate buildings to be maintained, and large community responsibilities. Victorian trade and charity did nothing to reduce these, and Wratislaw reports that in 1888 the Smyrna establishment consisted of a consul-general, a vice-consul, a chaplain, three clerks, a dragoman, and three cavasses; attached to the consulate was a British Seamen's Hospital in the charge of an English surgeon, and a post office: 'quite an extensive establishment as Consulates go'.[3]

But the real expense arose out of demands from three different directions—British political interest in the whole area, the judicial duties undertaken by consuls under the Capitulations, and H.M. Government's interest in the extension of British trade. In the early days of official responsibility for the service, trade was the main basis for consular expansion. William Huskisson, supporting the extension of the consular service in Asiatic Turkey, had argued that 'the obvious, perhaps the only wise method of attempting to open these regions to British adventure, is by planting Consuls in the principal Towns, which are numerous and well-peopled'.[4] At the time he was writing, Smyrna and Beirut were the only Levant Company consulates still retained in the area, but Damascus and Trebizond were added in 1830 for the development of British trade.

It was at this point that Russia became a real source of anxiety to the Foreign Office, and posts created originally for trading purposes, such as Trebizond itself and later Diarbekr and Monastir (in Turkey's eastern and northern provinces respectively), were retained as political consulates. When

---

[1] *The Times*, 4 May 1825, 3a.
[2] Minutes of Evidence, *Report of the Select Committee on Miscellaneous Expenditure*, PP 1847-8 (543) XVIII, Q 6232.
[3] A. C. Wratislaw, *A Consul in the East* (Edinburgh, 1924), p. 70.
[4] Memorandum dated March 1828: PRO.FO/95/592.

Sir Henry Elliot was defending the size of the Ottoman consular establishment (in reply to Clarendon's request of 1869 to consider a rationalization of the posts), he admitted that the importance of Trebizond as a seaport had materially diminished since it was raised to the rank of a consulate in 1856. At the same time he justified retaining W. Gifford Palgrave as consul because of his intelligent and most interesting reports 'which may prove of great value at some future time, if, as is generally considered probable, the next attack on Turkey by Russia should be made by the Asiatic frontier'.[1] The problem in setting limits to the service was that practically any post, in the atmosphere of unintelligent alarm which enveloped Anglo-Russian relations in the Near and Middle East for so much of the last century, could be justified on political grounds, and if there were no political grounds, jurisdictional crises served as well. C. M. Kennedy explained from Cairo in 1871 that

> the necessity which exists in Turkey for Consular intervention in very many instances not required in countries where society is constituted on the basis of European civilization; the extra-territorial jurisdiction which exists for the benefit of foreigners, and which cannot be relinquished; the necessity for constant watchfulness over their interests, and the extension of those interests throughout the whole Empire—render it imperative that Consulates should be more numerous, be placed nearer together, and be provided with a larger staff than is wanted in most other countries.[2]

In these circumstances there was an obvious danger of overexpansion. Once a post had been created it was difficult to close, whether because its existence had already attracted British subjects to the district, because H.M. Government had been persuaded to take under its protection certain local interests, because other Powers had appointed consuls, or because the consular district might overnight become of great political interest. The effect was to create a body of officials quite out of proportion to the real trading or strategic importance of the Levant area. In 1826 the Levant establishment amounted to two consuls-general and eleven consuls and vice-consuls, with salaries totalling £8358. By 1855 it had risen to three consuls-general and forty-one consuls and vice-consuls, at the cost, in salaries, of £21,150. Taking trade as a standard of comparison, British exports to

---

[1] Sir Henry Elliot to Lord Clarendon, Constantinople, 14 August 1869: PRO.FO/366/1132.
[2] C. M. Kennedy to Lord Granville, 10 February 1871: *ibid.*

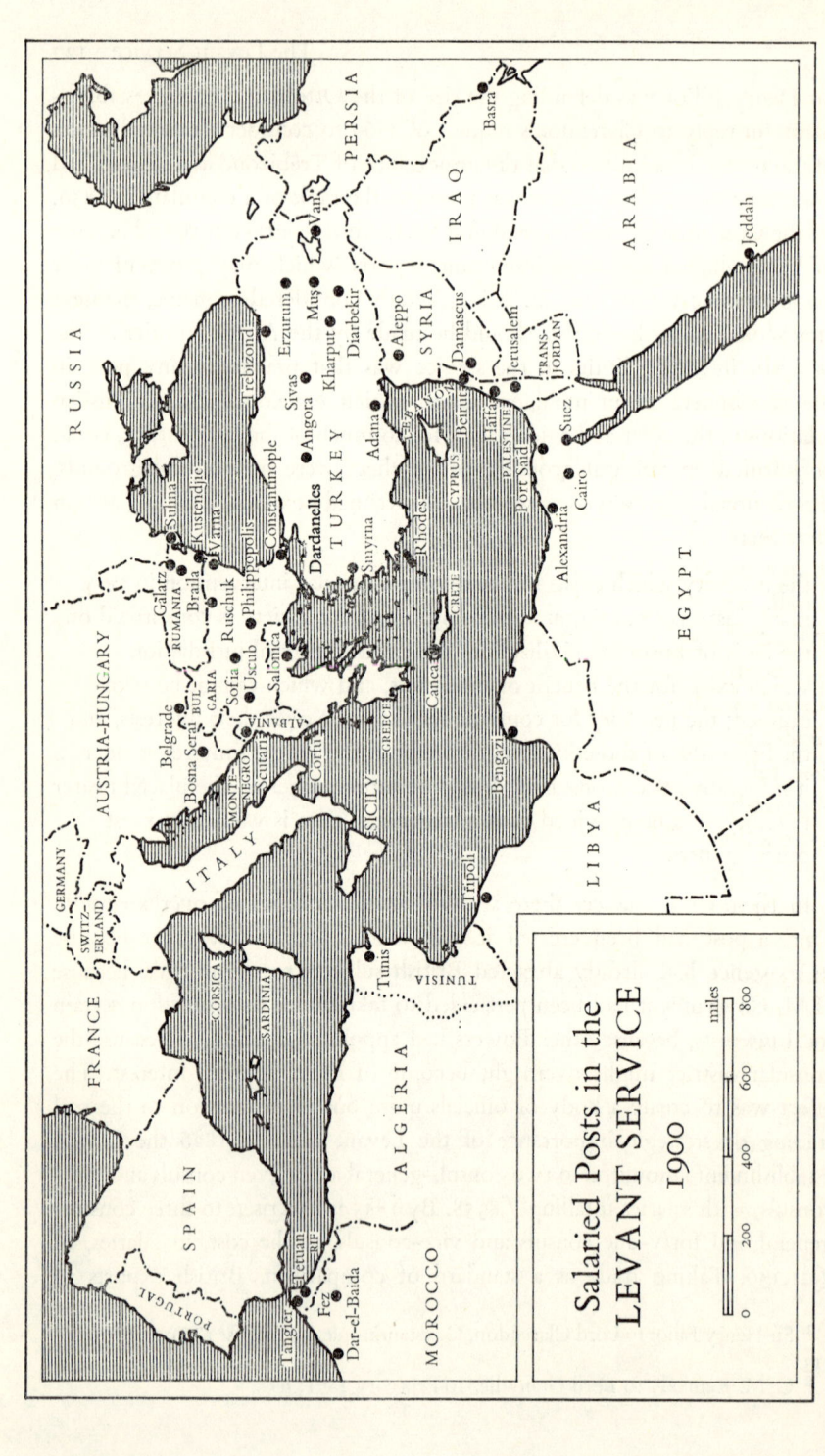

Turkey in 1855 were worth about £2 million; exports to the United States, where consular salaries amounted to £5000, had reached £23 million.

Palmerston, replying to criticism along these lines in the Commons, made some obvious points in defence of the exaggerated size of the Levant establishment—its judicial and political functions, the fact that in civilized countries so many burdens were removed from the shoulders of foreign consuls, the requirements of a trade which had to be extended where no trade had existed before.[1] These did not amount to a complete justification of what, after all, was to some degree an inherited obligation, and often an embarrassing inheritance at that. Lord Russell, speaking to the same point at the Supply debate of 18 July 1861, 'lamented that the system had gone so far as it had done', but argued that it would be 'plainly impolitic' to leave British interests in those parts of the world unprotected, particularly where there were so many consuls appointed by the other Powers. He hoped that change would come gradually through administrative reform in Turkey herself, which would make the presence of so many foreign consuls unnecessary.[2] Other statesmen felt the same, and the Select Committee of 1872 was positive that improved rail and telegraph communications and the altered condition of European political affairs in the Levant were tending rapidly to weaken the official arguments for keeping the Levant consuls at their full existing establishment. Yet when it came to the point, the Turks obstinately refused to reform their administration; Europeans insisted, often hysterically, on maintaining their full capitulatory rights; political conditions were as unpromising and as potentially explosive as ever; and the British consular establishment remained undiminished.

It was an experience common to the specialized services, all of which had a judicial and political rationale. The China Service in the last century expanded on a similar scale, and then found it impossible to contract. In the twentieth century the consular establishment in Persia rose to absurd levels. There were, according to Colonel Howard Bury, twenty-nine consuls-general, consuls and vice-consuls in Persia in 1930, more than in Germany but with one-fortieth of the trade.[3] The Russian threat to Persia was a thing of the past and Germany, in 1930, was no problem. Yet it was in answer to both that the inflated services had been established before and during the First World War. There was always a painful timelag. Government

---

[1] 138 *Parl. Deb.*, 3s, 216-17 (7 May 1855).
[2] 164 *Parl. Deb.*, 3s, 1079 (18 July 1861).
[3] 236 *HC Deb.*, 5s, 908-9 (10 March 1930).

services were not easily disbanded, even if, as Howard Bury said, the chief work for British consuls in Persia was to find work for themselves.

Political functions One of the recurrent objections to the promotion of consuls into the diplomatic profession was that it would induce them to attempt to establish a reputation for clever diplomacy, whereas it was not desirable to encourage consuls to meddle with political matters. Nevertheless, in the Levant politics became one of the main consular functions. 'Every consul in the East', said a former consul in 1903, 'bears a more or less political character, and is daily engaged in the conduct of negotiations with the native authorities which require all the tact and intimate knowledge of men that are supposed to be the essential qualifications of the trained diplomatist.'[1]

The ratio of political to commercial functions in the Levant varied from post to post. Some were almost exclusively political, others equally commercial, while most fell, in different proportions, somewhere between. A Foreign Office official, asked by the 1872 Committee to give a rough indication of the nature of each post, went through the list before him. In Turkey in Europe, Belgrade, Bucharest, and Jassy were political posts; Galatz was commercial; Rustchuck, political, but to some degree commercial in that it superintended three commercial vice-consulates, Sulina, Varna, and Kustenje; Bosnia, political, Constantinople, commercial and judicial; Adrianople, as the capital of the Vilayet and a place of importance, rather political than commercial; the Dardanelles, commercial; Enos, commercial; Salonica, commercial; Cavallo, commercial; Larissa and Volo, as posts of observation on the Greek frontier, political; Monastir, political; Janina, political; Preveza, political and commercial; Scutari, political; and Crete, political and commercial. As for Asiatic Turkey, Brusa was commercial; Smyrna, commercial; Rhodes, commercial and political; Erzurum, political; Trebizond, political; Mosul, political; Damascus, Aleppo and Beirut, political and commercial; Cyprus, commercial; Jerusalem, political; and Jaffa, commercial.[2] The Barbary consulates, in Tripolitania, Tunisia and Algeria, which the Foreign Office had taken over from the Colonial Office in 1836, were mainly political and judicial, and the consulates in Morocco commercial to some extent, but again very largely political and judicial.

---

[1] *Quarterly Review*, April 1903, 610.
[2] Minutes of Evidence, *Report of the Select Committee on Diplomatic and Consular Services*, PP 1872 (314) VII, QQ 154-5.

'Political' was a flexible adjective covering a miscellaneous selection of duties. Some of the main consulates and consulates-general, in semi-autonomous vassal states such as Romania, Serbia, Bulgaria, Egypt, Tripoli, and Tunis, were simply diplomatic missions under a different name. Diplomatic etiquette debarred them from the status of missions, just as it did for Warsaw, Belgrade, Budapest and Oslo (Christiania). Their functions were diplomatic none the less. Even at the smaller Balkan posts there were no commercial duties to speak of. Wratislaw writes of his pleasant years as vice-consul at Philippopolis (Bulgaria) in the 1890s, where there were only eight British subjects (all good citizens and causing no trouble), very little routine work, excellent shooting, an interesting political situation, a decent climate, and Constantinople a night's journey away. He sometimes wondered what he was there for, and his one preoccupation during his six years at the post 'was lest some Ahab should set the eye of covetousness on my little vineyard and I be dispossessed'.[1]

Other consulates were not Foreign Office appointments at all but the responsibility of different colonial governments. The East India Company, for political and commercial reasons of its own, had maintained a limited consular establishment in Iraq, Persia, and the Gulf since the late eighteenth century. In the 1830s H.M. Government took a share in the Baghdad consulate and assumed responsibility for consular representation in Persia (at Tabriz, Tehran, and Resht), receiving in return £12,000 p.a. from the Company to meet the main expenses of the Persian Mission. When the Company was wound up after the Mutiny, the shared arrangement continued with its successor, the Government of India. Later, by the Welby Agreement in 1900, the total cost of the diplomatic and consular establishment in Persia was divided equally between Indian and Imperial funds—an expensive arrangement for the Foreign Office, as it turned out, since the Indian Government's consulates and residencies were maintained on a particularly lavish scale. Baghdad and Bushire, by 1914, were traditionally Indian Government appointments, and there were shared posts at Meshed, Ahwaz, and Kermanshah. The formidable Sir Percy Cox, consul-general (1904-14) at Bushire under the Foreign Office and, as political resident in the Persian Gulf, the representative of the Government of India, had powers described by his biographer as 'intermediate between those of an official guardian and an ambassador'. He exercised 'an undefined but often decisive influence upon the affairs, and more particularly upon the foreign relations, of the Arab

[1] Wratislaw, *Consul in the East*, pp. 89, 92.

Sultanate of Muscat, the Trucial States of the Pirate Coast, Bahrein and Kuwait'.[1]

After the First World War the situation remained much the same, though the re-emergence of Arab and Persian nationalism sometimes made the position of Indian 'politicals' at these posts an embarrassing anomaly. The Government of India survived its embarrassment, and in spite of strong anti-Indian pressure in Persia, maintained its hold over the consulates until the Second World War. Indeed in 1931 the Political Resident in the Persian Gulf, Major T. C. W. Fowle, felt that the Indian Government (which, he argued, was commonly acknowledged to have paramount interests in South Persia) should take over direct consular control of the whole area and place it under the supervision of an officer of the Indian Political Department.[2] The Indian Government at the time was contributing similarly to posts in Afghanistan, and paying and appointing to the consulate-general at Kashgar in Chinese Turkestan; certain consular posts in Ethiopia were filled by civil servants from Kenya and the Sudan; and all such posts were created primarily for political reasons and for the protection of the subjects of the colonial governments directly concerned.

Within the Levant area itself, consulates were intended to serve a number of important political functions. They acted first as centres of political intelligence, whether in the Balkans or on the frontiers of Asiatic Turkey and Russia. An effective Foreign Office strategy for the containment of Russia needed constant information, and the information came largely from outlying consulates. Iasi (Romania) was an important frontier post, a centre of information on the border of Austria-Hungary, Russia, and the Balkan Principalities. Scutari (Albania), commercially insignificant, was one of the most important political posts in European Turkey, remaining so as long as Montenegro was the spot to which the eyes of all Pan-Slavs turned and in which their hopes were centred.

The 'military' consuls, appointed for a brief period after 1878 to the area known as Kurdistan or Armenia ostensibly to supervise the 'reforms' promised by the Porte in the Cyprus Convention, were posted primarily to act as military observers, to watch Russian progress and defend the frontiers. They were an able group of men: Herbert Chermside, Charles Wilson, and Herbert Kitchener were later to achieve great professional distinction. But they were withdrawn by the Gladstone Government after 1882, and by 1889

---

[1] Philip Graves, *The Life of Sir Percy Cox* (London, 1941), p. 93.
[2] Letter dated 3 August 1931: PRO.FO/369/2278.

there was only a single consulate at Erzerum and a vice-consul at Van. Their military experience proved unnecessary; they caused annoyance in Turkey; they were expensive; and, as one consul put it, experience showed that the measure of reform introduced under the eye of the military amounted to what it would have been without them—that is to say, nothing at all.

The experience of the military consuls was typical enough. But one of the main political functions of the Levant consuls in general was, and continued to be, the encouragement of social improvement and administrative reform. Kennedy, after his tour of the Levant consular establishment, reported that the beneficial influence exerted by British consuls during the current transition era of the Ottoman Empire was in itself 'one of the most active powers of social improvement in Turkey'—a fact, he continued optimistically, which 'has ever been fully appreciated by the Government of the Sultan: for the Porte receives gladly, and attaches much weight to, the Consular statements which are frequently communicated by Her Majesty's Embassy'.[1] The Porte, as it turned out, had very different ideas, but *The Times* convinced itself that even if the Turkish Government did not appreciate British consular efforts, the Turkish people did. 'We can scarcely wonder', it said, after surveying native mismanagement in Asiatic Turkey, 'that the miserable inhabitants should still ask, as we are told they have long asked, when the English are coming.'[2]

British consuls were probably more successful in keeping the peace than they were in persuading the Turks of the advantages of European-inspired administrative reform. It was obviously important in the interests of British trade and investment in the area to avoid, so far as possible, expensive interruption by massacre, riot or war. But the intention went further than that. The amount of British trade in the interior of Asia Minor, Earl Percy reminded the Commons in 1900, had never been very great, and it was perfectly notorious that, but for political reasons, we would never have placed any consuls there at all.[3] Over the entire span of the Ottoman dominions the astonishing mixture of creeds and nationalities, in an age of fanaticism and general intolerance, created a constant danger of racial or religious conflict. Consul Holmes argued from Bosnia in 1872 that the most valuable and important function of a political consulate was preventive. With so many different creeds and races, of the most turbulent dispositions,

---

[1] Despatch dated 10 February 1871: PRO.FO/366/1132.
[2] *The Times*, 28 October 1879, 9d.
[3] 84 *Parl. Deb.*, 4s, 213 (15 June 1900).

there was constant danger of collision between governors and governed, and among the governed themselves. This had to be watched, and if possible controlled, since it might at any moment involve half Europe in confusion, and what affected Europe interested England.[1] In circumstances where a serious political complication was imminent with a probable loss of lives, the direct interests of British trade had often to be sacrificed. Consul-General Eldridge reported from Beirut in 1870 that he had frequently to put aside his commercial and judicial duties in order to devote his whole energies to preventing or mitigating a revolt against the government or a religious civil war, so as to save the country from the return of the disasters it had so often suffered in the past.[2]

Nor would British public opinion, Turkish alliance or not, tolerate the massacre of Christians; and consulates were established to protect Christians first in the Balkan states and then, when fanaticism turned once more against the Armenians, over a wide area of Asia Minor. In 1895, for example, as a direct consequence of the recent appalling Armenian massacres, vice-consulates were established at Van, Sivas, Adana, Kharput, and Mûsh, and a salaried officer was appointed in place of an unpaid vice-consul at Diarbekr. There was no commercial work at Diarbekr. Telford Waugh, whose second appointment in the Levant Service was to the Diarbekr vice-consulate, reported that there were only two other Europeans living there in 1897, the French vice-consul and an old Capucine monk. But Diarbekr was right in the heart of the massacre area, and Waugh's duty, together with the other vice-consuls in the eastern provinces of Turkey, was to watch and report on the reforms and to see that the Armenian amnesty was respected.[3]

While the consuls were at their posts, they undoubtedly had a most important restraining effect. Captain Townshend described a visit to Marash, in the vilayet of Aleppo—a large town of mixed Turk, Arab, Armenian, and Circassian population, which had been the scene of massacres in recent years and where the Christians lived in a constant state of apprehension:

> When I arrived there in November 1903, after six days' march from Adana, I found all the Armenian shops closed and none of the Christians abroad in the street. ... As we rode up the main street people turned out to see us, saying, 'Shapkali, shapkali' (a wearer of a hat), and when

[1] Report dated 30 March 1872: Appendix, *Reports Relative to British Consular Establishments, 1858 and 1871*, Part III, pp 1872 (c. 530) LX.
[2] Report dated 2 May 1870: PRO.FO/366/1132.
[3] Sir Telford Waugh, *Turkey, Yesterday, Today and Tomorrow* (London, 1930), pp. 58-9, 51.

the word had gone round that a foreigner, a Consul, had arrived, shops were opened, and in a few hours the market was thronged with Armenians who had not left their houses for days.[1]

The Armenians at Marash were afraid of tax extortions rather than massacre, but the effect of the mere presence of a European consul was remarkable. And the same could be said of any area within reach of consular authority and jurisdiction, often within a radius of many days' ride. Mrs Finn had reason to exaggerate her husband's virtues as consul at Jerusalem, but what she said of his protection of the Samaritan, Jewish, Abyssinian, and Syrian minorities within his district was not far from the truth. So certain, she explained, were the natives that tales of trouble brought before the British consul would be listened to and acted upon, that cases were known in which the evildoer, on seeing his victim taking the street leading to the British consulate, would run after him saying, 'Don't go in there, I'll attend to you. If you go to the Consul he'll go to the Pasha, and the Pasha must send for me; and I shall have to spend money on the police, and the officers, and everybody. Better give you a little than much to them.'[2]

From the British point of view the real anxiety was that a European war might develop out of national or religious conflict within the Ottoman Empire. The Crimean War began with just such a conflict at Jerusalem, and there was every prospect of something of the same kind happening again, whether or not it served as a mere cover for irreconcilable Anglo-Russian or Russo-Austrian rivalries in the Levant and Balkan areas. When Edmund Hammond was questioned on the Levant establishment in 1871, he explained that Britain had a very great interest in keeping things quiet in Turkey. He realized that though there was always clamour for economy in the northern posts, which was justified if trade alone were taken into account, the Levant consuls were a most valuable safeguard for the peace of Turkey, and therefore for the general political interests of Britain.[3] Some days later, W. H. Wylde, Senior Clerk of the Consular Department, argued that there was no room for economy even among the smaller consulates: 'As long as we are interested in keeping peace in the East, so long do I think that you must continue to maintain consular establishments in those countries.'[4]

[1] A. F. Townshend, *A Military Consul in Turkey* (London, 1910), pp. 116-17.
[2] Editorial note to James Finn, *Stirring Times*, ii, 284.
[3] Minutes of Evidence, *Second Report of the Select Committee on Diplomatic and Consular Services*, PP 1871 (386) VII, Q 1762.
[4] Ibid., Q 2295.

Judicial functions There was something in *The Economist*'s complaint, inspired by the political activities of Levant consuls in general and by those of Consul Plowden in Abyssinia in particular, that such consuls, placed in remote and independent positions, either recognized that there was nothing to do, or by doing something, ended by pledging the country to obligations it had not desired, policies it had not considered, or enterprises from which it would instinctively have drawn back:

> We are at this moment pledged in some vague and, therefore, highly dangerous way to protect tribes whose names no European ever heard, who are as much beyond our reach as if they lived in the Moon, from undescribed dangers, arising from undefined Mahomedan oppressors.[1]

Was it possible, *The Economist* asked, that a consular agency which produced results like these could be considered a valuable agency? Yet was it possible that such an agency should not periodically produce such results? The answer was that it did, but that quite apart from the danger of assuming responsibility over new native tribes, a readier instrument for intervention in the Levant already lay to hand in the Capitulations. It was the Capitulations, rather than political activities, which occupied Levant consuls (even in the major ports) to the exclusion of their commercial duties, and which ended by creating the worst political complications of all.

When exterritorial rights were first assigned to Europeans in the Levant, they were the concessions of powerful sovereigns to weak, foreign trading communities, enabling foreigners, as Christians, to trade and receive justice in countries where the law and Islam were synonymous. Formal capitulations were obtained in 1580 by the first British ambassador to the Porte, William Harborne. The right to settle disputes between Englishmen before their own authorities was extended, by the Capitulations of 1675, to the further principle that the British ambassador or his representatives were to be present at civil cases between Englishmen and Ottoman subjects, and at cases where Englishmen were tried on criminal charges.

This remained the position until the Capitulations were abandoned in the early 1920s. As the European powers became stronger and the Porte relatively weaker, the right of the ambassador's representative to be *present* at Turkish tribunals was converted into a right of *veto*, after which the court had no alternative but to send the papers to the Porte for diplomatic negotiation. Criminal and civil cases between British subjects and foreigners other than

---

[1] *The Economist*, 30 November 1867, 1352.

Turkish subjects were tried before the consular courts of the defendants' nationality.

All this made some sense in the small, restricted communities of the Levant Company's factories, where it suited the Ottoman authorities to delegate authority over an alien race of a different faith, and where an ultimate sanction existed, in the case of misbehaviour by the community as a whole, of expulsion or even massacre. But a concession from strength, in the interest of a useful trade, became a serious weakness once the relative power of the Ottoman Empire and the European states was reversed, and once, for Britons, the compliant Levant Company was replaced by salaried officers of the Crown. Furthermore, laws well suited to small communities became a very different matter when, by the middle of the nineteenth century, they were enforced in favour of 50,000 Europeans of all callings in Constantinople alone and twice as many in the provincial cities, 'in pursuit, one and all', said Sir Adolphus Slade, *per fas et nefas* of one object—gain, and though divided by clashing interests, united by the common bond of rancour against the dominant race'.[1]

Unfortunately, there seemed to be no limit to the gloss which might become attached to the original capitulatory rights. As each power, taking advantage of a moment of weakness or defeat at the Porte, negotiated a further extension or concession, its gains were immediately claimed by all other powers on the basis of the most-favoured-nation clause in their treaties. One of these extensions was the local veto at courts. Others amounted to a perfectly incredible series of restrictions on the tariff autonomy of the Porte, on its right to levy taxes and dues, on the right of its officers to enter foreign property and arrest foreign subjects—in fact, on its ability to intervene in any way with the lives and affairs of a large, turbulent, and almost totally unregulated foreign community.

The situation was absurd. A foreigner suspected of a crime, taking refuge in another foreigner's house, could not be arrested until the Turkish authorities could persuade the consular representatives both of the criminal and of his protector to accompany them, by which time, of course, the criminal had made good his escape. When some gipsies, in encampment just outside Mersina, began fighting between themselves, the Turkish police sent out a force to arrest them. Townshend reports how they turned on the police and cried: 'You have no power to touch us. We are French subjects.' The police returned with a cavass from the French consulate. The gipsies shouted: 'Go

[1] Quoted by Henry Layard: 193 *Parl. Deb.*, 3s, 1047 (10 July 1868).

away, we are most of us British subjects and you have no power to give us orders.' When the British cavass arrived, the gipsies, undeterred, screamed: 'If you come nearer we shall fire. We are Russians and you must not interfere with us.' The gipsies were finally overpowered and arrested, and Townshend dealt with the six British passport holders as well as he could, shipping them off to different parts of the Levant.[1] It was obvious that the passports in this case, as in so many where foreign nationality was claimed, had been through a dozen different hands and were useless as a means of identity or as a guarantee of nationality.

A tax of any kind, municipal or national, might not be levied on foreigners without the consent of their governments. Reader Bullard tells how one of his first jobs as a consular assistant in 1908 was to call on the Governor of Pera in protest against a tax on a British Maltese who had erected some swings at a local fair. The Governor had excused himself on the grounds that the money collected from the Maltese was not (God forbid!) a tax, but a municipal rent for the pitch occupied—'an explanation which our Consulate-General, more reasonable than some other foreign consulates, was glad to accept'.[2] There was the characteristic situation against which Admiral Slade, an officer in the service of the Porte, had complained so bitterly in 1867. The powers were constantly affronted by the condition of the harbour at Constantinople, yet the port dues for European vessels at Constantinople were fixed immovably by the powers themselves at from one to two shillings; twelve piastres was all that it would cost in anchorage for the *Great Eastern* to lie in the Golden Horn for a year. The European powers appointed their own harbour-masters, and the English had made theirs 'out of a servant in search of a place, out of a shipchandler in difficulties, out of a hydropathic doctor in want of patients, but never out of a sailor'.[3] Right up to the First World War the powers (Britain included) were using their capitulatory rights to block all tariff increases and tax changes within the Ottoman dominions.

What was already distressing when applied to genuine European nationals was infinitely more so when extended to their multitude of protégés. Originating once again as a useful delegation of unwanted authority, the Ottoman Empire had conceded to foreign consulates the power to receive under their protection foreign travellers and residents, not of their own

---

[1] Townshend, *Military Consul*, pp. 198-200.
[2] Sir Reader Bullard, *The Camels Must Go: an autobiography* (London, 1961), p. 58.
[3] Quoted by Layard: 193 *Parl. Deb.*, 3s, 1033 (10 July 1868).

nationality, whose religion and social habits did not assimilate with Islam. What had begun as a contemptuous concession became a gross abuse as corrupt or power-hungry European consuls drew increasing numbers of local inhabitants under their protection. The worst period came in the early decades of the nineteenth century, when a weakened and obviously declining Empire allowed hosts of foreigners to settle, abuses to multiply, and protégés to be numbered in tens of thousands. Though the Russians and the French were the worst offenders, Britons were not far behind. Sir Henry Rawlinson, on his first visit to Turkey in 1835, found that British consuls gave protection indiscriminately to almost anyone who applied; there were great numbers of people living under the protection of the different British consulates in the Levant 'who had really no claim to it, but had received it in virtue of some obsolete passport, and in many cases merely for the asking'.[1]

The range of the protection extended was astonishing. All Turkish servants, whether of consuls or of foreign merchants, could claim consular protection. After the 1850s protection was limited to consular employees, but even these could be multiplied dramatically if the consul wished. Hobart Pasha told of a certain foreign vice-consulate on the coast of Syria which had no less than thirteen cavasses and twelve dragomans, 'all independent of Turkish law, all allowed to pass their goods free of duty—all, in fact, foreign subjects, who snap their fingers at the Turkish authorities'.[2] Servants were only the beginning. At Jerusalem the first British consul in 1839 had been instructed by Lord Palmerston 'to afford protection to the Jews generally', and left to work out the details for himself. By the middle of the century protection had been extended to a special category of Polish Jews, ex-Russian subjects, who had been granted British protection in Palestine by an agreement concluded between the British and Russian governments in 1848, and to all Europeans who, having no other consul, chose the British consul as their own.[3]

Protection, originating from the best of motives, could end by covering the most fearful abuses. When Kennedy inspected the Damascus consulate in 1870, he found that the consulate was committed to the protection of a group of moneylenders, who under cover of their 'protected' status, were growing rich on unbridled usury. Their practice was to add about 20 per

---

[1] Minutes of Evidence, *Report of the Select Committee on Consular Service and Appointments*, PP 1857-8 (482) VIII, QQ 2853-6.
[2] Letter, dated from Constantinople, 10 January 1879, and printed in *The Times*, 17 January 1879, 6b.
[3] Finn, *Stirring Times*, I, 97-8, 106.

cent to the sums advanced for services supposed to be rendered, then charge compound interest of sometimes up to 30 per cent on the whole amount, and begin the account afresh every third month. These were sums advanced to villagers for payment of taxes on the date due, and the interest alone soon exceeded the original tax; one moneylender was said to have ruined more than forty villages. Kennedy, while proposing a limit on the interest rate above which the consulates would give no support or protection, argued that the protection should be continued if only to safeguard the debtors, who might well be even worse off should the moneylenders seek the protection of another consulate.[1]

Although it was always possible to withdraw protection from non-British nationals in such cases, the consuls had no alternative but to accept responsibility for the mass of British subjects created by Britain's expanding empire. Gibraltarians, Maltese, Indians, and Afghans, of whom large numbers lived and worked within Ottoman dominions, could all demand British consular protection as of right, and the Ionians, perhaps the most troublesome of all, also came under British consular authority until the Ionian Protectorate was abandoned in 1864. The Ionians and the Maltese, according to Henry Layard, were probably the most dangerous sector of the foreign population; it was Britain's failure to control them which had made life and property so insecure in so many parts of the East: 'They defied both the Turkish and British authorities—committing murders, robberies, and every manner of crime with impunity. They claimed protection from the British Consuls, and exemption from the Turkish laws, under the capitulations, and our Consuls were quite unable to deal with them.'[2] British protégés, chiefly Ionians, made substantial fortunes by lending their names, as protected persons, to Ottoman subjects. Assignments, partnerships, endorsements, technically accurate but in reality fictitious, transferred Turkish property to British consular protection. Ten per cent on the amount of the bill was the recognized consideration to an endorsee for the use of his name.[3]

In order to cope with the increasing volume of police and court business, some of the larger British consulates in the East developed into full-scale police stations for their consular districts. The consulate-general at Tunis

---

[1] Despatch dated from Beirut, 11 January 1871: PRO.FO/366/1132.
[2] 193 *Parl. Deb.*, 3s, 1027-8 (10 July 1868).
[3] The system is described by Consul R. Stuart in his return from Janina (Albania), dated November 1871: *Reports relative to British Consular Establishments, 1858 and 1871*, Part III, PP 1872 (c. 530) LX.

was open from 8 a.m. to 11 p.m., and urgent applications were received at any hour. Ordinary petty police cases against the large numbers of Maltese immigrant labourers were summarily disposed of, while criminal cases heard and judged annually ranged from 280 to 350, with civil cases rising to 1100.[1] It was never easy for a British consul to distinguish genuine claims of nationality from false. A British subject from Pakistan looked much like an inhabitant of the eastern provinces of Persia; an Arab from Egypt or the Sudan was not unlike a Turkish subject from Arabia. For many Arabs, Afghans, and British Indians, British consular authority was recognized and British nationality claimed only when it suited; then, on receiving a tax demand, they would come, as one consul said, rushing to the consulate crying 'Sahib! Save us from the Turks; we are British subjects, and the Consul-Sahib is our only protection!' The French had the same problem. The traveller, Gaston Deschamps, described how, since the conquest of Algeria and the establishment of the French protectorate over Tunisia, 'on a vu des Arabes, émigrés de l'Yemen et du Fezzan, se draper magnifiquement dans leur burnous et se réfugier au jardin du consulat de France, quand le moment était venu de payer l'impôt'.[2]

Not unnaturally, the Capitulations were fiercely resented in Turkey. But there were critics, too, among the Europeans. *The Times*, in the 1850s and 60s, was strongly opposed to the whole capitulatory system. 'Next to the Koran and the harem', its correspondent complained from Constantinople in 1854, 'the greatest obstacle to Ottoman improvement is this pernicious system, which makes the independence and integrity of Turkey an empty name.'[3] In a series of leading articles in July and August 1868, spanning the important Commons' debate of 10 July, *The Times* pointed to the abuses of a system of exceptional jurisdiction, which (somewhat prematurely) it claimed to be at an end, as much out of date as the ecclesiastical tribunals of the past. Whatever the chaos of Turkish laws or the vices of its tribunals, there was no justification for the demand that Eastern governments should abdicate their 'most inalienable sovereign rights' and submit to 'abnormal institutions which grew up out of circumstances now no longer in existence, to which their consent was never explicitly obtained, and in which they acquiesced in consideration

---

[1] Return dated 14 December 1871: *ibid.*
[2] *Sur les Routes d'Asie* (Paris, 1894), p. 181.
[3] *The Times*, 3 May 1854, 10d.

of advantages now deemed by them inadequate to the sacrifice they entailed'.[1]

In the correspondence provoked by these articles, Hyde Clarke, who had had considerable experience of the Levant, expressed the opinion that if the Capitulations were abandoned forthwith, Turkish and Egyptian administration would be so vastly improved by the enforcement of the real responsibility of their officials and by the more effective, because more disinterested, cooperation of the European consuls, that no Englishman, foreigner, Levantine, or protected subject would actually leave the country, nor would one English lady hesitate to visit Constantinople or the Nile as before. The Capitulations, he argued, were 'very convenient for jobbery, but not essential for the safety or comfort of residents'.[2] Unfortunately, his opinion, though probably entirely justified, was not shared by the majority of politicians or officials at the time. Most were prepared to admit the harmful effects of the Capitulations, particularly on Turkey herself. But they could not see their way to abandoning the judicial safeguards which the system provided. 'The real question', the Foreign Secretary (Lord Stanley) told the Commons in July 1868, after agreeing with the greater part of Layard's criticism of the operation of the capitulatory system, 'is not whether you desire to give up these rights, but whether you can find an effective substitute for them.'[3]

At Paris in 1856 the Allies had recorded their intention, indefinitely postponed, to open negotiations at Constantinople for the revision of the Capitulations, and Lord John Russell went so far as to instruct the British Ambassador in May 1860 to take the initiative in proposing from time to time such relaxations as he thought fit. At the same time, Russell warned the Ambassador that the rights embodied in the Capitulations, which were based on the principle that Turkish rule and justice were so barbarous as to require exceptional privileges, could be relinquished only in proportion to administrative and judicial improvements in Turkey herself: 'So long as law in Turkey is undefined, so long as Pashas are allowed to sell justice and protection, so long will the privileges of consular tribunals be necessary.'[4]

---

[1] *Ibid.*, 6 August 1868, 8c; two leading articles on the same subject had already been published on 2 July and 13 July. The occasion of the first was Nubar Pasha's proposal for Mixed Tribunals in Egypt in place of the Consular Courts.
[2] *Ibid.*, 10 August 1868, 12c.
[3] 193 *Parl. Deb.*, 3s, 1050 (10 July 1868).
[4] No. 40, *Instructions addressed to H.M.'s Embassy at Constantinople respecting financial and administrative reform, 1856-75*, PP 1877 (c. 1740) XCII.

The difficulty was to decide precisely when concessions became due. In 1880 British consular officers in the Levant were called on to report whether any improvement had taken place in the administration of justice since the latest round of reforms (the new Law of 1879). Between ignorance and corruption, replied the Embassy dragoman (G. C. Stavrides), the administration of justice in Turkey 'laisse encore beaucoup à désirer'. The consul at Trebizond concluded that the 'reformed' courts in his district were 'a mere mockery'. The consul-general in Anatolia spoke of the Turkish prisons as 'almost too horrible for description'. The consul at Aleppo described justice as open to the highest bidder. The consul at Jerusalem spoke of the administration of justice as tainted by three evils—corruption, professional incompetence, and creed antagonism—of which the most serious was the first. In report after report, the failures of the administration of justice, the corruption of officials, the continued inequality of Muslim and Christian before the law, were repeated, emphasized, and driven home, in considerable detail. Clearly, the evidence was partial and sometimes ill-informed. But confronted with such evidence, H.M. Government had no alternative except to press for further reforms and for more adequate inspection, both in fulfilment of the Treaty of Berlin and as a precondition of any relaxation of capitulatory rights. The reports, taken together, formed a powerful and virtually unanimous indictment of the current administration of justice before Turkish tribunals.[1] It was more than likely, as Hobart Pasha argued, that the Turks had never had an opportunity fairly to administer to their own laws: 'At every step they have a dragoman from this or that Embassy or Consulate, threatening, coaxing, or pleading with the ill-paid Turkish judge, who does not know where to turn.'[2] But it was the old dilemma of the chicken and the egg. Which came first, the abolition of the Capitulations, or the regulation of Turkish police and tribunals?

Rightly or wrongly, the Capitulations remained in force. But efforts were made within their framework to limit the number of protégés and to improve the operation of the consular courts. H.M. Government's conscience had been disturbed for some time already when the Crimean War, and the Turcophil feelings it created, persuaded Lord Clarendon to take the initiative at Paris of suggesting the revisions of the Capitulations with respect to protégés. The Turks grasped the opportunity, and the 1856 Treaty

---

[1] *Reports on the Administration of Justice in the Civil, Criminal, and Commercial Courts in the various Provinces of the Ottoman Empire*, pp 1881 (c. 3008) C.
[2] *The Times*, 17 January 1879, 6b.

substituted, on paper, a Five-Power collective protectorate of the Christian subjects of the Porte in place of the exclusive protectorates of the past. Furthermore, by an Embassy instruction of 19 June 1858, British consular officers were commanded to refuse to register any person who was not able to justify his claims to British protection.

By this time, as Hammond told the 1858 Committee, there were very few Turkish subjects under British protection other than consular dragomans and the personal servants of British merchants.[1] But he was speaking of those who were officially registered as protected persons and who came, as such, under British consular jurisdiction. The net of what was called 'officious' protection (in this context, the claim of a right to make representations, but not to exercise jurisdiction) was spread much wider. W. R. Holmes, consul at Diarbekr in Asiatic Turkey, who gave evidence immediately after Hammond, spoke even of intervening in disputes between Muslims, and certainly regarded it as one of his main functions to give 'officious' protection to all Jews and Christians in his consular district, whether Armenians, Papal Armenians, Jacobites, Papal Jacobites, Syrians, Chaldeans or Papal Nestorians, Greeks, Papal Greeks, or Protestants.[2]

The return of the Ionian Islands to Greece in 1864 reduced very substantially the number of persons entitled to British protection, to the undisguised relief of the consuls themselves. Vice-Consul J. E. Blunt, explaining the reduction of judicial business at his consulate, described the Ionians at Adrianople and Philippopolis as 'very troublesome to deal with', requiring more looking after than any other subjects. Most of them kept wine and spirit shops and overburdened the consulate with claims arising out of drunken brawls on their premises; many mixed themselves up with public affairs, with religious and racial questions which gave a great deal of trouble both to the consulate and to the local authorities. Civil and criminal cases at Crete, in the five years before and after 1864, fell from fifty-three to four. At Monastir four-fifths of consular business vanished with the Ionians. At Janina the consul had been continuously occupied with the affairs of the 200 to 250 Ionians settled in his district; by 1870 his functions were limited to acting as a point of observation in a Turco-Grecian frontier province. Consul W. Gifford Palgrave reported from Trebizond that the effect of the cessation of the Ionian Protectorate had been threefold: 'firstly, deliverance

---

[1] Minutes of Evidence, *Report of the Select Committee on Consular Service and Appointments*, PP 1857-8 (482) VIII, Q 2245.
[2] Ibid., QQ 2358-64, 2378, 2477-83.

from a quarrelsome and disreputable sect; secondly, some diminution in the fees; thirdly, increase of respectability'.[1]

But the departure of the Ionians still left the Maltese, the Gibraltarians, the British Indians, and many descendants of earlier generations of protégés. The British ambassador might complain of 'the vicious system of protections, which I have been striving to keep within the narrowest bounds';[2] the Earl of Clarendon might agree that it was 'undesirable to return to the practice of granting protection on religious grounds to other than British subjects';[3] but 'officious' protection remained more or less freely extended to all Jews and Christians, even to the remote Nestorians, according to the ability or inclination of the local British consul.

Since these groups formed the trading class in so much of the Ottoman Empire, this was no light obligation. When Richard Burton was in Damascus, the Jews and the Christians between them, though only forty-two in number, had claims for settlement amounting to six million piastres. The Ottoman authorities, said Burton, were 'extremely charming to you so long as you saw them as visitors, but the moment you talk of piastres, it is the touch of Ithuriel's spear'.[4] In Morocco consular protection was traditional over an absurdly wide area. Protection could be claimed, not simply by British subjects of any kind, but also by foreigners or natives of Morocco while acting as agents for houses in Gibraltar and England, by the native agents or brokers in the employ of British merchants who were sent into the interior to buy produce, and even by the shepherds in charge of the flocks.[5] The Levant consulates generally became the focus of all kinds of grievances, many of which were totally unconnected either with their own nation or with any of the minorities which they claimed to protect. Captain Townshend relates how at Adrianople he received a message from some Circassian artillerymen that eight of them intended to come to the British consulate to state their complaints about pay; in the meantime they would do no work, as they intended to return to their villages. On another occasion,

---

[1] Returns respecting Consular and other Fees in British Consulates in the Turkish Dominions, requested by the Foreign Office on 31 March 1870: PRO.FO/366/1132.

[2] Sir Henry Elliot to Lord Granville, Constantinople, 14 February 1871: *ibid.*

[3] Clarendon to Barron: No. 183, *Instructions addressed to H.M.'s Embassy at Constantinople respecting the protection of Christians in Turkey, 1856-75*, PP 1877 (c. 1740) XCII.

[4] Minutes of Evidence, *Report of the Select Committee on Diplomatic and Consular Services*, PP 1872 (314) VII, QQ 2041-2.

[5] Report by H. L. Dupuis, Vice-Consul at Dar-el-baida, 23 October 1871: *Reports relative to British consular establishments, 1858 and 1871*, Part IV, PP 1872 (c. 544) LXI.

a mob of mutinous local reservists, who had grabbed a steamer, imprisoned their officers, and returned home from the Yemen, gathered outside the vice-consulate at Mersina to relate their grievances, apply for redress, and demand protection.[1]

'We are always getting into quarrels by protecting somebody', the *Examiner* complained in 1857: 'We were nearly involved in war with the United States by protecting those dear Mosquitoes. We are now at logger-heads with Persia to protect Herat and the precious Afghans; but above all to protect Mrs Hashem. Well might Sydney Smith say he was weary of protecting, worn down by defending all the world.'

Consular courts For all that, the main abuses of the protégé system were much reduced during and after the 1850s, and attention was turned simultaneously to the reform of the consular courts. Clause IV of the 1825 Act, by which the rights and properties of the Levant Company were transferred to the Crown, had invested the Levant consuls with 'all such Rights and Duties of Jurisdiction and Authority over His Majesty's Subjects resorting to the Ports of the Levant for the purposes of Trade' as they had lawfully exercised and performed while still in the Company's employment. Though it was soon obvious that these powers were too vague and undefined to be of much use in a real emergency, it was not until 1843 that the Foreign Jurisdiction Act (6 & 7 Vict. c. 94) gave consuls in certain parts of the world the same power and jurisdiction over British subjects as if those areas were Crown colonies.

By the orders in Council of 2 October 1843 and 19 June 1844, Levant consuls were given jurisdiction over both civil and criminal cases. Lord Aberdeen, in despatching copies of the 1844 Order to consuls, warned them that the state of affairs in Turkey was an exception to the system universally observed among Christian nations; they were under an obligation to the Ottoman Government to exercise this exceptional jurisdiction responsibly and effectively. The 1844 Order in Council, Aberdeen continued, was issued for the purpose of maintaining order and punishing crime. Consuls were to bear in mind that these comprehensive and unusual powers of jurisdiction were not to be 'needlessly or lightly employed'. Differences were to be settled as far as possible by arbitration, and whenever crimes had to be

---

[1] Townshend, *Military Consul*, pp. 167, 187.

punished, 'certain and speedy, rather than severe, punishment [was] to be preferred'.¹

The general reaction among consuls, who had long been pressing for formal powers, was most favourable. In the short run, at least, the new powers seemed to have a stabilizing effect on the turbulent Maltese and Ionians. Consul-General Warrington reported from Tripoli in February 1845 that the Christmas holidays had always produced riot, drunkenness and stabbing among the Maltese, but that they were now more on their guard. In the holidays lately passed, not one instance of assault, intemperance, or irregularity had been brought before him.²

But there were problems, both with respect to place of imprisonment and to the power of deportation. Consulates were seldom provided with adequate prison facilities, and a consul was likely to be deterred from passing an appropriate prison sentence when he knew, as Consul Blunt wrote from Salonica, that Turkish prisons were 'of a most wretched description', and that 'the horror of such places increases the degree of punishment to a greater extent, perhaps, than the case may demand'. It would be cheaper and more expedient, Blunt suggested, to have a prison attached to the consulate for the confinement of turbulent seamen whose offences were not serious enough to warrant a sentence in a 'filthy, damp Turkish prison, where, added to the vermin which prisoners collect, rendering it almost necessary to destroy their clothes, they run the risk of being disabled for life by getting confirmed rheumatisms, or other diseases which sleeping on damp stones generally produces'.³ Lord Stratford de Redcliffe described Turkish prisons some years later, as still 'wretched in the extreme, and no less objectionable on the score of morals than on that of humanity'.⁴ But adequate funds for the construction and maintenance of independent consular prisons were seldom available.

More serious was the lack of effective powers of deportation and the difficulty of obtaining convictions at the colonial courts to which, under the 1843 Act, serious crimes were sent for trial. Consuls had always been prepared to deport difficult subjects; their powers were put on a regular

---

¹ Memorandum dated 2 July 1844: Inclosure 2 in No. 2, *Papers relative to the Jurisdiction of Her Majesty's Consuls in the Levant*, PP 1845 (127) LII.
² No. 23, Section B, *ibid*.
³ Despatch dated 15 August 1844: No. 3, Section B, *ibid*.
⁴ Memorandum on Reforms in Consular Legal Jurisdiction in the Levant: Appendix 4, *Report of the Select Committee on Consular Service and Appointments*, PP 1857-8 (482) VIII.

basis in the 1843 Order in Council and in a further Order of 24 April 1847. But there was absolutely nothing to prevent a deportee from taking the first boat back to some other port in the Ottoman dominions or even, in large communities, back to the consular district itself. Henry Layard, speaking of the period before 1856, observed that there was no real restraint on murders, robberies, and other crimes in the Turkish dominions, because criminals were either not punished at all or were removed for a time, returning to commit the same crimes again: 'Especially in the case of British subjects, it was shown that the power of the Consul to punish and remove them from Turkey was so limited that they virtually escaped with impunity.'[1]

Even where it was found possible to send a criminal to a colonial court at Malta or Corfu, the cost was high and the likelihood of conviction slight. Both juries and judges in English colonies were extremely reluctant to convict on purely written evidence, without oral cross-examination of the witnesses in their presence. It was inconvenient, no doubt, to the consuls. But there were good reasons, summarized by Sir Henry Jenkyns as the cost to the private individual of procuring witnesses (whereas witnesses for the prosecution were brought to the court on public money), the separation of the accused from the sympathy of his neighbours and his trial among strangers, the personal hardship of removing an accused person from the spot where the offence was committed, and the fact that the nature of an offence might be viewed differently by people at a distance than by those on the spot.[2]

The only real solution, and the one ultimately adopted, was to establish a Supreme Consular Court at Constantinople. The occasion was supplied by the Crimean War. For many years before, legal business at the consulate-general at Constantinople had been almost more than the consul-general and his staff could handle. The war, with a vast increase in legal, shipping, and commercial business at the consulate, brought the old system to a standstill. Edmund Hornby, a barrister with some previous diplomatic experience who happened to be in Constantinople at the time supervising the expenditure of the 1855 Guaranteed Loan, was asked to prepare a report. He advised that a consular judge should be appointed at Constantinople, who would form a regular civil and criminal court, hold circuits in the provinces once

---

[1] 193 *Parl. Deb.*, 3s, 1029 (10 July 1868).
[2] Sir Henry Jenkyns, *British Rule and Jurisdiction beyond the Seas* (Oxford, 1902), p. 127.

The Levant Service 149

or twice a year to judge the more important cases, and sit on appeals from the decisions of the consuls (themselves acting still as magistrates in cases of minor importance).[1]

Hornby's suggestions were accepted by H.M. Government, and Hornby himself was appointed as the first Judge of the Supreme Consular Court at Constantinople, established by the Order in Council of 27 August 1857. *The Times*'s Correspondent, writing from Constantinople a couple of years later, reported that in spite of some teething troubles, 'Her Majesty's Supreme Consular Court is decidedly a popular institution'; it had gained the confidence of all classes of Englishmen at Constantinople and of the general public, judging by the large number of foreigners who submitted their cases to the Court for its decision. In spite of the value and importance of the civil cases which had come before it, not a single appeal had yet reached the Judicial Committee of the Privy Council.[2]

The Supreme Consular Court was not always to be so popular. But it answered a real need for a Court of Appeal within reasonable distance of the majority of the Levant consulates; its decisions were generally respected; it paid for itself out of its fees; and, above all, it acted as a professional core to what had been, and continued to be, a painfully amateur system for the administration of justice. C. M. Kennedy, during his tour of inspection in 1870-71, observed that at the British vice-consulates, where a regular consular court was not held, he could find no uniform system in operation either as to form of procedure or as to fees charged. As for the consulates, the British community wanted a closer control by a system of local assessors, and felt that the Rules based on English law were being applied too inflexibly and without sufficient consideration of local usage and custom.[3] From the consuls' point of view, the obstacles to the professional administration of justice were formidable. George B. Ward, consul at Galatz (Romania), explained in his 1872 report that the procedure at British consular courts was governed by the Order in Council of 30 November 1864 and the Rules of 23 January 1863, while the law was the Common Law, the Statute Law, the Rules of Equity, and other law for the time being in force in England.

Let it be premised [Ward continued] that the Consulate is not supplied with a copy of any one of the laws it is called upon to administer, that

---

[1] Hornby's report is summarized in *The Times*, 10 July 1856, 10b, c.
[2] *The Times*, 3 December 1859, 8e.
[3] Despatches and private letters from Kennedy to Lord Granville, 22 November 1870, 10 January 1871, 1 February 1871: PRO.FO/366/1132.

the Consul himself is not a professional man, that he is unassisted by any person having legal knowledge, that there is no English lawyer of any description in the district or nearer than Constantinople, that only one copy of the Rules of Court exists in the whole town, and that is at the Consulate, and that no suitor who ever appears in court has the slightest knowledge of procedure and practice, and then some idea may be formed of the difficulty of holding a court at all.[1]

Consular courts in the Ottoman dominions were responsible not only for cases between British subjects, but also for mixed cases between foreigners where a British subject was the defendant. In some of the outlying provinces, the principle that all cases concerning *Ottoman* subjects, whether as plaintiffs or as defendants, were to be tried before *Ottoman* courts had been relaxed, and foreigners, if defendants, were tried before their own consular courts. In Alexandria, for example, foreign consulates had always maintained the right of their fellow-subjects to be sued in the consular courts, just as Europeans sued natives in the Egyptian courts—the rule *actor sequitur forum rei*. Consul J. L. Stoddart admitted in his 1844 report that this did not accord with the ordinary interpretation of the Capitulations, but the pretension had generally been allowed in Egypt and had long usage in its favour. He added that as it was a very important advantage, 'we are not perhaps called upon to discuss too curiously our right to its enjoyment by sufferance, nor to arouse attention to the subject'.[2]

The same applied to consular jurisdiction in Tripoli and in Jerusalem. F. R. Drummond-Hay explained from Tripoli in 1871 that the privilege of exercising exclusive jurisdiction over British subjects in mixed cases with Ottoman subjects, though not sanctioned by treaty, had been practised by consuls, and tacitly accepted by the Ottoman authorities as a continuation of a system in existence long before the occupation of Tripoli by the Turks in 1835.[3] In Jerusalem, Consul James Finn reported that it was an established rule, never transgressed, that in mixed cases, whether with Turks or with foreigners, the case came before the court of the defendant: 'There was no confusion at all about it.'[4]

---

[1] *Reports relative to British Consular Establishments, 1858 and 1871*, Part VI, PP 1872 (c. 661) LXI.

[2] No. 18, Section A, *Papers relative to the Jurisdiction of Her Majesty's Consuls in the Levant*, PP 1845 (127) LII.

[3] Report dated 30 November 1871: *Reports relative to British Consular Establishments, 1858 and 1871*, Part III, PP 1872 (c. 530) LX.

[4] Finn, *Stirring Times*, i, 91, n.1.

This extension, although on the face of it not unjust and in accordance with exterritorial practices elsewhere in the world, was entirely disastrous in large, miscellaneous, and utterly undisciplined foreign communities such as existed in Egypt in the middle years of the nineteenth century. Egypt was the classic case of the total and unprincipled abuse of the system of consular courts. By the end of the 1860s, in addition to the local tribunals, there were sixteen or seventeen foreign consulates in Egypt claiming the right of jurisdiction over their nationals. Some courts refused to hear causes brought at the suit of a subject of others. Other courts, such as the Italian and Greek courts, were, as a contemporary said, 'notorious for the most shameful injustice'. At each of the courts a different code of laws and different standards of justice applied, and in some courts there was no justice at all. The British consular court at Alexandria enjoyed a high reputation, but its effect was to multiply the injustice so far as British subjects were concerned. A letter in *The Times* on 21 October 1868 pointed out that the subjects of other consulates could be sure that even if they were unable to obtain justice as plaintiffs in another consular court, the position would be reversed if they appeared as defendants before their own consul. An Englishman, on the other hand, denied justice in a foreign court, could be 'sure only of the most rigid justice in his own'.

As for the Egyptians themselves, if a band of criminals, foreigners but of different nationalities, committed an armed robbery or sacked an Egyptian village, the Egyptian authorities had to proceed against each man individually before his own consular court. If an Egyptian were knocked down in the street by a foreigner, he could take action in that foreigner's consular court, but he could not compel the attendance of a single witness other than those of the defendant's own nationality. If an Egyptian wanted to bring an action for debt against an association of persons of different nationality, and if he failed to get justice before each of the consular courts, his only recourse was by appeal to the several Supreme Courts, perhaps as far-flung as Washington, Rio de Janeiro, Brussels, and Berlin. Even where an Egyptian was the defendant he could not depend on trial before his own courts. Consular representatives at native courts could and did block an acquittal or a settlement in favour of the accused; cases coming before native courts were taken up as diplomatic questions, and summary settlements demanded on the consul's word alone. In the many cases brought against the Egyptian Government, against the Khedive and the princes, or against high government officials, foreigners refused to accept the jurisdiction of the local tribunals which they regarded as incapable in these circumstances of giving them justice. Their claims were taken automatically and directly through diplomatic channels.

The International Commission upon Consular Jurisdiction, recruited from Egyptian officials, foreign diplomats and lawyers and appointed in 1869 at the instance of Nubar Pasha (the Egyptian Minister of Foreign Affairs), agreed that Egyptian government action was null in matters of police:

> That when a crime is committed the police must ask for authority to arrest the foreign culprit, unless he should be caught in the fact. That when the foreign culprit is arrested the investigation is made by the consul, and the accused is sent far away from the country which has been troubled by his crime; that proved criminals are often known to go about at liberty, in the sight and to the knowledge of everyone. That this state of things is discouraging to the administration, dangerous to all.[1]

The Commission concluded that there was no certainty of the repression of offences in such a multiplicity of jurisdictions; and it was as a result of the Commission's report that, in 1874, a single judicature was finally established. The Mixed Courts of Egypt (Egyptian tribunals with two-thirds of the judges foreign and one-third Egyptian) exercised jurisdiction over all mixed cases, whether exclusively foreign, or foreign and Egyptian. The consuls retained only their original jurisdiction over disputes between their own nationals.

The 1874 settlement marked an important advance, even if for some years the Mixed Courts became mere instruments for the destruction of the Khedivial government. The Capitulations, in their modified form, still remained in force, and it is ironic that when Britain took over the administration of Egypt in 1882, she found herself hampered and restricted in precisely the same directions as she herself was hampering and restricting the autonomy of the Porte. It is difficult to feel much sympathy with Lord Cromer's complaint that the Capitulations protected 'the smuggler, the keeper of a gambling hell, the receiver of stolen goods, the retailer of adulterated spirits'. Britain was well and truly hoist with her own petard.

The condition of the consulates before 1877 The political and judicial duties of Levant consuls left them with little time or inclination for the

---

[1] *Report of the International Commission upon Consular Jurisdiction*, PP 1870 (186) LVI.

routine functions of their colleagues in the General Service. At the same time, these imposed exceptional burdens and responsibilities for which very special qualities were, ideally, required.

The Levant consuls, even in the early part of the nineteenth century, were never as disastrously bad as they were made out to be. Certainly by the third quarter of the century there was much to be said in their favour. Kennedy, after inspecting the consulates, concluded his report by observing that he had had the opportunity to see British consular officers in action in different parts of the world, and that he felt it to be an act of justice to H.M.'s consuls in Turkey (who were, generally, 'preeminently able and conscientious public servants') to place on record his testimony to the value of their great services:

> The nature and importance of these services, so well understood alike by Her Majesty's Embassy at Constantinople and Her Majesty's Government, is necessarily not of a character to acquire for them fame at home; they are, therefore, both as regards themselves personally and their work, little known. But no body of men are more usefully employed in securing the extension of commercial enterprise, the welfare of the people among whom they live, and the maintenance of peace.[1]

The government consuls had been imposed on the members of the Levant Company resident in the East. Local merchants, who had been accustomed to have some hand in the Company appointments (or at least to exercise some sort of indirect control over them), resented the new official authority; and much of the criticism of the Levant consuls in the early years was a legacy of the 1825 takeover. This was particularly true of large, old-established commercial communities like Smyrna, where the English community was reported to have worried two consuls into their graves. It was the case, too, that many of the complaints against the consuls were never substantiated, that others were published anonymously by Englishmen, Maltese or Ionians themselves of questionable standing and authority, and that more were derived from a misunderstanding of consular functions. Exeter Hall seems to have believed that consuls were bound to defend missionaries even when they chose to denounce the Prophet from the steps of St Sophia, and too many British subjects in the Levant, as one consul complained, were persuaded that a consul held the Queen's commission,

---

[1] Despatch to Lord Granville, Cairo, 10 February 1871: PRO.FO/366/1132.

as a lawyer held his brief, for the protection of British interests just or unjust.

Nevertheless, the condition of the Levant consulates at the time of the Crimean War was a public scandal. An 'Anglo-Levantine' declared in 1855 that 'most of our Consuls in the East are worthless individuals'. He listed a number of abuses, including promises of protection in return for generous bribes, the harbouring of criminals at consulates, the ignoring of quarantine regulations, and general corruption and injustice.[1] His pamphlet was too luridly expressed to be convincing on its own, but there was plenty of evidence from elsewhere to confirm much of what he said. That same year *The Economist*, reviewing an anonymous work, *The Roving Englishman: sketches from life*, noted that the author had been connected with British diplomacy in the East; he knew all about Lord Stratford's mode of managing business, all about the behaviour of junior diplomats, consuls, vice-consuls, and consular agents, 'and his account, probably true, but rendered doubtful by fictions and exaggerations, makes us blush for our Government and our country.... Turkey is already treated by our subordinates like a conquered country, and worse than any petty State in India.'[2] J. A. Wise, in the course of a long speech criticizing the consular establishment in 1856, attacked the Levant consuls in particular, some of whom were 'wholly unfit to represent the interests of a great country like England', and cited in support Lord Carlisle's *Diary in Turkish and Greek Waters* (1854) and Dr Humphry Sandwith's *A Narrative of the Siege of Kars* (1856).[3] J. White, welcoming the appointment of the Select Committee of 1858, quoted Lord Carlisle's report that the ladies in the Levant accounted for the eccentricities of English consuls by the theory that, as soon as a man was nominated a British consul, he went mad. White was not himself prepared to go so far, but he assured the House that he 'could state facts of the doings of British consuls to which the House could scarcely give credence'.[4] Lord Strangford, who as one of the pioneer student interpreters at Constantinople, knew his subject well, wrote a paper in 1863, under the title 'Chaos', in which he incorporated some particularly acid comments on the British public service in the Levant. His conclusion,

---

[1] *Our Consuls in the East: a parliamentary inquiry into their proceedings imperative* (London, 1855).

[2] *The Economist*, 16 June 1855, 654 [the author was, in fact, Grenville-Murray appointed Consul-General at Odessa in 1855 and a bitter critic of Lord Stratford de Redcliffe].

[3] 141 *Parl. Deb.*, 3s, 1016-17 (14 April 1856). He had criticized the consuls as sternly the previous year: 138 *Parl. Deb.*, 3s, 214-15 (7 May 1855).

[4] 149 *Parl. Deb.*, 3s, 553 (22 March 1858).

after listing the abuses, was that there were 'other sick things in Turkey besides the sick man, though they are not half such good subjects for declamation'.[1]

The most convincing testimony of all came from Sir Edmund Hornby, the Judge of the new Supreme Consular Court, whose task it became, after the Crimean War, to 'sweep clean the Augean stable'. He recalled that apart from Carlton Cumberbatch, consul-general at Constantinople, Charles Blunt, consul at Smyrna, and Robert Campbell, consul at Rhodes, the occupants of the principal seacoast consulates were 'one and all evidently disgusted with myself and my mission'. The condition of the consulates, it seems, was quite deplorable.

> They had few archives, few vouchers, and absolutely no records or even notes of the cases they had tried, or in fact any evidence of their official or judicial action for any number of past years. Appeal cases there were, tied up in bundles which had never been forwarded, money deposited unaccounted for, estates unadministered, and, worse than all, any number of protected subjects who had no shadow of right to the passports they held, and in respect of which they paid an annual fee.

Complaints reached Hornby from all sides, and he claimed that if he had attempted to enquire into one tithe of them, he would have had to spend months rather than hours at each consular district. On his next inspection tour Hornby investigated and suspended the consul at Jerusalem, whose wife, amongst other things, was conducting an ingenious land fraud selling plots in the Holy Land to credulous Anglican clergymen. He enquired into the activities of Assaad J. Kayat, consul at Jaffa, who had acquired, it seemed, any number of wives, had a somewhat ambiguous interest in girls' schools, and conducted a flourishing marine business by which in his consular capacity he condemned vessels, in his private capacity acted as auctioneer, and finally bought the vessels himself. He tried the vice-consul at Cyprus for scuttling a ship, said to be laden with silk, to defraud an insurance company, and gave him two years' imprisonment. And he sent another consul, an Englishman and otherwise a valuable public servant, to prison for insuring a ship called *Poseidon* which had never existed.[2]

The fact was, as Hornby said, 'the whole Levant service had got out of hand', and the fault was not entirely that of the consuls. Recruitment was

---

[1] Viscountess Strangford, ed., *A Selection from the Writings of Viscount Strangford* (London, 1869), I, 65.
[2] Sir Edmund Hornby, *An Autobiography* (London, 1928), pp. 97-100, 131-8.

haphazard and ill-conceived. Large numbers of unpaid vice-consuls or consular agents had been appointed all over the Ottoman dominions solely on the recommendation of British consuls. The consular title gave its holder, usually a local merchant, virtual exemption from local authority, an exemption which he extended to his clerks ('dragomans') and to his warehousemen, doorkeepers and servants ('cavasses'); it was, in fact, a licence to print money, the easiest path to a fortune in the Levant. But the recruitment of salaried career consuls itself left much to be desired. Sir Henry Elliot, the Ambassador at Constantinople, agreed in his evidence before the 1870 Committee that the French system of appointing consuls direct from France was on balance preferable to our own (that is, of picking up Levantines or travellers with some acquaintance with the East). The real difficulty, he said, was to strike some balance between on the one hand the wish to find people who could speak the language, and on the other the desirability of getting a real Englishman. He had no solution to offer. If an Englishman were to be trained up to the language, he would have to be promised and given a consulate after a period of years, and the service might find itself saddled with incompetent men as a result.

Elliot, who was speaking after the general cleaning up of the service in the 1860s, was able to insist that, although there were some people in the Levant 'who are not such as we would like to have', the consuls on the whole were efficient men, and some of the very best were those generally known as 'Levantines'—that is to say, men of English descent domiciled, sometimes over several generations, in the Levant.[1] His opinion of the Levantines was not, unfortunately, widely held. Lord Strangford, for example, was strongly of the opinion that in Turkey most particularly (in view of the nature of the duties performed), Britain should be represented by 'the most perfect and highest type of English manhood'. The consulates in European Turkey, because of their political character and because most of them, under political pressure, were of relatively recent creation, were generally filled by 'Englishmen of a higher stamp than the once common run of bankrupt merchants'. But there were comparatively few Englishmen 'of full English blood and rearing' in the Levant as a whole, and those brought up in the Levant visibly acquired the 'uniform low Levantine moral type ... their narrowness of mind, their follies, even their crimes'.[2]

---

[1] Minutes of Evidence, *Report of the Select Committee on Diplomatic and Consular Services*, PP 1870 (382), VII, QQ 1129-39, 1387.
[2] Strangford, *A Selection from Writings*, I, 55-7.

The Levant Service

It was the variety of the consuls, as much as their quality, which was so disturbing. As Strangford pointed out in a review written in 1867, our consuls in the Levant included 'Levantine lads, men of statesmanlike abilities, ex-Bashi-Bozuk officers, half-breeds, Scotchmen with hard heads, Scotchmen who are all heart, men like Mr Gifford Palgrave, of world-wide fame, and men like Colonel Sankey, fortunate in strictly local fame.'[1]

The criticism of Levantines as British consuls was almost universal. The main point, which was a perfectly valid one, was that these consuls were too closely linked by family, business interest, and social contacts to the districts in which they served. They were not, and could not be expected to be, wholly independent, prepared on every occasion to back general British interests against a local interest. When, as was often the case, they were salaried but with permission to trade, their business interests became a formidable barrier, in a real crisis, to independent action. There was also the point, for which British prejudices rather than the Levantines themselves were to blame, that English merchants and travellers disliked dealing with officials of Levantine or Maltese descent, whether in their ordinary consular capacity or, more particularly, in their official capacity as judges.

A further argument, that Levantine consuls did not carry the same weight in the East as consuls recruited direct from England, had some truth in it. Lt.-Col. Sir Henry Rawlinson, one of the more eminent of the East India Company consuls and a former consul-general at Baghdad, told the 1858 Committee of the great advantage which France enjoyed over England in this respect. Rawlinson had always appreciated the higher standing enjoyed by the French consular agency at Mosul in contrast to the agency under his own supervision, and this standing was entirely one of individual character. The French officer employed at Mosul was sent out direct from the French Foreign Office, whereas his own was a native of Mosul, who had been educated at Malta but who would always be considered, whatever his consular title, a local man. In Turkey, Rawlinson added, the more one could keep oneself to European habits and European position the better, and he deplored the tendency by which Englishmen, isolated in the East, became orientalized, adopting the dress and habits of the orientals: 'As they do adopt these habits, by so much they really lose in the respect of the people for their European character.'[2]

---

[1] *Ibid.*, p. 162.
[2] Minutes of Evidence, *Report of the Select Committee on Consular Service and Appointments*, PP 1857-8 (482) VIII, QQ 2867-8.

Rawlinson was sensible enough to realize that this 'orientalizing' had its advantages as well as its disadvantages; the Mutiny, he argued, would never have taken place in India if the relationship between officer and sepoy had remained as it had been fifty years before. But the isolation of the consular life in the East, where a man might spend decades at the same remote Asiatic post almost entirely deprived of European company, had curious effects on men, even on those with the most irreproachable English upbringing. In some cases, Stratford de Redcliffe explained, where a consul was left to himself, 'he takes root, and, branching in proportion, casts a deep shade on all around him. In others he sinks into discredit, and, whether his reign be closed by death or a recall, leaves finally nothing behind him save the character of a sot, or the balance of an insolvent.'[1]

Too often, it was the level of consular salaries which was ultimately responsible for personal deterioration and disaster among the Levant consuls. In 1858 the consul at the Dardanelles was paid £300, at Salonica £350, at Crete £300, at Rhodes £400, at Trebizond £300, at Jaffa £300. Even the more senior consulates were less than generously treated. The consul-general at Beirut had £500 p.a., the consul at Jerusalem £550, at Smyrna £700, at Damascus £600, and at Aleppo £500. At posts with the lower salaries, consuls were generally permitted to trade. But it was a permission of which they could not necessarily avail themselves. Trade in the Levant was a speculative affair at all times, with uncertain deliveries, pilferings, highway robberies, civil disturbances, violent fluctuations both in tastes and in the means to gratify them. Its advantages were much diminished for individual British traders, away from the main seaports, by the undercutting of Armenian, Greek, or Jewish shopkeepers and merchants, content with a substantially lower profit margin and in closer contact with local needs. An Englishman might build up a trade, as Consul Holmes had done at Trebizond, only to see it taken away from him almost immediately. While English importers at the seaports and English manufacturers at home continued to benefit by the expanded trade into whichever hands it fell, the position of an Englishman trading in the interior was precarious unless he chose to take the role of a continual innovator—for which few consuls had the wit or financial resources.

As it was, consuls found themselves trying to make ends meet on salaries which bore no relation to the real cost of living, European style, at their posts. Foreign officials, to maintain influence in the East, were expected to

---

[1] Despatch dated 30 January 1857: Appendix 4, *ibid.*

keep up a large and imposing establishment. European servants were to be had only at double the wages paid in Europe. Native servants were careless with property, asked more for their services than they would of their compatriots, and, as they considered their foreign master fair game, augmented his expenses by robbery and cheating. Richard Wood complained from Tunis in 1871 that over the past fifteen years he had had to renew no less than five times his dinner and breakfast services, each service for twenty-four persons, and the last for seventy-two persons in order to allow a margin for breakage; his table and house linen were three times replaced.[1]

Wood, as consul-general and political agent, was better off than his colleagues. Most Levant consuls, faced with this kind of domestic expense, were left without the means to educate their children or return home on leave. If they had permission to trade, they could not look forward even to the prospect of a pension at the end of it all. In the Ottoman dominions, where bribes were the normal path to official business, and where bribery itself had reached such a level of sophistication that it was often difficult indeed either for an outsider to detect it or for the recipient himself to be aware of his own corruption, it was hardly to be wondered at that consuls frequently gave way to the temptation. Once they had begun, they found it extraordinarily difficult to stop. The dismissal in 1868 of E. C. Grenville-Murray, consul-general at Odessa, was perhaps the most notorious case in the reformed service. The charges against him, investigated at great length by the Foreign Office, included implication in some curious financial transactions, the issuing of British passports to those not entitled to them, and the mishandling of consular marriages and registers. Grenville-Murray's register showed the birth of Jane Sarah at Steblow (near Kiev) on 24 August 1863, the day after her father and mother were registered as married at Odessa. The Registrar General agreed that that Miss Fletcher should give birth the day after her marriage to Mr Oakley was intelligible and, he feared, by no means unprecedented. But that Jane Sarah should have been born at such a distance from the place of marriage was strange. Still stranger was the birth, forty-seven days later, of her little brother, Richard Thomas. In all the 18 million births recorded at the Registrar General's office over the last thirty years, George Graham could not recall a similar occurrence as to the birth of twins. So extraordinary did he find it that he was, he said, meditating bringing it to

---

[1] Return dated 14 December 1871: *Reports Relative to British Consular Establishments, 1858 and 1871*, Part III, pp 1872 (c. 530) LX.

the notice of the recently established Obstetrical Society in London where it would, he was sure, attract the attention of the many celebrated *accoucheurs* of the metropolis.[1]

If a career consul could surrender to the temptations of the Levant, his servants were always ripe for the fall. It was customary in the Levant to employ native dragomans as interpreters and go-betweens. Other than Arabic, in which a number of mid-Victorian consuls were competent, very few British officials, even those brought up in the East, had more than a slight colloquial knowledge of the native languages. None spoke Serbian or Bulgarian; very few knew Turkish; fewer could manage modern Greek. Even if they knew the language, there were many functions which were better performed, in the special circumstances of the Levant, by a subordinate. On-the-spot enquiries into complaints or grievances were worse than useless when conducted by a uniformed consul supported by his panoply of armed cavasses. Gossip and local news came more easily to the ears of a native with his private contacts throughout the consular district. Daily visits to the pasha's palace would, for the consul, have meant the full, elaborate, time-wasting ceremony of pipes and coffee. For his dragoman, the same formalities could be dispensed with, and the business despatched with as much speed as could be expected in the East, even if, as Kinglake once said, you might suspect that your dragoman was 'habitually fighting your battles for you in a way that you can hardly bear to think of'.

Dragomans were indispensable; at the same time, they were wide open to corruption. The office allowances available to British consuls in the Levant, averaging around £150 p.a., were intended to cover every kind of office expense, from stationery to wages, to the rent of the consular office itself. They had to support the dragoman, the Turkish scribe, interpreters, cavasses (armed guards), doorkeeper, and cleaners. There was never any shortage of local applicants for these posts, however miserable the salaries, since the official protection gained by employment at a foreign consulate was much coveted throughout the Ottoman dominions. Unless a man had private resources, which was occasionally the case among employees taken from the rich Armenian or Jewish communities, he had to make his living somehow; and the line between what he did as an employee of the consulate and as a private citizen was extraordinarily difficult to draw. It was almost impossible to expect a man, paid virtually nothing by the

---

[1] No. 165, *Papers relative to the complaints made against Mr Grenville-Murray and his dismissal*, PP 1868-9 (4163) LXIV.

consulate, to put his official duties first, and as impossible to expect him to avoid using his official position to promote his private business or family affairs.

There was the further temptation, which many, if not most of the consular dragomans in the Levant found irresistible, of taking their percentage even on their official work. The *cause célèbre* was the scandal which broke round the head of Peter Meshullam, Consul James Finn's chancelier (private secretary and factotum) at Jerusalem at the beginning of the 1860s. Meshullam, a great personal favourite with Mrs Finn, was generally known and feared, both among the natives and among the British residents at Jerusalem, for his bullying behaviour and open corruption. In reply to a series of petitions against him (including one from his own father), Lord Russell sent Lt.-Col. A. J. Fraser on a special mission to Jerusalem in the summer of 1862 to investigate the charges. Fraser had a great deal of difficulty in collecting the evidence, since Meshullam had thoroughly intimidated the witnesses. After a prolonged enquiry, Fraser came to the conclusion that the charges against Meshullam were well founded, and that he had used his position at the British consulate (and the servile deference to that position displayed by the local Governor) 'to carry out a system of oppression and spoliation towards the unfortunate peasantry'. Fraser pointed out that whatever the facts of the present case, it was not to be expected that a man of very defective education, receiving no salary from his consular employer and in character a compound of the wily, city Syrian and the desert Bedouin, could be qualified to occupy the position of a British chancelier. Nor might it be supposed that he would avoid the temptation to profit from this position in a manner likely to compromise the government he was intended to represent.[1] Meshullam was dismissed, and Finn transferred to Trebizond. With his protector removed, Meshullam was murdered by angry peasants early the following year.

The Meshullam affair, unfortunately, was one of many. The cases were seldom brought out into the open. The British consul himself had such weight and authority among the Turks that he was virtually a free agent:

> There is no press to watch his doings; no society to cry shame on him; no means by which an ignorant Maltese or Ionian can make a grievance

---

[1] Fraser to Russell, Beirut, 10 September 1862: No. 6, *Correspondence respecting the Murder of Mr Peter Meshullam, and the Removal of Mr Finn from the Consulate of Jerusalem*, PP 1880 (c. 2608) LXXXI.

known and obtain redress. There is indeed no control of any kind over your British Consul; and a very august and singular personage he has become in consequence.¹

And whatever his own moral probity—and Grenville-Murray, the author of these criticisms, was to show what another decade in the Levant could do even to the best of intentions—the consul was often in no position to be aware of the corruption among his own staff, in his own name, and under his very nose. It was simple enough, especially under a weak consul such as Finn, or even under a stronger man without either an adequate command of the many languages of the East or the time to investigate each of the many hundreds of cases coming before him, to terrorize a community into silence, and to establish a regular percentage on consular transactions. Consul-General Richard Wood was an outstanding official, one of the best men Britain had in the Ottoman dominions. His duties at Tunis were very largely political, and his chancelier, one of the ubiquitous Pisanis, seems to have had his own way with the large, local Maltese community. Any monetary claim coming before the consulate was subject to a deduction—perhaps a third of the claim itself, or 500/1000 Tunisian piastres. 'Woe to him', wrote one of Pisani's victims, 'who would open the Consular tabernacle without this golden key; unfortunate he must be who ignores the secret or who has not the courage to use it.'²

The complaints against Pisani lost much from the tone in which they were expressed, as was generally the case in such affairs where the only witnesses were men of limited education often with burning personal grievances to avenge. But when Kennedy made his tour of the Levant consulates a few years later, he found much the same state of affairs. He fully realized the need to employ dragomans, but he saw too that if, under the present office allowance system, they could be paid only a retaining fee (or even nothing at all), they had no alternative other than to levy their own scale of fees. It was said, he reported, that it was the general custom for dragomans to undertake the settlement of claims (over and above those which they officially supported) on their own private account, receiving half or more of the amount recovered. In the current state of judicial administration in many places, he added, this might well be so: 'Mr Abcarius, the first dragoman

---

¹ E. C. Grenville-Murray, *The Roving Englishman in Turkey: sketches from life* (London, 1855).
² Luigi Demech, *The British Consulate in Tunis: Critical Remarks* (pamphlet published privately in Malta, 1868), pp. 22-3.

of the Consulate-General, has spoken very openly to me on these matters.'¹

All this was most regrettable. But it was largely unavoidable so long as H.M. Government refused to recruit systematically, to pay an adequate salary to the consuls, or to make sufficient provision for office expenses and subordinate staff. Problems such as these existed at any consulate throughout the world. The peculiar temptations and corruptions of the East, centering around the whole question of exterritorial rights, made them generally much more urgent and damaging in the Levant. It was in answer to these that a separate Levant Consular Service was established in 1877.

The formation of the Levant Consular Service The Levant consuls, whatever their individual misfortunes, had always enjoyed a higher status than their seaport colleagues in the General Service. Richard Burton, disgruntled with his position as a seaport consul in Brazil, was 'quite *dans son assiette*' at Damascus, where his political and judicial functions, the high respect with which foreign consuls were treated by the natives, the scale on which it was felt necessary to live (with dragomans, cavasses and interpreters), were in sharp contrast with the social standing of Her Majesty's Consul at Santos. Criticism could be directed individually at many British consuls in the Levant in the 1850s. But it was probably true, as John Green argued from Alexandria in 1857, that collectively their standing was high in relation to their foreign colleagues. He added, however, that 'we are irregulars, without system, without discipline, and continually reinforced by raw recruits, who must obtain their experience at the expense of the public'.²

At the same time, the siting of the Levant consulates in an area of great political importance to Britain, and the considerable powers given to consuls over their countrymen and protégés by the Capitulations, made it the more necessary to work out some system of control. The absence of such control, to a much greater degree in the Levant than in normal consular areas, could lead rapidly to corruption, petty tyranny, bravado, and inflammatory political complications.

The main criticism hammered home in a series of powerful articles by *The Times*'s Constantinople correspondent (1856-58) was the lack of any

¹ Despatches dated Beirut, 12 January 1871, and Cairo, 30 January 1871: PRO.FO/366/1132.
² Memorandum dated 3 December 1857: Appendix 4, *Report of the Select Committee on Consular Service and Appointments*, PP 1857-8 (482) VIII.

direct, controlling relationship between the embassy, the consulates-general and the consulates. He compared the consular body in the Levant to a rosary, the string of which was broken and its beads scattered all over the Ottoman empire; and he called for something on the lines of the distinct consular services established by Russia and Austria in the Levant, with a strictly defined organization and officers specifically recruited and trained for a career in the East.[1] The subject was investigated at some length by the 1858 Committee. The Committee concluded in favour of the employment exclusively of British subjects, who were to be maintained at full strength in future by the recruitment in London of a limited number of consular students. The students would be trained at Constantinople and at the larger consulates and eligible, when vacancies arose, for promotion to vice-consular and consular posts in the Levant area.

The Committee's recommendations fell on stony ground. Lord Russell accepted the principle that consuls in the Levant should be British subjects. But the proposal of a system of education and promotion for a consular service covering North Africa, the Levant, and Eastern Europe was not even seriously considered at the Foreign Office. Officials stuck to their argument, expressed in evidence in 1858, that they could not offer consular *élèves* a career in a small service with few subordinate posts, and cited the failure of Palmerston's training scheme for interpreter attachés at Constantinople as a satisfactorily damaging precedent.

Palmerston's scheme had never had a fair trial. Four young men altogether were sent out, two in 1841 and another two in 1845, nominated on each occasion by the Vice-Chancellors of Oxford and Cambridge. The idea was to make the Constantinople embassy entirely independent of foreign dragomans for its political functions, and the students seem to have made good progress in this direction. But the scheme collapsed when Stratford de Redcliffe consistently refused to trust the student dragomans with interpretorial functions. He merely absorbed them into his Chancery machine, employed them as political attachés, and left the interpretorial work with the family traditionally employed as dragomans at the British Embassy, the Pisanis. One of the student dragomans, Almeric Wood, the most promising linguist of the four, died in 1850 while employed on General Williams' frontier survey in south-western Persia; another, Lord Strangford, resigned, disgruntled at the poor prospects of promotion open to the attachés; of the remaining two, only Thomas Hughes was actually for long employed as

---

[1] *The Times*, 10 July 1856, 10b, c; 22 May 1858, 10b, c; 14 September 1858, 7a.

Oriental Secretary at the Embassy. William Doria joined the diplomatic service in Europe, and recruitment ceased after 1845.

The Constantinople scheme had been intended to replace the Embassy dragomans, not the consular. The arguments in both cases were the same, and it was the expense of a specialist consular system, rather than doubts as to its expediency, which proved the main obstacle. Kennedy, both in a report during his tour of inspection and in his evidence before the 1872 Committee, urged the training of a small corps of dragomans, British subjects, who would proceed by way of minor posts to the more important posts in the Levant.[1] But it was not until a real stimulus was provided by the recurrence of serious political trouble in Turkey in the mid-1870s, that the Foreign Office found itself compelled to act.

Sir Philip Currie, who as the senior clerk at the Foreign Office in charge of the Eastern Department had accompanied Lord Salisbury on his special mission to Constantinople in 1876, used this opportunity to enquire into the particular responsibilities and efficiency of the Levant consuls. On his return, he prepared a scheme, accepted by the government, which was intended to rid the service, so far as possible, of its local Levantine elements. They were to be replaced by natural-born British subjects, recruited by competitive examination, trained in the appropriate languages, promoted to vice-consulates, and employed, once fully trained, at the more important consular posts in the Ottoman dominions, in Greece and in Morocco.

Currie's scheme brought a new, distinct service into existence in 1877, the Levant Consular Service. Thirteen years later the Ridley Commission felt able to report that although the new training arrangements, like those for the China Service, were costly, they had already produced good results. Twenty-six officers had joined the service since it began, 'serving as consuls, vice-consuls, or assistants in various places throughout these countries, with a good knowledge of the languages, and an excellent training for consular work'. The native dragoman, by the turn of the century, was extinct at the embassy, though not as yet at all the consulates. 'We all of us know enough of the language of the country that we work in', Robert Graves, a senior member of the service, told the Reay Committee in 1908, 'to be able to conduct our business without an Interpreter, without having to call in

---

[1] Despatch dated from Cairo, 30 January 1871: PRO.FO/366/1132; Minutes of Evidence, *Report of the Select Committee on the Diplomatic and Consular Services*, PP 1872 (314) VII, Q 407.

somebody to talk for us; we can transact business in the languages of the country.'[1]

Recruitment and training For the first thirty years of its existence, recruitment to the new Levant Service was by open competition, without nomination or interview. Limited competition was substituted only as late as 1909 to bring the service into line with the General and China Services, and to give the Foreign Office some control over the personal qualities of its Levant recruits.

There was some point in 'limited' competition—that is, in competition restricted to those who had previously secured a nomination at the Foreign Office—if only to counteract by interview some of the less desirable effects of the extraordinary written examination devised for entry into the Levant Service. Candidates were expected to qualify in Arithmetic, Latin, and English composition at intermediate level, with the option of Ancient Greek at the same standard. In addition, they had to offer three, and in practice, four, modern languages at a very fair standard. The effect, as Algernon Law told the 1914 Commission, was to recruit 'what you may call a number of Mezzofantis—men of extraordinary linguistic powers'. But there was no guarantee that great linguists would make good consuls.

In any case, the examination excluded all but those who were willing and able to spend several years abroad preparing for language tests—unless, that is, like Reader Bullard (one of the very few working-class candidates to reach the service), they were exceptionally gifted as linguists, or unless they belonged to that category, so distrusted at the Foreign Office, of Englishmen brought up abroad. The 1914 Commission described the entrance examination for the Levant Service as 'a peculiar one, not to be defended on educational grounds', and recommended that the method of recruitment intended for the General Service should be applied, with suitable alterations in subsequent training, to the Levant. The Levant examination was assimilated into the general Class I entrance examination on the restoration of Civil Service competitions after the war.

Linguistic ability had been the main, perhaps the *only* criterion for recruitment over the first forty years of the new service. The results were better than the system deserved. It was probably true that the years of training to

---

[1] Minutes of Evidence, *Report of the Committee on Oriental Studies in London*, PP 1909 (Cd 4561) xxxv, QQ 5786-7.

which the Levant recruits were subjected tended to counteract some of the intellectual deficiencies of the background demanded by the examination itself. The first recruits under the new system were sent out direct to Constantinople, where they were established with a large staff of native teachers in a house at Ortakeui, three miles from Galata, and set to work for two years at Turkish, Arabic, Persian, modern Greek and Bulgarian. It was optimistic to expect them, in that short time and in the relaxing circumstances of life at Constantinople, to become competent interpreters, and the quality of their teachers made it no easier. The teachers, fine scholars in their own language, had no conception of how best to pass on their knowledge, or even how to explain the simplest of grammatical points. Walter Baring, who as a Secretary at the Embassy had served part-time as superintendent of the first student dragomans, told a committee many years later that it was a case of reversing the rules: the pupil had to extract information from the teacher:

> There were very few men . . . who could impart knowledge, and if you asked an ordinary teacher there, 'Give me an explanation of why you use such and such a phrase or construction,' he would smile and say, 'Well, because it is so.' That is what it amounted to.

On one occasion Baring found one of his Persian teachers, a considerable scholar, starting two young men on readings from Gulistan of Sa'di, the prose introduction to which could be read and understood only by a very profound Oriental scholar—'Yet his pupils had not learned the ABC'.[1]

It was partly for this reason, but rather more on account of the high cost of the Ortakeui establishment, that it was decided in 1894, after a lapse of several years in which no recruitment had taken place, to send the new recruits alternately to Oxford and Cambridge for a preliminary two-year training in languages before posting to the East. Oxford proved unsatisfactory, and after a few years all student interpreters were sent to Cambridge, where, under the control of the Board which superintended the instruction of students for the Indian Civil Service, they studied Turkish, Persian, Arabic, French, and Russian, the history of Turkey and Persia, and the elements of English law. This, at any rate, was the intention, but the remarkable E. G. Browne, Professor of Arabic at Cambridge and director of studies to the student interpreters, was no systematic purveyor of knowledge. As a teacher in the narrow sense, one of his best students described him as a joke. But,

---

[1] *Ibid.*, QQ 3812-17.

Bullard added, 'this mattered little in the light of the erudition which fountained from him in amusing and stimulating coruscations'.

> A skilful question would set him off in pursuit of some golden hare—Persian poetry, the early caliphs or the Abbasids of Baghdad, and the end of the hour came all too soon. I think that a few systematic lectures on Islam might have been useful to us, but Browne had to be taken for what he was: a meteor, not a locomotive.[1]

The two years at Cambridge were followed by stiff examinations, after which successful candidates were raised to the rank of consular assistants and posted either to a mission or to one of the more important consulates in Turkey, Bulgaria or Egypt. Twelve months later they were examined in the local language, and, after another year, required to pass a further searching examination (on which their promotion and subsequent seniority depended) in the civil, criminal and commercial law of Turkey, and in the history, language, and administration of the country in which they served.

If they survived all this the Levant consuls were as fully trained as any British public servant overseas. It was a patchwork of learning, with gaps in some of the most important places. No provision was made for formal instruction or examination in their magisterial duties. When the student dragomans (later known as student interpreters) received their training at Ortakeui, they had had an arrangement by which twice a week they attended the chambers of a local British barrister, Sir Edwin Pears, for legal instruction. Some law was taught at Cambridge, but the elaborate provisions made in the parallel China Consular Service for legal instruction were not extended to the Levant, and relatively few members of the Levant Service were actually called to the Bar. Nor was there any instruction in trade and commerce. Such knowledge as Levant consuls possessed was picked up by the light of nature. The result, Harold Satow explained, was that they were 'naturally unacquainted with business customs and practice, and sometimes even with the meaning of its phraseology'.[2]

Movement towards amalgamation By 1914 the Levant Consular Service had established itself as a close service with its own internal promotion ladder, staffed by highly competent, well-trained specialists, and

---

[1] Bullard, *The Camels Must Go*, pp. 47-8.
[2] Memorandum on the Duties and Training of Consular Officers in the Levant, 10 August 1918: PRO.FO/369/1319.

carrying out functions largely political and judicial in character. For purposes of recruitment, it had replaced the China Service at the peak of prestige, and unlike the China Service (which was having difficulty in finding recruits of sufficient quality), competition for entry to the Levant Service, right up to the outbreak of war, was keen and persistent.

The relative unpopularity of both specialized services *after* the war, when successful candidates at the amalgamated examination almost invariably selected the General Service, the Levant Service, the China, Japan and Siam Services in that order, was symptomatic of a change which was taking place in the whole position of specialization, a change which was to end in the amalgamation of the specialized services into the General Service in the mid-1930s.

Yet until as recently as 1918, it looked very much as if the tendency was in the opposite direction. There had always been a feeling among members of the consular service that the Latin American consulates, for example, with their affinities in language requirements, commercial and shipping duties, and political experience, might properly be brought together into a close service on the lines of the Far Eastern and Levant Services. The same was true, to some extent, of the African consulates.

The Levant Service itself, after the first years of this century, was tending to break down into even smaller self-contained components. It covered an area stretching from the Danube states in the north to Zanzibar in the south, and from Morocco in the west to Tehran in the east. Under pressure of the need for specialized knowledge both of the local conditions and of the widely different languages over so large an area, it had become the practice for officers to specialize in one or other of the areas—the Balkans, Asiatic Turkey, Persia, or Morocco—after which they tended to remain within those areas.

Russia, with its own language problems, was another obvious area for a specialized service, and recruitment for the Levant and Russian Services was brought together in 1914, with Persia and Russia becoming, for a brief period, a close service within the Levant Service. When the whole subject of the postwar reorganization of the consular service was considered at length in 1917, opinion at the Foreign Office and at St Petersburg was unanimously in favour of maintaining the Russian service as a distinct service with its own recruitment of student interpreters. The scheme was overtaken by events, but Russia remained within the area staffed by the Levant Service until the Service lost its independent status in 1934.

The 1914 Commission felt satisfied that nothing would be gained, while much would be lost, by any attempt to amalgamate the three traditional divisions of the service—General, Levant, and Far Eastern: 'Successive enquiries have confirmed the wisdom of this division, the reason for which is to be found in the differences of language, government and national customs in the countries in which each division works.' But there had always been good reason to dispute the division, and even the basic rationalization of language, government, and customs came under attack during the interwar period.

One of the fundamental objections to subdivision and to the formation of close services within the common consular service was the immobility which such partitions imposed. In the interests of the state, it was desirable to move consuls around more freely. Officers spending the better part of their career in one area would benefit by experience elsewhere; confined to one area, they tended to lose their flexibility and sense of proportion, to magnify the importance of their own particular areas, and to become absorbed in local detail to the detriment of the general interest. These arguments carried much weight in the interwar years, when conditions in the close services, particularly in China, became most arduous and oppressive. 'We must remember', said David Scott in 1933, 'that the idea nowadays is that Oriental Secretaries are liable to outgrow their utility if kept too long',[1] and one of the objectives of the 1943 reforms was to break down the strict specialization and give even the specialists 'all round knowledge and experience'.[2]

Quite apart from state advantage, mobility was important to the consuls themselves. Close services meant a career confined to one part of the world, not necessarily the most desirable. Long residence in isolated posts without civilized amenities and companionship could and did lead to demoralization and mental deterioration. After many years of deprivation, it might have been fair to bring consuls closer to home, to a kinder climate and to more of the amenities prized by Europeans. In practice there was virtually no such movement. A man who began his career in the Ottoman dominions or in Japan ended it there. However distinguished his services, he could expect neither promotion to the diplomatic service nor even a posting to a comfortable European consulate. Whatever its theoretical advantages, fragmentation, as Consul H. A. Cowper pointed out to the 1858 Committee, was in practice grossly unfair to individuals:

[1] Memorandum on the action to be taken following the Levant Committee' Report, Foreign Office, 1933: PRO.FO/369/2316.
[2] Richard Law, answering for H.M. Government, at the Foreign Service (Reform debate of 18 March 1943: 387 *HC Deb.*, 5s, 1434.

The fortunate man who commenced his career in Italy and ended it at Paris, ever amongst the charms and delights of life, would be in Paradise compared to him who, condemned to the *Inferno* of Africa, started as vice-consul in King Boy's dominions, and ended his barbarian course (if successful) as consul-general at Timbuctoo.[1]

The point was not lost on recruits to the service in the 1920s and 30s. Before 1914 the China and Levant Services were separately recruited by a higher standard of examination; they started with greater prestige, reinforced by the political and judicial nature of their employment, the tax and duty privileges brought by exterritorial rights, and in China at any rate by a higher scale of salaries. When, for one reason or another, these distinctions vanished in the interwar years there was nothing to persuade a man that his best interests were served by limiting his career to a narrow area of the world and by denying himself the possibility of a coveted post in Europe or North America. The best men, at the top of the mark sheet, selected the General Service, and the quality of the men recruited to the close services declined dramatically.

The retreat from the close services, however, had begun well before 1914. The smaller the service, the less the opportunity for transfers and promotions, and the more difficult it became to work out any systematic career structure. In recruiting for the Levant Service before the war, the very real problem in attracting graduates was not the initial salary, which (at £300 for an assistant and £400 for a vice-consul) was perfectly adequate for a young man presumably still unmarried. Rather, it was the prospects for promotion. By 1914 the experience on average over the last six appointments was that it took about sixteen years before a man was promoted to consul at £600, rising, even at the top of the service, to a bare £1000. This left nothing to spare for a married man with a family.

The promotion block created by the closing of so many posts in enemy-occupied territory during the First World War further delayed the average age of promotion to consul; and the expansion of the consular service, following the Steel-Maitland proposals, bypassed the Levant service. The political situation in Russia and Turkey was by no means clear, and the Treasury, ignoring the Foreign Office plea to allow a margin of extra posts to cope with unknown requirements, instructed the Foreign Secretary to carry on with his prewar establishment. Shortly afterwards economy set in,

---

[1] Minutes of Evidence, *Report of the Select Committee on Consular Service and Appointments*, PP 1857-8 (482) VIII, Q 4774.

and the Levant Service, though it escaped the cuts imposed on the General Service in the 1920s, remained saddled with a fixed establishment and a permanent block in its promotions. The recommended ratio of posts to secure a sufficient flow of promotion, as established by the Steel-Maitland Committee, was 38 per cent, 37 per cent, and 25 per cent for vice-consuls, consuls, and consuls-general respectively. In the late 1920s the ratio for the Levant Service, worse even than that for the China Service, was 58 per cent, 29 per cent and 13 per cent. By 1932, there were 100 senior posts (inspectors-general, consuls-general and consuls) in the General Service, and 66 junior posts (vice-consuls and probationers). In the Levant Service there were 37 senior posts and 47 junior posts.

The block in promotions in the Levant Service was not, as in the General Service, a temporary problem lasting perhaps no more than a decade and occasioned by an abnormally high number of postwar appointments followed immediately by a recession. It was a permanent block resulting from a totally inadequate proportion of senior posts, and it put promotions for Levant Service officers habitually ten years behind those of General Service entrants of the same generation.

Problems such as these had, after all, only recently been recognized to exist for the consular service, where career planning was virtually ignored before the war. But the increased scale of the service following the Steel-Maitland proposals, the wider range of the functions it was expected to perform, the new systems of control and accounting, the new salary scales and increased allowances, the destruction of the 'consul's freehold', meant a vastly expanded range of administrative functions which had simply never existed for the Victorians. It was this which drove home the incongruity of an organization of 350 men divided into no less than five watertight compartments—the General Service, the Levant Service (unofficially subdivided within itself), and the three independent and self-contained branches of the Far Eastern Service—China, Japan, and Siam. When Sir Maurice de Bunsen cabled home a proposal, from a Mr Holt at Montevideo, that a specialized branch of the service might be established for Latin America, Victor Wellesley was furious:

> Quite unnecessary to telegraph this. The idea is not a new one. It has been considered time and again. Whatever the advantages of a close service may be, and in many respects they are undeniable, the administrative difficulties arising from a system of watertight compartments in the Consular Service are even greater.

Wellesley admitted that for reasons not altogether of language but also of the semipolitical nature of the posts and the special duties imposed by exterritoriality, the close services in the Levant were 'a necessary evil'. But he concluded that he himself was strongly opposed to the creation of unnecessary, watertight compartments. Sir Eyre Crowe agreed.[1]

Language, political services, and the special duties created by exterritoriality were the surviving reasons, then, for the close services. But attitudes were changing even in this respect. The argument for the specialized services had been the homogeneity of their geographical areas. When the Levant Service came to include Russia at the one extreme and Zanzibar at the other, the argument lost much of its force. Real expertise in languages was far less vital than it had once been. Turkish ministers and officials were more commonly fluent in the main European languages. The days were gone when Lord Ponsonby could count solemnly up to fifty, modulating his voice and gesturing appropriately, and then back again to one, persuading the assembled Porte that he was delivering a graceful, ceremonial address. In ordinary consular business what was needed was a thorough and fluent knowledge of the language, rather than a mastery of classical Arabic; and this was more easily achieved *en poste* than at Cambridge. The *mezzofanti's* time was up, and in 1931 Levant probationers came under a new language-training scheme, much more modest in scope and intention, by which they went straight out for their first year to an Arabic-speaking post, and spent a second year at a post such as Constantinople, Athens, Tehran, Moscow, or Leningrad where they could acquire a second language. In place of the full-time training of the past, they were now expected to spend only some four hours a day at their studies under the supervision of a native teacher, with the rest of their time on general duties.

As for political and judicial duties, these too were in sharp decline. Turkey, her empire gone, was never again to reach the status of a great power; indeed, her position as a key to European security had disappeared as far back, arguably, as the last decades of the previous century. Britain's rivals, Russia and Germany, were temporarily *hors de combat*, and in the 1920s neither looked as if it had much chance of an early recovery. Some parts of the Ottoman dominions, of Persia and of the Persian Gulf were still of great interest to the British government for their oil, but the problems they created were diplomatic rather than consular. It was the abandonment of the Capitulations, however, which had the most immediate and dramatic effect

[1] Minutes on de Bunsen's telegram of 24 May 1918: PRO.FO/369/1052.

in reducing consular functions throughout the East. The special authority, expertise, and prestige of the Levant consuls had depended ultimately on their position as judges in their consular courts and as governors of their own nationals and protégés. It was for this that the array of dragomans and cavasses existed, and it was through this that the consuls enjoyed what amounted to full autonomy within a nominally sovereign state.

The Capitulations were intended to be coextensive with the Ottoman dominions. In practice, by the third quarter of the nineteenth century they were already restricted. The semi-autonomous Balkan tributaries, particularly Serbia and Romania, were understandably opposed to the exercise of consular jurisdiction within their frontiers. Consul-General Green reported from Bucharest in 1871 that the Treaties and Capitulations were 'virtually a dead letter in the Principalities, where Consular jurisdiction is resisted by the Government, disavowed by the Tribunals, and obstructed by the civil and military authorities'.[1] The acting consul-general at Belgrade, J. Watson, noted in his return for the same year that, though the Capitulations were still technically in force in Serbia, the Government was making every effort to set them aside, notably by inserting clauses in foreign contracts by which the contractors undertook to refer points in dispute to the Serbian courts.[2] Once both principalities had gained their full independence, after the Congress of Berlin in 1878, the British Government recognized what was already a fact. By the treaties of 1880 Britain surrendered (in the case of Serbia explicitly and for Romania by implication) the nominal privileges and immunities enjoyed by British subjects in those areas. Similarly, in French North Africa, capitulatory rights had disappeared with the establishment of full French government control. When France annexed Tunisia, for example, in 1881-83, all the European powers except the aggrieved Italy renounced their Capitulations and abolished their consular tribunals.

The Capitulations receded with the Empire, and even within it. But the powers refused to permit any relaxation for Turkey herself or for her Asiatic dominions. Even after the 1908 revolution, when Turkey had fallen under the reformed administration of the Young Turks, the position remained unchanged. *The Times*, by now (in contrast to its advanced opinions of the 1860s) a staunch supporter of tradition, felt that humiliating though the Capitulations might be to the new order in Turkey and cloak as they were to

---

[1] *Reports Relative to British Consular Establishments, 1858 and 1871*, Part III, pp 1872 (c. 530) LX.
[2] *Ibid.*

many abuses, they were a heritage from past periods of misrule, and could not be set aside until security and justice for foreigners were permanently assured: 'The Turks must earn their release, as Japan did, by steady and continuous reform and development upon lines which will win the confidence of Europe. There is no other method; and the surrender of ancient privileges would not be hastened by premature demands.'[1]

The Turks themselves were not prepared to wait that long, and they took the first opportunity of a division among the powers, the outbreak of the First World War, to denounce the Capitulations unilaterally in September 1914. A half-hearted attempt was made to re-establish capitulatory rights in defeated Turkey after 1918. But the powers finally renounced their rights at Lausanne in 1923, and a similar pattern was followed elsewhere in the former Ottoman dominions. With the establishment of the French mandates over Syria and Lebanon after the war, 'mixed' courts, in which the bench might have a majority of French judges, replaced the former Capitulations. Capitulations vanished in Persia in 1928, in Iraq in 1929, in Ethiopia in 1935 after the Italian conquest, in Egypt and French Morocco after the Montreux conference of 1937. Although the British Government never formally renounced its exterritorial rights in Saudi Arabia, Sir Andrew Ryan (the British Minister from 1932 to 1936) described them as 'no more than a slightly uneasy ghost'; he could not have invoked them without imperilling Britain's relations with Ibn Saud.[2]

It was obvious even by the end of the First War that the advantages of maintaining an independent Levant Service were already questionable, and likely to become more so within the next few years. A Foreign Office schedule of subjects for discussion by the Steel-Maitland Committee included, as its first question, whether any modifications were required in the scope of the existing special services, or whether any further special services should be created.[3] The Committee, when it came to report in March 1919, recommended that the organization of the Far Eastern service should remain as it was, but that the Levant Service, for the reason primarily of the disadvantage of a small restricted service with stagnant career prospects, should be merged into the General Service; officers needed within the combined service for duties in the Near East and Russia were to receive a year of language training.

---

[1] *The Times*, 31 August 1908, 7d.
[2] Ryan, *Last of the Dragomans*, p. 18.
[3] Prepared in June 1918: PRO.FO/369/1047.

It must have seemed at the time that this recommendation had been accepted. Certainly, when Steel-Maitland was announcing to the Commons in 1919 the reforms which had already taken place in the postwar consular service, he reported that the Levant Service had been incorporated into the General Service. There were to be no actual barriers within the new, enlarged General Service, but 'there will, inevitably, with wise administration, be a quite natural selection, so that the officers who are accustomed to Latin languages, Latin mentality, Latin customs, habits of thought, habits of trade, and the rest of it tend to circulate in the Latin and Latin-American countries, and similarly with the Slavonic and Teutonic countries'.[1]

But Steel-Maitland was speaking out of turn. The policy after 1919 was certainly to bring the specialized services, Levant and Far Eastern, as far as possible into line with the General Service. The grades of student interpreter and consular assistant were abolished in 1920, and recruits entered the Levant Service, like the General Service, as probationer vice-consuls, by the same examination and with comparable pay scales; the salaries of consuls-general and consuls were already the same. But in other respects—in staffing policy, training, seniority lists and promotion prospects—the services still remained on a different footing.

It was the endemic promotions block in the Levant Service which finally forced the issue. In both the Levant Service and the Far Eastern Service, the initiative for the amalgamation came not from the Foreign Office but from the members of the Services themselves, and in both cases the motive was to relieve an increasingly serious promotions block, with all its implications for recruitment and morale in the specialized services. In the case of the Levant Service this initiative took the form of a round-robin, signed by practically all the consuls-general in the Levant Service and addressed to Ernest Gye, head of the Consular Department, in the early summer of 1930. The round-robin suggested the need for an authoritative committee which would make recommendations for the removal of any legitimate grievances (in particular, the promotions block and the whole question of promotion policy) and for the future organization and conduct of the service; it proposed that such a committee might sit in the summer of 1930, when it could take the opportunity to examine the large number of Levant officers who should, at that season, be home on leave.

The Foreign Office procrastinated. That summer, Consul-General H. E. Satow, who had served as secretary to the reforming Steel-Maitland

---

[1] 116 *HC Deb.*, 5s, 528.

Committee and who seems, in this case, to have been the ring-leader in the revolt of the consuls-general, had a talk at the Foreign Office with Ernest Gye, Sir Hubert Montgomery, Sir Edward Crowe of the Department of Overseas Trade, and Herbert Hall Hall (an Inspector-General of consulates). The London officials did not feel that there were any real points which a special Levant committee might profitably discuss. But they left Satow with the impression, which they later denied, that they would hold an enquiry, and that the body which conducted that enquiry would concern itself mainly with the question of whether, under current conditions, the continued existence of the Levant Consular Service could be justified. The consuls-general had two possibilities in mind: either an amalgamation with the General Consular Service, or a new, combined Foreign Service in which both the diplomatic service and the consular service were fused.

Nothing happened, and three of the consuls-general wrote again to Gye in June 1931 to remind him of Satow's discussion and to enquire whether there had been any progress with the proposed committee. Hubert Montgomery, Deputy Under Secretary, was opposed to both forms of amalgamation. Amalgamation with the diplomatic service was, of course, unthinkable, quite out of the question. As for amalgamation with the General Service, which Montgomery conceded as a possible remedy, he argued that it was more than doubtful whether this would help matters, for there was, or shortly would be, a promotions block in the General Service also.

Gye himself was no great enthusiast for change, and both he and Montgomery readily agreed with James Morgan's conclusion from Ankara, 2 December 1931, that the Levant Service should be retained. Morgan explained that the chief point in the argument for amalgamation was that the Levant consuls-general were all, as it happened, relatively young, with many years to run before retirement. Consuls and vice-consuls saw their hopes of promotion long deferred, and this 'tinges their outlook with melancholy'. Furthermore, the old capitulatory privileges had served as some compensation for life in the East, while the end of exterritoriality had to a large degree dispensed with the requirement for special knowledge of local laws, English law and local languages. On the other hand, the balance against amalgamation was tipped, Morgan felt, by the value of a knowledge of Eastern customs, laws, and mentality, by the desirability of an acquaintance with the local languages, and by the importance of the personal contacts with local authorities open only to officers stationed continuously in the Levant. 'A very sensible letter', said Gye. 'Speaking generally, a very sound letter', Hubert Montgomery added. It was left to Sir Edward Crowe, of the Department of

Overseas Trade, to bring them to their senses again by reporting the arrival of a further memorandum from Harold Satow, in which Satow once more raised the question of a conference the following summer: 'I think we shall have to go into this.'[1]

The date was now February 1932. Foreign Office officials, though they had felt quite early on that they would be compelled, under pressure, to concede a Committee of Enquiry, had managed to stall it on the excuse, so favoured among civil servants, that until a current Royal Commission (the Tomlin Commission on the Civil Service, 1929-31) had ceased taking evidence, they did not know whether it would be enquiring into the sort of points which would be of interest to the Levant Service—a misleading argument, as they must have known, since the Levant Service was in need of rapid action to remedy what was very much a local problem, with little relevance to the Civil Service as a whole. The Royal Commission reported in 1931. Predictably enough, it had touched on only a couple of points relevant to the diplomatic and consular services. But the delays continued, and it was not until April 1932 that a committee was appointed, until June that it met, and until the following January that it reported, more than two and a half years after the original round-robin.

All this procrastination, frustrating though it was to the members of the Levant Service, had one valuable consequence: the report, when it came, went well beyond the original intention, covering points relevant to the entire consular service in all its branches. The general recommendations of the Committee have been considered elsewhere. As far as the Levant Service itself was concerned, the committee concluded that the arguments in favour of amalgamation had won the day. The report, accepted at once by Sir John Simon (the Secretary of State), proposed that the amalgamation of the Levant and General Services should take effect for all new entrants to the service. It recommended a short-term palliative for the promotions block in the Levant Service in the shape of increased salaries and allowances for senior vice-consuls, which, as watered down by the Treasury, amounted to an additional representational allowance of £100 p.a. for married vice-consuls on completion of thirteen years' service on the permanent establishment. The Committee held out no hope of relief through accelerated promotion, since the amalgamation was to apply only to new entrants; but in practice it was found possible to work out a joint seniority list for the combined

---

[1] The papers in which this preliminary argument for the Committee were conducted are in PRO.FO/369/2200.

service which went some way to applying the benefits of amalgamation to all members.

Once it had made up its mind, the Foreign Office was anxious to put the amalgamation into effect immediately (with the summer entry of 1933). The Civil Service Commission objected, and arrangements were postponed. But with the combined competition in 1934, the independent Levant Service ceased to exist.[1]

[1] The minutes on the Report and the subsequent negotiations with the Treasury are in PRO.FO/369/2316, 2317.

Chapter 5

The Far Eastern Service

British consuls in the Far Eastern Service (covering China, Japan, and Siam) were both like and unlike their colleagues in the Levant, and as distinctively different from the seaport consuls of the Victorian General Service. They were like in that they shared the burdens of exterritoriality; they acted as judges, governors, and guardian angels over British subjects and protégés within their consular districts. They were appointed initially, like so many Levant consuls, to provide the focus around which trade might develop, to 'open' trade rather than to supply services at well-developed, westernized commercial centres. Their establishments were on the scale at which much of the drudgery of detailed, consular work was delegated to subordinates. No China consul, any more than a Levant consul, found himself acting as a mere registrar of British ships and seamen.

But Far Eastern consuls in the nineteenth century were not, except marginally and accidentally, political officers. Whereas the Levant, with its weary preoccupation with the 'Eastern Question', was of a continued political importance to the powers until the last decades of the nineteenth century, China reached the hub of world politics only briefly at the turn of the century. Siam, as a buffer between French Indo-China and British pretensions in Burma, was of some political significance, and the small independent Siam Consular Service had in part a political rationale. But British consuls in China and Japan were not appointed for political reasons. They existed fundamentally for the protection and promotion of British trade.

Origins It was in 1833 that the British Government assumed responsibility from the East India Company for the care and protection of British subjects and their interests at Canton. Though the circumstances were rather different, the fundamental reasons for the replacement of the East India Company were the same as those for the Levant Company eight years before: the objection, under the new economics, to a monopoly officially upheld in the interests of a select group of English merchants, and the desire to throw open the trade to the energy and enterprise of any individual, British or foreign, who cared to take part.

The scale of British trade at the time, though obviously capable of extension, was still small and confined to a single outlet, Canton; and it was to Canton that the first official British representative was sent. Lord Napier arrived at Canton on 25 July 1834, but no effort had been made to prepare the Chinese authorities for the change of status and administration. So far as the Chinese were concerned, the East India Company's administration was perfectly satisfactory. The existing British trade, pleasant as an addition to Chinese revenues, private and official, was of no great consequence. The revenue, said the Governor of Canton, 'concerns not the Celestial Empire to the extent of a hair, or a feather's down'; English broadcloths and camlets were of no regard, in contrast to which 'the tea—the rhubarb—the raw silk—of the inner dominions, are the sources by which the said nation's people live, and maintain life'.[1]

England might have survived without rhubarb. But the Governor was right to the extent that those few Englishmen whom he saw around him— the representatives of the Company—were completely and abjectly dependent on Chinese official goodwill. It suited the Chinese authorities that they should remain so. Lord Napier, claiming to represent an authority greater than that of the Company and demanding, as such, to bypass the Hong merchants (the traditional and exclusive medium for communication between the Governor and the foreigners), posed a direct threat to a stable and satisfactorily defined relationship. Napier was the 'barbarian eye' who would spy out the land for future encroachments and conquests, after which China would share the fate of British India.

The tone which Napier adopted in demanding direct access to the Governor, and his precipitate and injudicious action in forcing his way up to Canton from Macao before obtaining permission from the authorities, gave the Chinese every reason to suspect his motives. His activities were far from pleasing to the British Government itself. When his complaints and requests for assistance reached London, the Duke of Wellington reminded him, coldly, that it was 'not by force and violence that His Majesty intends to establish a commercial intercourse between his subjects and China, but by

---

[1] Letter to the Hong merchants, 18 August 1834, printed in *The Times*, 2 February 1835, 3d.

the other conciliatory measures so strongly inculcated in all the instructions which you have received'.[1]

By the time Wellington's rebuke reached China Napier's mission had failed completely and, to the relief of the British merchants at Canton, he had retired to Macao, where he died after a short illness on 11 October. The Governor of Canton had merely applied that remedy, so effective against any threat of insubordination among foreign merchants, of calling a halt to trade; and there was nothing that Napier could do except get out of the way. The Chinese had no objection to a British representative. Indeed, when the Governor heard news of Napier's death, he at once asked for the appointment of a replacement to take responsibility for the English merchants and direct their trade. But what he wanted was a merchant, acquainted with the trade and with the traditions under which it was conducted: a taipan of the kind appointed over the English factory at Canton by the East India Company, not an official. 'It is unnecessary', he told the Canton factory, 'again to appoint a barbarian eye or superintendent, thereby causing hindrances and impediments.'[2]

Napier's misjudgments, not altogether surprising in a man ignorant of China and the Chinese, meant that in effect Britain was not officially represented in Canton between 1834 and the outbreak of the first Opium War in 1839. A successor was appointed as Superintendent of Trade, but he was seldom at Canton. Consular representation in China was the product of the Treaty of Nanking (negotiated by Sir Henry Pottinger at the end of the war in 1842, and ratified the following year) by which five ports—Canton, Amoy, Foochow, Ningpo, and Shanghai—were opened to world trade, and a consulate established at each. The consuls came under the direction of the Chief Superintendent of British Trade, stationed at the newly acquired colony of Hong Kong.

In a sense, then, the China Consular Service (which expanded later, with the establishment of consuls in Siam and Japan, into the Far Eastern Service) came first into existence in 1843, nearly a decade after the abolition of the East India Company's charter. From the first, it existed entirely apart from the General Consular Service. Consuls in China communicated not with the Consular Department at the Foreign Office but with the Chief Superintendent of Trade, who in turn communicated direct with the appropriate

---

[1] Quoted by Alexander Michie, *The Englishman in China during the Victorian Era as illustrated in the career of Sir Rutherford Alcock* (Edinburgh, 1900), I, 38-9.
[2] Edict of 19 October 1834, printed in *The Times*, 13 March 1835, 4a.

Political Department. Local administration was in the hands of the Superintendent, and later in those of his successor, the British Minister at Peking.

Recruitment In its early days the China Service was an *ad hoc* arrangement, surviving independently merely because of its homogeneity, its distance from London, and the obvious convenience of administration from Hong Kong. The first consuls, and their replacements over the years, were 'officers and gentlemen' with some claim or other on government patronage, but with absolutely no knowledge of China, of the Chinese, or of their language. By accident, some of them turned out to be men of great ability. Sir Rutherford Alcock, one of the original consuls, rose to be British Minister at Peking. Another, W. H. Medhurst, was a capable and willing official who, by the time of his retirement as consul at Shanghai, had reached the peak of the Chinese consular career. Sir Thomas Wade and Sir Harry Parkes, beginning as consular interpreters, both ended by taking charge of the Peking legation.

The China consulates, Stanley Lane-Poole once said, were 'a splendid school for men who were not afraid of responsibility; but a purgatory for cowards'. It soon became obvious that the peculiar dangers and responsibilities of those early years in China, and above all the impossibility of conducting consular business satisfactorily without a knowledge of the language, would make it necessary to train up a special class of officers for service in the Far East. Sir John Bowring, consul at Canton and later Superintendent and Plenipotentiary, pressed hard for the establishment of a strong China Service, recruited by examination and trained for the job, and in August 1854 Lord Clarendon took the first steps in this direction. The heads of a number of colleges, including King's College, London (which alone had a Chair of Chinese), and the three Queen's Colleges in Ireland (perhaps because Lord Clarendon was their Chancellor), were invited to submit nominations, and a number of young men were sent out, on recommendation but without examination, to begin their studies at consular posts in the East. In addition to those intended for the China Service, Clarendon made provision for six further young men at £200 p.a., to be posted to Hong Kong as 'supernumerary interpreters' specifically for service in Japan, once Japan was opened to trade.

The system of recruitment by nomination from the major schools and colleges continued for a number of years, though after 1860 candidates were expected to be examined by the Civil Service Commissioners. Once the

Service was better known it was no longer necessary to invite nominations, and applications received spontaneously were simply noted, held at the Foreign Office, and forwarded indiscriminately for selection when an examination was due to take place. In 1872, as a gesture towards the civil service reform favoured by the Gladstone administration, Lord Granville introduced 'open' competition for the China Service—the first of its kind under the Foreign Office—and the ample flow of applicants attracted by public advertisement made it possible to raise the standard of entry to such a point that, in the late 1890s, the quality was not substantially below that recruited for the Indian Civil Service.

After its first appointments the China Service was never regarded by the Foreign Office as a reservoir of patronage. It was difficult to persuade those in line for patronage to accept exile in China. But the main reason for throwing open the service in the late 1850s and 60s was the official recognition, with the appointment of student interpreters, of the supreme importance of language ability. A political patron could less easily persuade himself that a country cousin could master Chinese or Japanese than that the youth, though dull, had plenty of common sense and was good at handling men. The result was that the social composition of the China Service was unusually wide. The sons of gentry, clergy, and serving officers, who formed the great majority of recruits to the other branches of the consular service, maintained themselves in force. But a number of bright young scholarship men from the Scottish and Irish universities, the sons of the mercantile middle class, were also successful in the open competitions. The severity of the language test could be relied on, as for the Levant Service, to exclude working-class candidates. Of the fifty-two candidates for seven vacancies when Meyrick Hewlett was examined in 1898, the majority would have undergone a relatively expensive preparation parallel to his own—three months in France, three months in Germany, and a special cramming course of evening classes at King's College, London.[1]

Language training The central justification of an independent China Consular Service, recruited from young men in the age range of eighteen to twenty-four, was the creation of a supply of officers with an adequate working knowledge of the Chinese language.

There were no facilities for acquiring Chinese in mid-Victorian England,

---

[1] Sir Meyrick Hewlett, *Forty Years in China* (London, 1943), p. 1.

and it was natural enough that the first generations of student interpreters should have been despatched direct to the consulates, to pick up the language *en poste* with the help of locally employed Chinese teachers. The disadvantages were obvious enough. The standard reached depended on the ability of the Chinese teacher, on the distractions at the particular consular post, on the willingness of the supervising consul to spare the student from routine consular duties and to insist on adequate application to language studies. Results were uneven until, in the 1860s, with the establishment of a British Legation at Peking, arrangements were made to bring all the new student interpreters together for a preliminary two-year period of full-time language study at the Legation itself, under the supervision of the Chinese Secretary. Sir Thomas Wade, who (as Chinese Secretary at Peking after 1861) was largely responsible for the improved system, estimated in 1869 that as a result of recruitment to the Service from its own student interpreters since 1854, only six of the forty-eight officers currently holding consular appointments, were not, in greater or less degree, competent to act as interpreters.[1] By 1908 Sir Walter Hillier was confident that there were no consuls in China who had not a very fair knowledge of Chinese, though, as he admitted, 'many men do not care to keep it up'.[2]

The results, then, were not unsatisfactory, and in the early years, when Britain was pioneering the system of student interpreters, British consuls in the East were far better linguists than their foreign colleagues. It was characteristic, however, that the Foreign Office, having developed one system under a particular set of circumstances, should have become irrationally wedded to it when the original circumstances had changed. In the absence of genuine teachers of Chinese, students had to make do with whatever they could find—Chinese literati with no knowledge either of English or of the techniques of language training. Like the student dragomans in the Levant, the student interpreters in the East puzzled out the language from first principles, and it took them a full six months even to begin to make any progress. By the end of two years, aided by a 'teacher' whose only qualification for teaching Chinese (according to Sir John Pratt) was that he knew no English, they were lucky if they could do more than stumble along in colloquial Chinese. Unfortunately, this extraordinary system, adopted for lack of a better in the first half of the century, had acquired an inviolable

---

[1] Memorandum dated 10 March 1869: PRO.FO/366/341.
[2] Minutes of Evidence, *Report of the Committee on Oriental Studies in London*, PP 1909 (Cd 4561) xxxv, Q 470.

standing in the eyes of officials by the end of the second half. If a Chinese teacher knew English (Sir Ernest Satow argued before the Reay Committee in 1908) the pupil would take refuge in talking English to him. Satow's own experience, in Japan in the early 1860s, was that the less help of that kind one had, the better: 'Put a young Englishman together with a Chinese, and with a certain number of books, and let them puzzle it out together; the very fact that the Englishman has to make a great effort, I think, secures that he learns what he does learn more solidly and permanently.'[1]

With a man of Satow's ability, this might just have been true; it was not with the majority of consular recruits. The Foreign Office stuck grimly by the traditional methods, and the linguistic advantage which British consuls had enjoyed earlier in the century was lost by the end. It was clear to the Reay Committee (which was to be responsible for the establishment of the School of Oriental and African Studies in London) that if adequate instruction were provided, young men posted to the East would gain immensely by beginning their studies at home, whatever the language studied or their object in learning it.[2] Since 1894, this had been the method employed, most successfully, with the Levant students; and foreign consular services had long abandoned the native teacher in the East. By the turn of the century, the teaching of Oriental languages on the continent had reached a degree of sophistication unmatched in Britain. There was nothing in London directly equivalent to the École Spéciale des Langues Orientales Vivantes at Paris, to the Seminar for Oriental Languages at the University of Berlin, to the Imperial and Royal Consular Academy at Vienna, to the Lazareff Institute of Oriental Languages at Moscow, or to the Faculty of Oriental Languages at the University of St Petersburg. By the time English equivalents developed, the Foreign Office, on which they had hoped and depended for patronage, had discovered good reasons to scorn them. It is only since the Second World War that the School of Oriental and African Studies and the School of Slavonic and East European Studies have come into their own.

As for the China Consular Service, the traditional methods remained virtually unchanged to the end. The Hong Kong and Shanghai Bank had been training its young men at King's College, London, since the last decades of the nineteenth century. Between the wars British American Tobacco and Butterfield and Swire, two of the biggest employers of young

---

[1] Ibid., Q 1914.
[2] *Report of the Committee to consider the Organization of Oriental Studies in London*, PP 1909 (Cd 4560) xxxv, para. 6.

Englishmen in China, were sending some of their young men to the School of Oriental and African Studies. In the consular service, by contrast, both seniors and juniors were still, just before the Second World War, complaining of the system of training probationers at Peking. Sir John Brenan and Consul-General Phillips told the Consular Inspector (T. D. Dunlop), during his 1937 inspection tour, that few of the juniors had attained a satisfactory degree of proficiency in Chinese, and that when they left Peking they had had practically no training in consular work. Some of the juniors, in turn, criticized the lack of system in the teaching of Chinese at Peking, as a result of which each student wasted half his time in the first year groping for his own system. The remedy, they told Dunlop, lay in the provision of educated teachers who could speak English.[1] It was a remedy which would have sounded familiar to a mid-Victorian.

Legal training The decision in the early 1860s to concentrate the language teaching at Peking was at the expense, naturally, of practical experience at the major consulates. Though this gave rise to complaints among senior consuls, who found themselves saddled with consular assistants unprepared for their work and accustomed only to a mild degree of political work at the Legation, lack of practical experience was a small price to pay for reasonable progress with the language; there was time enough to train for routine consular duties at the first post.

But consular duties in China, as in the Levant, were in large part magisterial. The Order in Council of 9 December 1833 had transferred to the new Chief Superintendent all the powers exercised by East India Company representatives over the persons and trade of British subjects at Canton. A further Order of the same day created a Court of Justice at Canton, with criminal and admiralty jurisdiction over British subjects actually in China or within 100 miles of the China coast.

Unhappily, this left British official jurisdiction even less well defined than the similar transfer of the Levant Company's powers nearly a decade before. Sir George Robinson wrote to Palmerston on 1 July 1835 to point out the unfortunate effect on the expanding European trade at Canton should it become generally known that there was no way of enforcing on an unwilling party the settlement of *commercial* disputes, which had been ignored

---

[1] Notes on proposed administrative reforms in the China Service, prepared by Inspector T. D. Dunlop on 28 December 1937: PRO.FO/369/2461.

in the Order in Council. East India Company supercargoes, he explained, had found no call to intervene in commercial disputes between the few private traders in Canton; in affairs involving either political or commercial difficulties between a foreign trader and the Chinese authorities, they had ample powers, through the Company's monopoly of trade and shipping and through its authority to withhold a licence to trade, to subject British traders to whatever pressure proved necessary for the settlement of the case.[1]

Nothing seems to have come of Sir George's complaint, and Captain Charles Elliot, the Chief Superintendent, wrote to Palmerston a couple of years later to suggest that the current claims of some British merchants against one another might prove an appropriate opportunity 'respectfully to press the necessity for the early establishment of some formal and efficacious means of maintaining a state of good order amongst His Majesty's subjects in this country, and for the adjustment of disputes involving claims of money which may arise on the spot'.[2] A solution was deferred by the First Chinese War. With the restoration of peace by the Treaty of Nanking, consuls were established at the five Treaty ports, furnished, by the Jurisdiction Order in Council of 1843, with all necessary power and authority to exercise jurisdiction over British subjects within their districts. The Canton court, created by the 1833 Order, was transferred to the new colony of Hong Kong.

In China and in Japan (for which consulates with exterritorial jurisdiction had been created by the Treaty of 26 August 1858), the expansion of trade and the growing number of British subjects and protégés soon imposed an intolerable judicial burden on the more important consulates. Harry Parkes complained from Shanghai, the busiest of the consular posts, of the heavy judicial duties with which he was compelled to deal. Writing to his wife on 4 July 1864 he reported that he had convinced Sir Frederick Bruce, the retiring British Minister, of the heavy work at Shanghai; he thought Bruce would represent this at home, recommending the appointment of a legal adviser. Some months later he told his wife that the government was now alive to the need for a regular judicial officer at Shanghai to attend to the rapidly increasing judicial duties, already sufficient to engage the attention of any one man. Parkes had heard 'close upon a hundred stiff cases' since he returned to Shanghai in 1864, and though he tried to confine judicial work

---

[1] No. 1, *Papers relative to the Establishment of a Court of Judicature in China*, PP 1837-38 (128) XLI.
[2] Despatch dated 2 June 1837: No. 9, *ibid*.

to monthly sessions of about a fortnight each, it was difficult to keep it within these bounds.[1]

By the Order in Council of 9 March 1865 a Supreme Consular Court was constituted at Shanghai under a professional lawyer and judge, Sir Edmund Hornby, fresh from his successful organization of a similar judicial system at Constantinople. A few years later Sir Harry Parkes, promoted to the Tokyo legation, was pressing for a parallel subordinate establishment in Japan.[2] Certainly, the legal business had increased from one civil case and no criminal cases at Yokohama in 1859 to no less than 106 civil and 277 criminal cases ten years later; the total for the decade was 518 civil cases and 1001 criminal cases, with sixteen civil and five criminal appeals.[3] But it was not until 1878 that a Court was established at Yokohama, with a professional judge and assistant and general supervision over the consular courts in Japan.

Professional appellate courts, with an additional jurisdiction over all the more serious cases, reduced consular legal responsibilities to more reasonable proportions. But there was still, in the later part of the century as in the earlier, a clear need for legal training for recruits to the Service. Sir Alexander Johnston, in drafting Napier's first legal Instructions in the 1830s, had expressed his conviction that if the Instructions were precise and in plain terms, persons holding the office of chief superintendent in future, though not lawyers, would be able to execute their judicial powers without the assistance of a professional man.[4]

While this was probably true of the first years of jurisdiction when the volume of cases was still limited and the issues relatively simple, it was most certainly far from the case when civil jurisdiction was added to criminal jurisdiction, and when trade and British communities expanded all over the East. Lack of legal training rapidly became a serious handicap. Sir Edmund Hornby told his consuls from the beginning to become familiar with the principles of international law, for which 'the perusal of such works as those of Mr Wheaton and Dr Phillimore should be undertaken less as a task than as a recreation'. He recommended them further, if they sought to rise in their

---

[1] Quoted by Stanley Lane-Poole, *The Life of Sir Harry Parkes* (London, 1894), I, 473-7.

[2] General report on the Consular Service in Japan, 5 November 1869: No. 8, *Correspondencer especting Diplomatic and Consular Expenditure in China, Japan and Siam*, PP 1870 (c. 69) LXVI.

[3] Return dated 17 November 1869: Inclosure 2 in No. 11, *ibid.*

[4] Minute against the last paragraph of the undated draft Instructions, printed as Appendix No. 10, *Report from the Select Committee on Commercial Relations with China*, PP 1847 (654) v.

career or were anxious merely to perform their duties conscientiously, 'to devote some time to the study of "Stephen's Blackstone's Commentaries", the last edition of "Smith's Mercantile Law", "Chitty on contracts", "Arnould on Marine Insurance", "Byles on Bills of Exchange", "Taylor on evidence" and "Roscoe's Criminal Law".'[1] But when Hornby visited Yokohama in 1869, he found the judicial business of the consulate in a chaotic condition. He explained to Clarendon that he could not blame the consular staff for their lack of legal education, their youth, and their inexperience; they were conscientious enough in trying to get through the work. But the results were as unsatisfactory to them as they were to the public: 'Indeed, their position is very like what mine would be if your Lordship insisted upon appointing me to the post of chief surgeon to a London hospital.'[2]

Most of the legal business handled by the consulates could be settled with the use of a little common sense. 'Consuls by reading law may generally give fair and common-sense decisions', Sir Harry Parkes consoled an anxious consul at Nagasaki, 'and if they happen to be in error on technical points they can be set right on appeal ... I don't think you need indulge in self-depreciation, or at all events be disturbed by not being proficient in law.'[3]

But it was obviously more convenient if consuls could handle court cases confidently and without appeals, and in the last decades of the century elaborate provision was made for legal education. The subjects for which candidates for the Far Eastern Service were examined by the Civil Service Commissioners included the elements of English criminal law and the principles of mercantile and commercial law. Student interpreters, while at Peking, Tokyo, or Bangkok for their preliminary language training, were expected to pass searching examinations in the law of the countries in which they lived, and they were attached, when possible, to the staff of the Supreme Consular Court at Shanghai for a period of practical training. On their first long leave (due after five years' service) they were allowed an extra year in which they were expected to attend one of the Inns of Court and follow a course of law carefully prescribed by the Civil Services Commissioners. By making up the twelve terms during their second leave, they could finally be called to the Bar.

---

[1] Sir Edmund Hornby, *Instructions to Her Majesty's Consular Officers in China and Japan on the mode of conducting judicial business* (Shanghai, 1867), p. 2.
[2] Despatch dated 23 October 1869: No. 12, *Correspondence respecting diplomatic and consular expenditure in China, Japan and Siam*, PP 1870 (c. 69) LXVI.
[3] Letter to Consul Flowers, dated 27 November 1878, quoted by Lane-Poole, *Life of Sir Harry Parkes*, II, 252-3.

The results were satisfactory. By the turn of the century the administration of justice at the consular courts, with such reservations as are made below, was generally efficient and respected, and there had already been one Chief Justice and three Judges of the Supreme Consular Court in China who had begun their careers as student interpreters.

Career prospects From the mid-nineteenth century, the China Consular Service, administered from China with its own separate recruitment and training, was held up as the model to which all branches should aspire. The 1858 Committee expressed its 'unqualified approbation of this well-organized establishment', reporting that the new student interpreters had performed their duties with great efficiency. The 1872 Committee agreed with the Foreign Office, in the case of the Far Eastern Service, that the 'well-known close system of entry, education, and promotion, now long established, works well and gives satisfaction'. The 1890 Committee reported, briefly, that the consular service in China, Japan, and Siam, recruited from student interpreters selected by open competition, continued to be as efficient as when approved by the Select Committee of 1858.

The China Service was well in advance of the other branches. But it was far from perfect. The fact that it stood so well ahead of the others indicates only the distance which they had still to travel. For one, the China Service never developed a system of probationary appointments. Recruits were despatched straight to China, plunged immediately into surroundings and habits of mind quite distinct from those they had experienced at home, and expected to master an extraordinarily difficult language complicated further by a singularly unhelpful method of instruction. It was not surprising that a number of the student interpreters found their surroundings uncongenial and unsympathetic and their language problems insurmountable.

If the service were lucky, as it normally was, discontented or unsuccessful students resigned and sought their fortunes elsewhere. But there was no probationary period during which such men might be weeded out, and if they cared to stay, there was nothing that the service could do to eject them. A certain number of officers were always more or less in this position. Their promotion might be delayed or even withheld altogether, since permanent seniority depended on performance in the language examinations at Peking, but they could insist on remaining deadweights in the service until pensioned off at the full rate twenty years later.

These were the exceptions. Even for the majority, well-disposed though it may have been from the beginning, limited prospects, mediocre financial rewards, few prizes or distinctions, poor health, acted as positive disincentives to full and efficient service. Promotion in all three branches of the Far Eastern Service was extraordinarily slow. The service was what one senior consul called a 'death' service, with a fixed establishment of posts at all levels and promotion only on the occasion of a vacancy at one or other point in the establishment. Senior posts were few and far between, and junior posts out of all proportion to probable vacancies. During the 1860s, after the opening of a number of additional Treaty Ports, there were thirteen consuls to no less than five vice-consuls, eleven interpreters, twenty assistants, and an establishment of twelve student interpreters; and the remedy suggested at the time for understaffing at some of the consulates was not the creation of further senior posts (since these were limited by the number of Treaty Ports opened by the Chinese to foreign trade), but the addition of *six more* assistants. By 1890, when the subject came before the Royal Commission, some student interpreters had been in the Service for over ten years without promotion. One of the officers giving evidence, though he held the acting rank of consul at Tamsui, was in fact still a second-class assistant, and had received no promotion for ten years. There was at present, he said, an absolute block in promotion, which made it almost hopeless for those who were the juniors in the Service.[1]

Low salaries at the bottom of the profession increased the hardship of a promotion indefinitely postponed. To a young man in mid-Victorian Britain, with no means of his own, a salary of £200 p.a., his passage out to China, and two years of paid language study, seemed an attractive prospect. It became far less so when he arrived at his first post, faced the high cost of living, and had to put money aside for his passage home on leave. Furthermore, a student interpreter found himself surrounded by clerks in mercantile houses already better paid than himself and with better prospects. Young officers in the Imperial Maritime Customs Service, no more than his equals in education and far less selectively recruited, enjoyed double or treble his emoluments. In the late 1860s, according to Consul Caine of Hankow, a clerk in a mercantile house—for which only elementary educational qualifications were required—was provided (in addition to a salary of £250 by 100 to £700) with 'airy, well-furnished rooms, ice, punkahs, stable, and a well-supplied table, utterly beyond the reach of a junior Consular officer'.

---

[1] Minutes of Evidence, *Royal Commission on Civil Establishments*, PP 1890 (c. 6172-1) XXVII, QQ 29,904; 29,923.

The average salary of a bank agent at Hankow, excluding his house, servants, food, wines and coals, was about £1000 p.a. The Customs Service was salaried on the most liberal scale, with £2000 for the Commissioner, £1200 for the Acting Commissioner, and as much as £800 for Second Class Clerks, in addition to which they were provided with 'airy, roomy quarters rent free, and their expenses for chair coolie hire were also defrayed'.[1] Relative discomfort was endurable to the very young. It became intolerable when a consular officer grew older, thought of marriage and a family, yet found himself waiting for many years at a time between each meagre step on the promotion ladder.

Even at the more senior levels, the rewards and the prizes were slight. It was not until the end of the 1870s that Shanghai, a port of enormous consequence to British trade, was raised to a consulate-general—the first of its kind in the Service. And Shanghai, as the most important of the consular posts in China, was normally the peak of the consular tree.

At one point, before the diplomatic service stepped in and reclaimed its own, it looked as if the legations at Tokyo and Peking might be regarded as the prizes of the profession. There were obvious advantages, in posts so dependent on expert knowledge and so bound up with the administration of the local consular services, in taking the best and most experienced officers which those specialized services had to offer. Sir Rutherford Alcock, Sir Thomas Wade, Sir Harry Parkes, Sir Ernest Satow, and Sir John Jordan all began as consuls. As it turned out, they were the best of our diplomatic representatives in the Far East, superior by far to the tired and bewildered diplomats who replaced them. Lord Derby, indeed, told the 1870 Committee that it was, he thought, now the understood thing that the best of the consuls serving in China and Japan (of which countries, owing to the very special conditions in each, other diplomats knew very little) might fairly look forward to the missions at Peking or Tokyo.[2]

He underestimated the lure of a legation to the diplomatic service, even in the Far East. A timely reminder saved the day. 'No people in the world', Algernon Bertram Mitford, a Second Secretary in the Diplomatic Service, assured the same Committee, 'have such a keen eye for a gentleman, a man of high breeding, as the Asiatics':

---

[1] Inclosure 4 in No. 6, *Reports on Consular Establishments in China, 1869*, PP 1870 (c. 44) LXIX.

[2] Minutes of Evidence, *Select Committee on Diplomatic and Consular Services*, PP 1870 (382) VII, Q 2483.

Certainly in dealing with them I would employ men of as high breeding and birth as I could get to represent this country ... I would any day rather send a man who was a thorough gentleman, and a man of distinction (and ability, of course), to China, without any knowledge of Chinese, than I would send a man of the class to whom allusion has frequently been made in this Committee, as to whether they would not be proper men to appoint to the diplomatic service, however good his knowledge of Chinese might be.[1]

Deprived of an opening in the Diplomatic Service, consular ability might have found some reward in honorary distinctions, in that 'occasional bestowal of a C.B'ship, or honorary title' which Sir Rutherford Alcock had requested on behalf of the Service early in the 1870s. But the fact was that for more than thirty years after Sir Thomas Wade's C.B. in 1862, no distinction was awarded to a member of the Consular Service in China.

Salaries The original intention had been that the 'prizes' of the profession, so far as the Far Eastern Service was concerned, should be financial. The salary rates established for the first consuls, on the recommendation of Sir Henry Pottinger (the negotiator of the Treaty of Nanking), were substantially higher than the rate normally paid in the General Service. The Consul at Canton, at that time still the most important of the consular posts, received £1800 p.a., and his vice-consul £750; the consul at Shanghai, £1500 with a vice-consul at £750; and the consuls at the other three Treaty ports (Amoy, Foochow, and Ningpo), £1200 each. Although, under pressure in Parliament, these salaries were later scaled down, the consuls received substantial additional benefits in the form of free medical attendance, official residences provided and maintained at the public expense (or an allowance in lieu, calculated at the rate of one-sixth of their salaries), and a pension based not simply on salaries but also on the rent allowance.

There were several reasons for such exceptional treatment. East India Company salaries were on a generous scale, to which official salaries in turn had to bear some relation. The opening of the Treaty ports by force made it desirable that the new British establishments should be sufficiently dignified and impressive. Mercantile salaries in the East were high; even in the 1830s and 40s some of the clerks in the major mercantile establishments were

[1] *Ibid.*, QQ 4145, 4147.

earning as much as £1000 p.a., while the partners lived *en prince*. There was always the danger that consular officers might be attracted to Chinese or Japanese government service, or into trade. Sir Robert Hart, who was one of the first student interpreters to be appointed to China, was said to be earning between £10,000 and £12,000 p.a. in the 1870s as head of the Chinese Maritime Customs. John McLeavy Brown, Assistant Chinese Secretary at the Peking Legation, received £3000 p.a. when seconded in 1868 to the Chinese Government to accompany Anson Burlingame on his mission to Europe; soon afterwards he left the Consular Service altogether for permanent employment under the Chinese.

To some extent arguments for higher salaries in the Service were sustainable only in the short term; even in the case of competitive commercial salaries, the lavish standard of living of the early traders was severely curtailed under pressure of slow trading in the 1850s and 60s. But there were more enduring reasons. One was that in China, as in the Levant, far too many opportunities existed for a man to dabble in financial speculations. Consular officers, if kept too short of money in the midst of wealthy trading communities, could find it difficult to resist the ethos of Europeans in China—the overwhelming pressure to make a fortune by whatever means, however questionable, and to return with it as soon as possible to the West. There was the unfortunate case of George Whittinghame Caine, British Consul at Hankow, who was charged in 1873 before the Supreme Consular Court with embezzling £1041 14*s* 3*d* of public money. He was found guilty, sentenced to two years' imprisonment and died in gaol six months later.

High salaries were intended also to help compensate for the fact that China, for a Victorian at least, was exceptionally unhealthy. In the early years especially, the sickness and mortality rates were appallingly high. Rutherford Alcock estimated that the climate killed a consul every three years and juniors in proportion. Fifteen years after the opening of the Treaty ports, the total number of deaths was eleven, out of a consular establishment in China of twenty-five; four were consuls, one a vice-consul in charge, and all died at their posts, in the prime of life. Every European in China, Alcock explained, suffered from one of three maladies: he was covered from head to foot with sloughing boils of the most unpleasant and painful kind, lasting from three to four months; he was attacked by dysentery; or, in the freshwater valleys, he suffered from intermittent fever and was struck down with ague. These were the three penalties of life in China, and when they were repeated year after year, it was not astonishing that a man's powers were prostrated.[1]

In a despatch from the Peking Legation ten years later, Alcock calculated that allowing for sickness and leave of absence, the average proportion of non-effectives in the Service could not be taken at less than 25 per cent.[2] Sir Thomas Wade, writing the same year on the need to keep a sufficient supply of juniors at Peking, observed that from 20 to 30 per cent of the Service were generally absent from China on certificates of ill-health.[3] Even in 1928 it was estimated that some 25 per cent of the China Service suffered from impaired health; and the China casualty list, according to Inspector Dunlop in 1937, amounted to about two per annum over the past twenty-five years—ill-health, resignations, premature death, three suicides, three certified and sent to asylums, and ten compulsorily retired for such reasons as 'eccentricity' and native marriage.[4] Native marriages, though totally discouraged under the Victorians, became less of a disqualification with the arrival of a more rational age. Consul Wood, who married a Siamese girl during the First World War, was permitted to remain in the Service. But his career ended at Chiang Mai. The British Minister felt that Wood's marriage to a Siamese lady, simple, nice-mannered and pretty as she was, had not, rightly, commended itself to the Foreign Office. Wood had been told at the time that it would affect his promotion. He certainly would never be able to go to Bangkok, Batavia, or even Saigon with a Siamese wife—'the position would be intolerable'.[5]

It was the cost of living in China, and in the Far East generally, which was the ultimate justification of the higher salaries. Complaints of the high cost of living were constant and unremitting, so much so that in August 1869 Sir Rutherford Alcock despatched a circular to the China consulates explaining that since *every* consul was of the opinion that his was the most expensive post in China, and as they could not *all* be in that position, they should at once make a return of prices, provisions, wages, rents, etc., to guide H.M. Government in the approaching general revision of the China establishment.[6]

---

[1] Minutes of Evidence, *Report of the Select Committee on Consular Service and Appointments*, PP 1857-8 (482) VIII, QQ 1600-1.
[2] Despatch dated 29 October 1869: No. 4, *Correspondence respecting diplomatic and consular expenditure in China, Japan and Siam*, PP 1870 (c. 69) LXVI.
[3] Memorandum dated 10 March 1869: PRO.FO/366/341.
[4] Report dated 15 December 1937: PRO.FO/369/2461.
[5] Herbert Dering to Gregory, Bangkok, 2 July 1916: PRO.FO/369/896.
[6] The circular despatch of 12 August 1869 and the replies are printed in *Reports on Consular Establishments in China, 1869*, PP 1870 (c. 44) LXIX.

The response was overwhelming. Consul Charles Alabaster, writing from Swatow on 12 October 1869, observed that

> the appeals for allowances, and the impression your Excellency notes in every Consul's mind that his is the dearest port in China, are, truly considered, but evidence of the truth, that nowhere is the Consul's pay sufficient to enable him to take the position in society to which he is entitled and which he is supposed to occupy.

Actual living, Alabaster agreed, could not be expensive in a country where the people could live well for ten shillings a month and where foreign missionaries had survived on 120 dollars a year. Nevertheless, the scale of life demanded in the society of any port save those in which the missionary element was in the predominance was a problem, if not an impossibility, on the present salaries.

The details were filled out by other members of the Service. It was difficult and expensive to import stores from England, as much on account of extensive damage and destruction en route and in store as of freight. Yet Chinese fowls were small and tough, and there was 'about as much flesh on one English, as on four Chinese fowls'; 'one English is fully equal to two Chinese eggs'; pigs were such gross feeders that no foreigners could eat the meat; locally supplied meat was 'dry, tough, and juiceless'; fish, owing to the immense quantity of mud held in suspension both in the rivers and in the adjoining lakes and ponds, was 'scarcely eatable'; native flour was 'so coarse and full of grit as to be entirely unfitted for bread, or any culinary use whatever'. The high rooms in consular offices and residences, designed to be cool in summer, were difficult and costly to heat during the cold winter months, and coal, firewood and charcoal were the most expensive articles in daily use. Oil, for lighting the large houses, was another expensive item, and punkah coolies, for the hot months, had to be employed night and day. The consul at Hankow estimated that it cost him £88 a year for oil, wood, and charcoal alone. Life insurance was three times the price of the same insurance in England. Medical attendance for the consul's family, in a climate where the need for such attendance was frequent, was extraordinarily costly, even if the consul were entitled to claim free attendance for himself; and return tickets to Chefoo or Japan for wives and children on their annual change of air could come to £70, quite apart from expenses on the way and the cost of hotels. Fares home were high, and the expense of sending children to Europe for their education was formidable. Laundry, in a tropical climate, soon became a large item in the budget, increased by the rapid destruction of garments by the washerwomen; expensive imported woollen clothing, for the winter, was liable to the ravages of a great variety of insects. Even servants in China cost a great deal, 'on account of the number that must be kept'.

The fact was that cheap though China might be for the Roman Catholic missionary, unburdened with wife or children and prepared to live as the Chinese themselves lived, things were very different for those trying to live European style, in a society unadjusted to the needs of 'civilized' European existence. There was little or nothing in the way of organization at the majority of the Treaty ports for the cheap provision of the 'necessities' of European life. It was, one consul said,

> much as if a man, having to proceed occasionally by river from London Bridge to Westminster, had to buy a boat, purchase land, and build a boat-house on it, and hire a crew for that purpose, instead of being able to make the journey by the penny steamboats; or had to establish a soda-water manufactory in order to obtain aerated waters for his own use; or was obliged to purchase a valuable book that he had to refer to, instead of hiring it for a few days from a circulating library.

No doubt consuls were not inclined to underestimate the expense of life in China, particularly when they felt under popular pressure to economize. Alcock, in spite of all the evidence he had received, assured the 1871 Committee that though there were often representations of the difficulty of living and of the need for better remuneration, on the whole the China Service was considered a liberal service and fairly remunerated, even if the expenses of living were very high.[1] Yet he himself had told the 1858 Committee that liberally calculated though the salaries were, his expenses as consul at Shanghai had been £200 to £300 a year more than his salary.[2]

Losses on exchange might, from time to time, make the situation worse, even if consular salaries stood to benefit equally from gains. Salaries for the China consuls were paid in China, not in London, at an internal rate of exchange fixed by the Treasury. The currency situation in China was most diverse; market rates of exchange varied sharply from port to port, while dollars of one kind were acceptable at some ports and unacceptable at others. In 1858, for example, the British Government was paying 4s 9d for

---

[1] Minutes of Evidence, *First Report of the Select Committee on the Diplomatic and Consular Service*, PP 1871 (238) VII, Q 1451.
[2] Minutes of Evidence, *Report of the Select Committee on Consular Service and Appointments*, PP 1857-8 (482) VIII, Q 1571.

a Mexican dollar, which it then paid out to the consul at the official conversion rate of 4s 2d—a substantial gain for the consul. Yet at Shanghai, where the Mexican dollar was unacceptable and all payments were made in the pillar dollar, the consul, who nominally received a salary of £1500 p.a., did not actually draw (after the deductions and losses on exchange) more than £900 or £1000.[1] As a result of representations from the China consuls, the Treasury agreed to pay half the consular salary in London, for conversion as the consul himself saw fit. The boon, according to *The Times* in 1887, was more apparent than real, since it was accompanied by restrictions which placed the payments several months in arrear; very few consuls could afford this long delay, and in practice the great majority of them were obliged to go on drawing all their pay abroad, submitting to a discount which, during 1886, had ranged between 7 and 17·5 per cent.[2]

The problem of scale For all its faults the Far Eastern Consular Service by 1900 had developed into a relatively sophisticated organization, well in advance administratively of the General Service. The problem was to maintain for this organization, with its broad judicial, representational and administrative functions, some proper proportion between expenditure and return.

Early in 1869 three officials, J. Stansfeld, John M. Hay, and Louis Mallet, prepared a confidential memorandum for the Treasury violently attacking the scale and cost of the China Consular Service. Summarizing their criticisms, they found that there was a numerous and highly paid staff of officers posted at twelve or thirteen different ports; that the creation of the Supreme Consular Court at Shanghai had relieved these officers of the most responsible portion of the duties formerly imposed on them; that there were but few British residents at the majority of the ports; that the trade (which, judging by the fees, did not involve a very large amount of work) was largely coasting; and that the trend, which was for this trade to pass into the hands of the Chinese, would probably mean that it would require even less supervision in future. The officials concluded that consular establishments in China were unnecessarily large and costly, and that it would be possible to dispense with them in some instances without appreciable injury to trade. They expressed themselves as 'altogether opposed' to the opening of new

---

[1] Minutes of Evidence, *Report of the Select Committee on Consular Service and Appointments*, PP 1857-8 (482) VIII, QQ 642, 2010-29.

[2] *The Times*, 9 April 1887, 7d.

inland places to British trade: 'The course of commerce leaves room for doubt whether the foreign merchant would keep his footing if he got there; and, at any rate the experiment would not be worth the great risk which would attend it.'[1]

There was a great deal of truth in what they said. For reasons which have already been suggested, the original consulates in China had been established on a lavish and costly scale. It was, as the Foreign Secretary, the Earl of Clarendon, admitted in 1870, an exceedingly complicated and very expensive service indeed, not only on account of the cost of living, but also because of the difficulty of obtaining housing, the absence of so many officers on sick leave, and the absolute necessity of well-staffed consulates at the great Treaty ports for the protection of British interests.[2]

Staffing was indeed on a scale unmatched even in the Levant. When the consular establishment in China was discussed at the Supply Debate of 3 July 1857, J. Whiteside agreed that the Plenipotentiary should have £4000 p.a., and that Sir John Bowring could not be expected to dispense with the services of a secretary and registrar at £700 p.a., or with that secretary's first assistant and keeper of the records. But he was surprised to learn that on Sir John's staff this first assistant required a second assistant, that he required a third assistant, and that he again was helped by a fourth assistant. Then there was a chief secretary at £1000 p.a., no doubt a most important and dignified official, and 'as it was impossible for any man in that part of the world to do his duty without assistance', there was an assistant secretary at £600 p.a., supported by a corps of no less than thirteen supernumerary interpreters at £200 a year, assisted in turn by four Chinese writers or linguists. Whiteside supposed that these linguists were employed to teach the interpreters the language which they themselves, though interpreters, knew nothing about.[3]

Whiteside, as he himself confessed, was ignorant of conditions in China, and his remarks contained a number of misunderstandings. Yet at Shanghai in 1869, quite apart from the British consular officers, the staff of the Supreme Consular Court, and the consul's own domestics, the consulate employed a first and second linguist (Chinese), and a first, second, third and fourth writer (Chinese), a head gaoler and three constables (British), a Chinese compradore, ten office messengers, one gatekeeper, four coolies, four

---

[1] Treasury Memorandum, dated 4 February 1869: PRO.FO/366/341.
[2] Minutes of Evidence, *Report of the Select Committee on Diplomatic and Consular Services*, PP 1870 (382) VII, Q 3386.
[3] 146 *Parl. Deb.*, 3s, 938 (3 July 1857).

watchmen and a cook.[1] At Canton the subordinate Chinese staff consisted of a head writer, a writer, two linguists and a copyist, a constable, eight messengers, an office coolie, four boatmen, four watchmen, four chair-bearers, and a cemetery keeper.[2] British consular officers in China alone at the turn of the century, including assistants and student interpreters, numbered seventy-five; whereas the total strength of the salaried General Service was still rather less than 200.

The Treasury Memorandum of 1869 complained that the net annual expenditure on the China Service, after making allowance for fees (paid direct into the Exchequer), could not have been much less than £75,000 or £80,000, exclusive of the cost of so much of the naval squadron and military force at Hong Kong as was required to protect British trade—all this as a charge incurred on account of a direct trade of between £30 and £40 million. Indeed, according to Major Crossman's calculations for 1869, there was one consular officer at the Treaty Ports (exclusive of Shanghai) to every three firms, including banks, stores, hotels, etc., or one consular officer to every seven British subjects of the trading and missionary class.[3] For Siam, such a comparison became quite absurd. As J. Holms pointed out in the Commons early in 1870, British trade with Siam had averaged £10,500 exports and £12,000 imports over the last five years, while the expense for the Consular Service (the consul-general at Bangkok and his staff) was from £4000 to £5000 annually. In 1869, however, with a trade of only £3072, Britain spent £3450 on the consular establishment.[4]

But these were not the sort of terms in which the value of the Far Eastern Service could properly be expressed. The essential minimum of consular functions varied sharply from one part of the world to another. An 'uncivilized' or non-European area was immensely more costly in respect of protection, jurisdiction, and administration than a district in northern Europe or North America, where local justice and local facilities were more than adequate for most expatriate needs. Consuls in the Levant, in Africa, in Persia, and in the Far East were appointed often, and in China almost exclusively, to open up a new trade, and early trade returns could not hope to make much sense if related to the cost of the consulate itself. Of the five

---

[1] Return dated 21 July 1869: Inclosure 1 in No. 4, *Reports on Consular Establishments in China: 1869*, PP 1870 (c. 44) LXIX.

[2] Return dated 5 August 1869: Inclosure 3 in No. 5, *ibid*.

[3] Appendix 2, *Report of the Select Committee on Diplomatic and Consular Services*, PP 1872 (314) VII.

[4] 199 *Parl. Deb.*, 3s, 538-9 (18 February 1870).

original Treaty ports in China, Canton was already a trading centre, Shanghai rapidly became the major European trading centre in the East, but Amoy, Foochow, and Ningpo for years had virtually no trade at all. At Foochow during the first decade, the only foreign trade of any significance was opium, conducted (Alexander Michie noted) from a sea base beyond port limits, and invisible alike to Chinese and British authorities 'in the sense in which harlequin is invisible to clown and pantaloon'.[1] Consular posts, however, were kept open, and by 1870 Foochow, reduced at one point to a vice-consulate for lack of trade, had become the chief centre for the tea export trade; both Amoy and Ningpo, though ranking after Shanghai, Canton, Foochow and Hankow, stood with Tientsin and Swatow as ports of major commercial importance.

Further pioneer consulates were established as China gradually opened her doors to world trade. By the Chefoo Convention of 1876, H.M. Government was allowed to send consular officers up to Chungking to watch the condition of British trade in Szechwan (western China). Alexander Hosie was sent to man the post in 1881, but British merchants were not permitted to live there or to set up establishments and warehouses while the steamers had not penetrated so far up the Yangtsze, and it was many years before the first steamer reached Chungking.

Chungking became an important centre in time, but a post like Wuchow, down in the south, never justified itself. There was nothing to do at Wuchow except watch the mud and the river from the consulate, high on its banks, chat with the local representative of the Asiatic Petroleum Company or the British American Tobacco Company, register the mass of official papers arriving daily from Peking and London, and compile the quarterly accounts. H. A. Ottewill, who had spent twenty-one miserable months there in 1910-11, believed that a more benighted spot, from a consular point of view, could not exist: 'During the whole period, apart from some work done in the mornings, I worked one afternoon only. . . . Consular work at Wuchow degenerated into a dull struggle between a blighting boredom and a rotten climate.'[2]

But Wuchow's failure could not discredit the whole policy of planting consulates in advance of trade. It was a policy which had had a fair measure of success elsewhere in China. Outside China the Far Eastern Service in 1869

---

[1] Michie, *The Englishman in China*, I, 122.
[2] Minute on Vice-Consul R. A. Hall's report on Wuchow of May 1927: PRO.FO/371/12408.

included a consul-general and his staff at Bangkok, an envoy extraordinary and consul-general at Tokyo, and consuls at Yokohama, Nagasaki, Hakodate, Osaka and Niigata. Though Siamese trade was inconsiderable, important political considerations existed so long as Siam and the British Empire shared 700 miles of frontier to the west and the French were established at Saigon to the east. As Sir Harry Parkes told the 1872 Committee: 'Siam and Japan [where there was a total foreign trade of nearly £8 million in 1868] must be looked upon as the saplings of commerce, which, if you take care of them, will grow into great trees eventually.'[1]

Nor was the Treasury argument on the changing character of the China trade entirely acceptable as a reason for reducing the consular establishment. The Foreign Office argued in reply that the direct import trade (as well as the export trade) in articles of European consumption, was still in foreign hands; that the passing of the indirect and distributing trade to the Chinese might be expected to increase the demand for foreign goods and provide further employment for foreign ships; that the trade, direct or indirect, had been created by, and was dependent on, the continued existence of the foreign consulates; and that so long as the distributing trade was carried in foreign vessels, consular establishments would continue to be required at both subsidiary and primary ports for supervision and control.[2] Sir Rutherford Alcock, questioned by the 1872 Committee, conceded that the combined diplomatic and consular service in China and Japan might cost, on average, about £100,000 a year. This, he said, was in relation to a direct trade of £40 million, the employment of 3 million tons of shipping, and a revenue to the Indian Empire and Britain herself of very nearly £9 million. The £100,000 did not amount to two per 1000 of the trade and scarcely more than one per cent of the revenue.

> How is it possible to conceive [he asked] that this is not money well spent if, as I have the firm conviction (and I think I could establish it to the satisfaction of the Committee), that trade is entirely contingent upon the presence, and the protection, and the influence of centres of foreign powers, such as the consulates supply?[3]

[1] Minutes of Evidence, *Report of the Select Committee on Diplomatic and Consular Services*, PP 1872 (314) VII, QQ 1124-5.
[2] Memorandum dated 17 February 1870: No. 1, *Reports on Consular Establishments in China: 1869*, PP 1870 (c. 44) LXIX.
[3] Minutes of Evidence, *Report of the Select Committee on Diplomatic and Consular Services*, PP 1872 (314) VII, Q 1395.

Whatever the truth in this—and it is none too easy to imagine a complete halt to trade in the absence of consulates—there was certainly something to be said for the argument in the early days; and it was these early days, during which the Far East was opened to world trade, which in turn left Britain with the legacy of an expensive and elaborate Far Eastern consular organization. The real problem was the difficulty, experienced equally in the Levant, of reducing an existing establishment, even when the special conditions which had justified an inflated establishment in the first instance were themselves transformed. Back in 1850 Richard Cobden had moved the abolition of the Ningpo and Foochow consulates, on the grounds that there was no trade. Palmerston agreed that if this had happened at other ports around the world, he would have had no hesitation in abolishing the establishments. But, he added, there were some very peculiar circumstances attached to the China trade. The right to establish the consulates had been won by treaty, and the government was reluctant to surrender two of the five Treaty Ports without negotiating for substitutes, which it had already tried to do without success.[1]

Once a consulate had become rooted in an area, foreign interests and investments tended to gather and the occasional ship to call. It became difficult to abandon the post, not only out of a natural reluctance to desert a community which had established itself on the security of that post's existence, but also because an unsupervised group of Europeans, however small, could act as the spark for a dangerous and costly political explosion.

It was precisely the outlying ports which were frequented by the less respectable elements among the Europeans, away from the control and discipline of the larger European communities; it was here that the trouble was most likely to start, and here that there was most need for an experienced consul to anticipate it. There was only one British trader at Newchwang in the late 1860s, the agent of a large British firm. If importance had been measured by the fee book the consulate would have been closed at once. But consular duties in an outlying province could be most time-consuming. The investigation of a single case of homicide, in 1864/5, had occupied Consul Meadows for several days, since it had occurred at a town lying a considerable distance inland, to which he and two assessors had had to travel in the depth of a Manchurian winter. And there was a very troublesome class of English and American residents to be governed at Newchwang, the pilots, together with the crews of British vessels carrying bean-cake to

---

[1] 113 *Parl. Deb.*, 3s, 123, 125-6 (22 July 1850).

the south.¹ No one could tell what might happen if the consul were withdrawn. Four or five indiscreet or ill-conditioned residents, Alcock warned, might do more mischief in a week or a month in a country such as China, than Her Majesty's Minister or the Foreign Office could repair in a year.²

Relations with British residents Alexander Michie, who regarded himself as something of a spokesman for the British trading community in China, considered that it was no reproach to the China merchants that they should have seized every opportunity for gain, totally irrespective of the general policy of their country:

> It was not for them to construe portents, but to improve the shining hour. And if it should at any time happen that the action of private persons, impelled by the passion for gain, embarrassed a diplomatist in his efforts to bring about some grand international combination, the fault was clearly his who omitted to take account of the ruling factor in all economic problems. The trade was not made for Government policy, but the policy for the trade, whose life-blood was absolute liberty of action and a free course for individual initiative. . . . Nothing certainly could ever justify any trader in foregoing a chance of gain for the sake of an ideal benefit to the community, even if it were likely to be realized.³

It was with this kind of attitude that the consuls had to contend; without their interposition, it might have had disastrous consequences. The arrogance of the British commercial community in China increased rather than diminished with the passage of years. In the early days of the Company and of the first Superintendents, the merchants were still to some degree in awe of Chinese authority; they were aware of their dependence on Chinese goodwill, they made some effort to develop friendly contacts with the Chinese, and they even, it seems, attached some importance to acquiring a knowledge of the Chinese language.⁴ But as their exterritorial privileges

---

¹ Arguments included in Sir Thomas Wade's rebuttal of the Treasury report, 10 March 1869: PRO.FO/366/341.
² Despatch dated Peking, 29 October 1869: No. 4, *Correspondence Respecting Diplomatic and Consular expenditure in China, Japan and Siam*, PP 1870 (c. 69) LXVI.
³ Michie, *The Englishman in China*, I, 250.
⁴ Captain G. Balfour's evidence (former Consul at Shanghai): Minutes of Evidence, *Report of the Select Committee on Commercial Relations with China*, PP 1847 (654) V, QQ 4847-51.

and immunities extended, and as the foreign communities increased in size within their own, self-governed 'concessions', this contact (such as it was) between foreigners and Chinese was lost. Consuls and missionaries alone made any consistent attempt at closer relations. The traders conducted their business increasingly through Chinese compradores, and made contact with Chinese officialdom only through their consuls.

The military defeats suffered by the Empire, and the increasing gap between Chinese and Europeans created by technological advance, fed European contempt. Consul C. A. Winchester, in a bitter comment on the Treasury Memorandum of 1869, asked whether the Treasury officials really expected the policy of moderation towards the Chinese and the renunciation of force, which they so desired, to be executed by trading consuls selected from among the British merchants:

> I should like to place them for a few days, or even hours, in the society of one of the ports. They would discover, ere they left it, that what my friend Colonel Neale called the determination to resist pressure from those about him, was the first and most important duty an English Consular servant in China or Japan has to learn.[1]

While for consuls the importance of the language and the need to accumulate knowledge of Chinese habits and ways of thought was continually emphasized (forming, indeed, the ultimate rationale of their specialist service), for businessmen the opposite came to be the rule. British communities, whether in the Levant or in the Far East, tried to re-create English conditions of living, shutting themselves off further than ever from the natives. Valentine Chirol estimated that certainly not more than 5 per cent of the Englishmen in the big commercial houses at Shanghai in the first decade of this century had any knowledge at all of Chinese: 'In fact it is considered rather bad form to sweat at "beastly Chinese", or whatever it is, or to take any interest in what they do.'[2] Sir Ernest Satow, a former British Minister at Tokyo and Peking, felt that there was no difficulty whatever for any man in the East to learn the language if he wished to do so, but in China he would be looked upon as rather a strange creature for having such a desire: 'If a man, instead of going to the cricket ground or the tennis ground, or to the country club, or to the golf course, withdrew himself for the

---
[1] Memorandum dated 24 February 1869: PRO.FO/366/341.
[2] Minutes of Evidence, *Report of the Committee on Oriental Studies in London*, PP 1909 (Cd 4561) XXXV, Q 1427.

study of Chinese, people would shun him, probably—he would be socially shunned; that is not an exaggerated picture.'[1]

This attitude helped inevitably to widen the gap not only between the merchants and the Chinese but between the merchants and their own consuls. Consuls fluent in Chinese, accustomed to Chinese ways of thought, were suspected of becoming 'orientalized', of being inclined always to see things from a Chinese point of view. Even Sir Edmund Hornby, no linguist himself, felt after experience both in the Levant and in the Far East, that too much favour was shown to men of linguistic attainments in the Eastern Services: 'The study of languages, especially such languages as Turkish, Persian, Arabic, or Chinese, becomes an all-absorbing pursuit—nay, the latter language really seems to affect the brain.'[2]

It was true that the consuls, in exercising their jurisdiction and disciplinary powers over British subjects under exterritoriality, were aligned with authority sometimes directly against the interests of their own nationals. The Chinese Government, as one of the first British consuls pointed out, had given up the right of jurisdiction over foreign subjects, and it was 'therefore the duty of England to replace that natural authority which we have taken from China'.[3] Lord Napier's judicial Instructions of 1834 were prefaced by the observation that the British Government had two objects principally in view in conferring criminal jurisdiction. The first was, that by giving Napier authority over all British subjects in China, he would be enabled to maintain a proper respect among the Chinese for the British character, and thereby facilitate intercourse between the nations and increase British trade. The second was to satisfy the Chinese Government that the British Government had no desire to screen its subjects from punishment, if really guilty, but merely to provide that they should have a fair trial before conviction.[4]

In the desire to fulfil the second of these, it is quite possible that British consuls were inclined to bear too harshly on British nationals, especially in the days when a small incident might blow up into a major riot or even a massacre. It can be imagined how troublesome British sailors could be in an

---

[1] Minutes of Evidence, *Report of the Committee on Oriental Studies in London*, PP 1909 (Cd 4561) XXXV, Q 2079.

[2] *Autobiography*, p. 139.

[3] Minutes of Evidence, *Report of the Select Committee on Commercial Relations with China*, PP 1847 (654) V, Q 4875 (the witness was Capt. G. Balfour).

[4] Undated draft, prepared by the Rt. Hon. Sir Alexander Johnston and submitted to the Foreign Secretary, printed as Appendix 10, *ibid*.

explosive, xenophobic Canton, where in October 1845, according to the *Chinese Repository*, drunken sailors had done great damage, 'raving mad, beating themselves, beating one another, and like a Malay "running amuck" sauntering through the narrow streets, pelting the Chinese, and overturning and smashing whatever they could that came in their way'.

But sailors were a cross which all consuls in every part of the world had to bear. More serious in the long run was the arrogant, offensive behaviour which even the most respectable Englishman felt appropriate towards the Chinese. The Compton incident at Canton was an example of the extent of the problem, and of the complications which British consuls were likely to face when trying, in the interests of peace and fair play, to enforce discipline among British residents. In the mid-1840s Chinese itinerant salesmen had taken to frequenting the gardens in front of the factories at Canton, causing annoyance to the foreign merchants and to their wives, for whom these gardens were the only spot where they could take the air. But the situation was tense at the time, and the British consul, Francis McGregor, refused to take immediate action for fear of causing real trouble. One of the leading British merchants, Charles Spencer Compton, took it into his head to show his fury first by kicking over a fruit stall in a street near the factories and then, four days later, by striking a Chinese. The Chinese rioted, the Europeans were forced to defend their factories against imminent sacking and lived in hourly expectation of massacre, and several Chinese were killed.

McGregor, who bore the brunt of restoring sane relations with the Chinese, was understandably angry and fined Compton the maximum permitted to a consul, $200. Compton was a wealthy man and could easily have paid, but he was egged on by the other merchants to make an issue of it, and took the case to Hong Kong. McGregor's verdict was supported by Sir John Davis, governor of Hong Kong and British plenipotentiary in China, since it was obvious that, in the general interest, behaviour such as Compton's could not be tolerated. But the consul, and later Sir John himself, had interpreted the law mistakenly in certain respects, and the Chief Justice at Hong Kong had no alternative except to reverse the verdict. The strained relations between merchants and governor over this issue was a principal factor in Sir John Davis's resignation and retirement from China in March 1848.

The Compton case indicates how indispensable it became, whenever some part of China (however insignificant) was opened to Europeans, to plant a consulate on the spot to keep order. James Matheson, M.P., one of the most prominent of the China merchants and a resident in China from 1818 to 1842, explained when questioned about the Compton case that if a Chinaman had jostled Compton intentionally, he had no doubt that Compton would have pushed him off, and perhaps knocked him down; he (Matheson) would have done the same.[1] Matheson complained that in every case where an Englishman got into trouble in China, the British authorities, instead of protecting their own subjects, almost invariably took the side of the Chinese. His was a common complaint among British residents, and a correspondent, writing from Shanghai nearly forty years later, contended that British ministers had usually acted on the assumption that their function was to bridle and repress their countrymen, one after another succumbing to 'the curious delusion that on their pair of shoulders rested the onus of conserving the Chinese Empire, to which superstition all common mundane interests must be sacrificed'. 'Nothing', he concluded, 'more paralysing to all reasonable action could be conceived.'[2]

While there was just a hint of truth in the complaint, if not in the conclusion, since British consuls were inclined to go out of their way to prove to their Chinese critics the impartiality of British justice, there was equally, as Consul Balfour told the 1847 Committee, a serious responsibility on British consuls to see that justice was done to the Chinese, and a related responsibility on the British Government, if it wished to ask for further privileges for its subjects, to extend consular representation 'so as to insure to the Chinese perfect safety and security'.

Balfour's own solution back in 1847 was to impose on all British subjects a limit of travel beyond Shanghai of about thirty miles; he was not prepared to answer for peace between the two nations without some such restriction. It was the duty of the consul, he argued, to stand between his own people and the Chinese, and to see that both parties carried out their duties to each other. He quoted, as an illustration of the variety of opinion which existed on the subject of freedom, the example of a Reverend George Smith who had lived for some time in a Buddhist temple about twenty miles from Ningpo. Smith, who in other respects was moderately sane on the subject of the relations between Chinese and foreigners, described how he had gone one evening to an out-temple, a few hundred yards from his own, where two priests were stationed:

> They appeared to take pleasure in exhibiting the ugly little idols which were enshrined within the principal hall. As I remonstrated with them,

---

[1] Minutes of Evidence, *Report of the Select Committee on Commercial Relations with China*, PP 1847 (654) v, Q 2710.
[2] *The Times*, 11 October 1883, 3f.

in the presence of many other persons, on their folly in asking me to worship such senseless blocks, I proceeded to point to the idols with my umbrella, whereupon the principal idol soon gave way to the force with which, in my carelessness, I poked its various parts. The whole assemblage burst into a loud laugh, on which I was emboldened to show how little the other idols could help themselves. As I gave them a slight thrust they trembled, tottered, and tumbled from their thrones. The people laughed heartily, as the priests tried, for some time in vain, to make one of the idols maintain its sitting posture, the fall having disordered its component parts. Thinking this liberty might put their good humour to too severe a test, I became more serious in my manner, and spoke of the wrath of God on those who thus dishonoured His name. The only intelligible reply which I received was, that it was the Chinese custom to worship idols.[1]

Next to habitual criminals, Sir Edmund Hornby once complained, missionaries were 'the most troublesome people to deal with in the world'. He would, he said, back a Protestant missionary to do more harm in a limited space of time than any other human being.[2] And it was the consuls whose duty it became to restore order and sanity between the races.

Exterritoriality In the circumstances, it was not surprising that the focus of resentment against Europeans and their consular representatives, more particularly in the later years, was the system of exterritorial rights, privileges and immunities.

The Chinese Empire, like the Ottoman, had found it convenient to delegate responsibility for control and discipline to the leaders of the separate foreign communities. With the exception of cases of homicide, for which the Chinese Government insisted on the full penalty, this devolution continued, without serious difficulties, until the middle of the nineteenth century. Captain Elliot, the Chief Superintendent, in a memorandum on jurisdiction prepared before the first Chinese War (before, that is, any real pressure had been brought to bear on the Chinese Government) assured Palmerston that the Chinese Government was 'willing and anxious to devolve upon that of his Majesty the task of ordering these things according to its pleasure: indeed

---

[1] Quoted in Minutes of Evidence, *Report of the Select Committee on Commercial Relations with China*, PP 1847 (654) v, QQ 4326-8, 4433-5.
[2] Hornby, *Autobiography*, p. 124.

I have already ascertained that there would be no difficulty in securing from the Provincial Government, an Edict declaratory of its consent to the establishment of police and judicial institutions'.[1]

Formal consular jurisdiction began with the new consulates in 1843. Unlike the consulates, it was not a direct consequence of British victory in the Anglo-Chinese War; consular jurisdiction was a mere extension of a principle recognized as perfectly acceptable for the regulation of the British factory in prewar Canton. But the point was that the extension was out of all proportion to the original concession—a concession in any case intended at first only to cover foreign individuals, but which was now taken also to include foreign businesses. As the number of British settlers multiplied, as their commercial and financial interests increased, and above all, as they formed enclosed foreign concessions and settlements at Shanghai (1846), Canton (1859), Tientsin (1860), Chinkiang, Hankow and Kiukiang (1861), and Amoy (1903), what had originally been a sensible arrangement for the government of a small group of foreigners safely enclosed within their factories, became a radical infringement of Chinese sovereignty. The International Settlement and French Concession within Shanghai had developed, by the twentieth century, into the nucleus of a vast commercial and financial centre, with a population, under foreign control, of over one and a quarter million, less than 50,000 of whom were foreigners. Shanghai, as Sir Eric Teichman said, was 'the chief monument and citadel of the exterritorial régime'.

It was a situation which was bound to lead to trouble sooner or later. But the trouble, when it came, was aggravated by inequality of justice before the European and Chinese tribunals. On the whole, except in periods of real national hatred, the Chinese courts behaved fairly, often ruthlessly, towards cases brought by European plaintiffs against Chinese defendants. Where a complaint could genuinely be made, it was rather at primitive policing and at the failure to apprehend criminals than at any refusal to do justice in the Chinese courts themselves.

But policing was often equally inadequate among Europeans, before the twentieth century. It was simple enough to evade justice by flight, permanent or temporary, from the consular district, and consular constables were in no condition to cope with difficult arrests. In the early days, before constables were recognized as a necessary and allowable expense, the consuls had to

---

[1] Enclosed with despatch dated 2 June 1837: Enclosure in No. 9, *Papers relative to the Establishment of a Court of Judicature in China*, PP 1837-8 (128) XLI.

execute their judgments themselves. Sir Rutherford Alcock used to say that he had served as 'everything from a Lord Chancellor to a Sheriff's officer'. Questions of nationality were often raised to evade a particular consular jurisdiction, and even when a European was brought before his consular court, the punishment he received was likely to be substantially less than he deserved. When a Chinese murdered a European, he was pursued relentlessly into court and hurried to his execution. When a European murdered a Chinese, the consular court either acquitted altogether or declared the case to be one of manslaughter, for which the murdered man's relatives were compelled to accept a small money payment in lieu of punishment.

A typical case was that of the British merchant in Japan who, while illegally shooting wildfowl, was accosted by a Japanese policeman; he shot and seriously wounded the man. Rutherford Alcock, British minister in Japan at the time, imposed the maximum penalty—a fine of 1000 dollars, three months' imprisonment, and banishment from Japan. But the judgment, when brought before a jury of English settlers at Hong Kong, was reversed, the merchant was acquitted, and damages of 2000 dollars were declared against Alcock himself with the intimation (at the suggestion of the judge) that if the court had had full jurisdiction, the damages would have been from 15,000 to 20,000 dollars more.

Alcock, in his reminiscences, pointed to the contrast between England and the East. In England, if a man of good family became involved in a broil, he was arrested, kept in prison overnight, and fined or imprisoned by the magistrate the next morning—and nobody thought twice about it. But let the same happen at a Chinese or Japanese port, where the whole safety of the community depended on good behaviour, and let the consul try to inflict a fine or imprisonment on the British resident, and he was fortunate if the local press did not ring with denunciations of consular tyranny and if he did not find himself subjected to an action in the Supreme Court at Hong Kong, with the risk of vindictive and ruinous damages: 'This is an evil, not of yesterday, but of twenty years' duration, and one that cries very loudly for remedy.'[1] *The Times*, commenting on this and similar cases, concluded that the Supreme Court of Hong Kong was 'the greatest nuisance in the East'; its verdicts 'have sometimes been so whimsically unjust that they are fitter for a jest book than for a grave discussion'.[2]

---

[1] Sir Rutherford Alcock, *The Capital of the Tycoon: a narrative of a three years' residence in Japan* (London, 1863), II, 14-17, 26.
[2] *The Times*, 13 July 1863, 8e.

The worst abuses, where justice was denied altogether, expired with the creation of the new Supreme Consular Court at Shanghai, which assumed appellate jurisdiction in place of Hong Kong. But in other respects exterritoriality was as open to criticism as ever, and abuses multiplied as the European communities expanded. The British consular courts were always an imperfect instrument of justice. Underpaid subordinates were open to corruption. A Chinese writer, paid at the rate of $30 a month, had no alternative other than to take his cut from the Chinese appearing before the consular court; what is more, his consul was perfectly aware of the practice, but condoned it because he could not afford to pay more.[1] The consuls themselves were often inexpert in the law, and sometimes eccentric in applying it. Paul King, a commissioner in the Customs Service, described the procedure at Swatow. The consul, William Gregory, was notably weird, even for the China Service. He normally never changed out of pyjamas, but when King first saw him he was expecting a Chinese official call and was dressed in a strange mixture of bed clothes and uniform. A tubby little man, he disliked tight clothes, 'so his unfastened tunic displayed a sleeping shirt hanging out at the waist over a black leather belt that somewhat vaguely kept in position a pair of rather tumbly white duck trousers'. In his consular court Gregory insisted on using an extraordinary, archaic dialect which only he and his Chinese tutor could understand and which Gregory defended as the only true and unadulterated form of Chinese speech. The evidence (in Swatow dialect) was translated first into English for the benefit of the English defendant, then from English into mandarin, which the tutor could understand, and then from mandarin into the archaic dialect spoken by the consul; on a hot afternoon it was a positive miracle if justice were done. The British Government, King remarked in the context of a further example of consular eccentricity, 'seemed to give enormous latitude to the vagaries of its Consular officers in the Far East and appeared quite oblivious of the amount of mental and moral suffering a man charged with judicial functions, but off his moral balance, could cause in out-of-way places'.[2]

Political conditions The China Consular Service in the twentieth century faced all these problems, aggravated by the xenophobia so characteristic of the age. It was Britain's great misfortune, and the misfortune of the consular

---

[1] Consul Markham to Sir Rutherford Alcock, Chefoo, 20 July 1869: Inclosure I in No. 14, *Reports on Consular Establishments in China, 1869*, pp 1870 (c. 44) LXIX.

[2] Paul King, *In the Chinese Customs Service* (London, 1924), pp. 33, 37-8, 259-60.

service which represented her, that by occupying during the nineteenth century the principal place in China's foreign trade and investment, in the settlement and administration of the larger foreign communities, and in the creation of so many of the Sino-foreign administrative agencies—the Customs, the Postal Services, the Salt Gabelle, and the Railways—she attracted to herself the full force of Chinese resentment during the decades of bitter nationalism which followed the overthrow of the Manchu dynasty in 1911-1912. Sir John Pratt explained that

> All the aims and aspirations of Chinese nationalism may be summed up in the phrase—the 'unequal treaties'—and the unequal treaties were almost entirely the work of Great Britain.... Almost every question involving China's sovereign rights—exterritoriality, the International Settlement, the Mixed Court, tariff autonomy, the Customs Administration, foreign control of revenues—was primarily an issue between China and Great Britain.[1]

Conditions were not as bad for all three branches of the Far Eastern Service. By the 1894 Treaty, which came into effect five years later, Britain abandoned her exterritorial rights in Japan. In Siam, all British subjects, of European or Asiatic origin, were brought under the jurisdiction of the Siamese national courts by the Treaty of 10 March 1909. But Siam at the time was under very close tutelage to Britain, and Herbert Dering, Minister at Bangkok, told Gregory privately in 1916 that the Siamese were rather over-reaching themselves. Prince Srasti, the head of the Dikha Court of Appeal, to whom the Siamese judges kowtowed, was autocratic and highly corrupt; unfortunately, he was maternal uncle of the king and brother of the Minister of Foreign Affairs: 'He is an old Oxford man and ought to know better. A first class liar and humbug too.' The police and gendarmerie, Dering added, were under the command of a 'Serene Highness of considerable age and limited intelligence, chum of the Queen Mother'. The British Advisers, two former police officers, thought that things might yet right themselves without Dering's intervention, but if not, he proposed to 'speak to the king in person and tell him to get rid of his mamma's old dodderer'.[2] British interests in Siam were still in safe hands.

As for China, where British influence and control were far slighter, Britain had undertaken to relinquish her exterritorial rights by Article 12 of the

---

[1] Sir John Pratt, *War and Politics in China* (London, 1943), p. 200.
[2] Private letter dated Bangkok, 2 July 1916: PRO.FO/369/896 (f. 183655).

Mackay Treaty of 1902. But this was to come into effect only when H.M. Government was satisfied that the state of Chinese laws and the arrangements for their administration warranted it, and it was on this caveat that Britain rested her argument against surrendering her rights over the next twenty years.

The First World War, in respect to the Capitulations and the Powers, gave much the same opportunity to the Chinese as it had to the Turks. Before the war the Powers, whatever their disagreements among themselves, had maintained a united front against relaxations in their rights without substantial compensatory concessions. The war destroyed this front, permitting Turkey to denounce the Capitulations unilaterally, and China, encouraged by the Allies, to withdraw exterritorial rights from the Germans and Austrians. Since the rights had been founded on what was taken to be the unsuitability of Chinese courts and law for Europeans, and since the Germans, the Austrians, and now the Russians had been handed over without hesitation to their mercy, the foundations of the European argument were already insecure when the Washington Conference met and considered the point in 1921-22. At Washington, the Allies reaffirmed the intentions declared in the Mackay Treaty and passed conditional resolutions in favour of the restoration of tariff autonomy and the removal of exterritoriality.

Until now, every step had been taken reluctantly and under steady, increasingly well-informed and effective Chinese diplomatic pressure. But Britain was also under strong popular pressure in China herself. Constant riots, rough-handling and boycotts, directed particularly against the British, developed out of an increasing awareness of Chinese nationalism and of the degradation of China. In the mid-1920s the British Government at last decided to swim with the tide. In face of violent and sustained opposition from local British interests, more especially from the journalists and lawyers whose livelihood depended on the continuance of exterritoriality, Britain returned to China the Shanghai Mixed Court (taken under complete foreign control during the troubles of 1912), and handed over the Hankow municipal administration to a mixed body of British and Chinese; furthermore, Britain declared her readiness to sweep away some of her exterritorial rights without waiting for the Mackay caveat to be realized, to grant tariff autonomy to China, to modify other municipal administrations, and to surrender Weihaiwei.

There can be no doubt that the British Government would have been only too happy at this point to have abandoned administrative and judicial responsibilities altogether; the shift in policy at the Foreign Office was complete.

> Our difficulty [the Under Secretary of State told the Commons in 1927] is that there is no established Government with whom we can negotiate. China keeps on being a changing and shifting scene, and you may be negotiating with a general one day and the next morning he may have changed over with the whole of his army to the other side. Therefore, the only solution today is patience.[1]

By the late 1920s relative stability had been restored. The armies of the Kuomintang had fought their way up through China, most of the war lords were subdued and dispersed, and a common authority at last existed. Britain recognized the Nationalist Government of the Kuomintang in 1928, and conceded the first major step towards the end of the 'Unequal Treaties'— tariff autonomy (achieved in practice, subject to interim agreements on the chief articles of import, by May 1930). Though the civil wars continued, with the Kuomintang mopping up the remaining centres of opposition, the British Government made further moves towards the abolition of exterritoriality. The main obstacle was the very considerable foreign investment in the Treaty ports, particularly in Shanghai. Every concession was bitterly resisted by the resident foreigners, lawyers, property-owners and investors, and it was only in the face of strong local opposition that, in 1930, the safeguards and conditions imposed at the time of the rendition of the Shanghai Mixed Court in 1926 were abandoned.

Consular jurisdiction remained. The Chinese Government threatened the unilateral abolition of exterritorial rights, but it had no wish to force the issue, and Britain, still in full retreat, was anxious to continue negotiations. The Japanese coup in Manchuria in the autumn of 1931 put an end to further attempts at treaty revision. But Japanese encroachments and the invasion of 1937 meant that the troubles of the unfortunate consuls were far from over. China's entry into the European war on the side of the Allies in December 1941 strengthened, on both sides, the arguments for a renewal of negotiations, and by a treaty signed in Chungking, 11 January 1943, H.M. Government finally relinquished all exterritorial rights in China.

Conditions of service before 1914 The fate of the consular service in China was, of course, closely related to the disastrous politics of the period.

---

[1] 211 *HC Deb.*, 5s, 2385 (14 December 1927).

'Dissatisfaction with the local policies of the British Government', Sir Eric Teichman once said, 'has always been a characteristic of the British treaty-port communities',[1] and the dissatisfaction reached an hysterical pitch after the British Government's decision to adopt a sane policy of withdrawal and concession in the mid-1920s. Sir John Pratt believed that 90 per cent of the complaints of apathy, weakness, and lack of support were due merely to the fact that the consul was carrying out the new policy laid down by the Foreign Office.[2] But there was more to it than this. A great deal remained to be put right in the Service itself.

One of the problems investigated by the 1914 Commission was the serious decline in applications for the Far Eastern Service. The Chief Clerk, John Tilley, told the Commission that it was very difficult to get candidates at all for the China Service,[3] and it was certainly true that on one occasion, not long before, places had had to be offered, in default of direct candidates, to young men who had taken the previous Foreign Office examination. Yet only a couple of decades earlier, the Service had had no difficulty in recruiting at a high level in competition with some of the best openings under the Crown.

It is not difficult to see why this should have been the case. 'Open' competition, for one, had been replaced by 'nomination' as a result of the recommendations of the Walrond Committee in 1903. Some concern had been expressed at the social level of some of the recent entrants, under open competition, and nominations were intended to filter out the socially unacceptable. The effect on entry to the Far Eastern Service is difficult to measure. But 'nomination' meant that the examinations were no longer publicly advertised, while the field for recruitment was undoubtedly narrowed, even for those who were aware of the vacancies, by knowledge of an obstacle so formidable as a Foreign Office Board, fully equipped, as were all Englishmen at the time, with a battery of socially-sensitive antennae.

Furthermore, it was not at all unlikely that applications from any direction had declined as a direct result of political troubles, widely reported, in China. The Boxer Rebellion was one factor, since it had attracted great public interest at the time. The overthrow of the Manchu dynasty, followed by the unbroken civil troubles in China after 1911, could scarcely fail to be another.

---

[1] Sir Eric Teichman, *Affairs of China* (London, 1938), p. 283.
[2] As quoted by Inspector Dunlop, in his report on the Service, 15 December 1937: PRO.FO/369/2461.
[3] Minutes of Evidence, *Fifth Report of the Royal Commission on the Civil Service*, PP 1914-16 (Cd 7749) XI, Q 43,334.

Yet the most positive reason for the decline in applications was obviously a serious deterioration in the conditions of the China Service itself. At the turn of the century, the Far Eastern and Levant Services offered careers with all the prestige of competitive entry, with prospects of transfer, promotion and generous retirement. After 1903, conditions for entry into the General Service were much the same as for the specialized services, while further career prospects for General Service entrants were incomparably better. An effort was made to restore the differential in 1910 when, partly as a result of pressure from Professor Giles (the professor of Chinese at Cambridge and a former Far Eastern consul), the level of the examination for the China Service was raised to that of the Indian Civil Service, with the idea that the same class of men should be attracted. It was only in part successful. When the 1914 Commissioners questioned the Secretary to the Cambridge Appointments Board, he replied that what happened was that the China Service got those who came low down on the list; men were selected who were qualified for the Service, but they very often got the offer of an Indian appointment which they usually chose in preference.[1]

The preference was understandable enough. A young man joining the Indian Civil Service might normally expect to be an acting collector after ten years, at almost £1000 p.a., with prospects of promotion and pension far superior to those open to Far Eastern consuls. In the China Consular Service, by contrast, students began at £250 p.a., after which they were promoted to acting assistants at £300. It took about six years to get to the grade of second class assistant at £350, and ten and a half years in total to reach first class assistant at £400 p.a., the salary paid to a young man of twenty-two at a first-class Shanghai business house. Taking an average since the beginning of the century, it was calculated that it took about fifteen years for an officer in the Far Eastern Service to reach commissioned rank as vice-consul.[2]

Sir John Jordan argued from Peking, in the course of some general proposals for the reorganization of the China Service, that while £250 p.a. was adequate for students during the two years they spent learning Chinese (when free quarters were provided at the Legation), the period of greatest hardship came in the years immediately after leaving Peking. Jordan knew of at least one assistant with eight years' service who was in receipt of only £300 p.a.: 'This can scarcely be considered an attractive prospect for a

---

[1] *Ibid.*, Q 41,636.
[2] Foreign Office memorandum, dated September 1917: PRO.FO/369/972.

capable married man, thirty-two years of age, who after an expensive education has devoted himself to public service in a distant and undeveloped country.'[1]

It was not a living wage. Unless a man had some small private means, it meant that he had either to be prepared to remain a bachelor, or to drop out of society altogether (which was good neither for his work nor for his career). The situation for senior officers was rather better, but even here the salaries were out of line with those obtainable elsewhere. A businessman, writing to *The Economist* shortly after the war, explained that a new entrant to the Siam Service was paid £300 p.a. (equivalent to a local shipping clerk). He added that, since promotion was strictly by seniority, no consular officer had the least chance of receiving pay enough to marry and live in comfort until he was over forty years of age. Even at the top of the consular tree, the pay of £1200 p.a. was that of an accountant in the local exchange banks, and anyone with the faintest acquaintance with commerce in the Far East knew that a first-class commercial man could command triple this pay with infinitely better prospects.[2] The complaint was common to consular officers over the world. No consul, said George Michell from Pará (Brazil), could afford to live in the style of the managers and officials of the local British firms, nor could he hope to retire in comfort at the same age.[3]

There was only one grade of consul in the Far Eastern Service, with £800 p.a. Consuls-general were divided into three classes, £900, £1000, and £1200, with local allowances of £100, £200, and £600 respectively; but in China, only the consul-general at Shanghai was in the £1200 category. When Ernest Holmes, consul at Shimonoseki in Japan, was questioned before the 1914 Commission, he agreed that the leave question, which had recently been readjusted, was entirely satisfactory to the Japanese Service. But the level of pay, especially for senior officers, was far less so. It took a man, on average, between fifteen and seventeen years to reach full consul in the Japanese Service at £800 p.a. Since the days when Holmes first went out to Japan (in 1897) the cost of living had risen some 75 per cent, and salaries had not increased in proportion. It cost him a quarter of his salary to educate two children at school in Brussels, for though there was European education of a kind available in Yokohama, it was not advisable, for 'climatic reasons, social reasons, and various other reasons' to keep children in the East after

---

[1] Despatch dated 22 October 1917: PRO.FO/369/971.
[2] *The Economist*, 30 August 1919, 365-6.
[3] Memorandum dated 25 June 1918: PRO.FO/369/1047.

nine or ten years of age. Holmes complained that it was extraordinarily difficult and expensive to get a European-style house at Shimonoseki. One of the Commissioners asked him whether this expense was because he insisted on living in European style. He replied: 'Naturally. One cannot live in Japanese style. . . . That is impossible for Europeans.'[1]

Conditions of service after 1914 The more generous rate of allowances payable after the war was certainly an improvement. But recruitment remained painfully slow. In the Siam Service, with its very restricted opportunities for promotion, recruits were virtually unobtainable. A Foreign Office memorandum on 'Possible Economies in the Far Eastern Services', written in response to the pressure for economy in 1921, pointed out that there were still five vacancies for student interpreters in the Siam Service. Of the three sent out to Bangkok the previous year, two had resigned to take up more remunerative employment outside. The Siam Service had been 'literally starved', and it was impossible to cut down the personnel. If an economy had to be effected, it would be better to close down the Service altogether.[2]

The China Service, in spite of its greater size and flexibility, experienced much the same difficulty. After the war, when the General Service examination was brought into the Class I category, the examination for the China Service had been assimilated to that of the General Service. Successful candidates in the combined examination were extremely reluctant to go out to China. It was no longer right, or just to the China consuls themselves, Inspector Dunlop observed in 1937, to continue to regard them as an élite and to make special demands on them. Before 1914 they had entered the service by an examination superior in grade to the former examination for the General Service. Since the institution of the common entrance examination in 1922, China, as a rule, had been the field for entrants in the lower half of the examination lists.[3]

Sir John Pratt suggested that this was in part because the China consuls faced permanent exile from civilized ways of living and thought, finding their society either in a Chinese community with whom only the exceptional man could make intimate contact, or in a Treaty Port foreign community

---
[1] Minutes of Evidence, *Fifth Report of the Royal Commission on the Civil Service*, PP 1914-16 (Cd 7749) XI, QQ 42,754; 42,818; 42,843-6; 42,859-60.
[2] PRO.FO/369/1642.
[3] Report dated 15 December 1937: PRO.FO/369/2461.

'whose interests and outlook are limited'. In part also, it was because their work had become 'a constant battle against the encroachments of nationalism', putting consuls under a heavy strain and responsibility which might often involve the very lives of the communities under their charge. The most serious factor of all, Sir John added, was the fact that the proportion of senior posts to junior posts was so small that there was a perpetual block in promotions.[1]

Michael Palairet, writing from the Peking Legation a decade before, had argued along much the same lines, except that he felt that the existence of a waiting list of candidates for the Chinese Maritime Customs had proved that the lack of *consular* candidates could not be due merely to a general disinclination for service in China in the current disturbed political conditions. Palairet put it down rather to the whittling away of the various privileges and concessions which had formerly been enjoyed by the China Service in recognition of its more responsible, varied and onerous duties vis-à-vis the General Service, to the soaring cost of living in China, and to the extremely slow promotion. There was general dissatisfaction, he said, in the junior ranks of the Service, more particularly among veterans of the First World War, who had joined the Service at ages ranging up to twenty-eight and who could see little prospect, under present conditions, of attaining even a consul's rank before the age of fifty.[2]

Pratt had referred to a 'certain demoralization' which had 'crept over the service', and to the sense of grievance from which the members of the Service generally were suffering. The focus of this, in the China Service as in the Levant, was the chronic block in promotion. The 1919 reorganization of the General Consular Service brought no comfort to the Far East. No additional posts were created in the Far Eastern Services as a result of the Steel-Maitland proposals, and the effect of the postwar reforms was to level out the differences between the General Service and the China Service, leaving both under substantially the same conditions as regards pay and age of retirement with the China Service much inferior in respect to promotions.

By the mid-1920s, the promotion block was worse than it had ever been. Sir Miles Lampson formed a special committee at the Peking Legation in 1928 to investigate the whole problem and suggest a remedy. Its main recommendations were to readjust a number of posts, reduce the optional age of retirement, and improve remuneration by marriage allowances or

---

[1] Memorandum dated Foreign Office, 21 February 1935: PRO.FO/369/2400.
[2] Note dated Peking, 4 March 1925: PRO.FO/369/1867.

otherwise 'in order to compensate for the special difficulties and responsibilities of service in China'. The committee recognized the force of the argument that the tardiness of promotion in China was mitigated by the system of allocating 'acting' allowances and rank to officers in charge of posts above their grade during the absence of senior officers on leave. At the same time, while making the fullest allowances for this, it emphasized, that promotion in the China Service had been 'painfully slow'.

> During the past ten years, of the 17 officers promoted in that period to Consul's rank, only two became Consuls before the age of 40. The average length of service of all these officers at the time of promotion was 21 years and 4 months and their average age was 43 years and one month. Two of the number only received promotion at the ages of 47 and 48. The position has moreover steadily and progressively become worse; at the present moment the average age and average length of service of the ten Grade I Vice Consuls are 42 years and 6 months and 21 years respectively, including two officers of 45 years of age. Altogether there are 16 officers of over 40 who await promotion to Consular rank, including six who have not even yet attained the rank of Grade I Vice Consul.[1]

The situation in the 1930s, in spite of the creation of some additional higher grade posts as a result of the Legation Committee's recommendations, was no real improvement. The average age for promotion from vice-consul to consul was forty-three, in contrast to forty in the other Services, and for promotion to consul-general fifty-two, as against forty-nine. Steel-Maitland's recommended figures were thirty-five and forty-eight respectively.

The ratio of senior to junior posts in the service was so ill-conceived—twenty-eight senior posts to thirty-six junior (vice-consul and below), in contrast to one hundred senior and sixty-six junior posts in the General Service—that it was only the comparatively low retirement age for Far Eastern officers which prevented the promotion block from ending in total disaster. It had long been the practice for Far Eastern consuls to retire at about the age of fifty, a practice which made some financial sense to the consuls concerned because, allowing for the additional time calculated for service in an unhealthy climate (two years to count as three), a consular officer became entitled to a full rate of pension after only

---

[1] *Report of the Legation Committee on the Reorganization of the China Consular Service*, October 1928: PRO,FO/369/2020.

twenty-six to twenty-seven years' service. Technically, although entitled to the full rate at between forty-eight to fifty, consuls were not permitted to retire until they reached sixty-five. The Treasury was reluctant to consider any modification in the rule for fear, as one Treasury official put it, that 'such a change would involve legislation and legislation would be likely to provoke reactions both in other branches of the Consular Service and elsewhere in the public service'. But the official, who was speaking at a meeting at the Foreign Office in 1928, added that he thought that by not scrutinizing too critically the medical certificates furnished by consular officers and by accepting as sufficient a certificate that an officer was unfit to return to China, the Treasury already made it fairly easy for an officer who had earned a full pension to retire of his own accord, and for the Foreign Office to induce an inefficient officer to do so. The Treasury, he concluded, would be quite prepared to continue this practice while the China Service remained a close service.[1]

This was, admittedly, a recognized loophole in the regulations, and it was one which was widely employed. The Legation Committee of 1928 calculated, for example, that between 1893 and 1913, twenty-four officers retired between the ages of forty-six and fifty-five after twenty-seven years' service, in addition to four others who retired after a shorter term. If nothing else could be found, the Treasury was prepared to accept 'neurasthenia' as sufficient, provided it could be certified that it rendered an officer unfit for further service in China. In at least one case the doctors certified that a consul was suffering from 'peripheral neuritis of toxic origin', which, as the British Minister reported, was due, although he hesitated to say it, 'largely to intemperate habits'.[2]

The ease with which a medical certificate was obtained and accepted could, on occasion, create something of a public scandal. It was perhaps just a little provocative when an officer, who had retired on full pension on the grounds that continued residence in China would endanger his health, returned to the Far East, as robust as ever, to make his fortune in trade. But the real problem was that the advantage was all in one direction. Consuls could normally retire early if they wished; they could not be compelled to do so, though they might be persuaded. Short of outright dismissal, it was impossible to retire a man against his will before the age of sixty-five, and inevitably there were cases where officers who had really long outlived their usefulness remained at their posts to the bitter end. It was not until

---

[1] Note on a meeting at the Foreign Office, 4 December 1928: PRO.FO/369/2020.
[2] Sir John Jordan's despatch of 7 April 1916: PRO.FO/369/866.

1921, by the China Service Order in Council, that the Secretary of State was given the discretionary power to call upon officers to retire at sixty; subsequently, compulsory retirement at that age might almost be said to have become the rule.

The Legation Committee of 1928 recommended that the age of retirement should be reduced, optionally, to fifty-five, and Sir Miles Lampson, in forwarding the Report to London, added the comment that he himself attached more importance to this 'essential reform' than to any other proposal in the Report.[1] The Tomlin Commission again recommended that the limits of retirement for the Far Eastern Services should be reduced by five years from sixty/sixty-five to fifty-five/sixty.[2] But the reform was not completed until the Superannuation Act of 1935, and even then the motive was primarily to redress the injustice suffered by consuls since the 1876 Act by giving them the option of retiring at fifty-five, rather than to supply the state with the power to retire officers no longer useful to the Service: the state was still limited to compulsory retirement at sixty. By contrast, the principal firms in China during the 1930s aimed at promoting their future managers and directors to posts of major responsibility by the age of forty, and at retiring them between the ages of fifty and fifty-five.

Amalgamation Sir Arthur Steel-Maitland's Committee had recommended, in its 1919 Report, that the organization of the Far Eastern Service should remain as it was. There was to be no change in the existing system of entry and training or in the method of acquiring languages, other than the addition of a year of economic training before departure for the East with a further year on the occasion of the first long leave. Maitland's view, as he told the Commons, was that though there might be some point in considering whether the Siam Service, because of its very restricted career opportunities, might not profitably be amalgamated with the General Service, there was no alternative to retaining the China and Japan Services as separate services, for the reason that 'everyone conversant with the extraordinary differences of conditions in China and Japan, linguistic, racial, and others, knows that they have to be considered by themselves'.[3]

---

[1] Covering despatch dated 24 October 1928: PRO.FO/369/2020.
[2] *Report of the Royal Commission on the Civil Service 1929-31*, PP 1930-1 (Cmd 3909) x, para. 685-6.
[3] 116 HC Deb., 5s, 528 (21 May 1919).

It was true enough that exterritoriality in China, though not in Japan or Siam, survived through the interwar period, and that the China consuls continued to bear the exceptional responsibilities imposed by their judicial functions. It was true, too, that political conditions in China deteriorated even further after the time of which Maitland was speaking, and that consular duties required special political expertise, or at least a special capacity for physical endurance. Mob violence, strike pickets and boycotts were the common experience of consuls in the 1920s, and during the worst years, 1925-26, cases of direct violence against consular officers themselves were reported from Chinkiang, Swatow, Chungking, Têngyuëh, Hankow, and Amoy.

In other respects, the arguments against a common consular service covering the whole world, for the Far East as for the Levant, were losing much of their original force. The homogeneity of the areas covered even by the three separate branches of the Far Eastern Services was far less obvious as outside posts were added (both in recognition of the quality of the officers, and as some relief to the restricted opportunities for promotion in the two smaller branches). Even before the First World War, the Japan Service filled the posts at Manila and Honolulu and the Siam Service at Batavia and Saigon; the only outside post for the China Service was Weihaiwei, where an officer was seconded for duty under the Colonial Office. Korea and Formosa, now within the Japanese Empire, were staffed from Japan.

The extension and diversification of the Services not only weakened their claim to independent existence on grounds of regional expertise—three of the eight posts in the Siam Service in the interwar years were in the Dutch East Indies, and one at Saigon—but also, naturally, affected what had been the first reason for their existence, the common language. Siamese in any case was not a particularly difficult language, and, as it happened, in three posts Dutch was the only language necessary, and in a fourth, French. The Japan Service already had to cope with Korean, Chinese (in Formosa), and Spanish (in Manila). Furthermore, particularly in China and Japan, many nationals were now speaking far better English than consular officers could hope to speak Chinese or Japanese. In China this had had its effect comparatively early even at the level of the consular courts. Sir Walter Hillier explained in 1908 that a Chinese could occupy the position only of plaintiff or witness in a British consular court, not of defendant. If he came as plaintiff, it was up to him to suit the requirements of the court and to have his documents and evidence translated. Very few actions were brought by Chinese against British in the consular courts; the plaintiffs in any case were normally businessmen or Chinese compradores, fluent enough in English or in pidgin.[1]

Nor was it so obvious that the independent administration of the Services by the legations at Peking, Tokyo, and Bangkok was still such an advantage. In the early days of slow communications and comparatively simple, even primitive, administrative controls and techniques, there could be no doubt that administration was best done on the spot; the Foreign Office itself offered no competition. As the diplomatic service tightened its grip on diplomatic posts in the East, the legations tended to lose contact with, and control over, the consuls in the area; diplomatic officers serving short tours in the East were naturally unfamiliar with the merits of their subordinates and unequal to the organizational skills which such large and diverse services demanded. The main burden was taken by the Oriental Secretaries at the legations, promoted from the consular service, while the diplomats merely played at administration. In China the channelling of all consular correspondence and administration through the Peking legation had, by the interwar years, created a permanent bottleneck at which decisions were delayed and mishandled and information lost. Adequate staffing at the Far Eastern legations would no doubt have solved the problem. To this day it has been found worth while to maintain independent local administration of consular officers from such centres as Paris and Washington. But it is expensive to duplicate administrative services, and the Paris and Washington administrations almost certainly owe as much to history and to individual empire-building as they do to a genuine concern for the taxpayer's pocket.

All these points came under discussion during the 1920s, in conjunction with the more pressing problem of the promotions block to which the smaller services were peculiarly liable. The Levant Committee, taking into account both the ending of the special responsibilities attached to exterritoriality and the career problems of small services, recommended in its 1933 Report that the proposed amalgamation should include not only the Levant Service, but also the Japan and Siam Services. The Committee had taken some evidence on China, but the trend of the evidence, from Sir Miles Lampson, Sir John Pratt and Sir Eric Teichman, had been against amalgamation, and the Committee felt that, in view of the existing situation and the special requirements of the service in China, it might be 'inopportune to introduce any major changes in the China branch for the present'. The Japan and Siam

---

[1] Minutes of Evidence, *Report of the Committee on Oriental Studies in London*, PP 1909 (Cd 4561) xxxv, QQ 565-71.

Services became, as far as new entrants were concerned, a part of the amalgamated service in 1934. The China Service remained independent.

The Levant Committee had agreed, however, that the question of applying its recommendations to the China Service should be further explored in consultation with the Minister at Peking (now, 1933-35, Sir Alexander Cadogan). It was soon obvious that the China Service as a whole was in favour of amalgamation, and that the opposition came rather from some of the more senior and conservative officials within the Foreign Office. Sir Alexander Cadogan, in a despatch from Peking, 20 April 1934, reported that he had circularized the China consuls, the great majority of whom were strongly in favour of applying to the China Service the limited measure of amalgamation already put in force for the other specialized services. The general opinion was (a) that present conditions in China warranted amalgamation; (b) that language difficulties could be avoided if officers unable to speak Chinese were posted to the larger ports where there would always be a Chinese-speaking officer on the staff; (c) that amalgamation would make it possible to arrange transfers to other countries if this became desirable for reasons of health or in order to obtain a wider experience; and (d) that promotion would be accelerated. Cadogan was in full agreement, and added the further point that one unfortunate result of the current tendency in China to close down the consulates at so many of the smaller ports was that the China Service was unavoidably a service of contracting opportunity.[1]

The first reaction at the Foreign Office was favourable, and the suggestion was made that the amalgamation should go straight ahead, taking effect, with the other amalgamations, from the 1934 examination. To this there was dissent from two separate directions. Senior officials at the Foreign Office had always felt uneasy about permitting transfers between the Far Eastern and General Services for fear of blocking the expectations of officers in the General Service. Lord Dufferin had already shown himself most indignant at Consul-General H. H. Fox's proposal, in 1917, that China consuls might be posted to Europe as a reward for long and meritorious service in the East; the head of the Consular Department felt that provision for China consuls who were no longer fitted for work in their chosen sphere should be sought in some direction other than Europe, the preserve of their colleagues in the General Service. J. A. C. Tilley, the Chief Clerk, agreed.[2] When the

---

[1] PRO.FO/369/2358.
[2] Memorandum on proposed reforms in the Consular Service in China, 22 February 1917, and minutes: PRO.FO/369/922.

proposal was resurrected in 1934, Victor Wellesley did not believe that the theory of reciprocity between the General and China Services would work out in practice as smoothly as was hoped. He was inclined to think that the General Service was more likely to become a dumping ground for the senior members of the China Service, while the higher vacancies in China would continue to be filled from the China Service itself. Wellesley agreed with Sir George Mounsey's previous minute that it would be better to proceed gradually. Exterritoriality and the language difficulty, he had always understood, were insuperable obstacles against amalgamation; the language difficulty might have diminished, but exterritoriality still existed.[1]

The other objections were more serious, coming as they did from a better-informed quarter. Sir John Pratt, a former consul-general in China and for many years Adviser on Far Eastern Affairs at the Foreign Office, criticized the proposals on two main grounds: first, that there would not be a sufficient number of experts, under the original proposals, to provide the thirty or so officers with expert knowledge agreed as necessary for the efficiency of the service; second, that the scheme proposed by the Levant Committee, by which consular recruits sent to China would be kept there for only a year, was wasteful and liable to lose good young men to China. Sir John's objections were met by an undertaking to recruit at the rate of two a year (sufficient, when taken with the existing establishment, to maintain the necessary number of experts), while new entrants were to be put through the full, two-year training period.

The compromise which was to make the amalgamation of the China Service universally acceptable was summarized by David Scott in the following terms. Existing China consuls would remain members of the China Service, except that they would have the opportunity, in accordance with the recommendations of the Levant Committee, to take tours of service elsewhere in the world. All new entrants into the consular service would become members of a single service embracing all quarters of the world, including China. Those who, after passing the common examination, were sent to China would go in the knowledge that they would not be compelled to serve their whole career there; they would have the opportunity, as members of an amalgamated consular service, of spending at least a quarter of their active career out of China, 'thus avoiding the staleness and restricted outlook which is liable in certain cases to result from long years of service exclusively in China'. Such officers would receive their two years' language

[1] Minutes on Sir Alexander Cadogan's despatch of 20 April 1934: PRO.FO/369/2358.

training in Peking, be posted, until their first long leave, to a China consulate, and return, after that leave, for a further tour of duty in China. In this way they should be able to acquire such a knowledge of China and the Chinese as would not be obliterated by a subsequent tour of duty out of China.[1] Scott's Memorandum was approved by Sir Robert Vansittart and by the Secretary of State, Sir Samuel Hoare. It was put into effect in time for the Civil Service competition of the summer of 1935.

The results of the amalgamation are difficult to estimate, since the amalgamated consular service survived for less than a decade. Applying simply to new entrants, its effect on the promotion block was slight, and to this extent the opposition of the conservatives at the Foreign Office had been successful. The main reason for the failure to apply the amalgamation to all members of the service (as the China consuls, with a view to promotion opportunities, had themselves wished) was not the need to safeguard their rights or their *esprit de corps*—both of which were under strain at the time— or even to skirt round such tricky establishment problems as the different rate of outfit allowances and travelling expenses in the China Service, the distinct leave regulations, and the lower retirement age. It was to avoid an outcry from the General Service at the immediate creation of a joint seniority list, and at the subsequent flooding of consular promotions with senior officers from the East.

Certainly T. D. Dunlop, when he inspected the China Service in 1937, felt that the amalgamation process would have to be accelerated if it were to remove the real grievances of the China Service and the corresponding complaints from British merchants:

> The deadening effects of slow promotion, and the demoralizing and cramping effect of prolonged absence from western countries, which led to dissatisfaction and discouragement in the Levant Service, have operated on a larger scale in China, the land of misery and futility.

But, he concluded, if he had had any doubts as to the wisdom of amalgamating the China Service with the other consular services, they had been dispelled by his short tour in China and Japan.[2]

[1] Memorandum dated 31 May 1935: PRO.FO/369/2401.
[2] Report dated 15 December 1937: PRO.FO/369/2461.

Epilogue

Two deep-seated grievances were common to all consuls before 1943: their low status, and the inadequacies of the prospects and rewards open to them in the service. It was precisely these grievances which Anthony Eden's *Proposals for the Reform of the Foreign Service*, published as a White Paper in 1943, were intended to solve. By the amalgamation of the three branches—the Foreign Office and Diplomatic Service, the Commercial Diplomatic Service, and the Consular Service—into a single, new Foreign Service; by common recruitment from as wide a field as possible; by full training in economic and commercial affairs; by proper personnel management and control; by the exercise of new powers for the early retirement of officers unsuited to the highest posts; by a fair provision for subordinate staff, it was

> intended to re-equip the Foreign Service to meet modern conditions and to create a Service which shall be better able not merely to represent the interests of the nation as a whole, but also to deal with the whole range of international affairs, political, social and economic, and so constitute an adequate instrument for the maintenance of good relations and mutual understanding between the United Kingdom and other countries.[1]

The millennium had come at last ... or had it?

The 1943 reforms were designed to broaden the social basis of recruitment to the Foreign Service. Full amalgamation was to apply only to new entrants to the Service. At this level there was to be complete equality of opportunity, both in the initial selection and in the career openings, whether commercial, consular, or political.

The intention was laudable, but there is no evidence, even now, that it has been fulfilled. The consular service before 1943 may have lacked the

---

[1] *Proposals for the Reform of the Foreign Service*, PP 1942-3 (Cmd 6420) XI, para. 4.

standing of the Foreign Office or the diplomatic service. But it offered a red-brick, middle-class point of entry into the public service overseas. The effect of the amalgamated recruitment into the new Branch A of the Foreign Service—the equivalent of the Administrative Class of the Home Civil Service—although democratic in intention, was, ironically enough, to close this point of entry, or at any rate to make it much narrower and more demanding.

What happened was that a reform which was designed to open posts in the senior branches of the Foreign Service to a wider field of recruitment, in practice opened the best of the former consular posts to the sort of candidates who, before the war, would have been satisfied only with a diplomatic position. More candidates in total may have entered for the new, combined diplomatic/consular/commercial competitions. But whereas before the war social barriers streamed that competition into independent channels, after the war the candidates who had formerly entered only for the diplomatic competition tended also to scoop the pool of the amalgamated consular and commercial vacancies.

The tendency was emphasized, unfortunately, by the new Method II competitions, adopted at first experimentally by the Foreign Office but later as the main form of entry into the Service. The old prewar Civil Service entry, Method I, had depended first and foremost on severe academic tests. A *viva voce* examination was introduced as part of the competition after the First World War, but it was academic performance which contributed by far the greater proportion of marks to the total. An unprepossessing youth from the lower middle class, if academically gifted, might still win his way into the Civil Service on academic performance alone. To safeguard against this, the Foreign Office had insisted on its own selection board to weed out the socially unacceptable. The board had operated to great effect on entry into the Foreign Office and diplomatic service, but it had not been felt necessary to apply quite such high social standards to the consular service.

The 1943 reforms dispensed, democratically, with the Foreign Office's own selection board. But the Foreign Office remained convinced of the value of what it preferred to call 'character and personality' in the conduct of relations abroad. When it came to the choice between the Method I and Method II competitions, the Foreign Service predictably selected Method II, where the emphasis was placed almost exclusively on interviews and personality tests, with a relatively elementary qualifying examination as the first stage of the process. It is ironical that it should have been a Labour Foreign Secretary who made himself responsible for the experimental adoption of Method II. Ernest Bevin, in this respect at any rate, was a simple man; he believed that what he was doing was to open the door to simple souls like him, sound in mind and limb but indifferent performers at examinations. The Foreign Office saw no reason to dissuade him.

No doubt it is true that the panels of interviewers at the preliminary testing centre and at the final interview before the Civil Service Commissioners have made every effort to be objective; they have no reason to be otherwise. But it is equally true that young men of upper-class origin and home background, of expensive and superior education, have a substantial advantage in personality tests of this kind. A candidate of less fortunate circumstances, and particularly a candidate from the working class, has still a great deal of leeway to make up by the age at which he is likely to be examined for entry to the Foreign Service. Furthermore, the requirements laid down for the preferred candidate for the Foreign Service, which must serve to guide the C.I.S.S.B. examiners and the final selection board, are likely to mirror the persons responsible for drawing up the requirements in the first place. A man selects another for what is familiar in him, not for what is exotic, alien, or strange.

Whatever the reasons, the facts speak for themselves. Dr Alan Thompson, introducing a debate on the subject of the selection and training of Foreign Service officers, 22 March 1960, pointed out that over the first years of the new, combined Foreign Service competition, 1948-56, nine out of ten successful candidates were from the Registrar General's occupational classes I and II (that is to say, they were the sons of company directors and members of the professional and managerial classes); only the last came from the semi-skilled classes; and there were no sons of unskilled workers. Moreover, 94 per cent of successful candidates were from Oxford or Cambridge, 3 per cent from the Scottish universities, and the remaining 3 per cent from London and abroad. Eight out of ten successful applicants came from public schools.[1] The Plowden Committee found that, over a ten-year period, only 28 per cent of the successful applicants for the senior branch of the Foreign Service came from direct grant and state schools; from the universities Oxford contributed 59 per cent, Cambridge 35·2 per cent, and all the remaining universities only 5·3 per cent between them.[2] The Committee declared its dissatisfaction with both school and university background

---

[1] 620 *HC Deb.*, 5s, 459-60.
[2] *Report of the Committee on Representational Services Overseas*, PP 1963-4 (Cmnd 2276) XI, paras. 357-65.

of new entrants to the Service, but in 1968 Oxford and Cambridge were still supplying two-thirds of the entry.[1]

Whether or not it is possible to accept the official view, put to the Commons by a Labour Minister of State in 1967, that 'the selection process is completely non-discriminatory and it selects the best people who come before us',[2] it cannot be disputed that the class of candidate accepted for the consular service before the war stands little chance of finding a place in the expanded Branch A as it has existed since 1943. The 'democratization' of the service by the 1943 amalgamation has had the outcome, paradoxically, of *raising* the social tone of the combined service, rather than of depressing it. Amalgamation has meant, in effect, more posts in the Foreign Service for the 'diplomatic' entry. It has not opened the upper ranks to members of the old, 'consular' class.

The circumvention of the 1943 reforms is best seen in the grading which the Foreign Office has chosen to give to commercial and consular posts. Eden had intended to up-grade commercial and consular work. His reforms, as interpreted by the Foreign Office, had precisely the opposite effect.

While consular officers and members of the Commercial Diplomatic Service before 1943 were inferior beings, at least their educational qualifications (normally a degree, and certainly success in the Class I examination before the Civil Service Commission) were not dissimilar to those of officers in the Foreign Service or in the diplomatic service. In 1943 the intention was that the commissioned consular posts should rank as Branch A posts, and that Branch A officers should be responsible for the commercial as well as the political work of the service. Commissioned consuls and members of the Commercial Diplomatic Service joined the senior branch of the new, amalgamated Foreign Service. When David Eccles, in 1945, asked for an assurance that commercial secretaries would not be placed on a lower level than diplomatic secretaries, the Prime Minister (Clement Attlee) entirely agreed with him on the importance of the commercial branch: 'There must not be separate grades and a grade below, because it is of vital importance to the country.'[3]

[1] Civil Service Commission, *Annual Report 1968* (London, 1969), pp. 51-52.
[2] 745 *HC Deb.*, 5s, 71 (17 April 1967).
[3] 417 *HC Deb.*, 5s, 920 (17 December 1945).

Nevertheless, as the commitments of the Foreign Service increased, it was not the political posts which were reduced in number or status under pressure for economy, but the less glamorous commercial and consular posts. In 1951 there were still 170 Branch A officers serving as consular staff overseas, concentrated, as might be expected, in the 'plums' of the old service in France, Germany, Italy, Spain, Switzerland and the United States, and in the specialist areas of the Levant and the Far East. In 1953/4, out of a total of 306 consular officers, 109 were Branch A and 197 Branch B (equivalent to the Executive and Clerical Classes of the Home Civil Service). By August 1963, when the subject was investigated by the Plowden Committee, only 7 per cent. of consular posts abroad and 5 per cent at home were retained by Branch A; the rest were Branch B. Similarly, only 37 per cent of the economic and commercial posts were Branch A, as compared with no less than 91 per cent of the political posts. If anything, the position is even worse today. It is clear from the Duncan Report (1968/9) that consuls are now drawn almost exclusively from Branch B. Of the 276 consuls-general, consuls and vice-consuls, only fourteen are Branch A, and of the 254 home-based officers of Grade 5A (principal level), only forty-two are in posts specifically designated as commercial.

The most senior of the consular posts, the consulates-general, have remained the preserve of Branch A, where, as often as not, they have shared the function of minor Missions as a convenient refuge for the second-rate. But the standing of consular officers in general, which the 1943 reforms were designed to raise, was in fact reduced to the level proposed by the 1914 Commission and subsequently rejected as totally unsuitable to consular duties: the level of the school-leaver. The stigma of inferiority, attached from the earliest days to consular work, was transferred from consuls in relation to diplomats to the even more unpleasant, because more genuine and deep-rooted, division between Branch A and Branch B, between the Administrative and the Executive Classes. Consuls, suspended in Bruce Lockhart's day between the Heaven of the First Division and the Hell of the Second, had descended into Hell.

With Branch A officers falling over themselves to avoid commercial and consular postings, it is not astonishing that the integration of functions, which had again formed a major part of the 1943 reforms, never took place. Eden agreed that consular, commercial, and diplomatic functions would continue to be distinct. What he wanted (as his Under Secretary, Richard Law, reported to the House) was that there should be 'the fullest possible interchange and the fullest possible fusion between the three branches of the Service'. He wanted this for three reasons: so that there would be some fair distribution of agreeable and disagreeable posts among members of the Service; so that, in the interests of the new Service, the highest posts should be open to all members of the Service, from whatever branch they came; so that all members of the Service, in whatever branch they served, should have an all-round knowledge of foreign affairs as a whole (commercial, consular and political) and of the economic as well as of the political side of each question.[1]

The downgrading of consular and commercial posts to Branch B destroyed any chance of this happening. With only fourteen out of 276 consular posts in 1968/9 held by Branch A officers (and those primarily at the most senior level, often as a final post in a less distinguished career), the idea of heads of mission with previous consular experience and of consuls who had themselves served as diplomats, anticipated and celebrated so warmly by Lord Strang in his account of the Foreign Office in 1954,[2] was simply absurd. Indeed, in the words of the Duncan Report, 'the figures suggest that there is still some hang-over from the period when commercial work was at arm's length from important matters of policy such as concern those likely to reach the higher ranks of the Service'.

It might have been reasonable, with the abandonment of a genuine interchange or cross-fertilization between types of posts, to have looked for some substitute for experience through training. The 1943 proposals had included, beyond the actual interchange of functions, an elaborate scheme of training for all entrants into Branch A of the Foreign Service. Successful candidates would be given travelling studentships for eighteen months to study history, economics and at least two languages. They would then be examined again and subjected to interviews, with the object of assessing their 'personal suitability' for the Foreign Service. Finally, having qualified as members of the Foreign Service, they would spend six months in training at the Foreign Office and a further six months visiting centres of industry and studying economic, industrial, social and labour questions in other government Departments. The Plowden Report noted that the scheme was 'never carried

---

[1] 387 *HC Deb.*, 5s, 1364-5 (18 March 1943).
[2] Lord Strang, *The Foreign Office* (London, 1955), p. 125.

out and was from the first impracticable, if only because the manpower which such a scheme would require has never been available'.¹ The pressure to fill long vacant posts after the war—some 200 in all, to be recruited over three years—meant that it was impossible to spare appointees for more than a brief period of training (amounting to a course of lectures on the Foreign Service, and a special crash course in French for those who needed it). Arrangements for language study were later put in hand, but economic and commercial training remained virtually non-existent. All new entrants to the Foreign Office were given a course lasting three weeks with the limited aim of providing some knowledge of the work of the service. Their knowledge of economics, history, international relations, or developments in science depended largely, as the Plowden Committee observed, on what they had read at university or learned, perhaps from travel abroad, before entering the service.²

Vocational training, where it was given at all, was in practice limited to officers actually posted to commercial or consular posts—a rapidly declining number, so far as Branch A officers were concerned. The preparation considered adequate in the early 1960s for a first consular post would have outraged reformers a century before. New consular officers were to take a consular course of seven weeks covering such functions as the registration of births and deaths, the performance and registration of marriages, the administration of estates, and the duties prescribed under the Merchant Shipping Acts, which in turn was to be followed by a three-month attachment to a busy consular post in Western Europe. Yet even this does not appear to have been universal, since the Plowden Committee found it necessary to recommend specifically that no one taking up a consular appointment for the first time should do so without completing a consular course.³

'The reforms introduced into the recruitment and training of the Foreign Service', said the Earl of Perth, a former ambassador, in 1944, 'will, in due

---

[1] Nor has it become so since Plowden. The Plowden Report recommended a manpower margin of 10 per cent. Despite acceptance of the Report, 7½ per cent is the maximum so far authorized. This, says Duncan, continues to inhibit adequate programmes for training and secondment.

[2] *Report of the Committee on Representational Services Overseas*, PP 1963-4 (Cmnd 2276) XI, para. 410.

[3] *Ibid.*, para. 429.

time, ensure that all the members of that service will become commercially minded.'[1] 'Above all', said Lord Strang, ten years later,

> the amalgamation has put an end to segregating barriers which in the past created exclusiveness and a spirit of clique.... Prejudices were the inevitable outcome of segregation. They cannot survive the effects of intermingling and a common basis of training; and their demise would by itself suffice to make the reforms worth while.[2]

But the 1943 reforms, while they unified the personnel of the Foreign Service and placed them under a common direction, did not amalgamate functions. In the postwar Foreign Service a very clear differentiation of functions was recognized within each Mission, and the expenditure for each function—Diplomatic Establishments, Commercial Diplomatic Establishments, Consular Establishments, and Public Information Services—was separately set out in the estimates. This may have been logical and necessary, but it has meant that many of the snags of the old system have remained substantially unchanged. The separation of commercial from political functions, consular from diplomatic, has helped to perpetuate the snobberies and distinctions which had always existed between the services; the one remained quite recognizably 'inferior' to the other. As a further refinement in snobbery, 'economic' posts are now, it seems, considered more suitable for Branch A, 'commercial' for Branch B.

The real change in 1943 was in the method of entry and in the greater *theoretical* possibility of an interchange between the differentiated functions. In practice this became limited almost at once, both by the downgrading of commercial and consular posts to Branch B status, and by the fact that those Branch A officers who showed any talent or liking for commercial or consular work were too rare and valuable to be lost, and tended to remain within their chosen branch of the Service. For all the publicity given to the opening of a 'new era' in 1943, it was almost as rare in the early 1960s to find a senior diplomat with genuine commercial and consular knowledge or experience as it had been before the war. The Plowden Committee, with its recommendations for the upgrading of consular and commercial posts and its emphatic claim, supported by H.M. Government, that economic and commercial work must now be regarded as a first charge on the resources of the overseas services, has done much to bring the Foreign Service back to

---

[1] 134 *HL Deb.*, 5s, 286 (13 December 1944).
[2] Strang, *Foreign Office*, p. 79.

the intentions of the 1943 reforms. But Duncan has been compelled, 'by the arithmetic of the situation', to acknowledge that 'even with some increase in the number of commercial posts the proportion of senior officers without direct experience will always be more than half'.

The main enemy of the consular service has been the contempt in which the job itself was held. So long as the service could recruit separately from candidates for whom, for class or intellectual reasons, there was no hope of better things, it was able to command some respect and loyalty on its own. Its performance, variable though it was, was far better than the Foreign Office deserved. Most of its commissioned officers were honest, conscientious men who, if underpaid and unregarded, did their work as well as might be expected; some, particularly in the specialized services, were genuinely first class. But there was always the draw towards politics, towards distinction and recognition, towards national rather than local affairs, and it was a draw which could be regulated only while the two branches, diplomatic and consular, remained distinct. Once, after 1943, the barriers were down, the result, predictably, was a flight from consular work, the more desperate because the new recruits to the Combined Service who were to be asked, after the war, to take on consular duties, were generally of a higher calibre than the prewar consuls, and certainly of higher expectations. No successful candidate in the Combined Branch A examinations, with his wits about him, could have been expected to select a career so clearly second-rate as the consular. It was Eden's mistake to imagine that a mere paper reform, however logical and timely, would banish the contempt of 150 years, create new interests, and fuse such irreconcilable elements into a common Service.

Might it, in the end, have been better to have retained the independent Consular Service? Amalgamation had always been the ambition of the true consular reformer. But it was to be amalgamation on terms of *equality* between the two branches, diplomatic and consular. When, finally, it came, the fear that the senior and more attractive consular posts would simply pass to the diplomatic class while the remainder were downgraded to a standing below that even of the prewar consuls was amply realized. There were many injustices in the old system and there was every reason to welcome the improvements in personnel administration, in salaries and in allowances, which formed a part and parcel of the 1943 reforms. But, for all its faults, the effect of the old, independent consular service had been to staff British consulates overseas with specialists of higher standing and greater local expertise than the transient, three/four year Branch B consuls of the postwar generation.

Appendix

Sir Hughe Knatchbull-Hugessen to Sir Alexander Cadogan

The following is the text of a private letter from Sir Hughe Knatchbull-Hugessen to Sir Alexander Cadogan, the Permanent Under Secretary. The letter, dated from the Foreign Office, 20 January 1939, was in amplification of the minority report signed by the diplomatic service members of the 1938 Departmental Committee. Hugessen began by explaining that he and his fellow dissenters were 'anxious to draw your earnest attention to certain considerations which for various reasons it would have been difficult and delicate to include in the body of our report'. The letter continues:

In the course of our discussions we have, on occasions, found difficulty in emphasizing certain requirements of the Diplomatic Service which, though to our minds of the first importance, are in some sense intangible and difficult to state without creating an impression of exclusiveness. It is indeed this very suspicion of exclusiveness which to certain sections of opinion constitutes in itself a reason for widening the present basis of recruitment.

It would be easy to show that the Diplomatic Service as at present constituted is recruited on a very wide basis and that ancient and ill-informed criticisms of it as a preserve for candidates born in a certain station, possessed of independent means and educated at certain favoured public schools and universities are entirely false. It would be easier still to show that the implications of such criticisms, which (though perhaps unintentionally) suggest a surplus of opportunity and a deficiency of intelligence are still less justified. But, when these legends are disposed of, there remains a fact which is of intrinsic importance and which in the past at any rate may have been responsible for the legends which we condemn.

This fact is admirably described in a passage in Mr Boutwood's reservation published with the MacDonnell Report of 1914 [Cmd 7748]. The passage has been quoted briefly in our report, but we will here venture to quote it *in extenso*.

Mr Boutwood mentions the need for a diplomat to have the capacity 'to deal on terms of equality with considerable persons and their words and works'. He continues:

> Sometimes, very rarely, this capacity is given in its highest form by something which is hardly examinable—by very great intellectual powers. Ordinarily, however, this capacity is a result of nurture in an atmosphere of independence. Unfortunately, it is scarcely too much to say that the present condition of society provides this atmosphere of independence only where there is financial independence. . . . Whenever, as in the Diplomatic Service, there is a general need for such freedom, the mode of recruiting should conform to the social conditions which produce that freedom.

In our report we have expressed the view that personality is necessary both in the Diplomatic and the Consular Service but that a higher standard is expected in the former. We have found ourselves in a certain minority on the Committee where direct personal knowledge of the conditions and functions of the Diplomatic Service abroad is concerned, but we feel that those four colleagues who are most familiar with conditions of service abroad will agree with our view. It is this view which Mr Boutwood expresses in such well-chosen words. Though we should be far from suggesting that personality, 'address', and *savoir-faire* are not of great importance in the Consular Service, it is in the Diplomatic Service that these rather intangible qualities are most essential. A diplomatic officer must be prepared on all occasions to represent the most representative orders of his own countrymen. He must be able to deal as an equal with foreign colleagues, Cabinet Ministers, Prime Ministers and Heads of State; to hold his own with Sovereigns and other royalties and to fraternize with the governing class in no matter what country. This means that all suspicion of an inferiority complex must be absent from his make-up. It would be absurd to pretend that these qualities are exclusively the product of certain public schools and universities or that they are in the slightest degree an exclusive attribute of the Diplomatic Service as at present constituted. The point we wish to emphasize is that in increasing the numbers and thereby widening the range of choice of entrants to the Diplomatic Service there is a danger that the Service may suffer by the admission of candidates who lack the qualities which we have tried to describe.

As regards the ill-informed criticisms still prevailing, we should greatly deplore any concession to an ignorant public opinion holding views of the kind indicated above which besides being entirely antiquated are, as we hope you will agree, unfair and unfounded. The right way to deal with such unintelligent opinion is to see that it is better informed. While dealing with these less definable requirements for the Diplomatic profession, we should like to draw attention to the great importance which we attach to the suitability of the wives of Diplomatic Officers adequately to second their husbands in all that concerns the representative and social side of the profession abroad. In many posts the part played by the wife is fully as important as that of the husband, and in all an immense influence for or against British prestige is exercised by the wife. By this we mean by the wife in her capacity as 'Chefesse'. Women have their own and that a most important part to play in diplomatic life, a part which is quite distinct from that of men but no less essential. We feel that in selecting officers for service abroad, whether in an amalgamated service or not, great attention should be paid to this consideration.

You will see that our main object in writing this letter has been to bring out certain points which it would have been difficult to discuss satisfactorily in a Committee where administrative considerations inevitably came uppermost. A Mission abroad is not merely an exported government office on a small scale. Over and above the routine of the Chancery work, which can to a certain extent be limited to defined hours in the day, there are duties which are incapable of any such limitation and which are not easy to define. The representative and social duties, the power to understand the psychology, character and conditions of a foreign people and its leaders, to forecast their reactions, to explain to them our own outlook and policy and in general to contribute to increased mutual understanding—these tasks are of the first importance, and it is the ability to perform these properly at least as much as a capacity to deal with correspondence and paper work which should be the main test of suitability for service abroad.

This letter has been written after consultation with Howard Smith and Hoyer Millar and has their full support.

Bibliography

The Cinderella Service: British consuls since 1825 is based on material from the Foreign Office archives at the Public Record Office, on government publications (Parliamentary Papers and Debates), and on the contemporary press. Each item is footnoted as it occurs. The bulky minutes of evidence taken before the consular committees are difficult to handle without a specific reference, but it has seemed unnecessary to cite the reports themselves, most of which are short and easily scanned. A point can be traced without difficulty from the list of principal reports and memoranda printed below.

This is the first history of its kind for the British Consular Service. Such material as already exists takes the form of consular memoirs or manuals for the guidance of consuls and traders. Some of the more spectacular consuls—men like Richard Burton—have attracted a substantial literature on their own, but it is a literature which has little to contribute, directly or indirectly, to consular affairs; a sample only is listed in the second section of this bibliography, together with a selection from the vast literature on exterritoriality. A few consuls have reached the pages of the *Dictionary of National Biography*, some are in *Who Was Who*, while brief biographical details on all can be found in the annual volumes of the *Foreign Office List*.

Principal Reports and Memoranda on the condition, development and reorganization of the Consular Service

Report from the Select Committee on Consular Establishment, PP 1835 (499) VI.

Report from the Select Committee on Consular Service and Appointments, PP 1857-8 (482) VIII.

Report to Lord Malmesbury on Mr Murray's plan for the revision of consular fees, PP 1859 (2554. Sess. 2) XV.

Memorandum by the Official Committee on the Consular Service, 16 December 1859: printed in full as No. 11, *Correspondence on the subject of the Report of the Consular Committee of 1858*, PP 1860 (2661) XXXIX.

Report from the Select Committee to enquire into the Diplomatic Service, PP 1861 (459) VI.

Report of the Select Committee on Trade with Foreign Nations, PP 1864 (493) VII.

Correspondence respecting Diplomatic and Consular Expenditure in China, Japan and Siam, PP 1870 (c. 69) LXVI.

Reports on Consular Establishments in China, 1869, PP 1870 (c. 44) LXIX.

Report from the Select Committee on Diplomatic and Consular Services, PP 1870 (382) VII.

Reports from the Select Committee on Diplomatic and Consular Services, PP 1871 (238, 386) VII.

Report from the Select Committee on Diplomatic and Consular Services, PP 1872 (314) VII.

Reports respecting the Consular Services of Foreign Countries, PP 1872 (c. 498) LXII.

Reports relative to British Consular Establishments, 1858 and 1871, Parts I-III, PP 1872 (c. 497, 501, 530) LX.

Reports relative to British Consular Establishments, 1858 and 1871, Parts IV-VI, PP 1872 (c. 544, 551, 661) LXI.

Memorandum (by James Bryce) respecting the question of Diplomatic and Consular Assistance to British Trade Abroad: printed as No. 1, *Correspondence respecting Diplomatic Assistance to British Trade Abroad*, Part II, PP 1886 (c. 4779-1) LX.

Fourth Report of the Royal Commission on Civil Establishments (the Ridley Commission), PP 1890 (c. 6172) XXVII.

Report from the Departmental Committee on Commercial Intelligence, PP 1898 (c. 8962) XXXIII.

Report of the Committee appointed to inquire into the Constitution of the Consular Service (the Walrond Committee), PP 1903 (Cd 1634) LV. Minutes of evidence printed separately as Foreign Office Confidential Print 79737.

Report by Sir Eldon Gorst and Mr Llewellyn Smith on the System of British Commercial Attachés and Commercial Agents, PP 1907 (Cd 3610) LXXXVII.

Report of the Foreign Office Committee on the Consular Service (1912): printed as Appendix XC, *Fifth Report of the Royal Commission on the Civil Service*, PP 1914-16 (Cd 7749) XI.

Fifth Report of the Royal Commission on the Civil Service, PP 1914-16 (Cd 7748) XI.

Report of the Foreign Office Committee of 1916 (the Eyre Crowe Committee): printed as an Appendix to *Memorandum on the future organization of commercial intelligence*, PP 1917-18 (Cd 8715) XXIX.

Reports of the Committee on Commercial Intelligence in Foreign Countries (the Faringdon Committee): printed as Annex to *Memorandum on future organization of Commercial Intelligence*, PP 1917-18 (Cd 8715) XXIX.

Memorandum by the Board of Trade and Foreign Office with respect to the future organization of commercial intelligence, PP 1917-18 (Cd 8715) XXIX.

Report of the Committee on the Consular Service (the Steel-Maitland Committee), 19 March 1919, PRO.FO/369/1319.

Report of the Committee to examine the Question of Government Machinery for dealing with Trade and Commerce (the Cave Committee), PP 1919 (Cmd 319) XXX.

Report of the Legation Committee on the Reorganization of the China Consular Service, Peking, October 1928: PRO.FO/369/2020.

Report of the Foreign Office Committee on the Levant Consular Service, 11 January 1933, PRO.FO/369/2316.

Memorandum (by Sir David Scott) on the Amalgamation of the Diplomatic and Consular Services, 21 January 1938: PRO.FO, Confidential Print 15334.

Reports (majority and minority) of the Departmental Committee on the Consular Service, January 1939: PRO.FO/366/781.

Report (by Sir Malcolm Robertson) on the Reform of the Diplomatic Service, 12 May 1941: Foreign Office Library, FO Print No. 16050.

Proposals for the Reform of the Foreign Service, PP 1942-3 (Cmd 6420) XI.

Seventh Report of the Select Committee on Estimates (Foreign Service), PP 1950-1 (242) V.

Seventh Report of the Select Committee on Estimates (Foreign Service), PP 1953-4 (290) VI.

Report of the Committee on Representational Services Overseas (the Plowden Committee), PP 1963-4 (Cmnd 2276) XI.

Report of the Review Committee on Overseas Representation 1968-1969 (the Duncan Committee), PP 1969 (Cmnd 4107).

Books, pamphlets and articles

A., C. J. *A Sailor-Consul's Work for his Country and for Humanity* (privately printed, n.d.)

ALCOCK, SIR RUTHERFORD. *The Capital of the Tycoon: a narrative of a three years' residence in Japan*, London, Longmans, 1863, 2 vols.

ALLEN, BERNARD M. *Sir Ernest Satow: A Memoir*, London, Kegan Paul, 1933.

'ANGLO-LEVANTINE'. *Our Consuls in the East: a parliamentary inquiry into their proceedings imperative*, London, 1855.

ANON. *Foreign Office, Diplomatic and Consular Sketches*, London, W. H. Allen, 1883.

ANON. 'A Plea for Cinderella', *Royal Colonial Institute Journal*, new series, 8, 1917.

BARBOUR, VIOLET. 'Consular Service in the Reign of Charles II', *American Historical Review*, 33, 1928.

BEAWES, WYNDHAM. *Lex Mercatoria Rediviva or, A Complete Code of Mercantile Law*, 5th edn, London, R. Baldwin, 1792.

BINDOFF, S. T. 'The unreformed Diplomatic Service, 1812-1860', *Transactions of the Royal Historical Society*, 4th ser. 18, 1935.

BINDOFF, S. T., ed. *British Diplomatic Representatives, 1789-1852*, London, Royal Historical Society, Camden Third Series, vol. 50, 1934.

BONHAM, M. L. *The British Consuls in the Confederacy*, Columbia College Studies in History, 43, no. 3, 1911.

BOREL, F. *De l'Origine et des fonctions des consuls*, St Petersburg, 1807.

BORGOMALE, H. L. RABINO DI. *Diplomatic and Consular Officers of Great Britain and Iran*, 1946.

BROOKS, L. A. E. AND HAY, A. E. DRUMMOND, eds. *A Memoir of Sir John Drummond Hay*, London, Murray, 1896.

BULLARD, SIR READER. *Large and Loving Privileges: the Capitulations in the Middle East and North Africa*, Glasgow, David Murray Foundation Lecture, 1960.

BULLARD, SIR READER. *The Camels Must Go: an autobiography*, London, Faber, 1961.

CAMPBELL, SIR GERALD. *Of True Experience*, London, Hutchinson, 1949.

CAWSTON, G. AND KEANE, A. H. *The Early Chartered Companies, 1296-1858*, London, Edward Arnold, 1896.

CHAFY, R. E. W. 'Consuls in Barbary', unpublished typescript in the Library, Foreign Office, London.

CHITTY, JOSEPH. *A Treatise on the Laws of Commerce and Manufactures, and the Contracts relating thereto*, London, Henry Butterworth, 1820-4, 4 vols.

CLARK, SIR WILLIAM. 'Government and the promotion of trade', *Journal of Public Administration*, 1, 1923.

CUNNINGHAM, A. B. 'Dragomania: the Dragomans of the British Embassy in Turkey', *St Antony's Papers*, 11, 1961.

CUNNINGHAM, A. B. *The Early Correspondence of Richard Wood 1831-1841*, London, Royal Historical Society, Camden Fourth Series, vol. 3, 1966.

DEMECH, LUIGI. *The British Consulate at Tunis: Critical Remarks*, Malta, privately printed, 1868.

EDWARDS, H. SUTHERLAND. *Sir William White, his life and correspondence*, London, Murray, 1902.

FAIRBANK, J. K. *Trade and Diplomacy on the China Coast, 1842-54*, Cambridge, Mass., 1964.

FARWELL, BYRON. *Burton: a biography of Sir Richard Francis Burton*, London, Longmans, 1963.

FELLER, A. H. AND HUDSON, M. O., eds. *A Collection of the Diplomatic and Consular Laws and Regulations of Various Countries*, Carnegie Endowment for International Peace, Washington, 1933, 2 vols.

FINN, JAMES. *Stirring Times, or records from Jerusalem consular chronicles of 1853 to 1856*, London, 1878, 2 vols.

FISHER, SIR GODFREY. 'The Brotherhood of St George at San Lucar de Barrameda', *Atlante*, 1, 1953.

FISHER, SIR GODFREY. *Barbary Legend: war, trade, and piracy in North Africa, 1415-1830*, Oxford, Clarendon Press, 1957.

FISHER, SIR GODFREY. 'Our Old Consular Service. The Era of Mercantile Consuls, 1485-1648', unpublished typescript.

FYNN, ROBERT. *British Consuls Abroad*, London, 1846.

GASELEE, STEPHEN, see Tilley, Sir John and Gaselee, Stephen.

GLENNY, W. J. 'The Trade Commissioner and Commercial Diplomatic Services', *Journal of Public Administration*, 2, July 1924.

GOWAN, P. AND OTHERS. *The abuses of consular jurisdiction in the East: a complaint of British subjects resident in Siam*, 1889.

GRAFFTEY-SMITH, LAURENCE. *Bright Levant*, London, Murray, 1970.

GRAVES, PHILIP. *The Life of Sir Percy Cox*, London, Hutchinson, 1941.

GREEN, JOHN. *On the Nature and Character of the Consular Service*, London, W. H. Allen, 1848.

GREENBERG, MICHAEL. *British Trade and the Opening of China, 1800-1842*, Cambridge University Press, 1951.

HALL, W. E. *A Treatise on the Foreign Powers and Jurisdiction of the British Crown*, Oxford, Clarendon Press, 1894.

HAMBLOCH, ERNEST. *British Consul*, London, Harrap, 1938.

HAY, A. E. DRUMMOND, *see* Brooks, L. A. E., and Hay, A. E. Drummond.

HEARN, SIR WALTER. *Some Recollections: memories of 35 years in the Consular Service*, London, Nash & Grayson, 1928.

HEWLETT, SIR W. M. *Forty Years in China*, London, Macmillan, 1943.

HORN, D. B. 'The Board of Trade and Consular Reports, 1696-1782', *English Historical Review*, 54, 1939.

HORN, D. B. *The British Diplomatic Service, 1689-1789*, Oxford, Clarendon Press, 1961.

HORNBY, SIR EDMUND. *Instructions to H.M. Consular Officers in China and Japan on the mode of conducting judicial business*, Shanghai, 1867.

HORNBY, SIR EDMUND. *An Autobiography*, London, Constable, 1929.

HOSIE, SIR ALEXANDER. *Three Years in Western China*, London, G. Philip & Son, 1890.

HUDSON, M. O., *see* Feller, A. H., and Hudson, M. O.

HUMANN, C. M. *Das Konsularrecht Grossbritanniens*, Berlin, 1933.

HUTCHINSON, G. T., *see* Morison, Theodore and Hutchinson, G. T.

HYAMSON, A. M. *The British Consulate in Jerusalem in relation to the Jews of Palestine*, London, Jewish Historical Society of England, 1939, 1941, 2 vols.

INGLIS, SIR A. PERCY. *Consular Formulary*, 2nd edn., London, Harrison & Sons, 1898.

JACKSON, JOHN. *Reflections on the Commerce of the Mediterranean: shewing the policy of increasing the number of British Consuls etc.*, London, 1804.

JAYNE, M. S. 'British Consuls in Lisbon, 1583-1689' *Annual Reports of the Historical Association (Lisbon Branch)*, 1938, 1940 and 1941.

JENKYNS, SIR H. *British Rule and Jurisdiction beyond the Seas*, Oxford, Clarendon Press, 1902.

JOEL, L. *A Consul's Manual*, London, Kegan Paul, 1879.

JOHNSTON, SIR HARRY H. *The Story of My Life*, London, Chatto & Windus, 1923.

JONES, F. C. *Extraterritoriality in Japan and the Diplomatic Relations Resulting in its Abolition, 1853-99*, New Haven, Yale University Press, 1931.

KEANE, A. H., *see* Cawston, G. and Keane, A. H.

KEETON, G. W. *The Development of Extraterritoriality in China*, London, Longmans, 1928, 2 vols.

LANE, M. 'The Diplomatic Service under William III', *Transactions of the Royal Historical Society*, 4th ser., 10, 1927.

LEE, HILDA I. 'The supervising of the Barbary consuls during the years 1756-1836', *Bulletin of the Institute of Historical Research*, 12, 1949.

LEE, LUKE T. *Consular Law and Practice*, London, Stevens, 1961.

LOCKHART, R. H. BRUCE. *Memoirs of a British Agent*, London, Putnam, 1932.

LODGE, SIR RICHARD. 'The English Factory at Lisbon. Some Chapters in its History', *Transactions of the Royal Historical Society*, 4th ser., 16, 1933.

LONGFORD, J. H. 'The Consular Service and its wrongs', *Quarterly Review*, April, 1903.

MARGHETITCH, S. G. *Etude sur les fonctions des drogmans en Turquie*, Constantinople, 1898.

M'COAN, J. C. *Consular Jurisdiction in Turkey and Egypt*, London, William Ridgway, 1873.

MEAD, W. R. 'The birth of the British Consular System in Finland'. *The Norseman*, 15, 1957.

MICHIE, ALEXANDER. *The Englishman in China during the Victorian Era, as illustrated in the Career of Sir Rutherford Alcock*, Edinburgh, Blackwood, 1900, 2 vols.

MORISON, THEODORE AND HUTCHINSON, G. T. *The Life of Sir Edward FitzGerald Law*, Edinburgh, Blackwood, 1911.

NICOLSON, HAROLD. 'The Foreign Service', *Political Quarterly*, 7, 1936.

OLIVER, R. A. *Sir Harry Johnston and the Scramble for Africa*, London, Chatto, 1957.

OPPENHEIMER, SIR FRANCIS. *Stranger Within: Autobiographical Pages*, London, Faber and Faber, 1960.

PEARS, SIR EDWIN. *Forty Years in Constantinople*, London, Herbert Jenkins, 1916.

PIGGOTT, SIR F. *Extraterritoriality: the law relating to consular jurisdiction and to residence in Orient countries*, Hong Kong, 1907.

PLATT, D. C. M. 'The Role of the British Consular Service in Overseas Trade, 1825-1914', *Economic History Review*, 2nd ser. 15, 1963.

PLATT, D. C. M. *Finance, Trade, and Politics in British Foreign Policy, 1815-1914*, Oxford, Clarendon Press, 1968.

PLAYFAIR, G. M. H. *Compendium of Instructions to H.M. Consular Officers in China*, Shanghai, 1892; revised and reissued 1903 and 1915.

POOLE, STANLEY LANE. *The Life of Sir Harry Parkes*, London, Macmillan, 1894, 2 vols.

PRATT, SIR JOHN. *War and Politics in China*, London, Jonathan Cape, 1943.

RAWLINSON, GEORGE. *A Memoir of Major-General Sir H. C. Rawlinson*, London, Longmans, 1898.

RAWLINSON, H. G. 'The Embassy of William Harborne to Constantinople, 1583-8', *Transactions of the Royal Historical Society*, 4th ser., 5, 1922.

RIOCHE, YVES. *Les Jurisdictions Consulaires Anglaises dans les Pays d'Orient: Turquie, Perse, Mascate, Maroc*, Paris, Arthur Rousseau, 1904.

RODRIGUEZ, MARIO. *A Palmerstonian Diplomat in Central America; Frederick Chatfield Esq.*, Tucson, University of Arizona Press, 1964.

RYAN, SIR ANDREW. *The Last of the Dragomans*, London, Geoffrey Bles, 1951.

SATOW, SIR ERNEST. *A Diplomat in Japan*, London, Seeley & Co., 1921.

SELOUS, G. H. *Appointment to Fez*, London, Richards Press, 1956.

SHUTTLEWORTH, N. L. KAY. *A Life of Sir Woodbine Parish*, London, Smith, Elder & Co., 1910.

SMITH, SIR HUBERT LLEWELLYN. *The Board of Trade*, London, Putnam, 1928.

STOWELL, E. C. *Consular Cases and Opinions from the Decisions of English and American Courts*, Washington, J. Byrne, 1909.

STRANG, LORD, AND OTHERS. *The Foreign Office*, London, Allen, 1956.

STRANGFORD, VISCOUNTESS, ed. *A Selection from the writings of Viscount Strangford*, London, Richard Bentley, 1869, 2 vols.

TARRING, SIR CHARLES. *British Consular Jurisdiction in the East*, London, Stevens & Haynes, 1887.

TEICHMAN, SIR ERIC. *Affairs of China*, London, Methuen, 1938.

THOMAS, IVOR. 'Reform of the Foreign Service', *Political Quarterly*, 14, 1943.

TILLEY, SIR JOHN AND GASELEE, STEPHEN. *The Foreign Office*, London, Putnam, 1933.

TOWNSHEND, A. F. *A Military Consul in Turkey*, London, Seeley, 1910.

TUSON, E. W. A. *The British Consul's Manual*, London, Longmans, 1856.

TWISS, SIR TRAVERS. *On Consular Jurisdiction in the Levant, and the Status of Foreigners in the Ottoman Law Courts*, London, Association for the Reform and Codification of the Law of Nations, 1880.

VILLIERS, H. MONTAGUE. *Charms of the Consular Career*, London, Hutchinson, 1925.

WARDEN, D. B. *On the Origin, Nature, Progress, and Influence of Consular Establishments*, Paris, 1813.

WAUGH, SIR TELFORD. *Turkey, Yesterday, Today and Tomorrow*, London, Chapman & Hall, 1930.

WENDEL, HUGO C. M. 'The protégé system in Morocco', *Journal of Modern History*, 2, 1930.

WILSON, SIR ARNOLD. *S.W. Persia. A political officer's diary 1907-1914*, Oxford University Press, 1941.

WOOD, ALFRED C. *A History of the Levant Company*, Oxford University Press, 1935.

WOOD, W. A. R. *Consul in Paradise: sixty-nine years in Siam*, London, Souvenir Press, 1965.

WRATISLAW, A. C. *A Consul in the East*, London, W. Blackwood, 1924.

Index

Abcarius, dragoman, on corruption, 162-3
Abeokuta, 50
Aberdeen, Lord, on 1844 Order in Council, 146-7
Abyssinia, 132, 136
Abyssinians, and consular protection, 135
Accounts, control of, 60, 64-7; allowances and, 84; inspections and, 93; after Steel-Maitland, 172
Adana, 134
Administration (consular), 94; before 1825, 11; and consular finance, 30; Canning and consular remuneration, 33; and communications with Foreign Office, 62-3; personnel, 88-94; administrative reform, 114, 133; capitulations and Turkish and Egyptian, 142; of China Service, 183; of Far Eastern Service, 200-1; by Britain in China, 215; customs, 215; and arguments for amalgamation of Far Eastern Services, 227
Administrative class, examination, 117; after 1943, 234-5, 238
Adrianople, 130, 144, 145
Afghanistan, 132
Afghans, protection of, 140, 141, 146
Africa, appointments in, 17, 202; conditions of west coast of, 28, 43; Richard Burton and, 51; consular functions in, 120; specialized service in, 164, 169
Agencies, commercial, consuls and, 40-1
Agency system (Foreign Office), 60
Agents, commercial, 107
Ahwaz, 131
Alabaster, Charles, on cost of living in China, 198
Alcock, Sir Rutherford, on exile in Japan, 28-9; promotion of, 52; and career in China, 183, 194; and honorary distinctions for consuls, 95; on sickness in China, 196-7; and cost of living in China, 197, 199; on cost of China and Japan Services, 204; on consular jurisdiction, 213
Aleppo, 130, 134-5, 143, 158
Alexandria, 63, 163, 150, 151
Algeria, 130, 141
Algiers, 39
Allchin, G. C., on promotion, 98
Allowances, 198; evidence to committees on, 3; economy in, 17; allocation of, 33-6; inadequacy of, 39-40; compassionate, 47; for leave, 30; and accounting control, 64-7; as supplementation to salaries, 81-2, 83-8; allocation and control of, 83-4; rent, 86; representation and entertainment, 86, 88; proposal of local, 88; 'war bonus', 88; and clerical staffing, 112; and social objections to amalgamation, 114; and standards of living, 121; purposes of, 160; after Steel-Maitland, 172; and amalgamation, 178, 230; and perquisites in China Service, 195; and salary scales in Far East Service before 1914, 221, 223; 1943 reforms and, 239
Amazon, upper, Casement and, 35
America, Latin, consulates created in, 14; consular functions in, 16; and fares, 29; salaries for posts in, 31; political posts in, 53; specialized service in, 169, 172
America, United States of, 146, 202, 235; consulates in, 10, 14, 64; cost of overseas services in, 32, 129; need for allowances in, 87; commercial functions by consuls of, 107
Amoy, 29, 182, 195, 203, 212, 226
Anatolia, 143
Andalusia, 9
Anderson, Sir Percy, Ridley Commission and, 34, 43, 48; on inspection, 64
Ankara, 177
Antwerp, 12, 19, 82, 116
Appointments, royal authorization of, 6;

251

The Cinderella Service

Appointments—*continued*
by merchants, 6, 7, 8, 10; by state, 7-9, 22; by nomination, 8, 9, 22; Castlereagh and, 9; 1825 Act and, 14; Lord John Russell on economy in, 17; and functions, 19; and patronage, 21-3, 27, 49, 56; by examination, 25, 71, 185; 'freehold', 33; as replacements, 35; political, 37; and fees, 41; specialist, 52; Walrond Committee on, 69-70; Foreign Office attitude to, 73; social barriers to, 72-5; personal files and, 89; Sir William Tyrrell and, 95; after 1914-18, 101, 110-111; Government of India and, 131-2; by Levant Company, 153; and China Service, 183, 185, 192; legal, 189; and 1943 reforms, 231-9 *pass.*

Arabia, 141
Arabic, 160, 167, 173, 208
Archives, 63, 93, 113, 155
Argentina, 77; staffing in relation to trade with, 109; and 1916 Committee, 110
Armenians, protection of, 132, 134, 144, 158, 160
Arnould, on Marine Insurance, 191
Arundell, Isobel Burton and, 52
Asia Minor, consular functions in, 133-5
Asiatic Petroleum Company, 203
Athens, language training at, 173
Attlee, Clement, on status of commercial officers, 234
Austria-Hungary, Levant Consular Service of, 164; and exterritoriality in China, 216; political intelligence and, 132
Azores, 12

Baghdad, 131, 157
Bahia, salary at, 81
Bahrein, 132
Baldwin, Stanley, on patronage and recruitment, 70
Balfour, A. J., and entertainment allowances, 87-8
Balfour, Captain, on British justice in China, 210
Balkans, consular functions in, 131-2, 134, 135, 174; specialized service in, 169
Baltic consulates, inspection of, 63, 64
Baltimore, 53
Bangkok, 35, 197; law examinations for student interpreters at, 191; cost of service in, 202; staff at, 204; and Herbert Dering, 215; recruitment to, 221; administration from and arguments for amalgamation, 227
Barbary Consuls, 10n., 130
Barbour, Violet, 9-10
Baring, Walter, on language training of Levant recruits, 167
Batavia, 197, 226
Beawes, Wyndham, on appointments by state nomination, 9
Beira, 48
Beirut, Levant Company and, 126; political functions at, 130, 134; salary at, 158
Belgrade, consular functions at, 130, 131, 174
Bergne, Sir Harry, on commercial reports and the Foreign Office, 57
Berlin, 63, 151; language training at, 187
Berlin, Congress of, and judicial reform in Turkey, 143; and capitulatory rights in Serbia and Romania, 174
Bernal, Frederick, on diplomatic and consular duties, 118
Bernhardt, Gaston de, 70
Bevin, Ernest, and recruitment, 233
Bidwell, John, and Consular Department, 58
Blackstone's *Commentaries*, 191
Blunt, Charles, 155
Blunt, J. E., on Ionians and British protection of, 144; on Turkish prisons, 147
Board of Trade, 69, 106, 119; in eighteenth century, 11; and consular reform, 13, 16; attitudes to consuls of, 19; preliminary training at, 27; Poulett Thomson and, 32; and commercial reports, 54, 56, 57, 58; and shipping, 58; and recruitment, 80; and division of responsibility with Foreign Office, 91; *Journal* of, 104; Sir Roger Casement and functions of, 107
Bogotá, salary at, 37
Boma, 70
Bordeaux, consul's income at, 12; and shipping fees, 12; vacancy at, 24
Borel, F., on social position of consuls, 1
Bosnia, 130, 133
Boston, 41, 46
Boutwood, Mr, on social qualities of diplomats, 240-1
Bowring, Sir John, on patronage, 22; and pressure for special recruitment and training for China Service, 183; Staff of, 201

Boxer Rebellion, effect on recruitment for Far Eastern Service of, 218
Brackenbury, George, on shipping duties of consuls, 19; on Lisbon consulate, 20; on promotion, 49, 51
Brackenbury, John, 68
Brazil, shipping fees in, 13, 32; cost of living in, 40; Richard Burton in, 52, 163; and Instructions, 62
Bremen, political functions at, 18
Brenan, Sir John, and language training at Peking, 188
Brest, political functions at, 18; patronage at, 23; Lloyds' agency at, 41
British American Tobacco Company, 203; language training by, 187-8
Brown, John McLeavy, and salary with Chinese Government, 196
Browne, Prof. E. G., and consular training at Cambridge, 167-8
Bruce, Sir Frederick, 189
Brummell, Beau, 21
Brusa, 130
Brussels, 151, 220
Bryce, James, on patronage, 22
Buchanan, Sir Andrew, on social objections to amalgamation, 114-15
Bucharest, Sir William White at, 52; consular functions in, 130, 174
Budapest, 61, 131
Buenos Aires, Lord Ponsonby on, 28; consulate at, 36; salaries at, 37; allowances at, 82; Woodbine Parish on expense of entertaining at, 87; clerical staffing at, 112
Bulgaria, 131, 160, 167, 168
Bullard, Reader, 138; language abilities of, 166; on E. G. Browne at Cambridge, 167-8
Bunsen, Sir Maurice de, 120, 172
Burgess, Guy, 89
Burlingame, Anson, 196
Burma, 180
Burton, Isobel, 51, 52
Burton, Richard, 21; on Santos, 28; on salaries, 39, 40; leave and transfer for, 51, 52; private income and housing, 85; on claims of Jews and Christians in Damascus, 145; and status of Levant consuls, 163
Bury, Colonel Howard, on consular establishment in Persia, 129

Bushire, 131
Businessmen, *see* Merchants
Butler, Sir Frederick, and allowances, 84; on commercial functions, 105
Butterfield and Swire, language training by, 187-8
Byles, on Bills of Exchange, 191

Cadogan, Sir Alexander, 123; on early retirements, 103; and amalgamation of China Service, 228; letter from Knatchbull-Hugessen to, 116, 240-2
Caine, G.W., on mercantile emoluments in China, 193; imprisonment of, 196
Cairo, 86, 127
Calais, 29, 81
Callao, fees at, 41
Cambridge university, 164; Appointments Board and consular recruitment, 73, 77, 219; commercial education at, 80; language training at, 167-8, 173; Prof. Giles and China Service recruitment, 219; candidates from, 231
Campbell, Robert, 155
Canning, George, and Consular Act of 1825, 5, 13-15, 31, 41, 44, 45, 68, 125; and Consular Department, 11, 60; and intentions of Act, 16, 42; on functions of consuls, 18; on salaries or fees, 31, 32; allocation of salaries by, 33, 34, 81; and trading, 37; on pension rights, 44; and control, 58; and graded service, 68; and Levant Company agents, 125
Canton, British representation in before 1842, 181-2; consulate established at, 182; and Sir John Bowring on recruitment, 183; Court of Justice at, 188, 189; salaries at, 195; staffing at, 202; trade at, 203; riot of sailors in, 208-9; Compton incident at, 209-10; and consular jurisdiction, 212
Canton, Governor of, on revenue from British trade, 181, 182
Capitulations, *see* Exterritoriality
Carden, Sir Lionel, 52
Carlisle, Lord, on Levant consuls, 154
Casement, Roger, on replacements, 35-6; on consular furniture, 36; on consular functions, 107
Castlereagh, Lord, and consular appointments, 9
Cavallo, 130
Cavasses, 137-8, 139, 160, 163; consular

Cavasses—*continued*
protection of, 156; consular jurisdiction and employment of, 174
Cave Committee (1919), and commercial functions of consuls, 105, 109
Chaldeans, protection of, 144
Chamberlain, Henry, income of at Rio, 12
Chambers of Commerce, 76; President of Manchester on recruitment and training, 26-7; and strengthening of consular service, 107-8; Foreign Office officials on, 108, 109
Charles II, appointments by, 9-10; and consular remuneration, 12
Chefoo, 198
Chefoo Convention (1876), and opening of China to trade, 203
Cherbourg, political functions at, 18; patronage at, 23
Chermside, Sir Herbert, as military consul, 132
Chiang Mai, 197
Chicago, patronage at, 22
Chief Clerk's Department (Foreign Office), and personnel administration, 90
Childers, Hugh, and salaries, 43
Chile, 77
China Consular Service, 166, 169, 172, 180-230 *pass.*; fares to China for, 29; mortality in, 45; pensions and life assurance for, 48; inspection of, 64; and entertainment allowances, 86; promotions and career prospects in, 97-8, 103, 172, 192-5, 222-5; clerical officers, 113; cost and scale, 129, 200-6; training in, 165, 168, 187; as close service, 170; recruitment to, 171, 183-5, 192-3, 218-19, 221-2; origins of, 180-3; Lord Napier and, 181-2; and rewards for merit, 194, 195; salaries in, 195-200; temptations to corruption in, 196; merchants and, 206-211; jurisdiction of, 189, 211-14; political condition of China and, 214-17; retirement and pensions from, 223-5; and amalgamation, 225-30
China Consular Service, Legation Committee on the reorganization of (1928), and promotions block, 222-3; on retirement and pensions, 224, 225
China, Government of, employment by, 196; and exterritoriality, 208, 211
China Widows Pension Scheme, 48
Chinese, chair of, at King's College, London, 183; at Cambridge, 219

Chinese, language, patronage and problems of, 185; training, 185-8, 208, 219; in Japan Service, 226
Chinese Maritime Customs, 214, 215; Sir Robert Hart and, 196; applicants for, 222; salaries in, 193, 194
Chinese Repository, The, 209
Chinese Wars, First and Second, consequences of for consulates, 182, 189, 211-12
Chinkiang, 85, 212, 226
Chirol, Valentine, on businessmen and Chinese language, 207
Chitty, Joseph, on British attitude to consuls, 13; on contracts, 191
Christiania (Oslo), 39, 53, 131
Christians, protection of, 134, 136, 143-5
Chungking, 203, 217, 226
Churchill, Winston, and 1927 economies, 111
City (London), scheme for training in, 81
Civil Establishments, Royal Commission on (1890), *see* Ridley Commission
Civil Service Commissioners, 25; and recruitment, 70; and examinations, 72, 73, 77, 183, 234; and advertising of vacancies, 78; and clerical officers, 113; on social qualifications for diplomats, 115; and amalgamation, 179; and legal training, 191
Civil Service, Home, 117; examinations for, 71, 73; better prospects offered by, 79; system of salaries in, 81; clerical officers in, 113
Civil Service, Indian, 167; prospects offered by, 79, 185, 219, salaries, in, 82
Civil Service, The Royal Commission on (1912-14), 28; and office allowances, 36; and gulf between Foreign Office and Consular Service, 61; Algernon Law and, 71, 72-3, 96-7, 166; and examinations, 73; and advertising for applicants by Foreign Office, 74; on 1903 Committee's experiment, 76, 77; and commercial experience, 79; on promotions block, 100; and annual consular reports, 105; and commercial efficiency of consuls, 107-8; and social qualifications for diplomatic service, 115; and educational objections to amalgamation, 117; and overlap of consular and diplomatic functions, 120; on divisions of Service, 169-70; on decline of applications for Far Eastern Service, 218, 219; and

salaries, 219, 220, 221; Ernest Holmes and, 220-1; Mr Boutwood's reservations to on social qualifications for diplomacy, 240-1
Civil Service, Royal Commission on (1929-31), *see* Tomlin Commission
Clanwilliam, Lord, 61
Clarendon, Lord, 127, 191; on consular appointments, 17; and training, 26, 27; and Charles Lever, 29; and hospitality to travellers, 86; and capitulations, 143; and recruitment for China Service, 183; on cost of China Service, 201
Clarke, Hyde, on capitulations, 142
Clerical Class, Senior (Executive Class), 79
Clerical Officers, service of, 112, 113
Close Services, 169; objection to formation of, 170; and effect of, 170, 171; in Latin America, 172-3; reasons for, 173; China Service, 192; and Treasury attitude to pensions, 224
Clubs, consuls and diplomats in, St James's, Cercle d'Orient, Club de Constantinople, 2
Cobden, Richard, and move to reduce consular establishment in Far East, 205
Cocks, Philip Somers, 70
Coke, Sir John, on relationship between merchants and consuls, 6
Colenso, Bishop, 27
Cologne, political functions at, 18
Colombia, and 1916 Committee, 110
Colonial Office, salaried consuls from, 53; and Barbary consulates, 130; and Weihaiwei, 226
Colour bar, in consular appointments, 72
Commercial and Consular Affairs, Comptroller of, 71, 90, 95
Commercial Department (Foreign Office), 43, 57; and administration, 90; and overseas trade, 91-2; disbanded, 92
Commercial Intelligence Branch, 91, 104
Commercial Intelligence, Departmental Committee on (1898), and Second Division clerks, 112
Commercial Intelligence in Foreign Countries, Committee on (1917-18), *see* Faringdon Committee
Commercial Relations with China, Select Committee on (1847), Consul Balfour and, 210
Commonwealth, and consular appointments, 7-8

Competition (recruitment), limited and open, 25, 71-3, 78-9; Walrond Committee and, 72; language barrier, 74-5; Civil Service Class I, 74; for Levant Service, 166; for China Service, 185, 192, 218
Compradores, and British merchants, 207; and consular courts, 227
Compton, Charles Spencer, and incident in Canton, 209-10
Comptroller and Auditor General, and accounting control, 66
Congo, Roger Casement and, 35
Constantinople, 79, 131, 142, 150, 153, 156, 165, 190; posts at, 35; communications through, 62; C. M. Kennedy's inspection at, 63; consular functions in, 130; and capitulatory rights, 137-41; establishment of Supreme Consular Court at, 148-9; and Lord Strangford, 154; Carlton Cumberbatch at, 155; training at, 164-5, 167, 173
Consular Act (1825), and beginnings of a service, 5, 13-15, 31, 68; and notarial fees, 40-1; and pensions, 44, 45; and salary levels, 81; and Levant Company, 125, 146
Consular Appointments Committee, 109
Consular Department (Foreign Office), 43; social distinctions, administration and staffing, 2; creation of, 11, 15; Palmerston on promotion in, 49; and consular despatches, 56; Foreign Office and Board of Trade and, 57; communication and control, 58-64; Dufferin and, 59, 228; records kept by, 89; and administration, 90, 92; Sir David Scott at, 92-3; and promotions, 95; W. H. Wylde and, 135; and Ernest Gye, 176, 228
Consular Establishment, Select Committee on (1835), 24, 68; and consular remuneration, 32, 38
Consular Jurisdiction, International Commission upon (1870), on Egyptian policing and mixed cases, 152
Consular Salaries Committee (1917-18), 109; recommendations of, 110, 111
Consular Service and Appointments, Select Committee on (1857-8), and attractions of service, 24, and recruitment and training, 25-6; and private supplements to salaries, 39, 41-2, 199; and unhealthy climates, 45; and arguments against creation of service, 50;

Consular Service and Appointments, Select Committee on (1857-8)—*continued*
 and promotion, 52; and Foreign Office and consular despatches, 56; and contact with Foreign Office, 60; and accounting control, 65, 66; and appointments, 68; and consular and diplomatic functions, 118; and protection in Turkey, 139, 144; and recruitment for Levant Service, 154, 157, 164; and close services, 170-1; on China Consular Service, 192

Consular Service, Committee appointed to inquire into the Constitution of (1903), *see* Walrond Committee

Consular Service, Foreign Office Committee on (1912), 83, 90; and allowances and salaries, 87; and inspections, 93; on retirement, 102; on commercial efficiency of consuls, 107-8

Consular Service, Committee on (1919), *see* Steel-Maitland Committee

Consular Service, Departmental Committee on (1938-9), and distinctions between consuls and diplomats, 2; and diplomats' arguments against amalgamation, 115-16; and diplomatic functions, 118; minority reports of, 123; Knatchbull-Hugessen's letter amplifying minority report to, 240-2

Consuls, honorary, 37, 42, 53

Consuls, military, function of, 132-3

Consuls, trading, before 1825, 7, 12; 1825 Act and, 14; and relations with Chinese, 207; appointments in Far East, 202-4

Cooke, Henry, on allowances for hospitality, 87

Corfu, 148

Corruption, in Levant Service, 154-63; and consular jurisdiction, 214

Cotton, consular appointment to promote growing of, 50

Court, Mixed, and Chinese nationalism, 215-17

Court, Supreme at Hong Kong, 214; *The Times* on, 213

Court, Supreme Consular at Constantinople, establishment of, 148-9; and Sir Edmund Hornby (judge of), 154

Court, Supreme Consular at Shanghai, 190, 201; legal training for student interpreters at, 191; advancement in, 192; consul charged before, 196; effect of on consular duties, 200; consular jurisdiction and, 214

Courts, Chinese, justice at, 212; exterritorial rights and, 216

Courts, consular, and the Levant Service, 146-52; abuse of in Egypt, 151; abandonment of capitulations and, 174; at Canton, 188, 189; at Yokohama and supervision of Japanese, 190; administration of justice at in Far East, 192, 212, 214; and language requirements, 226-7

Courts, Egyptian, 150, 151

Courts, Ottoman, rights of ambassadors at, 136; condition of, 140-3

Courts, Siamese, jurisdiction of, 215

Cowper, Francis H., and promotion, 55

Cowper, H. A., on disadvantages of close system, 170-1

Cox, Sir Percy, powers of in Persian Gulf, 131-2

Crammers, and examinations, 77, 185

Crampton, Sir J., on communications, 62

Cranborne, Lord, on consular assistance to traders, 20; on patronage, 23; and Walrond Committee, 69; on career prospects, 90

Crawfurd, Oswald, 21; and objections to close service, 51

Crete, 130, 144, 158

Crimean War, 135; 1856 Treaty and protection of Christians, 143-4; and establishment of Supreme Consular Court, 148-9; state of Levant consulates at time of, 154; and after, 155

Cromer, Lord, on effect of capitulations, 152

Crossman, Major, on consulate at Tamsui, 85; on staffing of China Service, 202

Crowe, Sir Edward, and Levant Service and amalgamation, 177, 178

Crowe, Sir Eyre, on Association of Chambers of Commerce and consular reform, 108, 109-10; heading Foreign Office Committee, 108-9; Victor Wellesley on close services and, 173; *see also* Eyre Crowe Committee

Cumberbatch, Carlton, 155

Cumberbatch, Robert, on travel and leave, 29

Currie, Sir Philip, on assessment of consuls, 57; and training scheme for Levant consuls, 165

Curry, E. T., 34

Index 257

Curzon, Lord, on consulate at Muscat, 28; on appointment of Alan Napier, 71
Cyprus, 130, 155
Cyprus Convention (1878), 132

Damascus, 126, 130; need for appointment at, 16; cost of living at, 40; Richard Burton and, 52, 85, 145, 163; protection at, 139; salary at, 158
Danish, language, 75
Danubian Principalities, 169; consular functions in, 120
Danzig, consulate before 1825, 12
Dardanelles, 130, 158
Davis, Sir John, and Compton incident, 209
Delagoa Bay, Roger Casement on, 35, 36
Denmark, 10
Deportation, consular powers of, 147
Derby, Earl of, on promotions, 52-3; on accounting control, 67; on consular rewards in Far East, 194
Dering, Herbert, on political and judicial conditions in Siam, 215; on marriage to a native, 197
Deschamps, Gaston, on French consular protection in Tunisia, 141
Diarbekr, trading functions at, 19; political functions at, 126; protection of Jews and Christians at, 134, 144
Dikha, Court of Appeal (Siam), 215
Dilke, Sir Charles, on patronage, 22
Diplomatic and Consular Services, Select Committee on (1870-2), 60; and fees, 17; and Hammond on consular system, 17; and permission to trade, 42; and salary levels, 40, 43, 44; and pension rights, 45-6; on promotion, 51, 52-3; and inspections, 64; and accounting control, 66-7; on 1858 Committee, 68; and social objections to amalgamation, 114-15; and Levant Service, 129, 130-1; and Sir Henry Elliot on recruitment, 156; Kennedy and training scheme and, 165; on close system in China Service, 192; and consular rewards in Far East, 194-5; Sir Rutherford Alcock and, 199, 204; Sir Harry Parkes and, 204
Diplomatic and Consular Services, Memorandum on the Amalgamation of (1938), 122, 123, 229-30
Diplomatic Service, 51, 52, 95, 170; and distinctions between consuls and diplomats, 1-4; costs of, 32; and pension rights, 44; and arguments against creation of a service, 50-1; communications within, 54; superiority of, 62; and recruitment, 69, 72; examinations for, 71, 116; greater rewards for, 99; delegation of commercial functions by, 107; and amalgamation, 114-24, 177; and consular rewards in China, 194, 195; and administration in the East, 227; and 1943 reforms, 231, 232, 234; qualities for, 240-2
Diplomatic Service, Commercial, and Department of Overseas Trade, 91-2; and supervision of consular officers, 92; and amalgamation, 231, 234
Disraeli, Benjamin, in favour of amalgamation, 124
Distressed British Subjects, 18-19, 20, 112, 202
Dominica, 72
Doria, William, 165
Dragomans, 163, 174, 186; and Turkish justice, 143; protection of consular, 144, 156; corruption of in Levant, 160-3; training scheme for, 164-5, 167-8; for student dragomans *see* Interpreters, Student
Drogheda, Earl of, 92
Drummond-Hay, F. R., on consular jurisdiction in Tripoli, 150
Dufferin, Lord, and Consular Department, 59; on colour discrimination, 72; on need for clerical service, 113; on transfers of China consuls, 228
Duncan Report (1968-9) and Foreign Office grading, 235; and distribution of functions, 236, 239
Dunkirk, 79
Dunlop, T. D., and Peking language training, 188; on sickness rates in China, 197; on recruitment to China Service after 1914, 221; on amalgamation, 230
Dutch, language, 75, 226
Duties, *see* Functions

Eastern Department (Foreign Office), 165
East India Company, consular appointments of, 131; Rawlinson and, 157; in Canton, 180-1; and Chinese authority over, 181, 206; and establishment of China Consular Service, 182, 188; supercargoes of and commercial disputes, 189; and effect on consular salaries, 195

258 The Cinderella Service

East Indies, Dutch, Siam Service posts in, 226
Eccles, David, and status of commercial secretaries, 234
Economist, The, on Civil Service reform, 48; on commercial reports, 104-5; on activities of Levant consuls, 136, 154; and commercial salaries in relation to consular in Siam, 220
Eden, Anthony, and 1943 reforms, 3-4, 122, 231, 234, 235-6, 239
Egypt, 131, 141, 142, 150-2, 168, 175
Eldridge, on political functions of Levant consuls, 134
Elliot, Captain Charles, on disputes amongst merchants, 189; on consular jurisdiction, 211
Elliot, Sir Henry, on Ottoman consular establishment, 127; on appointment of consuls, 156
Embezzlement, and Public Accounts Committee (1892), 67; charge of, against G.W. Caine, 196
Emden, 12
Enos, 130
Entertainment, allowances and regulations for, 86-7; and information, 87, 88
Erzurum, consular functions in, 19, 130, 133
Estimates, Select Committee on (1937), and allowances, 84
Eyre Crowe Committee (1916), on shipping work, 106; formation of, 108; on trade policy and consular staffing, 108-9, 110
Examinations, 48, 71-9 *pass*., 112; and personnel control, 94; for Consular Clerk grade, 113; for Levant Service, 165, 166-8, 171, 176; for China Service, 171, 183, 192, 218, 219, 221; in Law, 191; and proposals for amalgamation, 229;
Examiner, The, on dangers of protection, 146
Exchange, rates of, and Chinese salaries, 199-200
Exchequer, 42; payment of fees into, 17, 64, 202
Exchequer and Audit Department, and accounting control, 66
Executive Class, 79, 117, 235-6, 238
Exeter Hall, and consular protection for missionaries, 153
Exterritoriality, 38; in Levant, 136-52, 172-5; in China, 206-17, 180; and legal training in China, 188-92; abandonment of in Far East, 226-7, 229

Faringdon Committee, 109
Featherstonhaugh, G.W., on salaries, 39
Fees, 200, 202, 205; before 1825, 6, 8, 11-13, 14; 1825 Act and, 13-15; notarial, 14, 31, 40; and salaries, 30-3; 40-3; and pension rights, 46; control of, 64-7; and clerical staffing, 112; end of Ionian protectorate and, 144-5; of Supreme Consular Court, 149
Fernando Po, 40, 51
Finn, James, consulate of in Jerusalem, 85; Mrs Finn on, 135; on consular jurisdiction, 150; scandal of *chancelier* of, 161, 162; and transfer of, 161
Finn, Mrs James, on Mr Finn and protection of minorities, 135; and Peter Meshullam, 161
Fisher, Sir Godfrey, on H.M.G. and early consulates, 5-6; on mercantile consuls, 6, 8-9
Fitzgerald, Seymour, on consular economy, 17
Flanders, 10
Fletcher, Miss, 159
Foochow, consulate at, 84-5; and establishment of, 182; salary at, 195; trade at, 203; move to abolish consulate at, 205
Foreign Jurisdiction Act (1843), and consular powers, 146
Foreign Office Committee (1916), *see* Eyre Crowe Committee
Formosa, staffing at, 226
Fowle, Major T. C. W., on Government of India and Persian consulates, 132
Fox, H. H., and European posts for China consuls, 228
France, 8, 185, 235; shipping fees in, 13; consular service of, 49, 68, 107, 156-7; inspection in, 63; ratio of staff to trade in, 109; protégés and, 137, 139, 141; consular appointments of in Levant, 157; end of capitulatory rights, 174-5; Concession in Shanghai, 212
Francis, Sir Philip, on travelling time from Levant, 29
Frankfurt, 18, 38
Fraser, Lt Col. A. J., 161
French, language, 167; examination in, 75, in Siam Service, 226

Functions, commercial, before 1825, 6, 7, 10, 11, 14; expansion of, 16; Canning/Huskisson and, 18; appointments for, 19, 50; neglect of, 20, 134; salaried service and, 30; Palmerston and, 53; returns and the Foreign Office, 56-8; and experience for, 72, 76; as sources of commercial intelligence, 31, 87, 104-5, 120; and administration, 91; before 1914, 103-10; and commercial reports 104-5; priority of, 109; after 1914, 110-13; and Second Division Clerks, 112; and objections to amalgamation, 117-21; of Levant consuls, 126-30; effect of Crimean War on, 148; in China, 181-2; and consular jurisdiction in China, 188-9, 208; trade returns and cost of consulates, 202-4; after 1943, 235-9 pass.

Functions, judicial, 104, 134, 202; and permission to trade, 42; in Levant Service, 126, 129, 136-46, 152-3, 169; effect of on recruitment before 1914, 171; decline of, 173; in China Service, 188-92; 208, 211-17, 226

Functions, maritime, in sixteenth and seventeenth centuries, 6-7; naval, 7, 8, 10, 16, 18; and neglect of commercial work, 20; and Board of Trade, 58; before 1914, 103, 105-6; delegation of, 106; Palmerston on, 117; in China, 204, 208-9

Functions, notarial, 31, 40; and inspection, 62

Functions, political and diplomatic, intelligence, 6-7, 8, 10, 18; and fees and salaries, 31, 37; and restrictions from trading, 42; and Foreign Office, 53, 56, 59; before 1914, 103-10 pass.; and objections to amalgamation, 117-21 pass.; in Levant Service, 126, 127, 129, 130-5, 152-3, 159, 164, 169; effect of on recruitment before 1914, 171; decline of, 173-4; in China Service, 180, 188, 189; after 1943, 235-9 pass.

Furniture, Roger Casement and, 36; and office allowances, 84

Galata, 167
Galatz, consular functions in, 130; consular jurisdiction in, 149-50
Galway, Captain, 28
Geddes Axe, 111
Genoa, shipping fees at, 12
Geography, commercial, education in, 80
German, language, 75

Germany, 129, 173, 185; consular functions in, 18; commercial functions by consuls of, 107; change of attitude to (1914-18), 108; exterritorial rights of withdrawn by China, 216; Branch A officers in, 235

Ghadames, consular functions at, 19
Gibbon, Edward, on name and status of consul, 5
Gibraltar, 145; consular charges and Gibraltarians, 65; protection of Gibraltarians, 140
Giles, Professor, and examination for China Service, 219
Gladstone, W. E., 40; and salaries, 43; government of and military consuls, 132; administration of and recruitment reform, 185
Golden Horn, 138
Gordon, Charles George, 21
La Goulette, accounting control at, 67
Graham, George, 159
Graham, Sir James, and financing the Service, 32
Granville, Lord, and inspection reports in France, 18; and open competition for China Service, 185
Graves, Robert, on language abilities of Levant consuls, 165-6
Great Eastern, 138
Greece, consular functions on Turkish frontier of, 130; and consular protection of Greeks, 144; training scheme for appointments in, 165
Greek, language, 160, 167
Green, John, on consular reform, 63; on inspections, 64; on Levant consuls, 163; on restriction of capitulations at Bucharest, 174
Gregory, William, consular jurisdiction of in Swatow, 214; Herbert Dering and, 215
Grenville, Lord, on dissolution of Levant Company, 125
Grenville-Murray, E. C., 21; and bribery charges against, 159; and corruption of Levant consuls, 162
Gretton, W. H., 45
Grey, Sir Edward, 115; and patronage in appointments, 70
Gye, Ernest, at Consular Department, 92; on promotion, 97-8; and Levant Service promotions block and amalgamation, 176, 177

Haiti, mortality in, 45

Hakodate, 204

Haldane, Miss, and advertising for applicants by Foreign Office, 74

Hall, Herbert Hall, and Levant Service and amalgamation, 177

Hamburg, shipping fees at, 12; difficulties of promotion at, 82

Hammond, Edmund, on satisfactory state of Consular Service, 17; on recruitment and training, 24, 25-6; on salaries, 39, 43; on mortality, 45; on mobility, 50; on promotion prospects, 53; and consular despatches, 55-6; and James Murray, 59; and Instructions, 62; and limitations imposed by consular salaries, 114; on functional distinction between consuls and diplomats, 118; on Levant establishment, 135; and Turkish subjects under British protection, 144

Hankow, salaries and perquisites in mercantile houses, 193, 194; imprisonment of G. W. Caine from, 196; cost of living at, 198; and trade at, 203; consular jurisdiction at, 212; surrender of exterritorial rights in, 216; violence against consuls in, 226

Hannay, James, 21

Harborne, William, and capitulations, 136

Harbour masters, English appointments of at Constantinople, 138

Hardinge, Sir Arthur, and consular and diplomatic functions, 120, 121

Hart, Sir Robert, salary of in Chinese Customs, 196

Hashem, Mrs, 146

Havre, Le, 39, 81; consular income at, 12; patronage at, 22

Hay, John M., on cost and scale of China Service, 200

Henderson, Arthur, on amalgamation, 121

Herat, 146

Hertslet, Godfrey E. P., 70

Hervey, Henry, and accounting control, 66-7

Hesse, 38

Hewlett, Sir Meyrick, and language training for China Service, 185

Hill, Sir Clement, and consular inspection, 64

Hillier, Sir Walter, on language abilities of China consuls, 186, 226-7

Hoare, Sir Samuel, on Foreign Service interviews, 73; and Sir David Scott's Memorandum, 230

Hobart Pasha, on protégés, 139; on Turkish administration of justice, 143

Holmes, Ernest, on leave and salaries in Japan Service, 220-1

Holmes, W. R., on political functions, 133; and 'officious' protection of Jews and Christians, 144; and opening a trade, 158

Holms, J., and scale and cost of Siam Service, 202

Holt, Mr, 172

Hong Kong, 183, 202, 214; Chinese consuls administered from, 182, 183; Canton Court transferred to, 189; and Compton case, 209; Supreme Court of and Rutherford Alcock, 213

Hong Kong and Shanghai Bank, language training by, 187

Hong merchants, and Lord Napier, 181

Honolulu, Japan Service and, 226

Hornby, Edmund, and establishment of Supreme Consular Court at Constantinople, 148-9; on condition of Levant consulates, 155-6; and Supreme Consular Court at Shanghai, 190; on legal training, 190-1; on judicial business at Yokohama consulate, 191; on language training 208; on missionaries, 211

Hosie, Alexander, at Chungking, 203

Hospitals, at Smyrna, 126

Housing, conditions of, 28, 30, 40; costs of, 37; allowances for and style of, 84-6; inspectors and, 93; and cost of housekeeping in China, 198-9, 201

Howard, Henry, 64; on functional distinction between consuls and diplomats, 118

Hudson, R. S., 103

Hughes, Thomas, as student dragoman, 164-5

Hull, 105

Hume, Joseph, on fees, 12; on salaries and fees, 32

Huskisson, William, and pressure for reform, 13; on extension of consular system, 16, 126; on functions of consuls, 18

Iasi (Romania), political intelligence from, 132

Ibn Saud, and exterritoriality, 175

Iliasu, A., 56
Iloilo, consular functions at, 19
Inchcape, Lord, *see* Mackay, Sir James
India, 154, 158, 181; attractions of business in, 77; cost to consuls of travellers to, 86; Government of and consular appointments, 53, 131-2; and Welby Agreement, 131; Government of and Persian nationalism, 132; revenue to from Far East trade, 204
Indians, British, and consular charges, 65; and consular authority, 141; consular protection of, 140, 145
Indo-China, French, Siam and, 180
Inland Revenue, and accounting control, 66
Inspections, consular, and consulates in France, 18; in nineteenth century, 58-64; of Levant consulates, 63-4, 149, 153, 165; for accounting control, 66, 67; and hospitality allowances, 87; personnel administration and, 88-94; and promotions board, 96; and Sir Edmund Hornby, 155; by T. D. Dunlop, 188
Instructions, consular, in eighteenth century, 11; and 1822 memorandum, 61; Foreign Office and, 61-2; on promotion 96; and Merchant Shipping Acts, 103; legal, 190, 208
Interpreters, student, Levant, Palmerston's training scheme for, 164-5; new training scheme for, 165-8; abolition of, 176
Interpreters, student, Far East, 183-8; legal training of, 188-92; career prospects of, 192-4; numbers of, 201-2; recruitment of after 1918, 221-2
Ionians, and consular charges, 65; and protection of, 140, 144-5; consular powers of jurisdiction in Levant over, 147; complaints against consuls by, 153; impotence of, against consuls, 161-2
Iraq, East India Company appointments in, 131; abandonment of capitulations in, 175
Ireland, 74
Italian, language, 75
Italy, 171; early appointments in, 8; consular functions in, 18; inspection in, 64; and capitulations in Tunisia, 174; Branch A officers in, 235

Jacobites, protection of, 144; papal, protection of, 144
Jaffa, 130; scandalous behaviour of consul at, 155; salary at, 158

Jago, Thomas, of consulate at Tripoli, 85
James, G. P. R., 21
Janina, 130; burden of Ionians to consul of, 144
Japan Consular Service, 180, 182, 207; Sir Rutherford Alcock on, 28-9; before 1914, 103; as close service, 170-2; end of exterritoriality in, 175, 215; functions in, 180; recruitment for, 183; and language training, 187; judicial burden in, 189, 190; career prospects in, 192; rewards in, 194; attraction of service with Government of, 196; and fares from China, 198; trade and, 204; case against merchant in, 213; 1894 Treaty and, 215; Manchuria and consular jurisdiction and, 217; leave and salaries in, 220-1; and amalgamation, 225-30 *pass.*
Japanese, language, patronage and problems of, 185
Jassy, consular functions in, 130
Jenkyns, Sir Henry, on consular jurisdiction at colonial courts, 148
Jerusalem, Finn's consulate at, 85; functions at, 130, 135; consular protection of Jews in, 139; administration of justice at, 143; consular jurisdiction in, 150; suspension of consul at, 155; salary at, 158; scandal of chancelier at, 161
Jews, 158; protection of, 135, 139, 144, 145; in consular employment in Levant, 160
Johnston, Harry, 21; on consulate at Tripoli, 85
Johnstone, Sir Alexander, and legal instructions, 190
Jordan, Sir John, promotion into diplomatic service of, 52; career in China of, 194; on career prospects in China Service, 219-20

Kashgar, 132
Kayat, Assaad J, 155
Kelly, Sir David, and Consular Department, 60; on Ernest Gye and consuls, 92
Kennedy, C. M., and inspection of Levant consulates, 63, 162; on consular jurisdiction, 127, 149; on consular influence in Levant, 133; on protection, 139-40; on consuls in Turkey, 153; on corruption, 162; on training of dragomans, 165
Kenya, 132

Kermanshah, 131
Kharput, 134
King, Mr, 45
King, Paul, on consular jurisdiction in Swatow, 214
King's College, London, nominations by, 183; language training at, 185, 187
Kinglake, Alexander William, on dragomans, 160
Kirk, Henry, 21
Kitchener, Horatio Herbert, 21; as military consul, 132
Kiukiang, consular jurisdiction at, 212
Knatchbull-Hugessen, Sir Hughe, on social objections to amalgamation, 116; letter to Sir Alexander Cadogan from, 240-2
Korea, staffing at, 226
Korean, language, 226
Küchen, Theodore, 38
Kuomintang, and exterritoriality, 217
Kurdistan, and military consuls, 132
Kustenje, 130
Kuwait, 131

Labour Party, and consular reform, 121-2
Lamont, William J., 70
Lampson, Sir Miles, on promotion, 97-8; and Legation Committee on Far Eastern Services, 222-3; on age of retirement, 225; and amalgamation of China Service, 227
Lane-Poole, Stanley, on China consulates, 183
Langley, W., on inspections, 93
Language tests, 74-5, 116, 166; effect of severity of, 185
Languages, and recruitment, 24, 26
Languages (Far Eastern Service), 201; ignorance of, 183; effect on social composition of service, 185; training for, 185-8, 191, 193, 219; problems of in China, 192, 214; attitude of merchants to, 206-8; and arguments for amalgamation, 225, 226, 228, 229; and 1943 proposals, 236, 237
Languages (Levant Service), and difficulties of recruitment, 156, 166; training for, 165, 167-8, 173; problems in Russia, 169, 175; and close services, 172-3
Languages, Schools of Oriental, 187-8
Larissa, 130
Lausanne, 175

Law, knowledge of, 24, 26; education in, 80, 167, 168, 188-92; and amalgamation arguments, 177; and international, 190-1; examinations in, 191
Law, Algernon, on pensions, 47; on outside appointments, 71; and Board of Selection, 72, 90; on inspections, 93; on promotions, 96-7; on retirement age, 102; on reorganization of consular service, 108; on university recruitment, 117; on language requirements for Levant Service, 166
Law, Andrew Bonar, and Walrond Committee, 69; on business experience for consuls, 76-7
Law, Edward Fitzgerald, on consular reports, 57
Law, Richard, and 1943 reforms, 122, 123-4, 236; on pensions from the Civil List, 47
Layard, Austen Henry, on fees, 40; and Richard Burton, 51; and criticism of capitulatory system, 140, 142, 148
Leathes, Stanley, on consular examination, 77; on social position of diplomats, 115
Leave, 60; entitlement and regulations, 29-30; and communication with Foreign Office, 54, 59; in China Service, 193; in Japan Service, 220; and effect on promotion in China, 223; training during, 225; and proposals for amalgamation, 230
Lebanon, French mandate and capitulations in, 175
Lee, Sir Henry Austin, on Foreign Office and consular control, 60-1; and society and diplomacy in Paris, 115
Leeds, University of, commercial education at, 80
Leghorn, mercantile consul at, 9; shipping fees at, 12, 13
Leipzig, political functions at, 18
Leningrad, language training at, 173; see also St Petersburg
Levant Company, 188; dissolution of, 14, 16, 125-6; consulates of, 85, 126; and capitulations, 136-7; and 1825 Act, 146; and government consuls, 153; reasons for replacement of, 180-1
Levant Consular Service, 120, 125-79 pass.; functions, 16; problems of leave from, 29; fees and salaries in, 31, 101-2; consular rights in, 35; and promotions,

Index   263

53, 97, 98, 176-9, 222; and Foreign Office, 54; inspection of, 63-4; and recruitment, 71, 166-9; as graded service, 68, 69; entry to, 72; housing for, 84, 85, 126; before 1914, 103; after 1914, 111; commercial functions in, 126-30; political functions in, 130-5; Indian 'politicals' in, 132; Kennedy and, 133; Edmund Hammond and, 135; judicial functions of, 136-46; inadequacy of prisons in, 147; and Supreme Consular Court, 149; scandalous condition of, 154-5; establishment as separate service, 163, 170-2; training for, 165-8, 186, 187, 197, 201, 202, 205, 207, 208; and movement towards amalgamation, 168-79, 226, 227; question of continuation of, 175; Foreign Office Committee on, 176-9; policy on after 1919, 176, 177; career prospects in, 176-9; 219, 222; Branch A officers in, 235

Levant Consular Service, Foreign Office Committee on (1933), and recruitment, 71; and promotion, 97, 98; Treasury and salary proposals of, 101-2; formation of, 176-8; recommendations of, 178-9; on amalgamation, 227, 228, 229

Levantines, criticism of as consuls, 153-63

Lever, Charles, 21; on Trieste, 28, 29; on La Spezia, 29; on salaries, 39

Liberia, 17, 70

Librarian, Department of (Foreign Office), 70

Lima, salary at, 37

Lisbon, early consulates at, 9, 10; shipping duties in, 19-20; promotion at, 49; and George Brackenbury, 51; appointment at, 70

Liverpool, 29

Livingstone, David, 21

Lloyds, fees from, 40, 41; agencies for, 41

Lockhart, Bruce, on social position of consuls, 55; on Consular Department, 59; and duties in Moscow, 78

Locock, Guy, on entertainment allowances, 87

Loftus, Lord Augustus, and inspection of Baltic consulates by, 63

London, 90, 121, 183, 199-200, 203, 225

London School of Economics, commercial education at, 80

Longford, J. H., on promotion prospects, 53

Lousada, Francis, 46

Lyons, 78

Lyons, Lord, on inspection reports from France, 18; on communication between legations and consulates, 62

Lytton, Lord, 29

MacAlister, Sir Donald, on distinction between consular and diplomatic functions, 120, 121

Macao, 181, 182

MacDonnell, Lord, on recruiting men with experience, 76; on salaries, 82; see also Civil Service, Royal Commission on (1912-14)

MacDonnell, E., on inspections, 93

MacDonnell Commission (1914), see Civil Service, Royal Commission on (1912-14)

Mackay, Sir James, and Walrond Committee, 69; on commercial experience of consuls, 76-7

Mackay Treaty (1902), and exterritorial rights in China, 216

Mackinnon Mackenzie, 69

Maclean, Donald, 89

Madeira, 12, 43

Madrid, 61, 118, 120

Malaga, salary at, 39; fees at, 40, 41

Malcolm, Ian, 64

Mallet, Sir Louis, and cost and scale of China Service, 200

Mallett, Sir Claude, and promotion to diplomatic service of, 52

Malmesbury, Lord, on consular appointments, 17; and Consular Department, 59

Malta, 157; consular jurisdiction and colonial court at, 148

Maltese, and consular charges, 65; and consular protection of, 138, 140, 141, 145; consular jurisdiction over, 147; complaints against consuls by, 153; dislike of as British consuls, 157; impotence of against consuls, 161-2

Manchester Chamber of Commerce, President of, on recruitment and training of consuls, 26-7

Manchu Dynasty, and Chinese nationalism, 215, 218

Manchuria, Japanese in, and consular jurisdiction, 217

Mander, Geoffrey, on amalgamation, 122

Manila, and Japan Service, 226

Manson, Allan, 113

264 The Cinderella Service

Marash, consular protection in, 134-5
Marine Superintendents, consuls as, 103; secondment of to consulates, 106
Mark, W. P., and salary and fees at Malaga, 39-40
Marriages, native, in Far Eastern Service, 197
Marsa, La, 85
Marseilles, income at, 12; as 'prize' in profession, 53; difficulty of promotion at, 82
Matheson, James, and Compton incident, 209-10
Mauritius, patronage at, 23
Maxse, Ernest, on allowances, 36; and duties at Rotterdam, 78
McGregor, Francis, and Compton incident, 209
McMaster, Mrs, and widow's pension of, 47-8
Meadows, T. T., and Newchwang consulate, 85, 205-6
Meagher, Jeremiah, 49
Medhurst, W. H., career in China, 183
Merchant Shipping Acts, consular functions under, 103
Merchants, and early consuls, 1-15 pass.; objection to government assistance of, 20; and recruitment as consuls, 25, 26, 76-7; fees and financing the service by, 30-1; as consular agents, 41-2, 156; and Consular Department, 59; servants of and consular protection, 144; and Levant consuls, 153; and commercial intelligence, 87, 104-5; dislike of Levantines and Maltese by, 157; trade monopoly of and origins of consular services, 180-1; Lord Napier and, 181-2; and commercial disputes in Canton, 189; salaries of compared to consuls, 193, 195-6, 220; and Chungking, 203; and exterritoriality, 206-13 pass.; and consular courts, 212, 226-7; and amalgamation, 230
Merit, salaries and, 33, 34; *The Economist* on, 48; reward for, 49, 50-1, 55, 195; and Richard Burton, 52; promotion according to, 53, 54; in F.O., 55; difficulties of rewarding, 82, 95, 231; seniority versus merit, 89, 96-9; lack of reward for in China Service, 193, 194, 228
Mersina, consular protection at, 137, 146
Meshed, 131

Meshullam, Peter, scandalous case of, 161
Michell, C. E., and agency money at St Petersburg, 40
Michell, George, and consular salaries, 30, 220
Michie, Alexander, and trade in opium at Foochow, 203; on attitudes of China merchants, 206
Middlemarch, 24
Milan, political functions at, 18
Millar, F. R. Hoyer, on appropriation of consular prizes by diplomats, 100n.; on social objections to amalgamation, 116, 242; on consular and diplomatic functions, 118-19
Missionaries, 202; and cost of living in China, 198, 199; and relations with Chinese, 207; and burden to consuls, 211
Mitford, Algernon, on social qualities needed for diplomacy, 194-5
Monastir, 126, 130, 144
Moneylenders, protection of at Damascus, 140
Montenegro, 132
Montevideo, patronage at, 22
Montgomery, Sir Hubert, and amalgamation, 177
Montreux Conference (1937), and end of capitulations, 175
Morgan, James and amalgamation, 177
Morocco, 130, 169; protection in, 145; training scheme for, 165; specialized service for, 169; abandonment of capitulations in, 175
Moscow, 78; and allowances, 83-4; language training at, 173, 187
Mosquito Indians, 146
Most-Favoured-Nation Clause, 137
Mostar, 19
Mosul, 130, 157
Mounsey, Sir George, on amalgamation, 229
Murray, James, on consular freehold, 35; on salaries, 43; and circulation of papers, 56; and staffing of Consular Department, 59; and accounting control, 66
Murzuq, consular functions at, 19
Muscat, 28, 132
Mûsh, 134

Nagasaki, 191, 204
Nanking, Treaty of (1842), 195, 205; and

consular representation in China, 182, 189
Nantes, 70
Napier, Lord, in Canton, 181; retreat to Macao and death of, 182; legal instructions of, 190, 208
Napier, Alan, 71
Naples, fees at, 12; appointment at, 61
Neale, Colonel, 207
Nestorians, protection of, 144, 145
New York, seamen at, 19; consulate at, 36; promotion at, 53, 61, 82; accounting control at, 66; salaries and allowances at, 82; delegation of shipping functions at, 106
Newchwang, consulate at, 85; consular functions at, 205
Newton, Sir Charles Thomas, 21
Nice, salary at, 39
Nicolaev, 39
Niigata, 204
Nile, 142
Ningpo, consulate established at, 182; salary at, 195; trade at, 203; move to abolish consulate at, 205
Northern Department (H.M. Government), consular administration by, 11
Norwegian, language, 75
Nubar Pasha, and Mixed Courts, 142n.; and International Commission on Consular Jurisdiction, 152

Oakley, Mr, 159
Odessa, shipping functions at, 19; consulate general at, 53; communications from, 62; dismissal of Grenville-Murray from, 159
Officers, Naval and Military, and hospitality to, 86
Opium, trade in, 203
Opium Wars, *see* Chinese Wars, First and Second
Oporto, 51
Oppenheimer, Sir Francis, on social position of consuls, 2
Orders in Council (Consular), 1833 and 1843, on Chinese consular jurisdiction, 188-9; 1843 and 1844 on Levant consular jurisdiction, 146, 148; 1847 on powers of deportation, 148; 1855 on examinations, 25; 1857 on Supreme Consular Court at Constantinople, 149; 1864 on consular jurisdiction, 149; 1865 on Supreme Consular Court in Shanghai, 190; 1896 on promotion, 53, 96; 1921 on retirement, 225
Oriental Studies, Committee on (1909), *see* Reay Committee
Ortakeui, language training at, 167, 168
Osaka, 204
Oslo, *see* Christiania
Ostend, salary at, 34
Ottewill, H. A., on conditions at Wuchow consulate, 203
Otway, A. J., on overlap of consular and diplomatic functions, 119
Overseas Representation, Review Committee on (1968-9), *see* Duncan Report
Overseas Trade, Department of, 105, 110, 177, 178; and Steel-Maitland, 80, 111; Victor Wellesley on, 91; creation and function of, 91-2; on Promotions Board, 96; and move towards amalgamation, 123
Oxford, University of, 164, 215; language training at, 167; candidates from, 233

Paget, Sir Augustus, on social objections to amalgamation, 114
Pakistan, 141
Palairet, Michael, on lack of applicants for Far Eastern Service, 222
Palestine, British protection, in 139; fraud in, 155; *see also* Fynn, Robert
Palgrave, W. Gifford, 21, 157; promotion of, 52; at Trebizond, 127; on protection of Ionians, 144-5
Pall Mall Gazette, 52
Palmerston, Lord, on consular system in 1855, 17; on patronage, 23; on training, 26, 164; on salaries, 37; trading consuls and, 38; on promotion, 49; and 1831 economies, 53; and consular despatches, 55-6; and consular functions in Danubian Principalities, 120; on Levant Service, 129; and instructions on protection at Jerusalem, 139; on powers of jurisdiction, 188-9, 211-12; and commercial jurisdiction, 189; on move to reduce China consulates, 205
Panama, salary and pension at, 34
Pará, Roger Casement on, 35; salaries from, 220
Paramaribo, 53
Paris, 18, 142, 143, 171; consuls general at, 61; society and diplomacy in, 115;

Paris—*continued*
  language training in, 187; administration of consulates from, 227
Parish, Woodbine, on salaries, 37; on expense of entertaining, 87
Parkes, Sir Harry, promotion of, 52; career in China, 183, 194; on judicial functions in Shanghai, 189; on need for Supreme Consular Court in Japan, 190; on judicial functions in Japan, 191; on trade in Siam and Japan, 204
Patronage, before 1825, 9, 10; 1825 Act and, 14, 33; and Secretary of State, 21-2, 23-5, 27, 51; and consuls general, 61; and Walrond Committee on, 69-70; Treasury on, 71; after 1903, 71; Tyrrell on, 95; and education, 117; and China consuls, 183, 185, 187
Pears, Sir Edwin, and legal training of Levant recruits, 168
Pedder, William Henry, on travel, 29
Peel, Sir Robert, on salaries and fees, 32
Peking, 97, 196, 203, 207; posts at, 35; and cost to consuls of travellers to, 86; and Henry Howard, 118; early consuls at, 183; language training at, 186, 188, 229-230; law examinations at, 191; language examinations at, 192; attractions of to diplomats, 194-5; sickness at, 196-7; career prospects in, 219-20; and promotions block, 222, 228; administration from, 227
Pensions, 59, 112, 192; Act of 1825 and, 13; in nineteenth century, 28, 44-9; inequalities in, 34; effect of on honesty of consuls, 65, 66, 94; and Walrond Committee, 81; and salaries, 82; and retirement of inefficient officers, 102-3; and permission to trade, 159; for consuls at Treaty ports, 195; and Indian Civil Service, 219; and retirement in China Service, 223-5
Pera, 2, 138
Percy, Earl, on consular functions in Asia Minor, 133
Pernambuco, fees at, 41; salary at, 81
Perry, William, 34
Persia, 141, 164, 202; E. F. Law in, 57; consular establishment in, 129; Indian appointments in, 131-2; protection in, 146; specialized service in, 169; abandonment of capitulations in, 175
Persian, language, 167, 208
Persian Gulf, East India Company appointment in, 131; Sir Percy Cox in, 131; Major Fowle in, 132; British interest in oil of, 173
Personnel, need for department of, 55; administration and inspection of, 88-95; and 1943 reforms, 231, 239
Perth, Earl of, and effect of 1943 reforms, 237-8
Philippopolis, Wratislaw on pleasures of, 131; Blunt on Ionians at, 144
Phillimore, on international law, 190
Phillips, Herbert, and language training at Peking, 188
Piraeus, patronage at, 23
Pisani, family of, and *chancelier* at Tunis, 162; Stratford de Redcliffe and, 164
Playfair, R. Lambert, 21; on salaries, 39
Plowden, Walter Charles, 136
Plowden Committee (1963), on overlap of consular and diplomatic functions, 119; and recruitment, 233; and grading, 235, 238-9; and training, 236-7
Poland, political consulates in, 18
Police, Levant consulates as police stations, 140-1
Ponsonby, Lord, on Buenos Aires, 28; and language barrier, 173
Ponsonby, Arthur, on social requirements for diplomacy, 115
Port-au-Prince, mortality in, 45; and colour discrimination in, 72; promotion at, 72
Port Said, 113
Portal, Lady Alice, widow of Sir Gerald, and pension of, 47
Portugal, early appointments in, 5, 7, 8, 10; shipping fees at, 13; inspection at, 64
Post Office, agencies for, 41; at Smyrna, 126
Pottinger, Sir Henry, and Treaty of Nanking, 182; and salary level in Far Eastern Service, 195
Pratt, Sir John, on language training in China, 186; on Chinese nationalism, 215; on popular discontent with consuls, 218; on recruitment to China Service, 221-2; and amalgamation of China Service, 227, 229
Precedence, diplomats and consuls, 2
Preveza, 130
Primrose League, 22
Prisons, Turkish, 143; at Levant consulates, 147

Index 267

Privy Council, Judicial Committee of, as court of appeal, 149

Probation (after appointment), salaries for men on, 76; lack of in China Service, 192

Promotion, 5, 106, 112, 168; 1825 Act and, 15; and patronage, 21, 22, 24; of locally-recruited officers, 27; and incentives, 48-54; and Foreign Office, 54-6, 59, 60; in 1903, 68; 1858 Committee and, 68, 164; Ridley Commission and, 69; and Walrond Committee, 82; and personnel administration, 89, 91; in twentieth century, 94-103; for student interpreters, 164-5; prospects in close services for, 170-1; block in Levant Service, 171-9; prospects in Far Eastern Service for, 192-4, 219-20; native marriage and, 197; in Indian Civil Service, 219; and recruitment to Far Eastern Services, 221-3; and arguments for amalgamation of China Service, 226-8; effects of amalgamation on, 230

Promotions Board (Foreign Office), 96, 99

Proposals for the Reform of the Foreign Service, White Paper on (1943), *see* Eden, Anthony

Protection, *see* Exterritoriality

Protestants, protection of, 144

Prussians, 38

Public Accounts, Commissioners for Auditing the, and office accounts, 65

Public Accounts, Committee of 1890, 119; Committee of 1892 and stamp system, 66-7; Committee of 1935 and inspections, 94

Puerto Rico, 55; Galway on, 28; agency fees in, 41

Quarterly Review, 53

Queen's Colleges, Ireland, and nominations for China Service, 183

Raikes, Thomas, 21

Rawlinson, Lt-Col Sir Henry, 21; on protection, 139; on appointment of Levantines, 157; on 'orientalizing' of consuls, 157-8

Reay Committee, 165-6; 187

Recruitment, before 1825, 5, 7-9; in nineteenth century, 21-5, 38, 48; pensions and, 44-5; and specialist appointments, 52; in 1903, 68; and Ridley Commission, 69; in twentieth century, 69-71; competition and, 72; interview for, 73; social barriers to, 71-5; proposal to advertise for, 74; training after, 75; widening of, 76; and Walrond Committee, 76-7, 90; and commercial experience, 79; 1914 Commission on level of, 79, 80; career planning and, 90, 95, 100, 171; and clerkships as backdoor entry, 112; difference from diplomatic, 116-17; and pressure for amalgamation, 122; Hornby on in Levant Service, 155-6; lack of systematic, 163; for Palmerston's student dragomans, 164-5; for Levant Service, 165-9; effect of close services on, 171; and promotion block, 176; for Far Eastern Service, 183-5, 192; by nominations, 183, 185, 218; and language training, 186, 187; and legal training, 190; decline in applications for, 218-20; after 1914 for Far Eastern Service, 221-3; Steel-Maitland on, 225; amalgamation and, 229, 240-2; and 1943 reforms, 231-2, 236-8

Redmond, William, on patronage, 22; on consular reports, 104

Reports, Commercial, 107; in eighteenth century, 11; and promotion, 54; and the Foreign Office, 56-8; value of, 104-5; *see also* Functions, Commercial

Representation Services Overseas, Committee on (1963), *see* Plowden Committee

Resht, 131

Retirement, 59; and replacements, 27; effect of Canning's reforms on, 34-5; control of accounts at, 66; lack of records on which to base early, 89; and career planning, 100, 162-3; and argument for amalgamation, 177; compulsory, 197; and career prospects, 219, 220, 222; after 1914 in Far Eastern Service, 222-5; and amalgamation, 230

Rezak, Abdur, on climate at Muscat, 28

Rhodes, 130, 155, 158

Ridley Commission (1890), and promotion, 34, 50, 193; and salaries, 43; and transfers, 48; and consular reports, 57; on a graded service, 69; and arguments against amalgamation, 117-18; and training scheme for Levant, 165; and recruitment for Far East, 192

Rio de Janeiro, salaries at, 12, 37; consulate at, 36; agency fees in, 41

Roberts, H. A., on examinations, 73

Robertson, Sir Malcolm, memorandum on consular reform of, 3-4, 123

Robinson, George, on consuls-general, 61; on scope of consular jurisdiction, 188-9
Rochefort, 18
Rochelle, 12
Romania, 131, 132, 149; restriction of capitulations in, 174
Rome, 114
Rosario, 19
Roscoe, on criminal law, 191
Rotterdam, income and fees at, 12; Ernest Maxse and, 78
Roving Englishman: Sketches from Life: 154
Royal Mail Steam Packet Company, consuls as agents for, 41
Russell, Lord John, on consular appointments, 17, 50; on promotion, 52-3; on consular despatches, 56; and instructions, 62; and Levant Service, 129; on capitulations, 142; and corruption in Levant, 161; and recruitment for Levant, 164
Russia, 10, 18; E. F. Law in, 57; difficulties of communication in, 62; allowances in, 87; Levant Service and, 126-7, 129, 171, 173; political functions of frontier consulates of, 132; and protégés in Levant, 138-9; Levant consular service of, 164; and specialized service for, 169; language training for officers in, 175; withdrawal of exterritorial rights of in China, 216
Russian, language, 75, 167
Russian Company, 40
Rustchuck, 130
Ryan, Sir Andrew, on distinction between consuls and diplomats, 2, 99; on capitulations in Saudi Arabia, 175
Ryan, Sir Charles, on accounting control, 66-7
Rye, 22

Saigon, 197, 204, 226
St John, Sir Spencer, and promotion to diplomatic service, 52
St Petersburg, agency money at, 40; and communication with consulates, 62; social qualities required for diplomats at, 114-15; opinion at on specialized service, 169; language training at, 187
St Sophia, 153
Salahiyyeh, 85
Salaries, 134, 156, 160; before 1825, 3, 10-13, 14; 1825 Act and, 13-15; economy in, 17; private income and, 23-4, 38-40, 43; and leave, 29; and agency system, 60; fees and, 30-33, 64, 65; allocation of, 33-6; levels of, 37-44, 53, 76, 171; and pensions, 46, 48; 1858 Committee and, 68; Ridley Commission and, 69; Baldwin and, 70; in twentieth century, 81-3; and allowances, 82, 83-4, 87; Treasury and 1933 Committee's proposals for, 101; reduction of salaried posts, 111; clerical, 112-13; and social objections to amalgamation, 114-16; difficulty of interchange of staff because of, 121; in Levant Service, 127-9, 158-9, 172; lack of and corruption in Levant, 161; and recruitment to close services, 171; and amalgamation, 178; and China Service, 193-200, 219-21; Steel Maitland Committee and, 222; 1943 reforms and, 239
Salisbury, Lord, 165
Salonica, 130, 147, 158
Salt Gabelle, 215
Salute, entitlement for consuls, 2
Samaritans, protection of, 135
Samoa, patronage at, 22
San Francisco, 82
Sandwith, Dr Humphry, and criticism of Levant consuls, 154
Sankey, Col Frank, 157
Santos, problems with seamen at, 20; Richard Burton at, 28, 39, 40, 52, 163
Sarell, Philip, and objections to businessmen as consuls, 79
Satow, Sir Ernest, promotion into diplomatic service of, 52; on language training, 187, 207-8; career in China of, 194
Satow, Sir Harold, on training of Levant recruits, 168; on promotions block and need to amalgamate, 176-7, 178
Saudi Arabia, end of capitulations in, 175
Saurin, Dudley E., 64
Savannah, salary at, 40
Schomburgk, Sir Robert, 21
Scott, Sir David, on distinction between consuls and diplomats, 1-2; at Consular Department, 92-3; and diplomatic functions, 118; memorandum by on amalgamation, 122, 123; on arguments against close services, 170; and amalgamation of China Service, 229, 230
Scutari, 130, 132
Seamen, 34, 102, 180; protection and regulation of, 6-7, 16, 19-20; at Santos, 20; and fees, 31; and nationality of consuls,

113; imprisonment of, 147; rioting by, 208-9; *see also* Functions, Maritime
Second Division, *see* Clerical Officer
Secondment, and training, 76
Selection Board, Foreign Office, and nominations for examination, 72; and recruitment to Far Eastern Service, 218; since 1943, 232
Seniority, 176; reward for, 50, 51, 89; promotion according to, 54, 96-9; and amalgamation, 178-9, 230; and career prospects in Far Eastern Service, 192, 220
Serbia, 131; restriction of capitulations in, 174
Serbian, language, 160
Servants, consular protection of, 139; cost of, 159, 199; corruption of, 160; *see also* Dragomans; Cavasses
Seville, 35
Shanghai, consulate established at, 182; Medhurst and, 183; judicial duties in, 189; establishment of Supreme Consular Court at, 190, 214; legal training of student interpreters at, 191; consular rewards at, 194; salaries at, 195, 199, 200, 220; staffing at, 201-2; trade at, 203; ignorance of Chinese by British merchants at, 207; and consular jurisdiction, 210, 212, 217; Mixed Court and surrender of exterritorial rights at, 216, 217
Shimonoseki, 220-1
Shipping, 17, 180; protection and regulation of, 6-7, 16; fees and, 11-13, 14; and 1825 reforms, 15; official duties of consuls and, 19, 58, 103, 105-6; and financing the service, 11, 30, 31, 40, 41; and Board of Trade, 58, 62-3; and distribution of posts, 109; and overlap of consular/diplomatic functions, 119; effect of Crimean War on, 148; in China, 189, 204, 205; clerk, salary of, 220; *see also* Functions, Maritime
Siam, 45, 180; ratio of trade to cost of service in, 202, 204; political importance of, 204; 1909 Treaty and, 215; and amalgamation, 225-30 *pass.*
Siam Consular Service, 103, 169, 172, 180, 182; career prospects in, 192; state and cost of, 202; 1909 Treaty and, 215; salaries in, 220; recruitment after 1914 for, 221; and amalgamation, 225-8
Simon, Sir John, and amalgamation, 178;

and separation between diplomatic and consular services, 121-2
Sivas, 134
Slade, Sir Adolphus, on exterritoriality in Turkey, 137, 138
Smith, *Compendium of Mercantile Law*, 27, 191
Smith, Rev. George, 210-11
Smith, Howard, on social objections to amalgamation, 116, 242
Smith, Sydney, on protégés, 146
Smuggling, consuls and prevention of, 11
Smyrna, 29, 130; consulate and staff at, 85, 126; consuls and English community at, 153; Charles Blunt at, 155; salary at, 158
Snowden, Philip, 115
Southampton, 18
South Eastern Railway Company, 23
Southern Department (H. M. Government), and consular administration in eighteenth century, 11
Spain, early consulates in, 5, 7, 8, 10; inspection at, 64; Branch A officers in, 235
Spanish, language, 75
Spanish Main, consular inspection in, 64
Spectator, 103
Spezia, La, 29
Spring-Rice, Edward, on overlap of consular and diplomatic services, 119
Srasti, Prince, and Siamese law courts, 215
Staffing (consular), at consulates in nineteenth century, 24, 25; and communication with Foreign Office, 62-3; value of, 109; difficulties of local clerical, 112-13; in Turkey, 127; policy, 176; scale and cost of in China Service, 201; and administration in East, 227
Stamps, and accounting control, 65-7
Stanley, Lord, on salaries, 38; on capitulations in Turkey, 142
Stansfeld, J., and cost and scale of China Service, 200
Stationery Office, H.M., and consular stationery, 84
Staveley, Thomas, at Consular Department, 58
Stavrides, G. C., on Turkish justice, 143
Steamship Subsidies, Select Committee on (1901), and consular reports, 57
Steblow, 159
Steel-Maitland, Sir Arthur, 93; on recruitment and training, 80; and salary

270 The Cinderella Service

Steel-Maitland—*continued*
scales, 83; and proposal for local allowance, 88; expansion promoted by, 91; reasons for resignation of, 111; and merging of Levant into General Service, 176; on organization of Far Eastern Service and amalgamation, 225, 226

Steel-Maitland Committee (1919), 109, 177; and recruitment, 79; and office allowances, 84, 88; on inspections, 93; on handling of personnel, 95; on promotion and career planning, 100, 222-3; scheme for increasing service, 110-11; and Levant Service, 171-2, 175-6; and clerical service, 113; ratio of senior to junior posts recommended by, 172; on Far Eastern Service, 222, 223, 225

Stettin, 12

Stevens, George, on salaries, 39

Stoddart, J. L., 150

Strang, Lord, on diplomats' contribution to consular reform, 122-3; on diplomats and consular experience, 236; on social effect of amalgamation, 238

Strangford, Lord, on poor state of Levant service, 154-5; on recruitment for Turkey consulates, 156-7; as student dragoman, 164

Stratford de Redcliffe, Lord, on Turkish prisons, 147; criticism of, 154; on effect of isolation, 158; and student dragomans, 164

Sual, 19

Sudan, 132, 141

Sulina, 130

Superannuation, *see* Pensions

Susa, 19

Swatow, cost of living in, 198; trade at, 203; consular jurisdiction at, 214; violence against consuls in, 226

Swedish, language, 75

Switzerland, 235

Synge, William, 21

Syria, consul-general at, 61; consular protection in, 139; French mandate and replacement of capitulations in, 175

Syrians, protection of, 135, 144

Szechwan, 203

Tabriz, 131

Taganrog, 19

Tahiti, 22

Tamsui, 85; promotion block at, 193

Taylor, on Evidence, 191

Tehran, 131, 169; language training at, 173

Teichman, Sir Eric, on consular jurisdiction in Shanghai, 212; on discontent in China with British policies, 218; and amalgamation of China Service, 227

Têngyueh, 226

Thomson, Poulett, on salaries and fees, 32

Thurstan, E. W. P., on social qualifications for consular posts, 78

Tientsin, entertainment allowances at, 86; trade at, 203; and consular jurisdiction, 212

Tilley, J. A. C., on qualifications for consular service, 78; on recruitment for China Service, 218; and transfers of China consuls, 228

Timbuctoo, 171

Times, The, on unsuitable appcintments, 9; on patronage, 23; on Bordeaux vacancy, 24; on training, 26; on New York consulate, 36; on promotion, 49, 50; and advertisements, 78; on poor conditions in service, 88; on treatment of consuls at Foreign Office, 92; on dissolution of Levant Company, 125; and consular affairs in the Levant, 133; on capitulations in Turkey, 141; and working of Supreme Consular Court in Constantinople, 149; on justice at consular courts, 151; and criticism of Levant Service, 163-4; and capitulations in Turkey after 1908, 174-5; and rate of exchange and salaries, 200; on Supreme Court at Hong Kong, 213

Tokyo, 207; posts at, 35; Parkes at, 190; law examinations for student interpreters at, 191; attractions of to diplomats, 194-5; staff at, 204; consular administration from, 227

Tomlin Commission (1929-31), 178; on retirement in Far Eastern Services, 225

Tonnay, 18

Townshend, A. F., on protégés in the Levant, 134-5, 137-8, 145

Trade, *see* Functions, Commercial; Merchants; Reports, Commercial

Trade, permission to, Palmerston and, 37-8; salaries and, 32, 40-2, 53; effect on pension rights of, 46; at lower-paid posts, 158-9

Trade and Commerce, Committee to examine the Question of Government

Machinery for dealing with (1919), *see* Cave Committee

Training, in nineteenth century, 25-7, 60; in twentieth century, 75-81; secondment for, 76; Henry Howard on, 118; 1858 Committee's proposals for, 164; for Levant Service, 165-8; language, for Levant recruits, 173; for Near East and Russia, 175; after 1919, 176; language, for Far East recruits, 183-92, 229-30; legal training, 168, 188-92; after 1914, 176, 225; and 1943 reforms, 231, 236, 237-8

Transfers, 121; before 1943, 5, 56, 91, 97; and reward by, 34; and inspections, 63; accounting control by, 66; in 1903, 68; and Walrond Committee, 82; lack of records on which to base, 89; and career planning, 100; and close services, 171; and career prospects, 219; and arguments for amalgamation

Transport, education in, 80

Travel, entitlement and regulations, 29-30

Travellers, 19; and consular fees, 31; and hospitality to, 36; in Ottoman Empire, 138; dislike of Levantines and Maltese by, 157

Treasury, and permission to trade, 42; and pension rights, 46, 47; and inspections, 64; payment of fees and, 64, 65; and patronage, 70, 71; and allowances, 82; and regulations on hospitality, 86; on local allowances, 87; and career planning, 89; and promotions block, 100-3, 171-2, 178; and retirement age, 102, 224; and opposition to expansion of posts, 111; and salaries for China Service, 199-200; and Memorandum on cost and scale of China Service, 200-2, 204, 207

Treaty Department (Foreign Office), 22

Treaty Ports (China), and China Service, 182, 189, 193; salaries at, 195; death and sickness at, 196-7; cost of living at, 199; cost of maintaining consulates at, 201, 202-3; and move to abolish Ningpo and Foochow; consular jurisdiction and, 212, 217; discontent with British government in, 218; and recruitment after 1914, 221-2

Trebizond, consular functions in, 19, 126, 127, 130; administration of justice in, 143; effect of end of Ionian protectorate for, 144-5; salary at, 158; opening of trade at, 158; Finn transferred to, 161

Trieste, Charles Lever on, 28; salary at, 39; appointment at, 70

Tripoli, consular housing at, 85; political functions at, 131; maintenance of order in, 147; consular jurisdiction in, 150

Tripolitania, 130

Trucial States, 132

Tunis, 99, 118, 131; accounting control at, 67; consular housing at, 85; police and court business at, 140-1; and corruption at consulate, 162

Tunisia, 130; and French consular protection, 141; and end of capitulatory system, 174

Turkestan, 132

Turkey, 125-79 *pass.*; consuls in after dissolution of Levant Company, 14; E. F. Law in, 57; Huskisson on extension of consular service in, 126; commercial functions in, 126, 127, 129; military consuls in, 133; Kennedy and consular influence in, 133; *The Times* on, 133; Armenian amnesty and consuls in, 134; Hammond on Britain and, 135; capitulations in, 136-7, 141, 142, 174; Rawlinson and protection in, 139, 140; consular jurisdiction and, 146-7, 148; prisons in, 147; Kennedy on consuls in, 153; and condition of Levant Service, 154-5; Strangford on recruitment of consuls for, 156; superior status of French career consuls in, 157; effect of trouble in on training and promotions, 165, 171; examination in law of, 168; decline of political and judicial duties in, 173; 1908 Revolution and Capitulations, 174-5; end of capitulations, 175, 216

Turkish, language, 160, 167, 173, 208

Tyrrell, Sir William, on promotion policy, 95-6; on social qualifications for diplomacy, 115

'Unequal Treaties', the, 215, 217

Uniform, distinction between consular and diplomatic, 2

United States, *see* America, North

Universities, 164, 237, 241; and competition for entry to consular service, 76, 77, 116; study at, for consular duties, 79; Steel-Maitland and commercial education at, 80; of Scotland and Ireland and recruitment for China Service, 185; language training at, 187; and recruitment to Foreign Service from, 233-4

272 The Cinderella Service

Ussher, Thomas, on mortality in Haiti, 45

Valparaiso, patronage at, 22; leave from, 29; fees at, 41
Van, 133, 134
Vanity Fair, 24
Vansittart, Sir Robert, and Scott's Memorandum, 230
Varna, 130
Venables, Mrs, widow's pension of, 48
Venice, 12
Vicars, Edward, 78
Vienna, 120; social qualifications for diplomacy at, 115; language school at, 187
Villiers, H. Montagu, on division of responsibility for consular service, 92
Volo, 130

Wade, Sir Thomas, career in China, 183, 194; and language training, 186; and rewards for merit, 195; on sickness in Peking, 197
Walrond Committee (1903), on consular recruitment, 22, 69-70; on an organized service, 69; on competition and nomination, 218; on commercial experience, 76-7, 79-80; and salaries, 81-3 (and pensions, allowances, transfers and promotions); and personnel administration, 90; and career planning, 90; and inspections, 93; failure to establish machinery for promotions, 95; on merit and seniority in promotions, 96
Ward, George B., on consular jurisdiction, 149-50
Warrington, on consular jurisdiction over Maltese, 147
Warsaw, 18, 61, 131
Washington, 79, 151; consuls general at, 61; Lord Lyons and, 62; consular administration from, 227
Washington Conference (1921-2), on exterritorial rights in China, 216
Watt, Vice Consul, colour discrimination against, 72
Waugh, Telford, on protégés at Diarbekr, 134
Weihaiwei, 216, 226
Welby Agreement (1900), on division of responsibility in Persia, 131
Wellesley, Victor, Maxse and, 36; on low morale of consuls, 58; and personnel administration, 90-1; on Treasury's attitude to promotion, 101; on Chamber of Commerce report, 109; on staffing recommendations from Missions, 110-11; and proposal of Second Division, 113; on close services, 172-3; and arguments for amalgamation of China Service, 229
Wellington, Duke of, reproof to Lord Napier, 181-2
West Indies, consular inspection of, 64
Wheaton, on international law, 190
White, J., on eccentricities of Levant consuls, 154
White, Sir William, and promotion to diplomatic service, 52
Whiteside, J., and staffing of China Service, 201
Wilhelmshaven, 18
Williams, General, 164
Wilson, Sir Charles, as military consul, 132
Winchester, C. A., on merchants' relations with Chinese, 207
Wise, J. A., and criticism of Levant consuls, 154
Wives (consular), 209; social distinctions, 2; lack of pension rights, 46-7; Knatchbull-Hugessen on, 116, 242; activities of, in Jerusalem, 155; fares for in China, 198
Wood, Almeric, 164
Wood, Richard, on contrast between rewards to consuls and diplomats, 99-100; on functions of diplomats and consuls, 118; on cost of servants, 159; corruption at consulate of, 162
Wood, Thomas, 24
Wood, W. A. R., and marriage with Siamese, 197
Works, Office of, and consular furniture, 84
Wratislaw, A. C., on Smyrna, 126; on pleasures of Philippopolis, 131
Wuchow, 203
Wyke, Sir Charles, and promotion to diplomatic service, 52
Wylde, W. H., on salaries, 43; on Levant consulates, 135

Yangtsze, 203
Yemen, 141, 146
Yokohama, 204, 220; accounting control at, 66; judicial functions at, 190-1

Zanzibar, 169, 173

DATE DUE	
6/20/11	
GAYLORD	PRINTED IN U.S.A.